A religion of the Word

MANCHESTER
UNIVERSITY PRESS

Politics, culture and society in early modern Britain

General editors
PROFESSOR ANN HUGHES   DR ANTHONY MILTON   PROFESSOR PETER LAKE

This important series publishes monographs that take a fresh and challenging look at the interactions between politics, culture and society in Britain between 1500 and the mid-eighteenth century. It counteracts the fragmentation of current historiography through encouraging a variety of approaches which attempt to redefine the political, social and cultural worlds, and to explore their interconnection in a flexible and creative fashion. All the volumes in the series question and transcend traditional interdisciplinary boundaries, such as those between political history and literary studies, social history and divinity, urban history and anthropology. They thus contribute to a broader understanding of crucial developments in early modern Britain.

Already published in the series

Leicester and the Court: essays on Elizabethan politics   SIMON ADAMS

Ambition and failure in Stuart England: the career of John, first Viscount Scudamore   IAN ATHERTON

The idea of property in seventeenth-century England: tithes and the individual   LAURA BRACE

Betting on lives: the culture of life insurance in England, 1695–1775   GEOFFREY CLARK

Home divisions: aristocracy, the state and provincial conflict   THOMAS COGSWELL

Cromwell's major-generals: godly government during the English Revolution   CHRISTOPHER DURSTON

Urbane and rustic England: cultural ties and social spheres in the provinces, 1660–1750   CARL B. ESTABROOK

The English sermon revised: religion, literature and history, 1600–1750   LORI ANNE FERRELL *and* PETER MCCULLOUGH (eds)

Londinopolis: essays in the cultural and social history of early modern London   PAUL GRIFFITHS *and* MARK JENNER (eds)

Inventing a republic: the political culture of the English Commonwealth, 1649–1653   SEAN KELSEY

The boxmaker's revenge: 'orthodoxy', 'heterodoxy' and the politics of the parish in early Stuart London   PETER LAKE

Theatre and empire: Great Britain on the London stages under James VI and I   TRISTAN MARSHALL

Courtship and constraint: rethinking the making of marriage in Tudor England   DIANA O'HARA

Communities in early modern England: networks, place, rhetoric   ALEXANDRA SHEPARD *and* PHILIP WITHINGTON

Aspects of English Protestantism, c.1530–1700   NICHOLAS TYACKE

Political passions: gender, the family and political argument in England, 1680–1714   RACHEL WEIL

A religion of the Word

The defence of the reformation in the reign of Edward VI

CATHARINE DAVIES

Manchester
University Press

Manchester and New York

distributed exclusively in the USA by Palgrave

Copyright © Catharine Davies 2002

The right of Catharine Davies to be identified as the author of this work has been asserted by her in accordance with the Copyright, Designs and Patents Act 1988.

Published by Manchester University Press
Oxford Road, Manchester M13 9NR, UK
and Room 400, 175 Fifth Avenue, New York, NY 10010, USA
www.manchesteruniversitypress.co.uk

Distributed exclusively in the USA by
Palgrave, 175 Fifth Avenue, New York,
NY 10010, USA

Distributed exclusively in Canada by
UBC Press, University of British Columbia, 2029 West Mall, Vancouver, BC, Canada V6T 1Z2

British Library Cataloguing-in-Publication Data
A catalogue record for this book is available from the British Library

Library of Congress Cataloging-in-Publication Data applied for

ISBN 0 7190 5730 2 *hardback*

First published 2002
10 09 08 07 06 05 04 03 02   10 9 8 7 6 5 4 3 2 1

Typeset in 10/12.5pt Scala
by Graphicraft Limited, Hong Kong
Printed in Great Britain
by Biddles Ltd, Guildford and King's Lynn

Contents

ACKNOWLEDGEMENTS—*vii*

SOURCES AND METHODOLOGY—*ix*

A NOTE ON THE TERM 'PROTESTANT'—*xx*

ABBREVIATIONS—*xxiii*

Introduction: historical perspectives on the reign of Edward VI

A religious revolution? Edward VI's reformations—*1*
Crisis or continuity?—*5*
The 'commonwealth men': reality or illusion?—*6*
Whatever happened to social conscience?—*6*
Edward VI: 'godly imp', ' young Josiah', or chip off the old block?—*8*
Somerset and Northumberland: a reversal of roles?—*10*
Unstable politics?—*12*
Conclusion—*13*

1 The struggle against popery

Introduction—*18*
Dichotomy—*21*
Inversion—*28*
Conspiracy—*34*
Disorder—*37*
Delusion—*41*
Repression—*47*
Conclusion—*51*

2 The threat of religious radicalism

Introduction—*67*
Who were the radicals?—*68*
Protestant images of 'anabaptism'—*73*
Conclusion—*79*

Contents

3   The reform of the church

Introduction: reformation by the Word—87
The ministry of the Word—88
The need for further reformation—106
The Christian body—114
Conclusion—127

4   The godly commonwealth

Introduction: models of order in the commonwealth—140
Godly judgement: the role of the magistrate—146
Obedience and its limitations: the duty of the subject—158
The social bonds: justice and charity—162
Conclusion—168

5   Signs of the times: hope and fear in the Edwardian reformation

Introduction—177
Assumptions—178
The ungodly commonwealth—197
Conclusion: England in the balance—214

Conclusion—231

APPENDIX: BRIEF BIOGRAPHIES OF AUTHORS—235

BIBLIOGRAPHY—247

INDEX—259

Acknowledgements

During the prolonged period in which this project has come to fruition, I have received considerable support, whether of an institutional or personal nature. My research was financed for the first three years by a DES–British Academy State Studentship, and from 1984–85 by a Scouloudi Research Fellowship awarded to me by the Institute of Historical Research. Newnham College, Cambridge, also awarded me a Caroline Turle Postgraduate Scholarship in 1981. I wish to thank them, and the staff of the following libraries, for making my research possible: the British Library; the Institute of Historical Research; the Public Record Office; Dr Williams's Library and Lambeth Palace Library, London; Cambridge University Library, Emmanuel College, and Newnham College, Cambridge; the Bodleian Library, Oxford; and the University of Birmingham's Library and the Shakespeare Institute. Special thanks go to Mirjam Foot of the Bibliographical Society for allowing me to consult the page-proofs of vol. 1 of the Revised Short Title Catalogue (RSTC). I wish to thank Newnham College, Cambridge, and St John's College, Oxford, for providing me with hospitality during a very productive month's work in the summer of 1984. On my return to transform the thesis into a book, the Open University Flexible Fund for Staff Development provided for me to attend a conference in Oxford on the Reformation in English Towns (January 2000). I wish to thank the staff of Manchester University Press for their help and forbearance, and the reader and series editors for their most valuable comments and corrections.

My work has benefited greatly from discussions with Maria Dowling, Pauline Croft, Jane Dawson, Joe Martin, Phillipa Tudor, Andrew Pettegree, Andrew Johnston, Joy Shakespeare, Andrew Hope, Jane Facey, Bryn Morris and Tessa Watt, and from the comments and suggestions of the members of Conrad Russell's and Michael Hunter's seminars in London, Sir Geoffrey Elton's seminar in Cambridge, and the biennial Colloquium for Reformation Studies. Research seminars at the University of Birmingham have kept me in touch in the years between thesis and book. John Fines was unfailingly kind and encouraging and was delighted to know that a book would be at last forthcoming. Diarmaid McCulloch very generously lent me the proofs of *Tudor Church Militant*, and boosted my confidence greatly with his words of praise. Special thanks to Alec Ryrie, for the last-minute loan of his thesis. In recent years my fellow associate lecturers at the Open University, Heather Swanson and Mary Bonwick, have given me enormous encouragement and have been super colleagues with whom to work. My students at the Open University and the University of Birmingham have challenged my ideas and made me explain them more clearly. It was a particular pleasure to teach the reformation to a group at the University of Birmingham's School of Continuing Studies, which included several church wardens.

My interest in the sixteenth century and in the history of ideas began as an undergraduate with the teaching of Quentin Skinner, who has been a source of much inspiration. My PhD supervisor Peter Lake was always boundlessly enthusiastic about my work and gave generously of his time to discuss it. It was Peter's suggestion, out of the blue, that the thesis was still viable for publication that has made me face up to some naggingly unfinished business. I hope the result meets with his approval.

Acknowledgements

My family have been the unsung heroes of this tale, putting up with the unbearably long time it has taken to produce this book, and all the vagaries of part-time employment in higher education which have been my attempt to square their needs with my work. To my parents I owe, besides all else, my love of history. They also provided practical assistance in the form of a word-processor, without which my thesis would not have been completed. My children Thomas and Elinor have welcomed me into the real world and been my constant delight. As in the kingdom of heaven, the last shall be first: my husband Jonathan has supported me in numberless ways (not least financially), and maintained faith and confidence in me and my work in difficult times. My biggest debt of gratitude is to him.

Sources and methodology

This book is a thematic survey of the printed material produced by English protestants in the period from c.1546–53. Protestants used print consciously as a means of reaching a wider audience, and making their case a matter of public debate and concern. They were well aware that before the advent of print ideas were disseminated by word of mouth, or by the circulation of manuscripts. The role of the oral tradition in Lollardy is well known, and yet there is increasing evidence of the part played by Lollards in networks of book distribution.[1] However, Lollards were, as is the nature of small heretical groups, scattered and few in number, and only known when they fell foul of the authorities. The sermon as a means of mass-communication was the preserve of the church, though ceremonies, festivals and processions were as important to catholicism as was preaching in communicating the religious message. As preachers and heretics, English protestants used both traditions of communication to spread their ideas; but, in contrast to both Lollardy and catholicism, the press was vital to protestantism from its beginnings. The new communication technology had significant practical and ideological parts to play in what is often described as a religion of the word.[2] Luther realised the potential of the press to reach a wide audience – one which did not even have to be literate, as Robert Scribner's study of Lutheran woodcuts has shown.[3] Studying the distribution of heretical printed books in England and the Netherlands is a useful means of tracing the growth and development of clandestine protestantism.[4]

This study, however, deals with the period during which protestantism for the first time was openly espoused by the English establishment, and was, however equivocally at times, government policy. The use of the press by the government in this period for propagandist purposes continued Cromwell's pioneering use of it in the 1530s. This was not just a narrowly official campaign, though: a wide range of publications promoted protestant views, not always harmoniously. Extensive work on the Henrician and Marian printed material makes a broad study of the Edwardian period long overdue, especially in view of the unusual printing history of the period.[5] The only recent study of Edwardian protestant printed material, by J.N. King, is a literary rather than a historical study: his selection of 'reformation literature' excludes sermons and polemic, and is based on a very small group of authors. His studies of

Sources and methodology

patronage are useful starting-points, though he tends to take dedication material at face value. His analysis of the limited iconographical material in print is, however, most perceptive.[6] Tessa Watt's *Cheap Print and Popular Piety 1550–1640* has a lot of pertinent information on the lower end of the market, though very little of it is about this early period.[7]

On the basis of surviving material, book production in the first two-thirds of the sixteenth century reached its highest peak in 1548 and 1550, only reaching comparable output by the 1560s (though Loach modifies these figures somewhat to the benefit of the Marian regime[8]). A large proportion of the works forming this first surge were religious books, and the great majority of these were protestant in outlook. The reasons for this phenomenon can be summarised as follows. The government was actively involved in using the press to prepare the way principally for the 1549 *Prayer Book*, but also for a programme of basic scriptural education, which included the publication of the *Paraphrases* of Erasmus and the first book of *Homilies*. The 1547 royal *Injunctions* insisted that every parish church should possess a copy of the Bible and the *Paraphrases*, an extension of the Henrician provision of scripture. In parallel with this use of the press, the abolition of the Henrician censorship legislation together with the Act of Six Articles in 1547 enabled protestants to publish without fear of reprisal.[9] A number of protestant writers and printers received the patronage of both Somerset and Cranmer; more expressed the hope that they would continue their 'godly policy' in dedications and prefaces.[10] However, the fall of Somerset, and Northumberland's reimposition of censorship in 1551, saw a return to the more cautious government attitude to the press seen in the later period of Henry VIII's reign.

Parallel to this official use of the press there was an extremely important 'unofficial' protestant press campaign, which has been perhaps too readily assumed to have been actively orchestrated rather than merely tolerated by the government as in its interests.[11] By 1548 many of the protestant exiles of the Six Articles' period had returned from the continent, and others emerged from 'internal exile'.[12] Work that had been printed abroad was reprinted in England, and some Henrician material came into print for the first time, which in part helps to explain the number of early Edwardian texts critical of the last years of Henry VIII's reign, and in particular answering Stephen Gardiner's influential *The detection of the devil's sophistry*.[13] There was not only a significant group of protestant writers; it is clear that many of the printers and stationers had protestant affiliations as well, and used their trade to help in the work of proselytising.[14] Their connections with protestant writers were close: a well-known example would be Robert Crowley, who was both a writer and publisher, and whose works were printed by John Day.[15] The numbers of protestant printers rose sharply by 1550 with the influx of foreign refugee printworkers, mainly from the Netherlands, the most notable of

Sources and methodology

whom was Stephen Mierdman. The commitment of some of these printers to protestantism has been shown not only in their output but in their exile and their involvement in the production of protestant books for the English market in Mary's reign.[16] But the commitment of such a large proportion of their output to protestant didactic and polemical works would not have been viable without a demand for it, however fleeting. The low production costs enabled very small businesses to cash in on the demand, especially in London, for cheap antipapal ballads and broadsheets. After 1550, this part of the market slumped, affected by a depressed economy and a glutted market, and many small printers were bankrupted.[17] The rise and decline in the market thus ran parallel to government use and censorship of the press but, remarkably, some of the later material is more fiercely critical of the regime.

The mention of a market raises the question of the audience for which this material was written. In general, this comprised anyone who could read plus the wider circle of those to whom the literate read aloud.[18] For the more sophisticated end of the market there were complex academic theological treatises in English and Latin, or dialogues like Ponet's translation of Ochino's *Tragedy of the bishop of Rome* that clearly emanated from the Court. There were very few illustrated books. Much of the material considered here, especially the ballads and short tracts, printed in the form of broadsheets or octavos of three or four signatures, was relatively inexpensive to purchase and aimed at a 'popular' market which might be attracted by the element of entertainment they offered. They were characterised by a style and a message which were at worst crude or scurrilous, at best simple and didactic. Many were clearly intended for London readers – Crowley's social critique *One-and-thirty epigrams*, for instance, or William Samuel's *A warning to London*. Susan Brigden's *London and the Reformation* has demonstrated how conditions in London provided for protestant writers a youthful audience which delighted in novelty and was entertained by the often salacious and usually topical and allusive nature of their work.[19] However, this is not to say that the provinces lacked presses, despite the fact that most printing activity took place in London. There were presses in Canterbury, Oxford and Cambridge; Humphrey Powell had a royal patent to print books for Ireland in Dublin and John Oswen had a patent to produce prayer books and godly books for Wales and the Marches. Oswen's press was in Worcester, and he also sold books in Shrewsbury. Earlier, he and Anthony Scoloker had presses in Ipswich.[20]

Very little is known about the ownership of such ephemeral books; even if books were bequeathed, it is most unlikely that the titles were recorded in wills.[21] Nor was this material prohibited, so there is no deposition evidence for book ownership comparable with, for instance, that of the Netherlands.[22] A rare instance was recovered by Margaret Spufford, who describes how a

Sources and methodology

villager from Orwell in Cambridgeshire possessed and read aloud a copy of a ballad called 'Maistres Mass'.[23] Philip Nichols, also a provincial protestant (from England's conservative west country), thought that there was a market for books, even though 'merry tales' were more popular than 'godly books':

> Understand now, gentle reader, that when I was about to write this matter that I have taken in hand, I considered what a number of books there be abroad in every man's hand, of divers and sundry matters which are very greedily devoured of a great sort. Whoso laboureth both writing and reading I do very much commend. But are the labours of all such writers thankfully received, think ye? Are their diligence and study gratified accordingly? Or doth every man read with such a purpose and intent that the commonwealth of Christ's flock might thereby be profited, and the people be brought to a Christian conversation and amendment of life, as the author intended? Do they read with such judgement that they receive the good and reject the bad? No, no. The weightier the matter the sooner passed over, and the less thanks to the author. But trifling matters, finely handled, are esteemed. So crooked and perverse is the nature of man and so little pleasure has he in following the doctrine of Christ. And so little profit have they also that labour therein.

He went on to give a useful insight into the close relationship between the press and the pulpit in the early years of Edward's reign:

> But what then, should the writers therefore leave off writing because the most part do not worthily receive it? God forbid: but rather would I wish those which never wrote before should also set themselves to work bestowing the talent that God hath lent them to most advantage. And seeing it is not lawful for any man (as yet) to preach in an open audience, unless he be or hath been an Apostata (an Apostle I should say), I purpose by the grace of God and his Holy Spirit to do that [which] lieth in me, to spy out the land of Canaan, and to bring such tidings as the Lord shall open to me in writing, by means whereof His people may know their Lord the better and at last be partakers of that pleasant land flowing with milk and honey.[24]

Books, therefore were not only printed pages: they could speak as preachers and even as prophets, bridging the gap between the oral and literate cultures. Crowley explicitly characterised his verse tracts as prophets:

> If books may be bold
> To blame and reprove
> The faults of all men,
> Both high and low,
> As the prophets did
> Whom God's spirit did move,
> Then blame not mine author
> For right well I know
> His pen is not tempered

> Vain doctrine to sow.
> But as Isaiah hath bidden
> So must he needs cry
> And tell the Lord's people of their iniquity.[25]

Thus the book personified the voice of the prophet, allowing more people to 'hear' him. The written word was the spoken word made accessible to all.

The starting point for this appreciation of the power of the written word was of course the Bible. It was axiomatic that it was written down by providential intention: 'God would have his word to be written that all men, of whatsoever degree they be [might be saved] by the word of God'.[26] That everyone should have the experience of listening to or reading scripture was the fundamental principle at stake throughout the reformation. As Cranmer explained,

> none be enemies to the reading of God's word, but such as either be so ignorant that they know not how wholesome a thing it is, or else be so sick that they hate the most comfortable medicine that should heal them, or so ungodly that they would wish the people still to continue in blindness and ignorance of God.[27]

So much for the point of view of conservatives, who saw only anarchy resulting when the laity did not have to rely on clerical interpretation of scripture. Printed vernacular Bibles were the key to everyone's spiritual emancipation:

> And truly we are much bound to God, that he hath set out his will in our natural mother tongue, in English, I say, so that now you may not only hear it, but also read it yourselves; which thing is a great comfort to every Christian heart. For now you can no more be deceived, as you have been in times past, when we did bear you in hand that popery was the word of God: which falsehood we could not have brought to pass, if the word of God, the Bible had been abroad in the common tongue: for then you might have perceived yourselves our falsehood and blindness.[28]

The laity did not have to be learned to appreciate the message of the gospel. The Bible in their hands was the ultimate weapon against the power of the popish clerical hierarchy. Foxe's well-known comment that the invention of print was a providential blessing for the true church was anticipated by an anonymous writer:

> For in the primitive church, and before such time that God had sent the print, it was a great thing for a man to write a Bible, yea as much as a man might do in his whole life. Wherefore, for lack of God's word, the people might not come to the knowledge of the Bishop of Rome's devilish invention ... But thanks be to the Lord our king's majesty may go further with £100 in printing than Constantine might have gone with £3000 in writing. For the lack of books caused the Bishop of Rome and his aiders to prevail in all councils

Sources and methodology

since the first ... Wherefore let us give God thanks and rejoice that he hath sent us in these our days that science whereby all those who love the light might have the same for a little charge; I mean the word of God who is the author of light.[29]

The evangelical thrust of policy was clear, and print brought true religion to a wider lay audience, whether as readers or as hearers. As the principal – and providential – weapon against the tyranny of the popish clergy, it had a unique ideological place in the protestant mind. For this reason, while we should be wary of unduly privileging books as evidence in reformation history, we should not slip into the equally false position of ignoring them.

The restriction of this study to the medium of print is counterbalanced by the extensive range of styles and approaches within it. The nature of this study suggests a broad banding of sources into three main groups: controversial, didactic and entertaining. The first group ranges from the scholarly debate of Cranmer and Gardiner on the Eucharist, to Crowley's rejoinder to Hoggard's attack on an anti-Mass ballad, which shows how format was no barrier to argument.[30] The second, rather larger, category includes scriptural and patristic compilations, such as Jean Veron's *Sayings of the old faithful fathers on the Sacrament* or Peter Pickering's definition of the role of the minister; sermons, some of which, like Latimer's *Sermon on the plough* or Lever's sermons are some of the most well-known sources of the period; didactic tracts, particularly those on the Sacrament and clerical celibacy; testimonies, from the anonymous *True judgement of a faithful Christian* to Hooper's *Godly confession of the Christian faith*; catechisms; Biblical commentaries; and histories.[31] The third group include satirical dialogues, ballads, and allegories.[32]

These groupings are however only used to introduce the reader to the range of sources under consideration rather than as an organising principle for the book. The aim of avoiding analysis by genre is to present a cross-section of material, in order to show how protestants using the press to appeal to a wide range of tastes and levels of learning, even though this method risks downplaying the differences in background and approach of the authors.[33] Even taking these into account, a striking similarity of ideas and assumptions emerges from a variety of formats, counterbalancing the conventional stress on dogmatic differences. This study thus breaks with previous works on similar material, which have analysed it by year,[34] or by controversy,[35] or by literary form, using representative authors,[36] or even by item.[37] At best these approaches explain the development of an individual's thought; at worst they remain purely descriptive. Too much was produced, and not enough of it of high quality, to make such approaches either illuminating or uncumbersome, so I have treated the material as a whole and drawn out the most important themes.

Sources and methodology

However, it is important to note that two significant types of printed protestant book are excluded here. Firstly, devotional material, which I have defined as all that concerned with spirituality and personal godliness. As this book is about public issues rather than private piety this seems reasonable; furthermore the subject has already been covered in Phillipa Tudor's thesis.[38] Nevertheless, where such material does refer to the public face of protestantism, such as polemical prayers by Thomas Becon, or Edmund Allen's *Catechism*, reference is made to it.[39] The second broadly excluded group is translations, though here it is even more difficult to draw more than a basic line, as many writers drew heavily on continental exemplars. Edward VI's reign was a peak period for the publication of translations from continental protestant theologians, whether of Lutheran writers (except on the Sacrament), or those from the Rhineland and Switzerland (including works on the Sacrament). Reference to these translations is kept to a minimum, since any more would extend the range of the book further than it is designed to go. It would be foolish to assume from this that they do not matter; the importance of continental theology to the Edwardian reformation is by now a truism.[40] But to include them would not provide an adequate study of their 'influence', since English theologians were primarily influenced by personal contact with their continental brethren, as various studies have shown,[41] and also by reading Latin versions of their works printed abroad.[42] In any case, a proper appreciation of the quality and content of translations requires a detailed knowledge of the originals, and is thus a study in itself. The intention is thus not insularity, but the need to limit the source material.

I wanted to look at a broad spectrum of protestant writers under a protestant regime, rather than singling out 'classic' texts – to establish a context and recover an ideological outlook and vocabulary, rather than set out a critique of a particular theory.[43] Clearly, as befits a study of protestant thought, the theological framework is important, but this is primarily a historical study. By the same token, it is not an attempt to isolate 'protestant political thought' or to look for intellectual originality. There was not much 'originality' among the writers under consideration here; indeed, it not an attribute they would they have thought desirable. This is not to say that in the political context of Edward's reign many of their utterances were not daring or radical in their implications. In reading a broad spectrum of material, and taking the writers on their own terms as motivated by religious zeal, this study aims to examine the Edwardian reformation through the medium of the reformers' own words and explanations.

Protestant propagandists saw their task as twofold: to defend the reformation from the onslaughts of its enemies, and to consolidate and extend its achievements. In following this framework, I begin by examining the struggle against popery, and then discuss the response to the real or imagined threat

Sources and methodology

of 'anabaptism', since these were the most obvious forms of 'false religion'. It is argued that protestants saw themselves not as constituting a 'middle way' between the two, as might be expected, but as defending 'true religion' against 'false'. Consequently, it is the polemical and rhetorical devices used by protestants to distance themselves from 'false religion', rather than purely doctrinal considerations, that are the centre of attention. An analysis of their attitudes to popery and 'anabaptism' reveals, to a great extent, protestants' view of what constituted true religion.

The confrontational nature of protestant polemic went further than this though, because even when popery and 'anabaptism' were not directly under attack, the language that was used against them was reused against other forms of false religion, notably the materialism and disobedience which protestants saw as new threats to the reformation. However, while this needs to be borne in mind, it is important to recognise that, when at work in the world, 'true religion' did have a positive content, which is explored in the chapters 3 and 4. These examine, firstly, protestant ideas of the church as both a proselytising institution and as a Christian body; and, secondly, the ideal of the godly commonwealth, paying particular attention to the role of the godly prince in supporting the reformation and executing God's law. This latter part of his role was a much more contentious area. Even if England was adequately provided with a reformed church and a godly magistracy (and protestants were clear that there was still a long way to go here), the nation was endangered from within, from the forces of false religion, and from without, from God's inevitable judgement on the people's sins. In order to understand the part which protestants saw themselves playing in all this, it is important to note the tension which existed between their new-found acceptance and support from the political elite, and their desire to distance themselves from actions taken by that elite in the name of the reformation. To a great extent they resolved that tension by seeing themselves as prophets, a role which rationalised both their direct criticisms of the establishment and the difficulties of influencing it, whether they were in positions of power or not. As prophets they could both intensify the immediacy of God's wrath by identifying England with Old Testament examples of plague and punishment, and explore eschatological realities which took the reformation out of human time. The final chapter brings criticism of contemporary events and problems into line with spiritual and providential explanations, and assesses Edwardian protestant hopes and fears for their country and their times.

NOTES

1 See C. Cross, '"Great reasoners in scripture": the activities of women Lollards, 1380–1530', in D. Baker (ed.) *Medieval Women* (Oxford, 1978), 359–80.

2 E. Eisenstein, *The Printing Press as an Agent of Change: Communications and Transformations in Early Modern Europe* (Cambridge, 1979), vol. 1: ch. 4; see also L. Febvre and H.-J. Martin, *The Coming of the Book: The Impact of Printing, 1450–1800*, tr. D. Gerard, ed. G. Nowell-Smith and D. Wootton (1976; repr. 1984). Andrew Petegree summarises succinctly the relationship of protestants with the press in a European context in *The Reformation World* (2000), 109–126.

3 R. Scribner, *For the Sake of Simple Folk: Popular Propaganda for the German Reformation* (Cambridge, 1981).

4 For the use made by Lollards of early reformation books, see A. Hope, 'Lollardy: the stone the builders rejected?', in P. Lake and M. Dowling (eds) *Protestantism and the National Church in Sixteenth Century England* (1987), 22–4; for the dissemination of protestant books in the Netherlands, see A. Johnston, 'The eclectic reformation: vernacular pamphlet literature in the Dutch-speaking Low Countries, 1520–65', unpublished PhD thesis, Southampton University (1987).

5 See below, nn. 34–7.

6 See J.N. King, *English Reformation Literature: The Tudor Origins of the Protestant Tradition* (Princeton, NJ, 1982), 443–56, for a rather strained comparison between Milton and the 'Tudor gospellers', especially 455. For his conclusions on dedications, see Chapter 4, n. 80.

7 Tessa Watt, *Cheap Print and Popular Piety, 1550–1640* (Cambridge, 1991; repr. 1996).

8 Figures for book publications are problematic, in that they vary according to survival rate (see F.B. Williams, 'The lost books of Tudor England', *The Library*, 1978) and whether reprints are counted as separate editions. P.M. Took, 'Government and the printing trade, 1540–60', unpublished PhD thesis, University of London (1979) gives figures based on the STC (vol. 1, unrevised) in Appendix 3: she concludes that Edward's reign saw levels of book production that were comparable with the Henrician and Marian peaks (1540, 1555, 1556) and were not equalled until the 1560s (average 120). However, in 1548 (227) and 1550 (260), peaks were reached which were not surpassed until well into Elizabeth's reign. Figures for print runs are also difficult to arrive at, but a comparison could be made with M. Spufford, *Small Books and Pleasant Histories* (1981), in which she estimates the size of the stock of chapbook publishers in the late seventeenth century, ch. 4.

9 A.G. Dickens, *The English Reformation* (1976), 280–2.

10 Took, 'Printing trade', 134–48, emphasises the patronage of Somerset and Cranmer but also notes the part played by John Ponet (patron of the eminent protestant printer John Day), William Cecil (collaborated with the bookseller William Seres, also censor, 1549), Catherine, duchess of Suffolk, and the royal printer Edward Whitchurch. King, *English Reformation Literature*, 103–12, gives greater emphasis to protector Somerset.

11 E.g. works produced by the Henrician exiles, Turner, Bale and Joye, who carried on producing material similar to that which they had produced in the earlier 1540s; also the work of the Ipswich group of propagandists centred on the Oswen and Scoloker presses (see below, n. 18). Note also that the major commissions were for the *Paraphrases* and *Homilies*; evidence from dedications suggests that suitable selections were made by translators with a view to official approval, rather than chosen by patrons; see chapter 4, n. 80.

12 E.g. Turner, Bale, Joye (exiles) Becon (internal exile), Latimer (prison, briefly, then internal exile). See Alec Ryrie, 'English evangelical reformers in the last years of Henry VIII', unpublished DPhil thesis, Oxford University (2000).

13 See Chapter 1, n. 5.

Sources and methodology

14 See Took, 'Printing trade', 144–8, 187ff. Took sees evidence of protestant attachment among 24 of the 80 printers and stationers.
15 J.W. Martin, 'The publishing career of Robert Crowley: a sidelight on the Tudor book trade', *Publishing History* (1983): 85–98. I owe this reference to the kindness of Dr Martin.
16 See n. 14 above.
17 Took, 'Printing trade', 9, 184.
18 D. Cressy, *Literacy and the Social Order: Reading and Writing in Tudor and Stuart England* (Cambridge, 1980), 14–15.
19 H.S. Bennett, *English Books and Readers, 1475–1557* (Cambridge, 1969).
20 A.G. Dickens, 'Peter Moone, the Ipswich gospeller and poet', *Notes and Queries* (1954): 513.
21 An example of an early book bequest in a protestant will can be found in Richard Holt et al. (eds) *Birmingham Wills and Inventories, 1551–1600* (University of Birmingham, Department of Extramural Studies, 1985), 11. P. Tudor, in a survey of London wills from 1318 to 1558, notes the extreme paucity of book bequests, and that service books and devotional literature were the most frequently named: 'Changing private belief and practice in English devotional literature, c.1475–1550', unpublished DPhil thesis, Oxford University (1984), 9. Watt, *Cheap Print*, 261, has some interesting calculations about cost.
22 I owe this information to a paper given by Dr A. Johnston in Prof. Swarts's Dutch history seminar at the Institute of Historical Research in 1984.
23 M. Spufford, *Contrasting Communities* (Cambridge, 1974), 245. Watt, *Cheap Print*, 221, describes how broadsheets were stuck on walls, using evidence from a Cambridge inventory of 1547.
24 Spufford, *Small Books*, chs 7 and 8; Phillip Nichols, *A godly new story of 12 men that Moses ... sent to spy out the land of Canaan* (1548), sigs A3vo–A4vo; cf. Robert Crowley, 'The book to the Christian reader', in *Pleasure and pain* (1551); also Thomas Becon, *The principles of the Christian religion* (1550), PS2 481.
25 Robert Crowley, *One-and-thirty epigrams* (1550), sig. A2. Crowley also used the image of the author as the last trumpet – *The voice of the last trumpet* (1550), sig. A2. Thomas Betteridge characterises this space as a 'public sphere' in *Tudor Histories of the English Reformations, 1530–83* (Aldershot, 1999), 30–2.
26 John Mardeley, *A declaration of the power of God's word, concerning the holy Supper of the Lord* (1548), sig. B1vo.
27 Thomas Cranmer, 'A fruitful exhortation to the reading and knowledge of holy scripture', *Homilies* (1549 edn), Book 1.
28 Hugh Latimer, *Fourth sermon on the Lord's prayer*, PS1 369–70.
29 'R.V.', *The old faith of Great Britain, and the new learning of England* (1549), sigs C1vo, C3vo–C4; cf. 'to restore the church again by doctrine and learning it pleased God to open to man the art of printing...', John Foxe, *Acts and monuments*, ed. S. Cattley (1837–39), vol. 4: 253; 'either the Pope must abolish knowledge and printing, or printing at length will root him out...', ibid., vol. 3: 720–1.
30 Thomas Cranmer, *Defence of the true and catholic doctrine of the Sacrament* (1550); Stephen Gardiner, *An explication and assertion of the true catholic faith of the Sacrament of the altar* (1550); Cranmer, *An answer to a crafty and sophistical cavillation devised by Stephen Gardiner* (1551). Robert Crowley, *The confutation of the misshapen answer to the misnamed, wicked ballad, called the abuse of the blessed Sacrament of the altar* (1548).
31 E.g. Jean Veron, *The godly sayings of the old ancient faithful fathers upon the body and blood of Christ* (1550); for sermons, see especially references to Latimer, Lever, Hooper;

Sources and methodology

for tracts, see e.g. Edmund Guest, *Treatise against the privy Mass* (1548) and John Ponet, *Defence of the marriage of priests* (1549); for testimonies, see e.g. 'J.B.', *A brief and plain declaration* (?1547) and John Hooper, *A godly confession and protestation of the Christian faith* (1550); for commentaries, see e.g. Anthony Gilby, *A commentary upon the prophet Micah* (1551); and for histories, see e.g. John Bale, *Acts of the English votaries* (1546).

32 Satirical dialogues, e.g. William Turner, *A new dialogue, wherein is contained the examination of the Mass* (1548); ballads, e.g. William Kethe, *A ballad declaring the fall of the whore of Babylon, entitled 'Tie thy mare, Tom Boy'* (1548); allegories, e.g. Robert Crowley, *Philargyrie of Great Britain* (1551) (with woodcut frontispiece, illustrating the giant Philargyrie using the Bible to rake money into a sack). See J.C. Devereux, 'Protestant propaganda in the reign of Edward VI: a study of Luke Shepherd's *Doctor Double Ale*' in E.J. Carlson (ed.) *Religion and the English People 1500–1640: New Voices, New Perspectives* (Kirksville, MO, 1998) for a detailed analysis of an antipapal ballad.

33 See E. Baskerville, 'John Ponet in exile – a Ponet letter to Bale', *JEH* (1986): 442–7. Though the letter applies to the situation under Mary, the range of material produced by protestants in Edward's reign shows the same impetus to appeal to a wide range of tastes and degrees of learning. See above, n. 11; chapter 5.

34 See e.g. G. Bowler, 'English protestant resistance theory', unpublished PhD thesis, University of London (1981).

35 E.g. R. Pineas, *Thomas More and Tudor Polemic* (Bloomington, IN, 1968).

36 See e.g. King, *English Reformation Literature*.

37 E.g. H. White, *Social Criticism in the Popular Religious Literature of the Sixteenth Century* (New York, 1944). The themes of the chapter headings disguise the item-by-item description of the material.

38 See above, n. 21, for details.

39 See P. Tudor, 'Religious instruction for children and adolescents in the early English reformation', *JEH* (1984): 391–413.

40 But see below, and 'A note on the term "protestant"', pp. xx–xxii.

41 For the importance of personal contacts between English and continental reformers, see e.g. P. Collinson, *Archbishop Grindal, 1519–83: The Struggle for a Reformed Church* (1979), ch. 3 (Bucer); E. Hildebrandt, 'A study of the English protestant exiles in north Switzerland and the Rhineland, 1539–47, and their role in the English reformation', unpublished Ph.D. thesis, University of Durham (1982), especially on Bullinger; J. Dawson, 'The early career of Christopher Goodman and his place in the development of English protestant thought', unpublished Ph.D. thesis, University of Durham (1978), ch. 2 (Martyr).

42 As shown by the sixteenth-century editions of the continental reformers in English cathedral libraries.

43 Q.R.D. Skinner, *The Foundations of Modern Political Thought* (Cambridge, 1978), vol. 1: x–xiv. I would define 'ideology' as a systematic body of concepts characteristic of a specific group (in this case Edwardian protestant publicists), which is used as the model on which to build their political, social (and religious) critique. For a postmodernist view of some of this literature, see T. Betteridge, *Tudor Histories of the English Reformations 1530–83* (Aldershot, 1999).

A note on the term 'protestant'

I am using 'protestant' as a convenient shorthand because, for the first time, protestants were part of the establishment and not a clandestine group forced to use allusive terminology – such as 'upholders of the gospel' – to describe themselves.[1] This decision was taken despite the fact that they themselves rarely used the term, preferring to refer to supporters of 'true religion'. As this was also claimed by traditionalists, and as it is clearly subjective, it did not appear to me to be a useful category for this study, so I have chosen 'protestant' on the ground that it is the most inclusive way of describing their doctrinal views,[2] rather than use the more anachronistic 'Anglican' or 'puritan', as M.M. Knappen did in his study *Tudor Puritanism*.[3] In the wake of J.K. Maconica's *English Humanists and Reformation Politics*, a somewhat misleading preference for describing all reformist or even all intellectual activity as 'Erasmian', or, even more vaguely, 'humanist', has arisen.[4] In Edward's reign, this idea of 'Erasmian reform' is given weight mainly on the basis of the publication of the admittedly important *Paraphrases*, in which a number of scholars and members of the royal family were involved; on an inflated perception of the learning and influence of Katherine Parr; and on Cranmer's *eirenic* attempts to bring continental protestants together.[5] It has even been applied to the social and economic reformers: Quentin Skinner, in taking the 'commonwealth men' as a group, including Smith, categorised them primarily as humanists.[6] However, I am working on the principle that however 'Erasmian' the principles of the open Bible and an educated nobility were, the use of the term in this period is anachronistic and also misleading, since English evangelicals by this time upheld the royal supremacy and did not believe in free will. My understanding of 'humanism' is that it is a term empty of doctrinal meaning, and more a matter of a radical attitude to texts and learning, both classical and biblical.[7] Therefore I have avoided using these terms. This is not to deny that humanism has a profound link with protestantism, nor to deny that many of the writers cited in this study, such as Cheke, Ponet and Salesbury, were also humanists. Others, for instance Bale and Latimer, were not humanists, though they were sympathetic to the 'new learning'. In this study I am examining the propagandist efforts of both types as a whole, in the context of an (even nominally) protestant regime, rather than singling out 'Erasmians' as being somehow more praiseworthy,

A note on the term 'protestant'

radical or congenial. It is also important to understand the humanist background to Zwinglian and Calvinist protestantism,[8] which makes those who have hitherto been considered *extreme* or 'puritan', like Hooper and Gilby, as worthy of consideration as humanists as was the *moderate* 'Erasmian' Cranmer.

Particular continental labels, such as 'Zwinglian', are used only when referring to distinctive doctrinal attributes. Lutheran influence in England was minimal by the late 1540s. This was partly a result of changing foreign policy considerations: Henry had turned his back on the Lutheran princes before the fall of Cromwell in 1540, and the Schmalkaldic league was severely defeated in 1548 by the emperor.[9] Henry's own religious attitude, as Alec Ryrie has recently shown, was doctrinally ambiguous, and the paradoxical combination of continued partial reform and a hardening attitude to evangelical reformers made the Mass the focus of religious conflict, especially after 1543.[10] Meanwhile those uncomfortable with the conservative tendencies of Henry's last years went to the Rhineland and Switzerland – with major implications for opinion forming.[11] Cranmer's own spiritual odyssey also took him away from Wittenberg, as MacCulloch has shown.[12] Traces of Lutheran influence remain in the Sacrament debate, in the discussion of the Real Presence, though there is no evidence here of the defining idea of the ubiquity of Christ's presence. However, this did not mean that the doors were closed to Lutheranism. Cranmer did invite Melanchthon to come and advise him on the reform of the English church – it was Melanchthon's reluctance to make the sea voyage rather than doctrinal antagonism that cut the link.[13] I have therefore sometimes used 'reformer' as an alternative to 'protestant' in response partly to its continental reformation associations, implying a more uncompromising stance along Swiss lines to the reformation of the church and society.

More recently Diarmaid MacCulloch has argued forcefully for the rejection of the term 'protestant' on the grounds that it was not used in England at this date, except to describe German Lutherans. He prefers the term 'evangelical' which is nearer to the meaning of the contemporary term 'gospeller' and conveys the biblical nature of the reform neatly without the need for doctrinal labels. It also links Erasmian and protestant attitudes in a convenient manner – after all, there was no dogmatic break, and the reform programme implemented by Cranmer had a strongly Erasmian strand, but it avoids the problems raised by using 'Erasmian'.[14] Jennifer Loach also avoids the term 'protestant'; she uses 'radical' instead, which I have restricted to the extreme doctrinal dissidents (see chapter 2).[15] After much agonising, I have decided broadly to retain my use of 'protestant', because it does imply acceptance of justification by faith alone, which at this date 'evangelical' may not. The implications of 'evangelical' may also be anachronistic, reading back a

A note on the term 'protestant'

particular kind of fundamentalism which is not identical to what is going on in this material. So while I have sometimes used 'evangelical', in reference to ideas which seem particularly to relate to the gospel, I have stuck with 'protestant' as the most convenient catch-all term.

NOTES

1. Terminology best described in M. Dowling, 'The gospel and the court: the reformation under Henry VIII', in P. Lake and M. Dowling (eds) *Protestantism and the National Church in Sixteenth Century England* (1987), 40.
2. I.e. Justification by faith alone, scripture as the prime authority, Communion in both kinds, a 'spiritual' view of the Eucharist. My definition would embrace the nuances of reformed opinion, but in the case of the Sacrament would exclude the Lutheran view, for which there is very little evidence. However, this did not prevent the publication and awareness of Lutheran works on other subjects. Care is to be taken with the remarks of zealots like John Burcher and Bartholemew Traheron – after all, they were writing to assure Bullinger of their own doctrinal purity. See *Original Letters Relative to the English Reformation*, PS1 323; PS2 651–2 and 662–3.
3. See M.M. Knappen, *Tudor Puritanism: A Chapter in the History of Idealism* (Chicago, 1970), ch. 4.
4. J.K. Maconica, *English Humanists and Reformation Politics Under Henry VIII and Edward VI* (Oxford, 1968); J. Booty (ed.) *The Godly Kingdom of Tudor England: Great Books of the English Reformation* (Wilton, CT, 1981); King, *English Reformation Literature*, 122–38. However, this use of 'humanist' as applied to intellectual/evangelical opinion in the Henrician period has been attacked by J. Guy and A. Fox, *Reassessing the Henrician Age: Humanism, Politics and Reform, 1500–30* (Oxford, 1986), part 1, especially 9–51. G.R. Elton began the process of exposing this 'excessive addiction to pattern making' in *Reform and Renewal: Thomas Cromwell and the Commonweal* (Cambridge, 1973), 3–5.
5. See esp. Maconica, *English Humanists*, chs 7, 8.
6. Skinner, *Foundations of Modern Political Thought*, vol. 1: 224–8.
7. *Ibid.*, 35–41; cf. Fox and Guy, *Henrician Age*, 31–2.
8. See G. Potter, *Zwingli* (Cambridge, 1976), 25–7, 39–44, 65–6; H. Höpfl, *The Christian Polity of John Calvin* (Cambridge, 1982), ch. 1.
9. John Guy, *Tudor England* (Oxford, 1988), 187.
10. Ryrie, 'English evangelical reformers', especially the Conclusion.
11. Hildebrandt, 'English protestant exiles'. For a contrasting view of the significance of the reformers, see Ryrie, 'English evangelical reformers', ch. 3.
12. Diarmaid MacCulloch, *Thomas Cranmer. A Life* (New Haven, CT, 1996), 182, 390.
13. *Ibid.*, 502, 518, 539–41.
14. Diarmaid MacCulloch, *Tudor Church Militant: Edward VI and the Protestant Reformation* (1999), 2.
15. Jennifer Loach, *Edward VI* (New Haven, CT, 1999) 18, 23–4, and *passim*.

Abbreviations

APC	Acts of the Privy Council
Archiv	Archiv für reformationsgeschichte
BIHR	Bulletin of the Institute of Historical Research
CH	Church History
CHR	Catholic Historical Review
DNB	Dictionary of National Biography
EcHR	Economic History Review
EHR	English Historical Review
HJ	Historical Journal
JEH	Journal of Ecclesiastical History
NAK	Nederlands archief voor kerkgeschiedenis
P&P	Past and Present
PS	Parker Society
RSTC	Revised Short Title Catalogue
SCH	Studies in Church History
SCJ	Sixteenth Century Journal
SP	State Papers

Spelling and punctuation have been modernised throughout.

Place of publication for all cited works is London except where otherwise stated.

TO THE MEMORY OF JOHN FINES

Introduction: historical perspectives on the reign of Edward VI

A RELIGIOUS REVOLUTION? EDWARD VI'S REFORMATIONS

RELIGIOUS extremity, in sharp contrast to the spirit of compromise and accommodation that seems characteristic of the Anglican *via media*, makes the Edwardian reformation seem an unfortunate experiment in the process of transforming the church. The intensity of the experience was increased by its short time-span – long enough to destroy a way of life, but too short to grow the roots of a new planting. The influence of continental churchmen on the leadership of the church and the presence in its midst of a 'Stranger church' that served as a model of reformed doctrine and discipline intensified the sense that these were aberrant, un-English times. While revisionist historians have in their pursuit of a traditionalist piety 'forgiven' Mary for the shortcomings of her reforms, they have either ignored the potential for change of the efforts of Edward's regime or deplored them as pointlessly destructive. The confessional pendulum swings in reformation historiography to a marked degree. For Elton and Dickens, Edward's reign was the culmination of twenty years of reform, so that by 1553 'England was almost certainly nearer to being a protestant country than to anything else'.[1] By contrast, Scarisbrick and Duffy have not merely catalogued the destruction but have emphasised resistance to the change and the persistence of the old ways.[2] The counting of protestants seems only to emphasise the undoubted fact that they only ever constituted a tiny minority.[3] The assumption that the reformation was a uniform and unitary process of protestantising and nationalising the church has been destroyed by Haigh's more convincing series of reformations, blown by the contingencies of politics and faction in conflicting and contradictory directions, making a serious impact only by the 1570s and later.[4] Perhaps, unintentionally, this makes it easier to justify a monograph on one of many reformations. MacCulloch's major reassessment of Cranmer and his study of Edward's reformation have brought the subject out of the shadows of historical obloquy. MacCulloch sees what happened as a religious revolution, which is a much more coherent model than previous accounts, and one which allows for a better explanation of the interplay of popular

Introduction

movements, factional elites and conflicting ideologies in this short but dynamic period. Religious policy changes are therefore seen as part of a cycle of openness followed by repression. He has restored the hope, and the festive and transgressive elements, to the story, which makes the tragedy all the more powerful.[5]

Edward's reformation overturned religious practice at all levels in society in pursuit of high ideals. The tide of freedom, danger and excess, rapidly turned to an ebb of repression and ruthlessness in 1549. High ideals combined with cynical profiteering to an unparalleled extent. The contradictory nature of this religious revolution was embedded in it before it began, for this was revolution from the top, in the name of the king – a king wielding a Bible as well as a sword.[6] The extent of the supremacy was fully realised in Edward's reign. The liturgy and doctrine of the church were systematically transformed; its assets were stripped, and its legal system was to follow. No other sovereign went further than this – the 1559 settlement only modified the Edwardian legislation. The revolutionary potential of the royal supremacy was largely fulfilled by Edward's regime, and there was every indication that the young king would have continued to use it in all its plenitude.[7]

The transfer of resources was massive: guilds and chantries, the liturgical treasures of the parishes, the spiritual–economic investment of generations were seized by the state. It was as if those that drove the money changers out of the temple were making off with the proceeds. Episcopal property was whittled away. By 1553, the church had lost approximately 60 per cent of its (1535) income.[8] Pastoral provision was severely affected.[9] The calendar was transformed as all but the major festivals were abolished.[10] Confraternities and guilds, the social and fundraising foci of parish life, were abolished and church plate taken. The opportunity for profit was seized by people across the religious spectrum, which made many of those who were otherwise conservative or religiously neutral stakeholders in the property transfer.[11]

Enforcement of the changes was uneven, but remarkably rapid – and remarkably orderly.[12] Iconoclasm was only rarely carried out by the mob – the peaceful mobilisation of churchwardens made this unnecessary.[13] Parishes bought the new *Prayer Books*, the *Paraphrases* of Erasmus, whitewashed the walls, removed stained glass and took down rood lofts, and bought new chalices for the Communion. Priests were able legitimately to marry, which those committed took as a badge of protestantism, and the less so as an opportunity to regularise their arrangements. Even so, it was only a minority who married; in East Anglia about 25 per cent were deprived under Mary for doing so – in York it was only 10 per cent of the clergy, though average age as well as the hostility of their congregations might explain this low figure.[14] The reform process was at its most effective in what were clearly designed as 'showcase' dioceses and deaneries, like Westminster and Worcester.[15] Duffy has described the stripping of the churches, and crucially their altars, as the focal point of devotion was wrenched from the Mass to the Lord's Supper, from the image to the word, from the rood to the royal coat of arms.[16] Outright rebellion for conservative religious reasons was comprehensively stifled in 1549. After that, 'passive' resistance was the only option possible, and it was as much about prudence in dealing with the twists and turns of policy, and the determination that the locality rather than the government should keep its treasures, as it was about uncomplicated devotion. Those who had endowed the church were often in a good position to reclaim their valuables. Quiet concealment of the artefacts of the traditional piety in hope of better times was common, but so was the transfer of assets for communal or private use.[17] But the combination of antitraditional reform and the extent of hostility to it made antipopery the overriding protestant concern (chapter 1).

The ramifications of religious change extended into the next life, as purgatory was finally closed. While the starker alternatives of heaven or hell were the predestined fate of all, the rhetoric of the reformers concentrated firmly on this life. Their triumph over the destruction of the old piety and their celebration of the end of the Mass was always qualified by disillusion and foreboding. The necessity for admonition and the powerful sense of the human failure to hear and act on the good news meant that doom was in-built from the outset. Plague and punishment were always imminent, but the pace of change in Edward's reign made it a dominant theme and one intensified by the real evidence of war, economic collapse and epidemic disease, as chapter 5 will reveal.[18]

Revolutions are not like neat equations, and this one anyway was incomplete. Stalled by political considerations, the reform of canon law was never passed.[19] Cathedrals retained their establishments, some vestments were still worn and ecclesiastical discipline was undeveloped.[20] The opportunity to abolish the episcopate altogether was not taken. On the more profound question of the transformation of popular religion, it could only be a beginning. A minority of people became committed to the cause. London and the southeast were where most of the committed were to be found – and also the highest degree of protestant radicalism or heterodoxy (see chapter 2). Given the influence of Cranmer and Ridley's active promotion of the reformation in their own dioceses, the importing of continental protestantism from the 1520s (magnified by the influx of refugees from 1548 on), and the persistence of a Lollard tradition, this should not be surprising. A more subtle but probably more fundamental factor was the youthful quotient of the population, especially in London. The experience of such a profound break with tradition in the formative years of adolescence make comprehensible the complaint of Marian polemicists, like Roger Edgeworth and Miles Hoggard, that the Mass

Introduction

was treated with juvenile contempt.[21] The difficulty experienced in marrying the priorities of evangelism and the constrictions of partially reformed institutions is explored in chapter 3.

The separation of the notion of a reformation of externals from the longer process of changing hearts and minds has given rise to a whole historiographical looking-glass world of conflicting *fast* and *slow* reformations. While this debate is particularly at issue in Edward's reign, it need not be, since the fact of reform and the reality of the response to it are different issues. No-one can have escaped the transformation of religion, the shift from image to word, the stark whitewashing of the churches, the extinguishing of the lights. The church simply did not belong in the same way as before, and yet compulsion meant there were still congregations. The process could be seen as analogous to moving from a long-inhabited house: stripped of all the familiar clutter, beloved furniture looks naked and diminished, the fading and wear on the pictureless walls is newly visible, the windows are empty holes. The connection of familiarity has been broken.[22] The new house may be comfortable, but it will take a long time before it is home. The pervasiveness of the transgression was as important as the violent break with tradition that it represented. The evidence of the suspension of commitment, the liminal nature of the space opened by the reforms is clear both from wills, where a neutral formulation became a frequent solution to religious instability,[23] and from the fall in clerical recruitment.[24] Perhaps it is also shown by the difficulties encountered by the Marian regime in trying to reconstruct catholic practice.[25] It should not really surprise us that the changes took so long to get established, and that the godliness of the nation should be such a contested issue. While the concerns of this book are those of the ideologically committed, it is much more difficult both to reconstruct and to explain the impact of all their 'high talk' on the rest.

The theological history of the reign has been dominated by discussion of the development of the 1549 and the 1552 *Prayer Book*. The key issue here is the nature of Cranmer's eucharistic theology, its evolution and the nature and timing of the various influences upon him. The debate has been an acrimonious one, since Cranmer, with his well-documented changes of heart and eventual martyrdom, is such an ambiguous figure in Anglican theology and polemic.[26] He has re-emerged as a guiding presence of these years in MacCulloch's monumental biography in which religious policy is seen as Cranmer's coherent programme of comprehensive and emphatically evangelical reform. The archbishop's own theological and spiritual progress are painstakingly documented and the outward-looking nature of his reformation reaffirmed.[27] The other major issue, one again in which the influence of Swiss protestantism has been seen as playing a major role, is the 'vestments controversy' between Hooper and Ridley. This has been dealt with in detail

Introduction

by J. Primus;[28] Andrew Pettegree has set it firmly in the context of the establishment of the Stranger churches in 1550.[29] The role of continental exile and the strategies necessary to survive the twists and turns of religious policy at home can be found in biographies, of which the best is Fairfield's on Bale; more conventional are J. Ridley on Nicholas Ridley, Allan Chester on Latimer, D. Bailey on Thomas Becon, and W.R.D. Jones on William Turner.[30] Lesser figures have been usefully outlined in John Fines's *Biographical Register of English Protestants*.[31] The presence of continental reformers as distinguished as Martin Bucer, Peter Martyr and John à Lasco in England in this period was undoubtedly significant, and the nature of their influence has been much discussed.[32] This study does not deny the power of that influence, althought it has a rather different focus. The effect of reading the works of English protestants collectively, and to focus on the ideological rather than the theological issues, is to bring out the attitudes protestants shared rather than the potential for doctrinal fragmentation.[33]

CRISIS OR CONTINUITY?

The short reign of Edward VI, dominated by the demands of war and a rapacious regency, dependent on a debased coinage and subject to epidemic disease, seemed for a long time to qualify as a period of crisis. Political instability was exacerbated by economic problems. External war led to an economic crisis and diplomatic confrontation. Internally, the regime was faced with major rebellions in the south-west and East Anglia. Religious conservatism combined with agricultural grievance to produce the most dangerous rebellions since the Pilgrimage of Grace, and this time unrest spread uncomfortably close to London. The elite failed to give a moral lead: financial and sexual scandal dishonoured a group grown rich on the asset-stripping of the church and the corruption of office. Factional politics was not new, but rule by a minor made the regime far more susceptible to coup and counter coup. Uncomfortable similarities with the latter years of Henry VIII and the reign of Mary persuaded W.R.D. Jones see the period 1540–60 as a 'mid-Tudor crisis', in which Edward's reign had a starring role: a time of political turmoil, economic collapse and loss of face abroad. Whether as a low point whose nature was unique, or as part of a more general trough in English fortunes, this was a black picture, contrasting with the splendour of the reigns of Henry VIII and Elizabeth I.[34] It is, however, difficult to sustain a model of crisis that lasts so long. More recently, the trend has been to emphasise the positive side of these years, throwing the periods of instability into sharper focus and contrasting them with both the successes of the regime and the continuities of policy and personnel in government.[35] This study re-examines material that has been used rather one-dimensionally as

Introduction

evidence of contemporary perception of crisis, and reveals its potential both as critique of reform (chapters 3 and 4) and as prophetic and providentialist discourse (chapter 5).

THE 'COMMONWEALTH MEN': REALITY OR ILLUSION?

The one chink of light in this gloomy picture of crisis was afforded by a group of critics of society and the economy. Seizing on their apparent radicalism the assumption was made that these individuals constituted a formal group, a political movement, and they became known as the 'commonwealth party' or 'commonwealth men' after their use of this concept as a means of putting the common public interest before private, selfish ones. R.H. Tawney and Helen White have documented their writings, and W.K. Jordan was shown their political influence.[36] G.R. Elton, however, poured scorn on the notion of a clearly defined 'commonwealth party'.[37] He clearly showed that the so-called commonwealth men were a group of disparate divines, politicians and pamphleteers, whose ideas lacked coherence, whose timing in presenting those ideas was unco-ordinated, and whose interests were diverse. Indeed, he disposed of all but(?) Thomas Smith's *Discourse of the Commonweal* as worthless efforts at formulating economic policy.[38] His critique of the sources was partial, but no more so than the critiques of those who had invented the commonwealth men. However, his contempt for preachers and divines as incapable of original economic and social thinking is perhaps a more serious failing: it plays down the topicality of their utterances and is insensitive to their use of the language of antipopery to describe what they thought was going wrong with the reformation.[39]

This study aims not to rehabilitate the 'commonwealth men' but to show that the protestant response to the problems of Edwardian government and society, and their own situation within it, was a coherent one. One of the reasons for the rise and fall of the commonwealth men is that, until now, historians have read a small number of 'classic texts' – notably Brinkelow's *The Complaint of Roderick Mors*, Latimer's *Sermon on the Plough* (or parts of it), Crowley's *Way to Wealth*, Lever's sermons and little else. By contrast this study allows us to see their writings in context as protestant works, whose shape is based on antipopery (chapter 1), rather than as half-baked economic theory – a rehabilitation which pays due regard to their own identification with the prophets rather than their imagined role as proto-socialists.

WHATEVER HAPPENED TO SOCIAL CONSCIENCE?

The problem of social and economic reform, given an added edge by perceived increase in poverty, was a major political issue, albeit one blunted by inadequate diagnosis of the reasons for inflation, which emphasised enclosure rather than the pressures of population increase, costly war and the debasement of the coinage. The measures taken can be seen as a continuation of the methods of Wolsey and Cromwell.[40] The results were mixed. The Vagrancy Act of 1547, notorious for envisaging the enslavement of the wandering poor, fortunately never came to anything.[41] The Enclosure Commission inadvertently and clumsily destabilised Somerset's rule, and was doomed to failure after its part in the 1549 'stirs'. Indirectly, Northumberland's policy of peace and his attempts to stabilise the coinage were more useful approaches, though they were only beginnings. More forward looking was the 1552 statute which demanded a weekly church collection for the poor. Concerns shown in parliament reflected the active measures that were being taken in towns, where the poor were being counted, given organised relief and work (censuses of the poor: Chester 1539, Coventry 1547, Ipswich 1551; compulsory levies: Norwich 1549; York 1550; work schemes: Oxford and King's Lynn 1546–48).[42] The role played by private philanthropy was still an important one, though Jordan's assumption that it was a growing and secular trend has been thoroughly revised to take into account inflation and a more appropriate consideration of the role of piety.[43] As with the reform of the church, the profiteers and the providers were often the same people: John Hales, the classic 'commonwealth man' and leading enclosure commissioner, founded the grammar school in St John's Hospital in Coventry and built himself a mansion in its Whitefriars.[44] The evangelical tone of poor relief reform was not narrowly protestant – Italian models of hospitals were important. But the most significant and lasting development came in London, where 'a fusion of royal benefaction, civic opportunism, Christian charity and educated patrician self interest' joined the refounded hospitals of St Thomas and St Bartholemew with the new school of Christ's Hospital and the institution of Bridewell in 1552, dedicated to the correction of sin and the provision of work.[45] Poverty, perhaps at its most acute in the capital, was being tackled on all fronts.

Education, the other major social concern of the reformers, has been a more contested area. The dissolution of the chantries was not principally of great profit to the crown: the urgent demands of the war in Scotland soon absorbed the surplus 'windfall'. A.F. Leach, the nineteenth-century authority on English schools, thought that the dissolution had a damaging effect on education at an elementary level by removing the chantry priests who helped to provide it, and that the Edwardian contribution to education has been overstated. Joan Simon has comprehensively overturned this view, showing that the provision of schools and teaching as a result of the dissolution of the chantries was the beginning of state intervention in English education. Twenty-three English counties had refounded or newly constituted schools as a result of the dissolution of the chantries.[46] The central role of education in a

Introduction

reformed commonwealth is clear from the letters patent constituting them.[47] Content as well as setting was a preoccupation of government – a royal Latin grammar was issued in 1549, and Ponet's Latin *Catechism* of 1552 was intended to help schoolmasters ensure that their charges could learn 'godliness together with wisdom'.[48] The universities were subjected to royal visitations in 1549 and the distinguished foreign reformers Martin Bucer and Peter Martyr were appointed as regius professors of divinity in the same year, though attempts to reorganise the colleges to improve the provision of civil law teaching and to restrict grammar teaching to schools were less successful.[49] The anxieties of Lever and Latimer that gentlemen were forcing out poor men's sons from university were not assuaged, but the large proportion of university protestant exiles in Mary's reign, especially from Cambridge, testified to the effectiveness of the promotion of the 'new learning'.[50]

Church and society needed further reform. The royal supremacy provided an ambivalent heritage of opportunity and frustration to the reformers. The accession of Edward did not ease the problem: the king was a child, his government was in the hands of a fractious and factious nobility, and the kingdom was prey to coups and rebellions. When protestants appealed to the godly magistrate, therefore, it was with a tense mixture of professions of loyalty and admonitions of disaster, but they also had enough space to debate the shape that the godly commonwealth might take (see chapters 3, 4 and 5).

EDWARD VI: 'GODLY IMP', 'YOUNG JOSIAH', OR CHIP OFF THE OLD BLOCK?

Ironically, given the image-making to which Edward has been subjected, he is the only sovereign for whom a distorted portrait, or *anamorphosis*, was made.[51] As a child king, he was vulnerable to the machinations of the politically powerful, the formative experiences of the nursery and the schoolroom, the image-making of propagandists and the wishful thinking of historians. But he also left a remarkable archive of autobiographical evidence, much of which is still extant: his 'chronicle' or journal, educational exercises and essays, and 'devises' for the reform of the Council and the Garter Statutes, and, most effectively, for the succession. More recent work has focused on the reinterpretation of this personally produced evidence.

Traditionally, Edward was seen as a sickly child, almost inevitably wasted away by tuberculosis. Such physical weakness made him the prey of powerful figures, especially Northumberland – who may even have poisoned him, so desperate was he to get his own family into power. His tutors were some of the leading humanist scholars of the day: Richard Cox, John Cheke, Roger Ascham and Jean Belmain.[52] The assumption that he was an exceptionally intelligent and bookish child sprang from the weight of evidence about his schooling. It also fitted nicely with the rather Victorian sentimental association of sickliness and intellectual precocity. The woodcut illustration of the king, in Foxe's *Acts and monuments*, showing him intent on Hugh Latimer's preaching from a specially built enclosure in Whitehall, gave him the lasting image of the king who led his Court in listening to sermons.[53] His piety was emphatically protestant – Elton went as far as describing him as bigoted.[54] MacCulloch has characterised it rather more sensitively as having all the intensity of teenage idealism.[55] His diary and exercises have been difficult to use as they were not designed primarily for self-expression. The combination of sickliness, precocity, religious fervour and apparent coldness has given rise to a portrait that is either sentimental or potentially frightening – the orphaned and emotionally stunted king who showed no feeling when his uncles were executed.

Loach has done serious damage to these impressions of the king. Her mission is the destroying of myths, and she carries it out effectively. On the medical side, she both disposes of either puerperal fever or caesarean section as the suggested causes of Jane Seymour's death, proposing instead haemorrage caused by a retained placenta, and confirms the king's relatively good health, until he developed the fatal infection of the lungs that developed into generalised septicaemia with renal failure.[56] While she accepts that the king's tutors were protestant she emphasises that while Henry was alive they did not show these leanings, and they were employed for their learning rather than their protestantism.[57] She dismisses the woodcut of Latimer preaching as a piece of propaganda (which it was, but based on evidence); but, more seriously, she understands that the royal portraits have been insufficiently noticed. These, by Holbein and Scrots, show Edward in the confident stance and the sumptuous clothing of the prince and young king, the son of Henry VIII rather than a 'godly imp'. The evidence for a young aristocrat growing up to enjoy the pageantry and sports of the court, very much in his father's mould, is strong and has been underemphasised for too long.[58] But here, too, there is a note of special pleading, as the evidence for royal piety is explained away as mere upbringing and attachment to Cranmer, his insistence on bringing Mary to heel as little more than a desire for obedience, and the 'devise' for the succession as a product of the combination of advisers, including Cheke and Goodrich as well as Northumberland, in which the king was a willing participant rather than its architect and prime mover.[59] The persistent notion that the young king would know better when he grew up was an illusion that religious conservatives, including Gardiner and Mary, consoled themselves with; after all, it allowed them space for resistance. She ignores both the king's reform of the Garter Statutes and the crucial missing document recording the sermons to which he listened.[60] The former combines nicely the protestant king and the prioritising of the reform of chivalry.

Introduction

The latter is dismissed as a mere list, but even this may be more revealing than she would allow. The emphasis on the king's conventionality is welcome, but it balances rather than wipes away the young Josiah. Upbringing is a strong base for future development, and there is no evidence that points to a change in policy in a more traditional direction had Edward lived. The two images, chivalry and piety, are not mutually exclusive – after all, Josiah died fighting. The militancy of the Edwardian reformation described by MacCulloch might well have turned into a protestant crusade.[61]

SOMERSET AND NORTHUMBERLAND: A REVERSAL OF ROLES?

The dominant figures of Edward's reign have been seen as neatly paired opposing archetypes: the good duke Somerset, seen an idealist with a genuine desire to improve the lot of the poor downtrodden peasant, exploited by rackrenting and enclosing landlords, displaced by the ruthless and treacherous Northumberland, whose ambition was first to plunder the church and then to attempt to divert the succession in favour of his family. His ambition thwarted, he cravenly abandoned the protestantism he had professed to such effect in a grovelling confession on the scaffold. These images had their roots in contemporary comment. Ponet scathingly described Northumberland as 'the ambitious and subtle Alcibiades of England'.[62] Pollard's study of Somerset, and Tawney's view of the agrarian problems of the sixteenth century together with his *Religion and the Rise of Capitalism*, set out this case eloquently, and it has been built on by Helen White, W.R.D. Jones and, above all, W.K. Jordan in his two-volume history of Edward's reign.[63]

But the case was too good to be true, and revision has modified the black and white images of the two leading figures. The result was not so much a transposition as a greyer picture, one that was morally less clear-cut but fairer to character and more politically sensitive. Elton considered Somerset 'high-handed and incompetent'.[64] C.S.L. Davies argued that his social policy was characterised by 'sheer impracticality'.[65] Bush's 1975 radical critique *The Government Policy of Protector Somerset* disposed of the notion that he was especially reform minded, but at the cost of over-emphasising the Scottish campaign as the engine of his policy.[66] Somerset's idealism has given way to his ambition: the extent of his profit from the diocese of Bath and Wells, his self-aggrandisement in the building of Somerset House, his strict control of the king and his increasing scorn for the mechanism of conciliar rule show this clearly.[67] His populism is newly revealed have been a reality, though interpreted not as idealist progressivism but as a dangerous alliance with rebellious interests that ultimately lost him the confidence of his aristocratic colleagues and led to his downfall.[68] Loach questions the extent of

Introduction

his protestant commitment, seeing more evidence of it in his wife, Anne Stanhope.[69]

While Somerset's stock has fallen in recent years, that of Northumberland has risen. Barrett Beer's 1973 biography was much more tolerant than the traditional view, pointing out that as lord president of the Council, and *not* lord protector, he was much more open to counsel and advice than was Somerset, was morbidly aware of his own shortcomings, especially his relatively poor education, and even that 'his acquisition of wealth was no crime in an age of grandeur and ostentation'.[70] Hoak's study of the Edwardian Council clearly showed the dictatorial nature of the Somerset regime, and the contrasting efforts of Northumberland to play by the rules. This view was further detailed in his essay aiming to 'rehabilitate' the duke's reputation.[71] Achievements in economic and foreign affairs show that he was capable of making tough decisions. The ending of war in 1550 with the two traditional enemies of England, Scotland and France, was once seen as his most cowardly act; but MacCulloch justifiably describes him as 'one of the great peacemakers of the century'.[72] Though his towering ambition, especially shown by his determination to build himself a power base in the north-east, cannot be denied, illness and exhaustion, indeed a major failure of nerve, seem to make desperation rather than overweening desire for power the engine of his actions in the summer of 1553, notably his support for the *devise* for the succession and his rapid capitulation to the Marian regime.[73] His confession is viewed less moralistically, and more as a last ditch attempt to save not his own neck but his children's property. It was more catholic than papist, and was 'vague and imprecise' about doctrinal considerations.[74]

Jennifer Loach is more restrained in her conclusions about Northumberland, seeing the main differences between him and Somerset in their methods of rule, rather than in character or policy. Both men were 'ambitious, greedy and corrupt', but Northumberland faced the problems of social unrest in the wake of the 1549 risings, a financial impasse brought about by the cost of war, the debasement of the coinage and a succession of bad harvests between 1549 and 1551. It was the need to govern defensively in the face of these threats that made his government seem more reactionary than it was.[75] Mark Nicholl explained the insecurities of the Dudley regime as springing from its 'essentially provisional' nature, seeing the establishment of the county lieutenancies and the 'gendarmes' as a reflection of anxiety about disorder, and the participation of the young king in Council business as a way of managing him, however deferentially.[76] The device for the succession was thus less the work of the dying king and more a desperate attempt to shore up Dudley fortunes. If so, it was a high-risk strategy, particularly in view of the disbandment of the gendarmes the previous October. Northumberland could not outface Mary's legitimate claim to the throne – in the face of this his nerve

Introduction

crumbled, and all his attempts to placate her were doomed to be remembered as cowardly backsliding, rather than as the continuation of a policy of pragmatic accommodation to adverse circumstances.

UNSTABLE POLITICS?

The influential role of faction in Tudor politics, particularly in the Court of the capricious and increasingly moody Henry VIII, has become a truism in recent historiography.[77] The result of that habit of political behaviour did not go away when Henry died – rather the space he left was almost inevitably vulnerable to the machinations of powerful individuals, however determined he was to protect it. The accession of the 9-year-old Edward exposed politics to palace revolutions – faction was not a new development, but came to be laid bare at key points throughout his short reign.

The origins of Somerset's rapid rise to power lay in the Court politics of the dying king Henry VIII. The nature of Henry's intentions for the governance of the realm and the safety of his son have been subjected to close scrutiny by Starkey, Miller, Ives and Houlbrooke, debating the extent to which the king's will was open to tampering with by Hertford and his allies in the Privy Chamber and the Council, in order to facilitate his rapid rise to the protectorship.[78] While it seems clear that Hertford was abetted in this process by Paget and that the executors were rewarded with new titles and a liberal distribution of crown lands, what is not clear is the extent to which Henry himself was in control. The process by which the conservative consensus of the mid-1540s gave way, with the fall of the Howards and the exclusion of Gardiner from the Regency Council, to victory for the reforming faction is indistinct.[79]

One significant individual to be sidelined in the process was Thomas Seymour, uncle to the king and brother of the lord protector, whose *amour propre* was satisfied by his rapid preferment to lord admiral in February 1547, and by £500 per annum in crown lands from the king's 'unwritten will'. Seymour was not content to ride on his brother's coat tails, but aimed to rise by preying on the emotional attachment of vulnerable members of the royal house – the king's widow Catherine Parr, who he married with 'unseemly haste', the princess Elizabeth, with whom he at the very least flirted, and the young king, who he flattered and gave money to in an attempt to secure the office of 'governor' of his person. While Edward 'showed precocious discretion' in handling his advances, Somerset took no chances in the light of the evidence of a potential coup, and signed his brother's death warrant. Latimer's sermons during the Lent of 1549, justifying this fratricide, show just how uneasy the protector and the Council felt about the proceedings, though the danger was real enough.[80]

More dangerous still, however, was the general rural unrest and the rioting that had gathered momentum by the summer of 1549. Demand for economic reform and the assertion of religious traditionalism meant that the protectorship was threatened on all fronts – and government policy was to blame. The destruction of hedges by those opposed to enclosure had become a feature of rural life in the 1530s and 1540s,[81] but government commissions of 1548 and 1549 precipitated the commons into direct action in widespread 'stirs' in the Midlands and East Anglia. In the west country, religious conservatism doused the Whitsunday inauguration of the new *Prayer book*, which was intended to be a gentle introduction to the reform of the sacraments. The ensuing risings were the worst threat to the progress of the Edwardian reformation, which ironically ensured a more vigorous assertion of protestant doctrine.[82] Elsewhere, and not only in Norfolk, as has recently been shown by Ethan Shagan, the authority of the government was deeply compromised by the protector's attempt to grant concessions to the rebels. Protector Somerset's 'populism' has been given a new face, but this time as the desperate strategy of a man whose power derived from the fact that he was the king's uncle, and who 'wanted to be uncle to the whole realm'. It was thus the need of his aristocratic colleagues on the Council to stop Somerset as much as it was to suppress the rebellion that led to the slaughter at Dussindale.[83] But the end, in 1549, of what MacCulloch has vividly described as the 'carnival time' of the Edwardian reformation had a direct consequence for its long-term health: the perceived betrayal of Somerset's promises by Northumberland led people eventually to support princess Mary rather than queen Jane.[84]

CONCLUSION

The verdict on Edward' reign is a contested one, partly as a result of the acutely confessional prejudices it evokes, partly because it was a period in which high ideals combined with low opportunism to a marked degree. This study does not aim to be another history of the reign; it attempts to reconstruct the presentation of the protestant case. It is not so much intended to put a new piece of the historical jigsaw in place as to show a shifting configuration of the historical kaleidoscope – the reformation seen through protestant eyes.

Why is it important to study these writings? They are conventional in many respects, and show clear continuities with the evangelical productions of the 1530s. What gives them their edge is not so much the secular content as the sense of urgency produced by the unstable political context, and the unalloyed biblicism of their response to it. The difficulty of needing both to influence or even curry favour with the regime and to retain enough distance to be critical was one that sooner or later would lead to conflict, but things were changing too fast for these tensions to be resolved. In retrospect,

Introduction

protestants would see Edward's reign both as an opportunity lost and, later, as a high watermark of reform.[85] In this, however, they were only working out positions which had been laid out in the reign itself.

NOTES

1. Elton, *Reform and Reformation*, 371; Dickens, *The English Reformation*, 2nd edn (1989), 230–42.
2. J. Scarisbrick, *The Reformation and the English People* (Oxford, 1984), 19–39; Eamon Duffy, *The Stripping of the Altars: Traditional Religion in England, 1400–1580* (New Haven, CT, 1992), Part 2, especially ch. 13.
3. John Fines, *A Biographical Register of Early English Protestants, and Others Opposed to the Roman Catholic Church 1525–58* (Abingdon, 1989), Part 1: *A–C*. I am very grateful to Professor Fines for giving me a typescript of Part 2 of his *Register (D–Z)*.
4. Christopher Haigh, *English Reformations: Religion, Politics and Society under the Tudors* (Oxford, 1993).
5. MacCulloch, *Thomas Cranmer*, part 3 and ch. 12; *Tudor Church Militant*, esp. 8, 14, 156–8 and *passim*.
6. Ibid., 71–4, 126–33; 140–1, and 155–6. A good comparison with the German reformation is to be found in S. Ozment, *Protestants: The Birth of a Revolution* (1993).
7. Ibid., 35–6, 163–5.
8. W.G. Hoskins, *The Age of Plunder. The England of Henry VIII* (1976). Chapter 6 traces the story from the monastic dissolutions to the plunder of episcopal estates continuing through Edward's reign. MacCulloch, *Cranmer*, 520–4, shows how ecclesiastical property was becoming a serious source of strife between secular and church leaders in 1553; Duffy, *Stripping*, chs 13 and 14 discusses the Edwardian reforms and associated plundering of the parishes.
9. Robert Whiting, *Local Responses to the English Reformation* (Basingstoue, 1998), 169–171.
10. Ronald Hutton, *The Rise and Fall of Merry England: The Ritual Year, 1400–1700* (Oxford, 1994), ch. 3.
11. Duffy, *Stripping*, 487–90.
12. Hutton, *Merry England*, 79–93.
13. Margaret Aston, *England's Iconoclasts*, vol. 1: *Laws Against Images* (Oxford, 1988), 246–77.
14. Eric Carlson, *Marriage and the English Reformation* (Oxford and Cambirdge, MA, 1994), 52–3; and H. Parish, *Clerical Marriage and the English Reformation: Precedent, Policy and Practice* (Aldershot, 2000). Ch. 8 modifies some of his conclusions.
15. Patrick Collinson and John Craig (eds) *The Reformation in English Towns* (1998). Contains articles by MacCulloch on Worcester and Julia Merritt on Westminster.
16. Duffy, *Stripping*, ch. 13; MacCulloch, *Tudor Church Militant*, 159–63; note the example of the Edwardian royal arms in plate 65.
17. Ibid., ch. 14.
18. See Chapter 5.
19. Maculloch, *Cranmer*, 533–4. For the result of this lack of action on marriage, see Carlson, *Marriage*, 82–5. For the reform of canon law, see J.C. Spalding, *The Reformation of the Ecclesiastical Laws of England, 1552* (Kirksville, MO, 1992).
20. See J. Primus, *The Vestments Controversy* (Kampen, 1960); C. Davies and J. Facey, 'A reformation dilemma: John Foxe and the problem of discipline', *JEH* (1988): 37–65.

Introduction

21 See J.F. Davis, *Heresy and the Reformation in the South-East of England* (1983), for the persistence of Lollardy, though his conclusions are somewhat overstated. See MacCulloch, *Tudor Church Militant*, 108-9, for an overview and Susan Brigden, *London and the Reformation* (Oxford and New York, 1989), 441-2, for the impact on the capital.
22 I owe this metaphor to Anne Waugh, a student on my English reformation course at the School of Continuing Studies, University of Birmingham, in 1998.
23 Duffy, *Stripping*, ch. 15; Hutton, *Merry England*, 94-5; Whiting, *Local Responses*, 125-6.
24 See above, n. 9; and Rosemary O'Day and Felicity Heal, *Princes and Paupers in the English Church, 1500-1800* (Leicester, 1981).
25 Duffy, *Stripping*, ch. 16.
26 Notably in the range of views found in C. Smyth, *Cranmer and the Reformation Under Edward VI* (Cambridge, 1926; repr. Greenwood, CT, 1970); C. Dugmore, *The Mass and the English Reformers* (1958); P.N. Brooks, *Thomas Cranmer's Doctrine of the Eucharist* (1965).
27 MacCulloch, *Cranmer*. Note especially 334, 354-5, 357, 379-83, 391-2, 467 for Eucharist, updating n. 26.
28 Primus, *Vestments Controversy*, chs 1-4; B. Verkamp, *The Indifferent Mean: Adiaphorism in the English Reformation to 1554* (Athens, OH, 1977).
29 A. Pettegree, *Foreign Protestant Communities in Sixteenth Century London* (Oxford, 1986).
30 L. Fairfield, *John Bale, Mythmaker for the English Reformation* (West Lafayette, IN, 1976); J. Ridley, *Nicholas Ridley. A Biography* (1957); D.S. Bailey, *Thomas Becon* (1952); Allan Chester, *Hugh Latimer. Apostle to the English* (Philadelphia, PA, 1954); W.R.D. Jones, *William Turner: Tudor Naturalist, Physician and divine* (1988).
31 See above, n. 3.
32 See above, ns 28, 29. See also C. Hopf, *Martin Bucer and the English Reformation* (Oxford, 1946), and MacCulloch, *Cranmer*.
33 See Conclusion, pp. 231-2.
34 A.F. Pollard, *The History of England from the Accession of Edward VI to the Death of Elizabeth* (1910); S.T. Bindoff, *Tudor England* (1950); W.R.D. Jones, *The Mid-Tudor Crisis, 1539-1563* (1973); G.R. Elton, *Reform and Reformation: England 1509-58* (1977), 298, 341; and W.K. Jordan, *Edward VI: The Young King* (1968) and *Edward VI: The Threshold of Power* (1970).
35 The reassessment of the mid-Tudor period is signalled in J. Loach and R. Tittler (eds) *The Mid-Tudor Polity, c.1540-60* (1980). See especially the Introduction, though the emphasis is rather more on the rehabilitation of Mary than the reassessment of Edward's reign. M.L. Bush, *The Government Policy of Protector Somerset* (1975), emphasised the Scottish campaign rather than idealism as the motivating factor behind the Protector's policy; Dale Hoak, *The King's Council in the Reign of Edward VI* (Cambridge, 1976) and 'Rehabilitating the Duke of Northumberland: politics and political control, 1549-53', in Loach and Tittler (eds) *Mid-Tudor Polity*, judges Northumberland more positively; J. Loach, *Edward VI* (Yale, CT, 1999), emphasises the essential continuity of the reign with this period. W.S. Hudson, *The Cambridge Connection and the Elizabethan Settlement of 1559* (Durham, NC, 1980), is a good example of tracing continuities in personnel.
36 R.H. Tawney, *Religion and the Rise of Capitalism* (1926; repr. 1943), 142-50; H. White, *Social Criticism in the Popular Religious Literature of the Sixteenth Century* (New York, 1944); N. Pocock, 'The condition of morals and religious belief in the reign of Edward VI', *EHR* (1895): 417-44. This curiously uses mostly Marian books as evidence.
37 G.R. Elton, 'Reform and the "commonwealth-men" of Edward VI's reign', in P. Clark, A. Smith and N. Tyacke (eds) *The English Commonwealth: Essays Presented to Joel Hurstfield*

Introduction

(Leicester, 1979), 23–38. Postscripts by B.L. Beer and R.J. Nash, 'Hugh Latimer and the lusty knave of Kent: the commonwealth movement of 1549', *BIHR* (1979): 175–8, modifies some of the details of Elton's arguments.
38 Since it can be convincingly argued that the *Discourse of the Commonweal* is primarily an economic treatise – see G.R. Elton, *Reform and Reformation: England 1509–58* (1977), 323–5 – it has been omitted from this study.
39 Compare Chapters 4 and 5, below, with Elton, 'Reform and the "commonwealth-men"'.
40 Paul Slack, *From Reformation to Improvement: Public Welfare in Early Modern England* (1998), ch. 1.
41 C.S.L. Davies, 'Slavery and protector Somerset: the Vagrancy Act of 1547', *EcHR* (1966): 533–49.
42 Paul Slack, *Poverty and Policy in Tudor and Stuart England* (1988), ch. 6.
43 W.K. Jordan, *Philanthropy in England 1480–1660* (1959), modified in J. Hadwin, 'Deflating philanthropy,' *EcHR* (1978): 112ff.
44 Slack, *From Reformation to Improvement*, 23.
45 *Ibid.*, 20.
46 Joan Simon, *Education and Society in Tudor England* (1966; Cambridge, 1979), 239.
47 *Ibid.*, 40; e.g. Louth.
48 *Ibid.*, 43; further detail on the state of learning, especially relating to books on travel, anatomy, arithmetic, biblical literature, humanist texts and school textbooks in ch. XI.
49 *Ibid.*, ch. X.
50 H.C. Porter, *Reformation and Reaction in Tudor Cambridge* (Cambridge, 1958), 78–92.
51 Jennifer Loach, ed. G. Bernard and P. Williams, *Edward VI* (New Haven, CT, 1999), plate 5. The distortion is on similar lines to the skull in Holbein's *The Ambassadors*.
52 Elton, *Reform and Reformation*, 318; MacCulloch, *Tudor Church Militant*, 20–1, 25.
53 Loach, *Edward VI*, 113; MacCulloch, *Tudor Church Militant*, 23–5.
54 Elton, *Reform and Reformation*, 371–2.
55 MacCulloch, *Tudor Church Militant*, 41.
56 Loach, *Edward VI*, 6–8, 159–62.
57 *Ibid.*, ch. 2; cf. n. 52.
58 *Ibid.*, plates 6, 7, 8 and ch. 11 on Edward's court.
59 *Ibid.*, 163–4; cf. MacCulloch, *Tudor Church Militant*, 39–41.
60 Loach, *Edward VI*, 158, dismissing the missing sermon notebook; MacCulloch, *Tudor Church Militant*, 23, is more positive about its potential. On reform of the Garter Statutes, see MacCulloch, *ibid.*, 30–4.
61 Thomas Audley envisaged the young king leading his troops to glory, but shrewdly advised caution in the process in British Museum Add. MS 23971, transcribed by Lieut. Col. W. St P. Bunbury, in *Journal of Army Historical Research* (1927), VI. Jonathan Davies kindly gave me this reference.
62 John Ponet, *A Short Treatise of Politic Power* (Strasburg, 1556), sig. Iiii.
63 Chapter 5, n. 1. see also G. Parry, 'Inventing "the good duke" of Somerset', *JEH* (1989).
64 G.R. Elton, *England Under the Tudors* (1955), 222, 209–10.
65 Davies, 'Slavery', 533–49.
66 Bush, *Government Policy of Protector Somerset*.
67 See Loach, *Edward VI*, 40, especially ns 5 and 6, on his rapaciousness.
68 MacCulloch, *Tudor Church Militant*, 44–52, 122, 147–9.
69 Loach, *Edward VI*, 43; MacCulloch sees the allegory of 'Edward VI and the pope' as connected with her (*Tudor Church Militant*, 200–4), as opposed to the alternative theories expressed by Margaret Aston in *The King's Bedpost: Reformation and Iconography in a Tudor Group Portrait* (Cambridge, 1993).

70 B.L. Beer, *Northumberland: The Political Career of John Dudley, Earl of Warwick and Duke of Northumberland* (Kent, OH, 1973), 164–5. Cf. David Loades, *John Dudley, Duke of Northumberland, 1504–1553* (Oxford, 1996).
71 Hoak, *The King's Council*; also 'Rehabilitating the duke of Northumberland: politics and political control, 1549–53', in Loach and Tittler (eds) *The Mid-Tudor Polity*, and 'The king's privy chamber, 1547–53', in *Tudor Rule and Revolution: Essays Presented to G.R. Elton by His American Friends* (Cambridge, 1982), 87–108.
72 Maculloch, *Tudor Church Militant*, 17.
73 Beer, *Northumberland*, 154–63.
74 *Ibid.*, 162.
75 Loach, *Edward VI*, 114–15.
76 Mark Nicholls, *A History of the Modern British Isles: The Two Kingdoms, 1529–1603* (1999), 133.
77 Eric Ives, *Faction in Tudor England*, Historical Association Pamphlet (1979); David Starkey, *The Reign of Henry VIII: Personalities and Politics* (1985); John Guy, *Tudor England* (Oxford 1988).
78 Starkey, *Reign of Henry VIII*, 160–4; Helen Miller, 'Henry VIII's unwritten will: grants of lands and honours in 1547', in E. Ives, R. Knecht and J. Scarisbrick (eds) *Wealth and Power in Tudor England: Essays Presented to S.T. Bindoff* (1978), 87–106; Eric Ives, 'Henry VIII's will: a forensic conundrum', *HJ* (1992): 779–804; Ralph Houlbroooke, 'Henry VII's wills: a comment', *HJ* (1994): 891–9; Eric Ives, 'The protectorate provisions of 1546–7', in *ibid.*: 901–14.
79 Loach, *Edward VI*, 26.
80 *Ibid.*, 55–7; George Bernard, 'The downfall of Sir Thomas Seymour', in George Bernard, (ed.) *The Tudor Nobility* (Manchester, 1992), 212–40.
81 R.B. Manning, *Village Revolts: Social Protest and Popular Disturbances in England 1509–1640* (Oxford, 1988), 31.
82 Loach, *Edward VI*, chs 8 and 10; MacCulloch, *Tudor Church Militant*, 141–56.
83 MacCulloch, *Tudor Church Militant*, 43–52; Ethan Shagan, 'Protector Somerset and the 1549 rebellions: new sources and new perspectives', *EHR* (1999): 34–63. Note the ensuing debate in *EHR* (February 2000) between Michael Bush, George Bernard and Ethan Shagan.
84 MacCulloch, *Tudor Church Militant*, 156.
85 *Ibid.*, ch. 4; and Conclusion pp. 231–3.

Chapter 1

The struggle against popery

INTRODUCTION

Anticatholic propaganda has too often been either ignored or dismissed as the regrettably bigoted face of protestantism.[1] This has been the case particularly with Edward VI's reign, where a disproportionate amount of attention has been given to the 'acceptable' concerns of social criticism and reform. The resulting image of reform was thus automatically distorted. A glance at the titles alone of protestant printed works produced in this period reveals antipopery to be (in terms of sheer quantity) by far the most important issue, one which dominates the surge of print during the years 1548–50, and this does not include a great deal of material to be found within works with 'neutral' or unpolemical titles.[2] Moreover, antipopery formed the polemical context which shaped protestant ideas on other subjects, notably about the nature of *church* and *state* and their relationship, about the direction and necessity of reform, and about the relationship of contemporary events to time and providence. Just as significantly, the concentration of attention on fighting popery largely explains 'polemical silences', or subjects that were not discussed.

It should not be assumed, however, that antipopery was an unchanging formulation of ideas. The shifting circumstances of the English reformation make it a highly topical subject. The issues of justification by faith alone, purgatory and the power of the papacy, characteristic of the 1520s and 1530s,[3] were less prominent than discussion of the Mass and clerical celibacy. This reflects in part a change in connections with continental protestantism, from Wittenberg to Strassburg and Zurich,[4] but – more significantly – changing political events at home. The establishment of the royal supremacy had made the papacy recede in importance just as the dissolution of the monasteries had reduced interest in satires on the regular orders and discussion of purgatory.

But the Sacrament and clerical celibacy were both subjects on which the Act of Six Articles had taken a conservative line, so that its abolition in 1547, in combination with Somerset's relaxation of censorship, allowed legitimate discussion in print of these subjects for the first time. Thus a significant proportion of the material published in the first two years of Edward's reign referred to the conservative 1540s, notably the refutations, by Hooper and Gilby, of Gardiner's important *Detection of the Devil's Sophistry* (1546) and Robert Crowley's *Confutation of Shaxton's Articles*.[5]

The subject protestants discussed most often was the Mass, as befitted a period of intense popular debate, public scholarly disputations (at Oxford and Cambridge in 1548, which were set up to ensure a protestant victory), and the publication and enforcement of the 1548 and 1549 Communion Services. The government's active involvement in encouraging protestant publicists, sponsoring a preaching campaign and muzzling the catholic opposition was in clear contrast to Henrician conservatism.[6] Protestants made use of the full range of literary forms at their disposal to attack the Mass. Some writers tackled it in terms of single issues. These included Edmund Guest, whose denunciation of private Masses coincided with the dissolution of the chantries, and William Salesbury, who timed his *Battery of the pope's buttress*, which attacked the doctrine of the re-enactment of the sacrifice of Christ on the cross in the Mass to coincide with the destruction of altars.[7] Other writers used a more general approach: Jean Veron described the main doctrines of the Mass in a blow-by-blow attack on the 'Five blasphemies' he alleged it contained, and in *Certain little treatises* used the liturgy of the Mass in evidence against it.[8] Tracts defending the Lord's Supper took the form of attacks on the Mass, although a more positive protestant emphasis emerged after the 1549 *Prayer Book*.[9] The contempt felt by protestants for the Mass allowed them to use it as a subject for entertainment as well as edification. Thus in ballads and dialogues the Mass was punningly satirised as mistress Missa, the harlot daughter of the pope, who was to be tried by Truth and sent ignominiously packing back to her father in Rome or even hell.[10]

However, the Mass did not lack defenders, despite the difficulties catholic writers faced in Edward's reign: Stephen Gardiner and Richard Smith were able scholarly controversialists, and Miles Hoggard wrote for a more popular market.[11] Gardiner's *An explication and assertion of the true catholic faith of the sacrament of the altar*, published in Rouen in 1551, attacked both the 1549 *Prayer Book*'s Service of Communion and Cranmer's 1550 *Defence of the true and catholic doctrine of the Sacrament of the body and blood of our saviour Christ*. Richard Smith also produced a *Confutation* of Cranmer in 1550, published in Paris, and Cranmer felt bound to produce a lengthy reply, in his *Answer to a crafty and sophistical cavillation devised by Stephen Gardiner* (1551), to which he appended his *Answer to Smith's preface*. The controversy extended into Mary's

A religion of the Word

reign when the tables were turned once again and Cranmer was on the defensive in the 1555 disputations.[12] A less sophisticated debate took place between Miles Hoggard and Robert Crowley, which started out with Hoggard's verse refutation of an anonymous protestant anti-Mass ballad and was confuted in prose by Crowley in 1548.[13]

While no other single issue compared with the Sacrament in terms of quantity or range of printed material, clerical celibacy stood out. This debate had simmered throughout the 1540s, when Gardiner defended it against Martin Bucer and George Joye. John Ponet wrote an elegant *Defence of the marriage of priests* to accompany its legalisation in 1549, which was later to prove somewhat embarrassing in the light of his own disastrous marriage. Vowed celibacy was the central theme of Bale's *Acts of the English votaries* (1546–48), which chronicled the rise of the regular orders in England on the basis of the 'feigned holiness' which vows of chastity gave them. He also debated the subject of vows with a 'rank papist'.[14]

Bale's obsession with the monastic orders was in part personal idiosyncrasy, part throwback to the 1530s. The lasting effect of the reforms of that era go a long way to explain the relative neglect of topics such as images and the cult of purgatory, despite their topicality in view of the Edwardian dissolution of the chantries and plunder of church plate and goods.[15] Though Gardiner's defence of images was attacked by Hooper (who also preached a funeral sermon against purgatory), a reluctance to be associated with anarchic popular iconoclasm, combined with increasing concern that the purging of the church was turning into sacrilege, seems to have inhibited denunciations of images.[16] What was new was the licence to confront the Mass itself as the supreme example of false worship, rather than the restriction of the attacks to the cult of saints.

Antipopery brought together a wide range of literary forms to attack a relatively narrow range of subjects. The same attitudes and themes can be found throughout the whole range, whether they be scurrilous ballads, short pamphlets, or more scholarly polemic. Analysis of these varied texts shows how consistent protestant attitudes to popery were, despite variations in the range of sacramental doctrines, and it is from this consistency that a pattern emerges which provides a key to the understanding of Edwardian reform mentality.

Fundamental to the structure of protestant polemic was the assumption that protestantism and popery were polarised opposites, on the basis of the dichotomy between true and false religion. This dichotomising method allowed protestants to disassociate themselves completely from popery. It was confirmed and extended by a process of inversion in defence of 'truth': those aspects of traditional catholic piety which had hitherto been regarded as constituting its unassailable virtues were revealed as hideous vices. Revelation of the truth was naturally and rhetorically shocking. But if such a monstrous lie had been perpetrated for so long, what had allowed it to persist? The explanation required a subtle balancing act from protestants, who could not simply dismiss generations of piety, yet could not condone them either. Hence the popularity of the notion of conspiracy, especially and pre-eminently that of a *clerical conspiracy*, which allowed the mass of the people to be quietly exonerated from blame. The clerical conspiracy was the earthly face of the conspiracy of Satan and Antichrist to destroy true religion. This appealed to and consisted in all that was corrupt and fleshly in fallen human nature. It was, in short, a religion of sin. It was supported by other means: by disorder, which explained the false worldview it imposed; by delusion, which explained its psychological hold over both ordinary people and the 'powers that be', and finally by repression, which obtained by open force the power it could not obtain by stealth. Using these themes – of dichotomy, inversion, conspiracy, disorder, delusion and repression – as analytical tools, a more rounded picture of the assumptions protestants held about popery will emerge, and in the process provide a context for their views on the reformation of church and state.

DICHOTOMY

The fundamental dichotomy between 'true' and 'false' religion grew out of the persistent need to distance the reform from popery and yet to be able to shrug off the charge of schism. In this way, protestants could associate themselves with objectivity, truth, and whatever was divine or spiritual in origin, while consigning popery to the realm of falsehood, subjectivity, the world, the flesh and the devil. The charge of schism was thus neatly side-stepped. The two religions were opposite poles, linked only by antagonism or conflict. On closer examination, the monolithic dichotomy between true and false religion can be seen to be a construction of a series of lesser dichotomies, which were closely related, the four most significant being that between scripture and human learning or tradition, between light and darkness, between spirit and flesh, and between the true and the false church.

If protestantism was a 'religion of the word', the most fundamental dichotomy was that between *scripture* and *human traditions*. What had begun as a humanist desire to return to the written sources of religion, to restore purity to a corrupted text and to base piety on that text rather than on traditional rituals, became in protestant writings a desire to make scripture the sole objective source of truth.[17] Protestant emphasis on the centrality of scripture sprang from the need to give saving faith a firm foundation: *sola fide* could only safely be predicated on *sola scriptura*. The result was the replacement of the authority of the church by the authority of the Word. The popish church

A religion of the Word

no longer enshrined the Word, according to protestants, but was a fundamentally different type of authority which all too often in the past had conflicted with the Word of God and even attempted to stifle its true message. The Bible, as the revelation of the divine will, was treated as a unitary document, a text that applied in all times and places,[18] whereas the traditions of the church were seen not as the proof of the presence of the Holy Spirit, but as historical and human developments subject to corruption and decay.[19]

In metaphorical terms, scripture revealed the light of truth, while tradition led men only into the darkness of lies. This implied a definite choice. As Elijah scorned the Israelites for trying to worship both God and Baal, and 'walk unrightly' between light and darkness, so Bale derided the English for refusing to choose between the Gospel and popery.[20] The protestant godly were in these terms those 'enlightened ones' who had either read the Bible or listened to its message, while papists were associated with the darkness of spiritual blindness, the ignorance and malice arising from their wilful preference for their own traditions.[21] The light of scripture was a valuable polemical asset: it alone could reveal the murkiness of their opponents' arguments. Hence Bale described the works of pagan philosophers as 'dark lights' on which true preachers have no need to rely, as they possessed the 'sun of righteousness' in the Bible. That same 'sun' showed the works of the schoolmen to be 'abominable lies and errors'.[22] In debate, they tended to focus attention on the meaning of biblical texts, dismissing tradition, patristics and reason to at best a secondary status.[23] The attempts of Smith and Gardiner to bring tradition back into the centre of the argument were largely ignored.[24]

'Light' and 'darkness' had both moral and rhetorical connotations. Great play was made of the lucidity, clarity and essential simplicity of a 'literal' interpretation of scripture in comparison to the contorted, complex and diverse arguments resorted to by papists. Cranmer pointed out that even when papists declared *Hoc est corpus meum* as a simple statement of fact, 'in expounding these words they vary among themselves, which is a token that they be uncertain of their own doctrine'.[25] Gardiner's attempts to avoid being labelled a papist only dragged him deeper into confusion. According to Joye, his doctrine of justification was 'so intricate, perplex and repugnant, that in many places ye fight against yourself...'.[26] On the Lord's Supper, Cranmer accused him of agreeing neither with 'the true catholic doctrine' nor with 'the papistical doctrine', but of making 'a song of three parts; you have devised a new voluntary descant, so far out of tune that it agreeth neither with the tenor nor mean, but maketh such a shameful jar that godly ears abhor to hear it'.[27] Building on humanist textual radicalism, protestants made their contempt for 'Dunsical learning' very clear: they dismissed scholastic traditions of 'glossing' or interpreting the Bible through commentaries as obscuring rather than deepening understanding.[28]

The struggle against popery

The popish clerical monopoly on theology was doubly iniquitous. Not only did it foster false doctrine: it made those who should be teachers and preachers into 'blind guides' who could only lead the people into darkness and error. There was thus a pressing need for preachers who expounded the literal text, not those who obscured the Word with human philosophy or 'fables'. Hooper described the fall of man as a paradigm of popery: 'And whereas he [i.e. Adam] would not for the love of God believe the texts of God's mouth, the pains that followed his transgression taught him to know that the gloss was diabolical.'[29] The ultimate fate of both those who created papistical glosses and those who believed them was consignment to the darkness eternal. Something of this punishment could be perceived in this world, however, since belief in false doctrine could not bring comfort. By contrast, the Bible sustained believers in a way that no human doctrine could, since it revealed the will of God.[30]

The comfort brought by scripture to the faithful introduces another dichotomy, that which existed between the *godly* and the *ungodly*. These would always exist: even the Gospel sorted out sheep from goats. To the godly the Gospel meant the good news of saving faith in Christ, but the ungodly closed their ears to it, for it brought them the painful truth of damnation. Bale described the process as a confirmation of faith and of disbelief:

> This song is the Word of the Lord, all new, both to the good and to the ill: the faithful it reneweth in the spirit of their minds, provoking them to put on a new man in Christ; the hearts of the unfaithful are so hardened that they in disdain and spite do call it new learning, as did the ignorant multitude at Capernaum, and the worldly-wise men at Athens.[31]

The ungodly, in turning away from the Gospel, sought the immediate satisfaction of works' righteousness and the apparent security of devotional rituals. Instead of being drawn to God by the message of the Bible, they were drawn away from him by worship and piety that they had invented contrary to his will. While the Word was life-giving, popish piety brought spiritual death. Hooper developed this contrast by showing how intentionally the imagery of the gospel was drawn from nature:

> Those things [i.e. nature] were made to be testimonies unto us of God's mighty power, and to draw men unto virtue; not these idols, which the devil caused to be set in the temple to bring men from God. Thus did Christ teach the people his most blessed death and passion, and the fruit of his passion, by the grain of corn cast into the earth ... He hanged not the picture of his body upon the cross, to teach them his death, as our late learned men have done.[32]

People's response to scripture and tradition on the basis of godliness or ungodliness indicated the dichotomy between *spirit* and *flesh*. Protestant writers

A religion of the Word

were well aware that this was a fundamental concern, especially of the New Testament, and also that conservatives often accused them of a scepticism characteristic of their carnality.[33] It was not surprising, then, that protestants were eager to re-appropriate spirituality from the definitions of traditional piety, and re-emphasise their links with scripture in the process. The possibility of open discussion, in print, of the Sacrament for the first time in 1548,[34] although amounting to licence for protestants to attack the Mass,[35] meant that the defining of 'spirit' and 'flesh', and of the necessary conflict between them, were at the forefront of the debate. This was a critical contrast with the earlier stress on *faith* and *works*, although the identification of spirituality with an inward and justifying faith, and carnality with external works and rituals meant that the justification debate lay only just submerged in the Sacrament polemic.[36]

Though the doctrinal niceties raised by discussion of the Sacrament were already causing problems among protestants,[37] the polemical contrast between spirit and flesh allowed these differences to be downplayed. Thus, for instance, Crowley showed that a symbolic understanding of the Sacrament was full of meaning: 'These are things of great importance and value in the eyes of the spiritual members of Christ, though in your fleshly eyes which cannot discern the things of the spirit, they be vile and of no value.'[38] Transubstantiation was a doctrine that sprang from a 'carnal' understanding of Christ's words during the Last Supper. Gilby wrote: 'These words ("This is [my] body which shall be given for you") were never meant so carnally, that every priest mumbling these words in a strange language with breathing and blowing should cause Christ to come down from the right hand of the Father, to be changed into bread, that he might sacrifice him new again to take away sins.'[39] Evidence of the 'carnal mind' was to be found in the uncomprehending response, both of the Jews of Capernaum and of the papists, to Christ's description of himself as 'the bread of life' in John 6.[40] Crowley found the papists more carnal than the Jews – 'You declare yourselves neither to favour the spirit nor yet to understand the phrases of the letter.'[41]

Popery, in the Mass, concerned itself with externals, resulting not in a developed spirituality but in mere hypocrisy, or pharisaism – an outward appearance of devotion. The protestant Lord's Supper, however, provided a focus for true worship, which was purely spiritual in character.[42] Edmund Guest wrote that the Sacrament should be taken as Christ had instituted it:

> that is to wit; with pure faith, cleaned conscience, with unfained repentance, charity and thankgiving, with full desire and purpose to be fed with Christ's flesh, to be thereby mortified to sin and sanctified, to be embodied to Christ and not to crouch before the bread, to his flesh, or to worship, invocate and solicit him as present in or under the bread.[43]

Faith was not a result of experiencing the Sacrament or believing in transubstantiation, but preceded the Sacrament and was confirmed and nourished by it. As the chief occasion when Christ's death and its meaning for the believer was preached and his command to 'Take and eat' was obeyed, the taking of the Sacrament was a spiritual act.[44] The faithful 'hungered and thirsted after righteousness' and it was this spiritual hunger that was assuaged by receiving Christ into their hearts.[45] The Lord's Supper was thus a heavenly occasion unlike the Mass, which required Christ's Real Presence in the flesh. Statements of faith were contrasted with questions of substance.[46]

The carnality of the Mass required altars, replete with connotations of blood sacrifice and Old Testament practices. In the spiritual liberty that followed Christ's supreme sacrifice, there was no need for them:

> The sacrifices that are allowed only for Christian men to be offered are these: the calves of our lips' prayers, thanks, praising of God, charitableness and mercy and alms to the poor, our own bodies mortified, a contrite heart and a troubled spirit. I pray you now what shall we need an outward and a stony altar to offer these sacrifices on?[47]

If altars were an irrelevance, transubstantiation was seen as the ultimate fleshly taboo – an act of cannibalism. This was intended to shock, especially when it was presented as the logical outcome of the doctrine. 'Tell me then', asked Gilby, 'whether it do not abhor nature that man should eat man's flesh. Yet seem you to have a cloak for this Scythian cruelty in that you change him into the form of bread.'[48] John Ramsey did not pull his punches: 'in his hands thou must hear his bones crack/ And thinkest thyself safe when he is down in thy maw'.[49]

While the Mass prevented true spiritual communion, the Lord's Supper prevented only the fleshly from communicating. The argument used here followed on directly from the rejection of the Real Presence. If 'carnal eating' were possible, 'then every idolater and whoremonger (who can have no part in thy kingdom) might make themselves sure of life by their own work'.[50] In this important respect, the Mass upheld ungodliness: while the ungodly may be present at the Lord's Supper, they could not be members of the body of Christ, because they lacked 'lively faith'. The church on earth had always contained hypocrites, ever since the Last Supper when Judas ate with the other apostles whilst fully intending to betray Christ. This did not prevent protestants from assuming that visible clues to godliness and ungodliness were discernable. The ceremonies and rituals of popery, as human inventions, set out to please the senses, and consequently were decked in the richest adornments that the world could provide. By contrast, just as the godly were concerned in the Sacrament only with spiritual eating, so they were eager to cultivate the spiritual virtues:[51] 'But seeing that we know God

A religion of the Word

(yea rather seeing that we are known of God) we will not return again to your weak idols and your beggarly ceremonies to the which you would have us slaves and do service afresh ... We have begun in the spirit and we neither will nor can be made perfect by the flesh (Gal. 3).'[52]

The humility of the godly contrasted with the pride and luxuriousness of the carnal. 'For whereas the wicked do seem to themselves to be witful, strong, learned, rich, righteous, religious and holy spiritual fathers; thou esteemest thyself but an abject of the world, wretched, weak, blind, poor, sinful and a miserable doer, as concerning the flesh.'[53] This contrast was not limited to prelatical pomp and humble lay faith, but this extreme form was often used. The clergy profited from a religion of externals:

> [T]hese sell no more but the sight, the sound and the shadow; as the looking upon their images, the noise of their bells, the spreading out of their ornaments, the show of their jewels, the use and occupying of their instruments, the kissing of their relics, the wind of their lips, the spittle of their tongues, their idle pratings and unholy merits. But still they keep to themselves the gold, the silver, the precious stones, the pearls and suchlike, though they never cost them money.[54]

More generally, the carnal person needed the comfort offered by an abundance of the goods of this world, and the satisfaction of an advancing career; he was frightened by the thought of struggle and death even if he realised that the Gospel was the truth.[55]

The godly, however, were 'the forsaken wretched sort' whom God sent into the world to admonish its sins.[56] Indeed, this often antagonised the world into persecuting them.[57] But even the godly, as fallen humans, had to suffer the temptation to resist God's will; according to Hooper only continual vigilance and mortification of 'this aversion and malicious obstinacy of the will' could prevent 'eternal displeasure'.[58] Their acceptance of worldly misfortune and persecution had to be seen in this context of personal spiritual struggle;

> The continual battle between the flesh and the spirit in every just man is not so easily fought as you dream in your pleasant slumbering security and wealthiness, as ye may see in the lives and examples of them whom you banish from their native country, persecute at home, imprison and burn, and in the lives of Christ and his apostles.[59]

Persecution was thus an externalisation of the spiritual struggle of the godly. The experiences of the godly and the ungodly, both in this world and in the next, were diametrical opposites.

So this series of dichotomies, between scripture and tradition, spirit and flesh, godly and ungodly, can be seen as aspects of the final dichotomy to be discussed here, that between the *true* and the *false* church. This is not to say that protestants believed in the existence of two churches. There could be only the one true church, outside of which there was no salvation. The false church was its negative image, like a mirage which seemed real but was not. Where the true church was governed by the Word of God, the false relied on its own invention of traditions.[60] Thus Cranmer defined the true church as follows: 'This Church is the "pillar of truth", because it resteth upon God's Word, which is the true and sure foundation, and will not suffer it to err and fall.'[61] The true church was spiritually the body of Christ; the false consisted of unredeemed, sinful flesh.[62] The dichotomy owed much to Augustine's theory of the conflict between the church and the world.[63] It was the conflict between the godly and the ungodly in its collective institutional form.

However, the dialectic between the true and the false church was seen as an observable historical phenomenon, for the persecution of the godly was a constant since the time of Cain.[64] The argument from history could work both ways, however; novelty was the main catholic taunt. Gilby retorted that it was popery, not protestantism, that constituted the 'new learning': 'And surely it is needful that you bishops, which build yourselves a new Church, clean contrary (both in life and learning) unto the Church of Christ should have all things new changed...'.[65] However, later in the same tract he emphasised the antiquity of idolatry – in this respect the Mass was only the most recent aspect of a phenomenon that stretched back to the days of the golden calf.[66]

Of even greater importance than the validation of history was the definition of the creed, that the true church is one, holy, catholic and apostolic. Clearly this required even more engineering.[67] Thus, for instance, Gilby's opponents could equally well have assented to his definition, but he distinguished the true church by its stark simplicity – the true church believed in Christ, but not in the Real Presence.[68] Cranmer contrasted the 'uniformity and constancy' of his doctrine with the 'variable and uncertain' nature of Gardiner's.[69] The holiness of the true church consisted in the faith and witness of its godly members, sanctified by the blood of Christ,[70] not in the feigned holiness of a priestly caste.[71] Its catholicity was shown in the dispersal of its members throughout the world, not its claim to universal worldly power.[72] Its apostolicity consisted not in a visible succession, but in following the example and instructions of the apostles. This was especially true of the sacraments of the Lord's Supper and Baptism, and the case for the marriage of priests,[73] but also in a more general sense. Phillip Nichols hoped that the church would follow the example of the apostles, those 'holy fathers and perfect true men', in questioning the authoritarian structure of the church of their day and being rebuffed by it.[74]

The true and the false church dichotomy was most fully worked out in Bale's *Image of both churches*, his commentary on the book of Revelation. It would not be safe to consider the prevalence of evidence for the dichotomy

A religion of the Word

(illustrated above) as the result of his influence alone. It was rather more a matter of its usefulness as a polemical device – after all it had been developed by Lutheran propagandists before Bale produced his commentary.[75] But it does offer a neat summary of the themes discussed in the foregoing section. The two churches were allegorised as Jerusalem, the pure Bride of Christ, and Babylon, the great Whore and paramour of Antichrist.[76] As Bride and Whore, the two churches–cities were the symbols of spiritual and carnal characteristics. The Bride was the 'woman clothed with the sun' who gives birth to a child and flees from the dragon into the wilderness:

> Her cry was the mighty and strong declaration of Christ's doctrine, the fervent zeal and desire of the glory of God, and of all men's health in Christ . . . And like as the pained woman in all her agonies is much comforted by the hope of a child; so are God's faithful witnesses, trusting that by their patient and glad sufferance Christ should be received and rightly fashioned in many.[77]

The Whore by contrast was the apotheosis of fleshly desire and worldly power.[78] Bale's intent in writing the commentary was 'the merciful forewarning of the Lord's elect'.[79] He envisaged his role as merely to show the true church the message that had already been revealed in Revelation. He anticipated that the false church would ignore both messages. Thinking itself invincible, and scorning and persecuting the godly, were the signs of its imminent ruin. This reversal of fortunes leads to the next stage of the analysis: inversion.

INVERSION

Distinguishing between the true and the false church was by no means the end of the matter. The distinction was reinforced and confirmed by overturning the claims of Henrician catholics that their conservative piety was the bulwark of divine order in the world. Inversion was a traditional satirical method which gave protestant propaganda its daring and liberating edge.[80] It was given graphic illustration in the woodcuts of the German reformation, but unfortunately comparable English illustrative material either never existed or has not survived.[81] However, the evidence considered here shows clearly that inversion was fundamental to the protestant outlook. It was not merely a polemical conceit. The world had been turned upside-down by popery; the task was to reveal this, and restore right order.

In 1546, Stephen Gardiner wrote *A detection of the devil's sophistry* to alert the people to the subversive dangers of protestantism.

> Consider, gentle reader, how full of iniquity this time is, in which the high mystery of our religion is so openly assaulted . . . Follow God and his ministers, whom he ordaineth to rule and rather conform knowledge to agree with

obedience, where God's truth repugneth not unto it, than with violation of obedience, which is a displeasant fault, to enterprise the subversion of God's honour and glory...[82]

Gardiner's attitude was challenged by many writers, who simply reversed his assertion, blaming reactionary discontent rather than protestant 'innovation' for contention.[83] Strife over scripture was a case in point: 'This should be a mean to set for ever amongst us a public quietness, true love, sure and faithful friendship. By this mean forsooth we should banish hypocrisy and ignorance, which be ever brawling and stand in contention for every cold ceremony and trifling tradition.'[84] Similarly the Eucharist was instituted by Christ 'to move and stir all men to friendship ... but the Devil, the enemy of Christ and of all his members hath so craftily juggled herein, that of nothing riseth so much contention as the holy Sacrament'.[85]

The strife stirred up by the Sacrament was only the tip of the iceberg. The Mass in itself encapsulated – and helped to generate – the false order inherent in popery, a false order that began with false doctrine and ended in cosmic disarray. As Hooper put it, the doctrine of the Real Presence 'makes heaven hell, and hell heaven, turns upside down and perverts the order of God'.[86] Those who supported it perversely upheld sinful human order instead of divine order and, worse, presumptuously imposed that order on God himself. As Isaiah had warned, there would be disaster in store for those who 'made light darkness and darkness light'.[87] Doctrinal untruth was reflected in the natural world; failure to perceive the truth in doctrine meant that creation itself was turned upside down.

Instead of enlightening their flocks, papist teachers lured them into the fog and darkness of the obscurantism of their own learning and traditions. Cranmer put this protestant commonplace to specific use in his debate with Gardiner:

> And where you pervert the order of the books setting the cart before the horse (that is to say the third and fourth books before the second, saying that the natural order of the matter so requireth) here the reader may note an evident mark of all subtle papists, which is under the pretence and colour of order, to break that order, whereby the falsehood of their doctrine should best be detected, and the truth brought to light. For when they perceive a window open whereby the light may shine in and the truth appear, then they busily go about to shut that window and to draw the reader from that place to some mystical and obscure matter where more darkness is, and less light can be seen.[88]

The obscurantism of the papists, a combination of scholastic learning and Latin liturgy, was intended to keep the people away from the truth contained in the Bible.[89] It was strengthened by a calculated use of 'lies' – even to the extent of misrepresenting its own liturgy[90] and the church fathers.[91] More

A religion of the Word

dangerously, it substituted 'lies' (i.e. its own laws and traditions, which could be changed at will, and thus were the antithesis of God's immutable truth) for scripture.[92] 'But what crafty teachers be these papists, who devise phantasies of their own heads directly contrary to Christ's teaching and then set the same abroad to Christian people to be most assuredly believed as God's own most holy Word?'[93] A church founded on such 'lies' could not provide comfort or assurance: 'Now poor wretched man and comfortless person, how canst thou believe the thing thou knowest not?' asked Hooper. 'Thy conscience is a jakes for every devilish bishop's decrees; and as they change their law, now for avarice, now for fear, and now for *placebo*, so thy faith changeth as inconstant as the wind...'.[94] No one was safe when the definitions of doctrine were constantly changing – at the hands of those who 'hath laws to damn one year and to save another; that that is good and catholic this year shall be heresy next year'.[95] Inconstant faith was false faith, and so the very mutability of popery indicated that it led to perdition.[96]

The popish church maintained what it called 'order', but it was a false order based on misinterpretation of scripture and a diminution of the role of Christ. It put the church hierarchy between Christ and his members. The true church obeyed Christ as the bride does the bridegroom; the disobedience of the false church made her punish infringements of her own traditions rather than those of the commandments.[97] Such fundamental disobedience led Bale to deny the church any right to exercise ecclesiastical authority; the only power of salvation belonged to Christ.[98] The final proof that the authority wielded by the popish church did not come from Christ was that it persecuted upholders of the gospel.[99]

Persecution of the gospel was characteristic of a church whose spiritual ancestors were not the apostles but the pharisees, men who opposed the message of Christ's freedom in favour of the bondage of Old Testament legalism. Denying the progressive nature of the revelation of God's will inverted the order of the scriptures. It reflected the ceremonial and ritual aspects of popery, which became more of an issue in the later 1540s,[100] but was also true of the definition of faith. When traditionalists insisted on the need for faith, what they really required was unquestioning acceptance of the popish clergy's commands.[101] Justifying faith was the converse of this, bypassing the burdensome demands of 'works' piety' to achieve a direct and liberating link with Christ. To put works before faith, like putting the law before the gospel, was to get the order of religious experience the wrong way round – to plant, as Joye graphically put it, 'your herbs with the roots upward... a backward order and a preposterous planting'.[102]

It was in discussion of the Sacrament, however, that the most disturbing inversions were revealed. Inversion went further than merely pointing the contrast between *spiritual* Lord's Supper and *carnal* Mass,[103] by showing how the Mass inverted man's relationship to God by misinterpreting both what a sacrament actually was, and what happened when it took place. Transubstantiation invalidated the nature of the Sacrament, which was to convey spiritual mysteries symbolically:[104] when symbol was made into reality, the Sacrament was no longer a sacrament. Conversely, to assert the Real Presence and then keep Christ in the pyx was self-contradictory, since 'A dumb thing without senses is no harbour nor dwelling place for Christ's precious body, nor for the Spirit of God; but in the penitent and sorrowful heart of the Christian lodgeth this ghostly and spiritual guest.'[105] The doctrine of grace *ex opere operato* was rejected by Hooper because it put the emphasis on the sign rather than the promise which it symbolised.[106] Faith preceded the sacraments and was confirmed by them; so to come to the Sacrament without faith was 'to set the cart before the horse'.[107] Veron wrote that the Mass made grace flow backwards, from man to God: 'For the Supper of the Lord is a gift which with thanksgiving should be received, whereas the sacrifice of the Mass is a price or reward offered unto God to be received of him for a satisfaction and amends.'[108] God and man changed places because papists subordinated scripture to fit the demands of their doctrine:

> But you ... remove the words, both out of the right place and the right sense. And can any man that loveth the truth, give his ears to hear you, that turn upside down both the order and sense of Christ's words, contrary to the true narration of the evangelists, contrary to the interpretation of all the old authors and the approved faith of Christ's Church, even from the beginning, to maintain your wilful assertions and papistical opinions?[109]

True worship was impossible in such a doctrinal context, yet papists claimed to be worshipping Christ in the Sacrament. According to Cranmer, the result was the very opposite, for by

> treading the son of God under their feet, and despising the blood, whereby they were sanctified, [they] crucify again the son of God, and make him a mocking-stock to all the wicked. And many professing Christ, yet having vain cogitations and fantasies in their heads, do worship and serve Antichrist, and thinking themselves wise, become very fools indeed.[110]

True worship ascended to heaven in spirit, but if Christ was present in the flesh then worship had to remain earthbound, and indeed the 'sacrificing priesthood' 'plucked Christ down' from heaven to make this possible.[111]

Thus the Mass was revealed as both blasphemous and idolatrous, the very obverse of true worship. It degraded God, the Lord of all, by making him a mere 'piece of bread' – and also man, since

> there is nothing so vile amongst all my creatures, but that you have essayed to set up the same as your God, despising therein, both my power, and the rule that I gave you over all other creatures; forgetting clearly that I have exalted

mine elect above the angels, and have sent mine heavenly spirits to do service unto them.[112]

The divine order was mocked by transubstantiation, which disregarded all the laws of nature.[113] The sanctification of things (both the Host and lesser parts of the ritual apparatus of popery) was an absurdity,[114] since only humans, 'being made after his image, and being his lively temples and Christ's mystical body',[115] could be made holy.

It was not only in the Mass that papists committed idolatry. Since idolatry was defined as worship of created things even in God's name,[116] it permeated every aspect of popery. Idolatry was the inverse of true preaching, since it did not edify, as preaching did, but led instead to destruction.[117] The emphasis on the Mass of conventional piety rather than the Word substituted burdensome observances for gospel freedom.[118] Idolatry was obviously present in the cult of images and saints,[119] but it also underpinned vows and (especially) clerical celibacy. Bale described the process of vowing as a degradation, not an opportunity for holiness: 'Whereas thou wert the Lord's before, thou becomest thine own by a new creation, as the tree that is hewn down and made an image, becometh of God's, the carver's. A miserable mutation is this if thou mark it. For by thy vow thou thus becomest of God's creature, an idol of thine own.'[120] And, as idolaters and blasphemers, God would punish them.[121]

The outward finery with which churches and clergy were bedecked during the celebration of these ceremonies may have been intended to signify the glory of God, but protestants inverted it, to serve as evidence of clerical hypocrisy and superstition.[122] This was not as radical as it might seem – they were here building on a satirical tradition of anticlericalism that had both traditional and humanist forebears.[123] Did not the clergy substitute worldly vices for apostolic virtues, using the church as a front for the cultivation of their own interests? This was the church as Whore: 'Many outward brags maketh this painted Church of Christ, of his gospel, and of his apostles, signified by the gold, precious stone and pearls, which is but a glittering colour: for nothing mindeth she less than to follow them in conversation of living.'[124] Wealth from land, tithes, multiple benefices and the selling of priestly services had been substituted for the poverty of the apostles.[125] The church did not comfort the poor, but exploited them:

> Thy coffers were filled
> With riches and treasure
> Thy chambers were delled
> With silks of great value
> Thy red deer were killed
> And slain out of measure
> Thus poor men were pilled
> To maintain thy pleasure.[126]

Careerism rather than unworldliness was rampant: 'ambition' and 'lordliness' were two of the commonest charges brought against the clergy.[127] John Ramsey pictured the Mass priest: *'gloria in excelsis* for joy doth he sing/ more for his fat living than for devotion', while the less fortunate 'sing not with merry hearts for lack of promotion./ Thus some be merry, some be sorry, according to their portion.'[128]

The poor priest ideal, whether deriving from the Gospel or from a traditional account of good works, was overturned by graphic descriptions of clerical laxity. Fasting was a case in point. Bale commented, sarcastically, that 'a platter-faced priest, with a pair of cheeks as big as a boy's buttocks, well vittled also, may conveniently stand forth and preach of good abstinence',[129] while Gilby was filled with social indignation:

> And why should we not as well do thus, as you bishops, to eat on the greatest fasting days; you have sweet sucket, green ginger, marmalade and such-like dainties for the punishing of your pope-holy carcases? Is a piece of beef or bacon more perilous for the provocation of fleshly appetite in us poor men of the country that labour all the day long, in hunger and cold, than these subtleties are to your slothful and idle bellies?[130]

Far more attention, however, was devoted to the question of clerical celibacy.[131] While the basic argument used in Bale, Ponet and Crowley's treatments of the question was the Lutheran one that vows made contrary to God's will were invalid and consequently could and should be broken, the evidence they presented for this was in the form of an inversion of clerical 'holiness': that is, that vowed celibacy was merely a front for all kinds of sexual debauchery. Bale concentrated on exposing the lack of chastity among the religious orders and the abuse of sexual power by the 'saints',[132] but elsewhere the secular clergy were described as whoremongers and sexual predators from whom no female was safe.[133] Ponet contrasted the 'willing chasteness and continency' of the church when priests had been able to marry with the 'feigned chastity, most filthily stained with the spots of fornication, adultery, incest and sodomitical abomination', of the contemporary church, 'bound by the law of wiveless life'.[134] The element of sensationalism in all this was 'justified' by the assumption that the exposure of such scandalous behaviour was the first step to humiliation and punishment. Just as the vision of the shameless triumph of the Whore of Babylon was the prelude to her humiliating downfall,[135] so these revelations about the 'celibate' priesthood were intended to destroy its reputation.[136]

The idea of the priesthood being a powerful and shamelessly exploitative group brings us to the final inversion, that of the worldly power and final end of the *true* and the *false* church. The domination of the temporal powers by the ecclesiastical increased the likelihood of secular tyranny:[137] true kingship

A religion of the Word

and right order were only possible when the ecclesiastical yoke had been cast off (a neat merging of the supremacist and protestant cases).[138] But the great power of the clerical hierarchy also indicated that theirs was not the true church. Paradoxically true power was the obverse of worldly values. Bale saw them personified in Anne Askew – 'Thus chooseth the Lord the foolish of this world to confound the wise, and the weak to deface the mighty; yea, things despised, and thought very vile, to bring things unto nought, which the world hath in most high reputation.'[139] It triumphed in persecution, not in domination, seeking suffering not worldly comfort,[140] and it was made up of the faithful few, not the fickle majority.[141] 'This Church suffereth always with her head Christ, wherefore she shall also reign with him always and be glorified.'[142]

However, in the last days, the positions would be reversed, and the true church would triumph, even in the face of incredible odds,[143] while the false church would be vanquished. The defeat of Antichrist was overshadowed in this period by the downfall of the Whore. The Whore symbolised all that was corrupt, venal, shameless and licentious in the false church.[144] She was 'drunk with the blood of the saints', was a great persecutor, and her seductive powers were so great that she held kings in her thrall.[145] As a personification of the carnality and seductiveness of the Mass, she was put on trial and sent packing, either to hell or back to 'her father' the pope, in several dialogues and ballads.[146] In its social context, it has been argued that the humiliation of the Whore was symbolic of a protestant 'restoration' of a patriarchal control over women. However, this interpretation overlooks its importance as a symbol of the purification of religion.[147] Certainly in the protestant literature of Edward VI's reign the humiliation of the Whore is a more recurrent theme than is the struggle with Antichrist. This was because the fall of the Whore was visibly happening, beginning with the enactment of the royal supremacy and the dissolution of the monasteries, and continuing with the marriage of priests and the attack on the Mass in Edward's reign. Inversion was not merely wish fulfilment, but description.

The consistent use of dichotomy and inversion enabled protestants to establish the essential polarity between true and false religion. Denunciation of popery implied the conclusion that true religion would be the opposite, without necessarily being explicit or detailed in saying so. Before examining these conclusions and their implications for true religion, however, it is necessary to understand protestant explanations for the persistence of popery.

CONSPIRACY

The problem of the persistence of popery was only partly explained by the assumption that the false church was in essence fleshly, and thus craved to dominate in the world. This Augustinian definition of worldly power was modified by the notion that in the case of popery it was supported by a malignant conspiracy of the clerical hierarchy headed by the pope. The stages by which this had developed not only revealed the cunning and political ability of the papacy, but had apocalyptic significance.[148] The intrigues of the popes revealed the supernatural plot of Antichrist to subvert true religion and destroy the godly: the visible conspiracy of popery was a key to the invisible conspiracy of Satan, the world and Antichrist to crush the true church.[149] However, except in the work of Bale, Antichrist remained a shadowy, background figure in this period – from which the overwhelming impression gained is of anticlericalism on a grand scale.[150] This had two main advantages – firstly, it allowed protestants to deny that they were breaking the bonds of charity in attacking their fellow clergy. For such a view of 'charity' was designed to conceal a common purpose to deceive Christendom into accepting the blasphemy that the popish priesthood could 'make God' in the Mass. Secondly, and more practically, it deflected attention from the radical implications of a 'priesthood of all believers'.

Anticlericalism, in England, had far more to do with the supremacist rhetoric of the 1530s than it did with the theological basis of the priesthood of all believers. While fear of anabaptism and the lessons of the German Peasants' War may have also played a part in this, it is just as likely that the many protestant polemicists who were clerics preferred anticlericalism to more radical alternatives involving lay self-determination.[151] It is also significant that ordination was not attacked, despite the snipings at its external ritual of 'oilings and shavings'. It was understood that the conspiracy drew strength from such externals rather than from ordination itself.

Direct reference to the debate around the introduction of the English Bible in the early 1540s indicated the way in which clerical monopolisation of scripture and its interpretation was seen as being crucial to the sucess of the conspiracy. Only the clergy's corrupt interpretations of scripture had been allowed to be taught.[152] This showed them to be 'enemies of God's word and of his truth',[153] as did their refusal to allow others to search for it.[154] Barriers to the laity were set up by the use of arcane scholastic language and the Latin liturgy.[155] Papist theologians allowed none but themselves to discuss the high mysteries of religion,[156] which Cranmer described as a sinister pact of silence.[157] Hooper went further, accusing papists of saying 'he that is unlearned cannot know or comprehend the true use of the sacraments in Christ's Church, and what they be, as well as a learned man, and say it shall be sufficient for them to trust unto other men's judgements'.[158] By contrast, all protestants believed that the Bible was accessible to everyone; all had the right to read 'their father's will and testament which he hath left in writing'.[159] The place of scholarship was to increase access, not to conspire to exclude ordinary

A religion of the Word

people.[160] Popular ignorance was indeed a disgrace, but it was less blameworthy than were the clergy's actions in maintaining it, which indicated a malignant purpose.

Nevertheless, the bulk of the clergy were not well-trained or subtle theologians, and equal scorn was poured on the ignorance of the 'mass-priests'.[161] Gerrard found them

> very idiots and of no knowledge and the occasion of this is, they are so choked with wilful ignorance that they will not once look upon the Bible. They so persuade themselves that they say all is well enough, and remain still even hard-hearted pharaohs toward the shining light, and as deaf as any door nail if a man will call them to study.[162]

Like Isaiah's 'wicked generation', they had rejected the Bibles which Henry VIII had ordered to be placed in every church.[163] William Salesbury showed how the doctrine of the sacrifice of the Mass transposed the Old and New Testaments 'to mislead the simple' and maintain the status of the sacrificing priesthood.[164] The retrograde establishment of sacrifices showed how 'the sinister corruption which continually did issue from the first father Adam unto all his offspring' obscured true knowledge of God's will.[165]

The Mass was crucial to the maintenance of clerical power in terms of both social status and religious function. Mistress Missa boasted in her 'recantation' that 'by the means of me they might increase their riches and fill their coffers, and by me Sir John Lacklatin that could do nothing but mumble up Matins [and] sing a Mass was held in as much reputation as a right honest and well-learned man'.[166] Communion in one kind, the consecratory and sacrificial powers of the priest, and especially the institution of private Masses, all combined to separate the priesthood from the laity. The presence of the laity was not necessary to make it an efficacious sacrament, and this led to various abuses: in the private Mass the laity received the benefit in their absence, while in ordinary Masses the devout could participate in only a peripheral way, and the ungodly received an equal benefit, however perfunctory their devotions.[167] Such doctrines made the Sacrament, according to Veron, not an occasion of unity but 'a very excommunication' of the laity.[168]

While both learning and ignorance as well as false doctrines combined to shut out the laity from a full life in the church,[169] the clerical usurpation of temporal powers was a more straightforward matter. The rise of the papacy was a classic example of conspiracy theory. Even though the ground covered here largely repeated the work of Tyndale and Barnes, and the establishment of the supremacy made it no longer a burning issue, it was the subject of three substantial tracts – all, incidentally, translations.[170] While these tracts saw Edward as putting the finishing touches to the Henrician triumph over the papacy, others saw a continued need for vigilance. The supremacist theme of the threat to the position of the king from the conservatism of the bishops brought the clerical conspiracy nearer to home.[171] Again, the work of Tyndale and Bale in the 1530s and 1540s reduced the novelty of this theme, and Bale continued to provide examples of it in his later works.[172] Henry VIII's religious conservatism was explained by the exiles of the 1540s as positive proof of the conspiracy's effectiveness and, in particular, of Gardiner's persuasive skill.[173] William Samuel's *The practice, practised by the pope and his prelates* described the pope as relying on episcopal intrigue to maintain his power in England, after the establishment of the supremacy. So far the papacy had succeeded in bringing about the Pilgrimage of Grace, the wars with France and Scotland, and the Six Articles, but the plot was backfiring on the papacy, since its activities had made the country so poor, that the king had to avail himself of the church's lands and wealth. But papal intrigues still gave cause for vigilance:

> God save the king his noble grace
> And send him to spy the subtlety of the bishops
> And that he may in any case
> Once thrust down these forked tops
> For as long as the [mag]pie in the king's chamber hops
> The silly sheep and the lambs all
> Are like to be devoured with [i.e. by] the priests of Baal.[174]

The persistence of support for the Mass and the political power of the church combined to provide considerable resistance to the forces of reform which the conspiracy theory explained. Cranmer summarised its ramifications:

> Now the nature of man being ever prone to idolatry from the beginning of the world, and the papists being ready by all means and policy to defend and extol the Mass for their estimation and profit, and the people being superstitiously enamoured and doted upon the Mass, because they take it for a present remedy against all manner of evils, and part of the princes being blinded by papistical doctrine, part loving quietness and loath to offend their clergy and subjects, and all being captive to the Antichrist of Rome, the state of the world remaining in that case, it is no wonder that abuses grew and increased in the Church . . .[175]

DISORDER

When the devil was in control, according to Latimer, there was apparent peace and security in the land. But when his authority was questioned 'by one greater than he' (i.e. Christ) then his consequent rage caused strife and contention, stirring up all the forces of malice and discontent. This explained Christ's paradoxical warning that he came not to bring peace but a sword.[176]

A religion of the Word

Religious strife was thus not caused by protestant 'innovation',[177] but by papistical reaction to the threat to Rome's hegemony from 'true religion'. Nicholas Lesse was one of those who denied the possibility of 'unity, concord and love' among the 'poor and simple people' while catholic preachers were still preaching works' righteousness: 'How is it possible', he asked, 'that the cart should go forward when the horse drawers do pluck and draw sundry ways?'[178] Moreover, 'bitter brawling and contention' was part of the very nature of clerical learning.[179] 'Glossing' the Bible naturally led to argument because it increased the ambiguity of the text.[180] John Mardeley, for instance, 'marvelled much' that the papists were so ready to write books which did not 'accord with God's holy Word', and concluded that their eagerness to descend into such 'profane ways' indicated their evil intent to 'sow discord'.[181]

The contribution of obscure or ambiguous theological language to the bitterness of the Sacrament debate was often noted.[182] To Cranmer, the entire argument about the nature of Christ's presence in the Eucharist rested on the meaning of technical terms: 'And as for pleading of those words "really", "corporally", "sensibly" and "naturally", they be your own terms and the terms wherein resteth the whole contention between you and me: and should you be offended because I speak of those terms?'[183] Gardiner's refusal to abandon these terms in the debate maintained the strife. Simply by refusing to go along with the reform, conservatives could be portrayed as generating disorder.[184]

More subtly, disorder was inherent in both the doctrine and the practice of the Mass. As an act of blasphemy it made war on God himself. Veron's *The five abominable blasphemies that are in the Mass* listed the substitution of the papist clergy for Christ's unique priesthood, denying the uniqueness of his sacrifice on the cross, obliterating the memory of his death and taking away its fruits, and cancelling his institution of the Lord's Supper.[185] If the Mass conjured up the disorders of pagan sacrifice, transubstantiation was caricatured as a cannibal feast.[186] On a less crudely shocking but ultimately more disturbing level, it overturned the transcendental certainties of the creed; Christ, instead of being bodily in heaven, was in thousands of pyxes throughout Christendom.[187]

The Mass was described by protestants as a series of confusions heaped one upon another. It confused sign with signified,[188] remembrance with the object of remembrance,[189] and Christ's humanity with his divinity.[190] Cranmer declared that Gardiner's writings may have included relevant analogies, but the resulting whole was a dangerous chaos, which would lead to 'very madness and impiety', because he was 'making a chain of gold and copper together, confounding and mixing together corporeal and spiritual, heavenly and earthly things'.[191] The origin of Gardiner's doctrine was clear:

[T]he Church of Rome is the mother thereof, which in scripture is called Babylon, because of commixtion or confusion; which in all her doings so doth mix and confound error with truth, superstition with religion, godliness with hypocrisy, scripture with traditions, that she showeth herself always uniform and constant, to confound all the doctrine of Christ...[192]

The contrast between the 'constant' aim of Babylon and its chaotic results is striking. The whole panoply of traditional piety was to protestants a concatenation of idolatries centred on the Mass. Idolatry was the prime form of disorder, as it directed worship away from God to his creation. Disordered worship resulted in the ultimate disorder of plague and punishment.[193] Hooper showed how the Hebrew word for idol 'signifieth either affliction, rebellion, sorrow, tristes, travail or pain, or else the wicked muck and mammon of this world, or the thing that always provoketh the ire of God',[194] and Gerrard cited the example of king Jehoram who was 'wonderfully plagued' for defiling himself and his kingdom with idolatry 'against the law of the Lord'.[195] The papist threat that 'the ceremonies of the Church are knit in such an order, that if ye take one away all the rest shall be in jeopardy of falling into destruction', bringing conservative rebellion in its wake was as nothing compared with God's wrath against idolatry.[196]

The worst punishment of all was God's abandonment of the idolaters, which was already happening, as St Paul had prophesied in Romans 1.[197] The inversion of worshipping the creatures of God rather than their creator gave rise to disorder and perversion. Paul emphasised the prevalence of homosexuality among the idolaters, and Bale in particular made use of this accusation,[198] but Paul also listed 'envy, murder, strife, malignity; they are gossips, slanderers, haters of God, insolent, haughty, boastful, inventors of evil, disobedient to parents, foolish, faithless, heartless, ruthless'.[199]

These verses from Romans 1 could stand as the epigraph for the protestant view of the disorder inherent in the popish church. Sexual disorder was treated with the usual mixture of prurient interest and censoriousness.[200] However, straightforward salaciousness was not the only reason for the sexual anarchy characterising especially the anticlerical material. It would be as insensitive to leave it at that as it was for Victorian editors of Bale to censor it out.[201] Not only was it an inversion of clerical celibacy,[202] it bore witness to the nature of idolatry, which broke faith with God, and thus unleashed the corruption of fallen human nature. This corruption was at its most potent in sexuality, and it is surely no coincidence that idolatry was frequently described as 'spiritual fornication'.[203]

Idolatrous worship was maintained and directed by an idolatrous and supposedly celibate priesthood.[204] Celibacy was a thin disguise. Vowed celibacy overturned God's institution of matrimony and replaced what should be a rare gift of grace with a mechanical exercise of the will. 'Away with that

A religion of the Word

wicked vow that setteth variance among virtues, and that places in their rooms most execrable vices', wrote Bale.[205] Doctrine as well as morality suffered, founded as it was on a confusion of Old and New Testaments:

> By this barbarous and strange coupling together of baptism and vows of the old law in one definition, he putteth no difference between the master and the servant, the free and the bond, the light and his shadow, the verity and his figure, the Church and the synagogue, Christ and Moses, but thrusteth them in together, making of them an hotch-potch, all contrary to the wholesome doctrine of Paul, Gal. 4 . . .[206]

Since God had not ordered the vow of celibacy, there was no way in which corrupt human nature could keep it. It was but a short step to suggest that this impossibility was intentional, as a means of gaining power. Far from being a sign of holiness and discipline it acted as a solvent of political bonds and social order.[207] In political terms, this meant treason.[208] In social terms the effect of celibacy was to undermine marriage – 'Do ye judge it a whoredom, an uncleanness, a beastliness?'[209] asked Bale, and went on to make a simple equation:

> God ordained marriage for his people to keep them in good order. Pope Hellhound [i.e. Hildebrand, Gregory VII] ordained vows against marriage for his professed cattle to bring them out of order. Thus is marriage an holy institution of God for the conservation of man. And vows against marriage are a wicked constitution of Pope Hellhound, for destruction of body and soul.[210]

The authority of parents was also undermined, since many 'holy' men and women took their vows without parental consent.[211] In *The acts of English votaries*, Bale chronicled the access monks gained by a false reputation for sanctity, whether to royal money or to aristocratic ladies.[212]

Thus sexual disorder indicated the conspiratorial and carnal nature of popery, although the worldliness of the popish church meant that it was disordered in many other ways.[213] The corruption of the church by wealth made disorder in worship advantageous.[214] Sin was licenced by payments to the church for prayers, Masses and indulgences – 'There is no sin found where you are fatted.'[215] Sin went unpunished as the clergy preferred to profit from it than teach the ten commandments.[216] Greed rather than apostolic poverty was the order of the church.[217] While Christ the good shepherd gathered and governed his flock, the 'idol shepherds' of popery cared only for their hire.[218]

The disorder generated by idolatry spread upwards as well as downwards in society, affecting both temporal powers and congregations. Behind the church's domination of kings lay the growing supernatural power of Antichrist, the personification of disorder. Bale described the process of increasing demands for worship as idolatry.[219] The next stage was the pope, as Antichrist, making the temporal powers 'in his image':

When such an image or idolous prince is thus upset or constituted by authority (his oath once made that he shall always defend them), he may in no wise speak but out of that spirit that their conjurers (confessors I should say) have put into him. He may make no laws but at their spiritual appointment, like as the emperor Charles doth now in these days.[220]

The resulting mayhem showed the papacy to be the unbridled apocalyptic horses that carried the persecuting princes wherever they wanted.[221]

When popery had the upper hand, then, corruption and disorder were rife. In these circumstances, the image of the Whore was extremely significant of protestant attitudes to popery. Disorder was synonymous with the unrestrained carnality she symbolised. She was the inverse of patriarchal order and male control – yet far from being a matriarchal figure! Her power was a form of devastating sexual thrall – 'She shall in this life have peace in the flesh, liberty in ungodliness, obedience of the world, and power in darkness, that she shall swim in wanton pleasures and bathe herself in innocent blood ... besides all godly wisdom is she, and forgetful of herself, through this same bloody drunkeness, so great excess has she taken'.[222] Her drunkeness and fornication symbolised the spiritual fornication of the priests. Ramsey's lewd description of the drunken Mass priest and his harlot turned the Mass into an orgiastic party,[223] in contrast to the ordered building of which Christ was the foundation.[224] If the triumph of the Whore was the celebration of anarchy, then her fall was a shambles.[225]

The moral was clear: the disruption caused by the fall of popery was the result not of protestant anarchy, but of the collapse of a disorderly structure. But we have already seen that the antithesis between the true and the false church assumed that popery was not objectively real. The explanation for its apparent reality thus had to go further than the antichristian conspiracy and the establishment of disorder, and on into the realm of the imagination and the senses, which popery had so cunningly deluded.

DELUSION

Delusion was a concept on which protestants relied heavily to explain the persistence of popery and the success of the clerical conspiracy. It should be explained that in this analysis it is used as an umbrella term, linking the acts of deceit which convinced both clergy and laity that popery was true religion with the illusory nature of popery itself. As an illusion, popery was at once powerfully convincing and yet insubstantial: both entrenched in the consciousness of the people and yet easily swept away by the irresistible truth of the Gospel. These concepts, deceit and illusion, are sometimes difficult to disentangle, but this itself is an important clue to the mixture of fear and contempt with which protestants treated popery, and especially popular piety.

A religion of the Word

The idea of an apocalyptic 'strong delusion', which would make the people believe Antichrist was the Messiah, was probably more important as a paradox which imbued the protestant critique of popery than as a narrowly eschatological sign.[226] Within its confines, protestants could successfully maintain and even resolve the apparent tension between their scorn for the vanity of popery and their fearful certainty that it constituted the most dangerous obstacle to the establishment of 'true religion'.

The acceptance of the conspiracy theory of popery makes clerical delusion an obvious starting-point.[227] Convinced that they had sacred powers, the priests proceeded to delude the laity as to the nature and extent of those powers. Becon's *Castle of comfort* was the one full-length attempt to deflate the doctrine of absolution,[228] and Bale and Ponet, as we have seen, ridiculed clerical celibacy.[229] The false perception of papal power was allegorised as intoxication: '... they shall strongly delude the kings of the earth and blind the governors of the universal world, making them drunken with the cup of all abominations.'[230] This proceeded by perceptible stages, including the Fourth Lateran Council, when the adoption of the dogma of transubstantiation and the institution of auricular confession increased the 'holiness' of the clergy[231] and the papal victories in the investiture contest, so that 'by taking from princes the investing of prelates they diminished more than half their authority, making them bond-servants to Antichrist'.[232]

The power to delude was used to cheat believers of their inheritance. Hooper dismissed the superstitious curate who taught that rituals and payments could buy off purgatory: 'Foolish be they that sell this abomination, but more fools be the buyers, seeing that Christ once cast such sellers out of the temple.'[233] The poor sick man in Hooper's sermon, believing he could reduce his allotted time in purgatory by endowing Masses for his soul, thus unwittingly condemned himself to hell.[234] Crowley showed how the sale of Masses tricked people into thinking they could be saved without true repentance – here too the clergy enriched themselves at the expense of the salvation of souls.[235] The author of the *Fall of the Romish church* compared the Mass priests to the priests of Baal whom Daniel had accused of eating the sacrifice themselves: 'you eat up all yourselves and make us believe we be partakers, and have part of your sacrifice, but we have nothing but the blessing of the empty cup'.[236] Cranmer characterised the priests as charlatan apothecaries, claiming professional competence but really 'accustomed with their merchandises of glistering glasses and counterfeit dredges to deceive the world'.[237]

The mutual delusion of clergy and laity was neatly illustrated by the figure of the 'idol priest'. The 'idol priest' indoctrinated his flock to believe in idolatry, so that he became part of the idolatry itself.[238] However, Gilby hoped that the flock would rise up and cast out their 'idol shepherd' and replace him with the good shepherd Christ.[239] God would see the truth, according to

The struggle against popery

Bale: 'Thou hast a name of life, an outward show of virtue and of goodness, and a shining pretence of much holiness; yet art thou before God a dead rotten idol, full of hypocrisy and falsehood.'[240]

Hypocrisy in its more straightforward form explained clerical self-deceit. Like their spiritual ancestors the pharisees, they were convinced of their own righteousness. The blurred line between hypocrisy and disguise could allow a contradictory picture to be drawn.:

> For those mocking Mass-mongers have counterfeited Aaron in their apparellings, altars and ceremonies, yet were they never as was Aaron, Eleazar, or Phineas. They have counterfeited Christ's sufferings in crossing one hand over another and in spreading their arms abroad, Judas in kissing, Caiaphas in prelating and Pilate in washing their hands, with a hundred toys more, yet were they never right Christs, but such disguised monsters . . .[241]

The 'blind guides' who preferred to ignore scripture in favour of their own traditions and inventions[242] took this action to delude the flock.[243] Not only the papacy but the doctors of the Church were guilty.[244] This did not prevent them using scripture at every opportunity, not as a sign of the faith of the church but to disguise their purpose. This explained the Scriptural texts that occurred throughout the doctrine and liturgy of the Mass. Gospel and epistle were read in the service. But these were described as cosmetic additions, not proper preaching, since the Mass was a human invention.[245] The scriptural elements in its doctrines were seen as deliberately misleading.[246] The Epistle and Gospel in the Mass were rendered worthless by the context in which they were read, according to Bale: '[W]ho can say but that it was the Scripture that Satan alleged to Christ upon the pinnacle of the temple? (Matt. 4) Yet remaineth it there still, after his ungracious handling thereof, as a false crafty suggestion, a devilish error, or a shield of his wickedness and shall do evermore.'[247] All seemed accurate and plausible enough, but when the evil intention was revealed, the scripture was rendered worthless. At the same time, the clerics had become the objects of the laity's faith.[248]

Papist sophistry did not stop at interpreting scripture. Patristic texts were also 'wrested' to fit false doctrine.[249] Obscurity was deliberately sought in the use of arcane theological vocabulary – hiding the truth made deception of the people an easy task. But even the use of the term 'Mass' itself was seen by Gilby as a deliberate ploy to 'hold men occupied in trifles, and keep them from the plains of the truth'.[250] In contrast to Cranmer's 'plain and manifest Scriptures', Gardiner had to make an extraordinary effort of concealment:

> But to avoid and dally away these words that be so clear and plain, must needs be laid on loads of words, the wit must be stretched out to the utmost, all fetches must be brought in that can be devised, all colours of rhetoric must be sought out, all the air must be cast over with clouds, all the water darkened

with the cuttle's ink; and if it could be, at the last as much as may be, all men's eyes must also be put out, that they should not see.[251]

Further concealment was made possible through the adoption of a pseudo-professional jargon:

> [A]s apothecaries, physicians, surgeons and alchemists use words of Greek, Arabic, and other strange languages, purposely thereby to hide their sciences from the knowledge of other, so do you in many parts of your book devise many strange terms and strange phrases of speech, to obscure and darken thereby the matter of the sacrament, and to make the same meet for the capacities of very few, which Christ ordained to be understood and exercised of all men.[252]

Gardiner's employment of Latinisms to maintain the authority of the church and limit theological understanding, while appearing to consent to demands for vernacular scriptures, was used as clear evidence that he was intent on deceiving the people.

A specific use of such obfuscation was image worship. Here, theological discussion was separated from religious practice, so that 'idolatry' was explained away in a mere form of words:

> And although the subtle papists do colour and cloak the matter never so finely, saying that they worship not the sacraments which they see with their eyes, but that thing that they believe with their faith to be really and corporally in the sacraments; yet why do they run from place to place to gaze at the things which they see, if they worship them not, giving thereby occasion to them which be ignorant to worship that which they see?[253]

The contradiction of words by practice threw the motive of deceit into sharp focus.

Protestant attitudes to the part lay-persons played in their own deception were somewhat more ambivalent. 'God hath given unto many men this prudence, to know the Mass is ill; yet ill as it is, they let neither to say it nor to hear it, which is very idolatry, and shall be cruelly avenged without they amend.'[254] While the effectiveness of clerical deceitfulness explained the extent of idolatry, there was also a strong element of wilful ignorance among the laity.[255] Ponet described the collusion of the laity as contributing to the successful imposition of celibacy:

> The cloud which hath so long blinded the eyes of the lay sort in this point, ws the opinion of holiness that they conceived in the priests, for that they married not as other men did, and the cloud that blinded the eyes of the priests was the gain that they got by their unworthy estimation. So the one being deceived by simpleness and ignorance, and the other by covetousness and vainglory, have by a mutual consent continued this devilish state of unchaste sole life . . .[256]

Conservatism was recognised as a difficult hurdle. It was one thing for ordinary people to reject the pope, who scarcely impinged on their lives, but quite another to reject the Mass.[257]

On the whole, however, protestants preferred to explain lay complicity by the deception argument, partly because it reinforced the conspiracy theory, and partly because its corollary was that exposure of the conspiracy by preaching the Gospel would set matters to rights. Credulity and ignorance had allowed the wily priests to take advantage; what simple layman could withstand the propaganda turned out by so powerful and eloquent a prelate as Gardiner?[258] But ignorance was something that could be overcome. Reform of the communion appeared 'strange' to the 'ignorant and unlearned'

> But if such persons to whom it appeareth strange would but ponder and weigh how our forefathers have been robbed and the commonwealth decayed through the abuse of the Mass, they should soon perceive the difference between the communion and it. And that the King's Majesty and his honourable council doth but as they be commanded by God's word.[259]

The trouble with the 'ignorance' argument was the implication that the religious delusion took place on a purely cerebral, intellectual level, so that a rational explanation would immediately convince. 'Reason' and 'truth' were linked very closely in this way by some writers,[260] but it must be stressed that this did not assume intellectual sophistication, rather that the gospel consisted of simple truths which were accessible to everyone. However, even the cold light of reason could not adequately penetrate the supernatural elements in the 'delusion'. Although mystery was on the whole alien to protestants, religion was not just a matter of words. The numinous power that surrounded the priesthood, especially in the Mass, was a significant element in the 'delusion'. In confronting it, protestants displayed a revealing mixture of fear and contempt.

The ambivalence of this response could be seen in their frequent allusions to 'magic'. These references are better evidence of protestant attitudes to traditional piety than of attitudes to contemporary magical belief and practice.[261] Priests were described as 'conjurers', the Mass as the greatest 'trick', or *legerdemain*, they performed.[262] Not only the wafer but the congregation were bewitched by the incantations and rituals practised by the priest.[263] The idea of the priest as illusionist was not all a matter of ridicule. A sense of fear and danger came over as well. Gilby marvelled at the ability of the priests to make people believe in transubstantiation, contrary to reason, nature and sense.[264] Cranmer urged his audience: 'Listen not to the false incantations, sweet whisperings, crafty jugglings of the subtle papists, wherewith they have this many years deluded and bewitched the world; but hearken to Christ, give ear unto his words which shall lead you in the right way unto everlasting life . . .'.[265] Only determined resistance founded on the stark simplicity of the

A religion of the Word

gospel could combat the seductiveness of papist rituals and arguments. But the idea that popery cast a spell over people was a useful way of absolving the laity from responsibility. Furthermore, it indicated the immanent evil power of Satan and Antichrist within popery that a purely sceptical account would not have countenanced.[266] The element of positive evil had to be destroyed by force as well as by laughter: it was fearsome as well as contemptible.

The persistence of the delusion sprang from the hold of Satan over the weakness of the flesh, manifest in the desire for gratification of the senses. The sense of sight was especially vulnerable,[267] as participation in the Mass usually meant watching rather than receiving communion. To the godly the body was an obstruction to worship, and the Mass was a 'strange sight',[268] but papists were blinded by flesh.[269] When communion did take place the corporal presence prevented a spiritual experience; according to Turner it was done 'only to feed the belly and not to feed the soul'.[270] Nor could it bring the spiritual comfort that it claimed – 'Such comfort have weak and sick consciences at the papists hands to tell them that Christ was with them and now is gone from them.'[271] Spiritual blindness meant that in their misguided zeal papists mistook a 'dead idol' for the living God. The Host may have been in itself a 'small and weak idol', but it exercised a powerful delusion on worshippers.[272]

From seeing the delusion as a magical trick, or the figment of human imagination, it was a short step to the conclusion that it had no objective existence. Popery was reduced to an empty, meaningless structure, which existed only in the minds of papists; it was literally vanity incarnate and could not be edifying since it was not founded on God's word.[273] After 'disproving' the corporeal presence, Cranmer concluded that papists were in a worse situation than he thought – they were actually worshipping not the Host but nothing at all![274] Even their external realities of a powerful clergy and glittering ceremonies were reduced to trivialities by knowledge of the simple Gospel truths. Doctrine and ceremony alike were derided as mere dreams and fantasies, completely imaginary and ephemeral.[275] These dreams might be vivid, but were empty of all spiritual content, and hence unsatisfying: 'This is much like a man that dreameth all the night long that he hath eaten quail, rail and curlew, and that he hath drunk pleasant wine his fill, and yet in the morning he is nevertheless hungry and thirsty, because he had nothing but the forms, shadows, outward accidents and qualities.'[276]

The sanctification of objects was derided as 'absurd'.[277] Even the massive wealth of the church, based as it was on 'idolatry', was effectively empty: 'Thus is your popish religion nothing, and worse than nothing, and shall come to nothing, even as your abbeys have done, which had their foundation of so many nothings and by their nothings had heaped together all things; riches, lands and tenements.'[278]

The struggle against popery

So popery was as mere smoke, blown away by the wind of the Gospel. Yet the absurdity and vanity at its heart did not exonerate, but increased, the guilt of those who manipulated the illusion. Idolatry was empty and absurd, but those who ignored the clear scriptural warnings and enforced it on the people were clearly oppressors as well as deluded fools. Indeed the necessity for their defence of idolatry sprang from the inherent impotence of the idol: if it was God, it could defend itself.[279] We are back with the idea of conspiracy again. The delusion of popery was a result of wilful blindness to the Gospel. The ungodly realised that the Gospel represented a mortal threat to their interests, and they resisted it accordingly.

REPRESSION

While delusion explained the psychological hold of popery, repression was its attempt to prevent the truth from spreading. If delusion was absurd then repression was futile, for persecution vindicated the truth. This allowed protestants to describe popery as a tyranny over body and soul, over secular powers, and epecially over the godly. Hooper described how 'the pope and his adherences with whip and fire beateth as many as call the people from this merchandise, and no marvel, for he is Christ's adversary'.[280] Moone averred that the papists 'persecute the gospellers in every town and city', 'spinning webs' to trap them in and 'hatching cockatrices' eggs' of cruelty.[281] William Kethe saw persecution of the preachers as part of a general oppression of the people:

> For he sent them preachers
> And they were disdained
> To death the true teachers
> Were always constrained
> [. . .]
> With bell, book and candle
> Ye gave us your curses,
> And would us so handle
> That walk should our purses.
> Some time for to strangle
> With ropes ye would truss us;
> No longer now dandle
> For we are past nurses![282]

These instances were intended to place the recent past of protestantism within a continuous history of persecution. From Cain's murder of Abel, through the persecutors of the prophets, the pharisees and Roman emperors, to the papacy, the false church always repressed the true. Hence the timelessness of Bale's description of the 'second age' of the church:

A religion of the Word

'And there went out another horse that was red.' This horse resembleth the said false teachers, born and brought up in flesh and blood, and taught of the same. Such went from the apostles and were not of them, they cursed the true preachers out of their synagogues, they persecuted them from city to city, they accused them as the stirrers up of sedition, they caused the rulers to imprison them, scourge them and slay them, thinking thereby they did God high service ... These were those bloodthirsty doctors and puffed-up prelates, which are partakers with their fathers in the blood of the prophets; whose succession for a token of the same is clothed in red scarlet to this day.[283]

No distinction was made between clerical and secular tyrannies when both served the purposes of the false church. The two main definitions of secular tyranny, of usurpation and oppression, were applied to popery. The usurpation of temporal power by the papacy was a well-worn supremacist theme, as was the excessive influence of clerics.[284] More recent conservative religious policy was seen as tyranny by oppression. Bale's hagiography of Anne Askew emphasised that she was denied the privileges of her rank and sex; she was not allowed to appeal, or to have unquestioned financial support in prison, and worst of all she was racked by Wriothesley and Rich when her gaolers refused to co-operate.[285]

The theme of repression occured most frequently in the protestant exile literature of the mid-1540s, but it did not disappear during Edward's reign. It was alluded to as a constant reminder of the sinister aspects of the traditional piety.[286] Gardiner was depicted as a monster of cruelty, who was prepared cynically to exploit false doctrine in gratifying his own blood-lust:

> But I can never think it that ye believe your own doctrine of works to justify, for if ye did, surely ye would work better works than ye do. For what else do ye than write and strive against the gospel; yea, ye work your brother Cain's work, slaying your brethren for the truth, ye imprison, ye persecute, ye burn, ye banish, ye condemn all good books and professors of God's Word, to set up your own Antichristian articles and damnable popish doctrine.[287]

Accused of attempting to bring back the pope into England via the 'back door' by maintaining popish doctrines and ceremonies,[288] he was a useful target for writers determined to find examples of clerical tyranny and unwilling to blame Henry VIII for conservative policies.

Persecution was a spiritual as well as a physical threat. Spiritual tyranny was exercised by restricting access to scripture and disseminating false doctrine. 'We are captives indeed. For we must ransome full largely if we either speak, write, or keep any book of the Christian religion contrary to your popish doctrine.'[289] Crowley described the burning of New Testaments and other godly books as stopping 'the sweet springs that lead to the head fountain Jesus Christ. In this they play the Philistines that stop up Abraham's wells'.[290] The combination of depriving people of the Bible and enforcing false doctrine led to 'soul murder'.[291]

Access to scripture was denied, whether by using the vulgate or by restricting the readership of the vernacular Bible on grounds of status and gender.[292] The latter policy was evidence, according to Gilby, of Gardiner's fear that the common people, applying the message of the Gospel, would come to 'despise your shameless pomp and pride, and utterly renounce all your wicked errors'.[293] On the other hand, it also led to suspicion of the gospel, as people were either prevented from reading scripture[294] or were cowed by the punishment of those who were caught.[295] The temporal authorities had been deluded into associating unrestricted Bible reading with subversion.[296] Propagandist preaching reinforced suspicion of the Bible; conservatives declared that it was a 'nose of wax, easy to be turned to all purposes'[297] and put a lot of effort into discrediting it: 'O bishop and idol, diddest thou not villainously at Paul's cross (not long since) seek and bring forth all the arguments of thy subtle brain for to stop the kingdom of Christ spreading by his Word and Scriptures, from the which thou didst affray men by the terrible inventions of thy devilish subtleties?'[298]

The traditionalist inconsistency of throwing the immutability of God's Word into doubt, whilst constantly changing their own laws and doctrines, was frequently emphasised. It could only be maintained through compulsion exercised by

> the papists [who] make and unmake new articles of our faith from time to time at their pleasure, without any Scripture at all, yea, quite and clean contrary to Scripture. And yet will they have all men bound to believe whatsoever they invent, upon peril of damnation and everlasting fire. And yet will they constrain with fire and faggot all men to consent (contrary to the manifest word of God) to these their errors...[299]

Yet they took good care to ensure that they remained themselves unbound by either Scripture or law. The history of clerical celibacy bore this out.[300] Ponet described Gregory VII 'heaping up his thunderbolts of cursings and excomnmunications' against all who resisted his enforcement of clerical celibacy.[301] It was not only notorious popes who behaved in this way – 'Is it not open and manifest to all the world that for the breaking of these trifling and foolish traditions they have punished men grievously even with death? And have we not seen the breakers of God's commandments punished at all?' asked Phillip Nichols.[302] The author of the *Fall of the Romish church* accused the papist bishops of suborning those justices whom they knew to be 'blind' (i.e. ignorant in scripture) to punish 'heretics' rather than criminals.[303] False doctrine required repressive methods: oaths, confession and catechising were all used to predispose the people to a suspicion of 'heretics'.[304]

A religion of the Word

False doctrine, however, was a greater threat in itself than these external acts of tyranny. The oppressive and burdensome nature of 'works' piety' showed continuity with pharisaism and Old Testament legalism.[305] Works' piety made not only the church but Christ himself a tyrant, which was an outrage to all who were in the liberty of the Gospel.[306] The people were oppressed body and soul: examples included hostility to marriage and the imposition of excessive tithes and fees.[307] 'For like as he deprived Job, a man that feared God, of his substance . . . so doth this greedy leviathan, this malicious murderer, the man of sin, and body of the devil, with his devouring locusts, rob the poor people of their sweat, labours, travail and necessary living, sparing neither sick nor succourless' and even demanding the profits of crime 'coming to them amiss in their private confessions,' whilst in return, 'they defile their souls with all superstitions, false belief and devilishness, leaving their consciences all doubtful, desperate and comfortless'.[308]

Even the Sacrament had been turned into an instrument of repression, by the restriction of communion to one kind, by forgetting Christ's institution, and by the re-enacting of his sacrifice. Gilby defined communion in one kind as a blasphemy defended by tyranny, and asked 'shall we suffer you thus to captive us still?'[309] In the Mass the church behaving as pharisees continued to crucify Christ, which was intensified by association with the actual persecution of the godly who were the 'members of Christ'.[310] 'St Paul [said that] with often shedding of blood there is no remission of sin (Heb. 9), by the which by her doctrine she crucifieth Christ every day anew, and not only in her doctrine but also she persecuteth him afresh in his faithful members . . .'.[311]

Persecution was the most blatant expression of the evil intent of the false church: 'At their pleasure shall it be to hang them, head them or burn them. And though they lay no hands upon them for soiling their consecrate fingers, yet must it be done by their ghostly counsel, and ordered also after their spiritual appointment.'[312] In the false church, Christian charity had been replaced by a 'burning love', which did not edify but destroyed.[313]

Although everyone was repressed by false doctrine and restrictions on the Bible, the godly bore the brunt of such tyranny.[314] They felt the oppression of false doctrine the more keenly because of their awareness of the truth, and their witness aroused the hostility of the ungodly.[315] In their acceptance of persecution, the godly were 'as lambs in the midst of wolves'.[316] This was the proving of their faith.[317] But the persecution of the saints would eventually prove the undoing of the papists, as Cranmer pointed out to Gardiner:

> And as for the prosperity of them that have professed Christ and his true doctrine, they prospered with the papists as St John the Baptist prospered with Herod, and our saviour Christ with Pilate, Annas and Caiaphas. Now which of these prospered best say you? Was the doctrine of Christ and

St John any whit the worse, because the cruel tyrants and Jews put them to death?'[318]

In persecuting the gospellers, the false church forgot the lesson of the crucifixion. 'For after none other sort reigneth his church here than he reigned afore them, whose triumph was greatest upon the cross.'[319] For the crucifixion was, after all the greatest inversion possible. By undergoing a cruel and humiliating death, Christ redeemed mankind. By imitating him, his followers were able to turn submission into triumph. In allying themselves with the martyrs, protestants were making it clear that they were on the side that would ultimately win. The problem with this, though, was that it was retrospective – there had been no change in perspective from protestant underground to protestant establishment.

CONCLUSION

Antipopery allowed protestants of varying theological types to fight together in the same war, and present a united front. Its themes and tactics could be used at every literary level, from street ballad to scholarly treatise. But from the miscellaneous and diverse sources investigated here one should not derive the impression of an incoherent or casual ideology. As I hope to have demonstrated, it was a carefully constructed web of assumptions and methods, which entangled all aspects of popery: papal and episcopal political claims, theological doctrines, practical piety and spirituality. Using antithesis and inversion, protestants revealed how the antichristian conspiracy worked to generate disorder in the world, by deluding and repressing princes and people alike.

An appreciation of the methods and assumptions underpinning antipopery is not just essential in its own right: it has important consequences in considering protestant ideology as a whole. For, to a great extent, the case against false religion was the mould in which the case for true religion was cast. While (in keeping with their understanding of antithesis and inversion) this undoubtedly had advantages, in that protestantism could be automatically invested with the virtues corresponding to the evils of popery, it also meant that the model was limited. Protestants could not easily break the mould of antipopery and work freehand to construct their ideal church and state. This is why it often appears that they had a better idea of what they wanted to destroy than what they wanted to put in its place.

This was not necessarily either deliberate vagueness or a disingenuous attempt to mask the manifold disagreements within the protestant camp. One of the fundamental themes of antipopery was that true religion was in essence spiritual and intangible, whereas false religion occupied the world of the flesh and the senses. Nowhere was this more evident than in the problem

A religion of the Word

of ecclesiology, where the image of the true church as a persecuted and hidden minority clashed with the demands of a visible, national, partly reformed church.[320] This was a clash founded in personal experience, as the exiles and covert evangelicals of Henry's reign came to terms with their new-found role as the protestant establishment. However, the continuing appeal of the true church as persecuted little flock, whether oppressed by papists or by mammon worshippers, reflected the persistence of antipopery. Similarly, the open-endedness of leaving the essential transformation of lives to the effect of the gospel was not so much an admission of failure to provide a programme as it was a statement of faith, made in deliberate contrast to the papist reliance on *human* institutions.

Antipopery profoundly affected the protestant understanding of the nature and distribution of power, both spiritual and secular. Thus, in the church, discussion of the issues both of a reformed spiritual discipline and of the nature of episcopacy was constrained by the strong association of those issues with papist tyranny and corruption. Maintaining respect for the protestant ministry in the context of the virulent anticlericalism inherent in antipopery also proved a difficult task. Protestants, as we shall see, did try to confront these issues, but could not risk the charge of reverting to popery.[321] Within the state, protestants gladly obeyed their godly prince while he defended 'true order' against the false claims of the papacy, but should he, as punishment for the nation's sins, be replaced by a creature of Antichrist, then he could no longer expect their unqualified obedience. The sense of threat to the political order from popery made true obedience a sensitive issue.[322]

Since antipopery was a way of understanding the world, its application did not cease with the abolition of the Mass. The Mass was but one form of idolatry; another, more insidious, form was the worship of worldly power and wealth, for which the plunder of the churches gave increased opportunity. It should not, therefore, be surprising that the same language was used to denounce contemporary ills as had been used to attack popery.[323] In this wider sense, the time could be interpreted as one of the struggle between the true and the false church. This sense of struggle did not diminish the sense of triumph in the achievements of both Henry VIII and Edward VI in ridding the realm of the papacy, providing it with the vernacular Bible and abolishing the religious orders and the Mass. Though these acts were part of the apocalyptic struggle, they were not final, for Antichrist was not yet overthrown. True order and true religion could not be established without conflict. This chapter has shown the fundamental nature of that conflict; the next three will show its consequences for the church, the commonwealth and the times. But first we take a move sideways, to look at how protestants dealt with popery's antithesis and their own close relatives, the religious radicals.

NOTES

1. E.g. A.G. Dickens's distasteful comments in *English Reformation*, revised edn (1976), 307–1; and G.R. Elton's dismissal of this material in *Reform and Reformation: England 1509–58* (1977), 343. Antipopery has only begun to be taken seriously as a phenomenon for the later sixteenth and the seventeenth century – even here, it is often regarded as significant only at times of political stress. See e.g. C.Z. Wiener, 'The beleaguered isle: a study of Elizabethan and early Jacobean anticatholicism', *P&P* 51 (1971): 27–67; also R. Clifton, 'The popular fear of catholics during the English revolution', *P&P* 52 (1971): 23–55. Betteridge, *Tudor Histories*, and Parish, *Clerical Marriage*, explore mid-Tudor antipopery through the lenses of history and celibacy.
2. This study draws on forty-three specifically 'antipapist' tracts (approximately one-third of all the material used); more antipapist material can be found in the tracts on the Lord's Supper (thirteen are used for this study), and yet more in sermons and commentaries – e.g. Hugh Latimer, *The sermon of the plough* (1548), PS1 73–7; John Hooper, *An oversight or deliberation on the holy prophet Jonah* (1550), PS1 513–37. There were also six reprints of Tyndale, as well as reprints of Frith, Wyclif (see Chapter 5, 'Time', pp. 180–3.), and Barlow's *The burial of the Mass*. Judging by their titles, about a quarter of the translations from continental reformers were antipapal polemic.
3. See W.A. Clebsch, *England's Earliest Protestants, 1520–35* (New Haven, CT, 1964) on the Bible and justification (Tyndale), 137–204, the church (Barnes) 58–73. See also R. Pineas, *Thomas More and Tudor Polemics* (Bloomington, IN, 1968) especially chs 2, 3, 5.
4. Clebsch, *England's Earliest Protestants*, shows the early influence of Wittenberg on Barnes and Tyndale (49–57, 137–53) but shows also the Rhenish influence to have been active from the early 1530s, especially in the work of Frith (78–136, 312–3). The itineraries and contacts of the exiles of the 1540s are traced in E. Hildebrandt, 'A study of the English protestant exiles in north Switzerland and Strasbourg 1539–47, and their role in the English reformation', unpublished PhD thesis, University of Durham (1982).
5. E.g. Anthony Gilby, *An answer to the devilish detection of Stephen Gardiner . . .* (1547); the Preface indicates that it may well have been written in 1546; Robert Crowley, *A confutation of thirteen articles to which Nicholas Shaxton, late bishop of Salisbury, subscribed* (1548), refers to an event of 1546, and also (approvingly) to Gilby's *An answer*, sig. A2. Peter Moone, *A short treatise of certain things abused* (1548), refers to the 'whip' of the Six Articles sig. A3vo. William Punt, *A new dialogue called the inditement against mother Mass* (1548), does not include the 1546 Askew–Lascelles group among its list of martyrs, sig. C4vo, which may indicate an earlier date of composition. Richard Tracy, *A brief and short declaration made, whereby every man may know what is a sacrament* (1548), is a good example of the 'censorship gap' between writing and publishing.
6. See especially Took, 'Government and the printing trade', ch. 2, section 2 and ch. 3; J.N. King, *English reformation literature*, ch. 2. See also above, Sources and methodology.
7. On private Masses, see Edmund Guest, *A treatise against the privy Mass, in the behalf and furtherance of the most holy communion* (1548); the 1545 Chantries Act allowed royal appropriation on grounds of financial expediency; the 1547 Act dissolved them on doctrinal grounds. See A. Krieder, *English Chantries: The Road to Dissolution* (Cambridge, MA, 1979), chs 7, 8. Communion in both kinds was ordered by a proclamation of 8 March 1548 – the *Order of Communion* had English prayers for preparation inserted in the Latin service. Ridley removed altars from St Paul's and the London parish churches in June 1550, less than two months after his consecration as bishop

A religion of the Word

of London – the Council ordered all bishops to follow his example in November (Dickens, *English Reformation*, 339–4; William Salesbury, *The battery of the pope's buttress, commonly called the high altar* (1550), sig. A4vo.

8 Jean Veron, *The five abominable blasphemies that are in the Mass* (1548), claimed them to be: (1) substituting the sacrificing priests for Christ's unique priesthood; (2) defacing the passion, Christ's unique sacrifice; (3) obliterating the memory of Christ's death; (4) destroying the benefits of Christ's death; and (5) cancelling the Lord's Supper as instituted by Christ. Veron, *Certain little treatises . . . for the erudition and learning of the simple and ignorant people* (1548), uses the liturgy to show 'how the Mass did creep into the church of Christ'.

9 E.g. E. T[?ilney]., *Here beginneth a song of the Lord's Supper* (?1550); Thomas Lancaster, *The right and true understanding of the Supper of the Lord and the use thereof . . .* (1550).

10 See below, n. 146.

11 Gardiner was an active force opposing Somerset's reforms until 1548, when he was committed to the Tower, where he remained for the rest of Edward's reign; however he was not deprived until December 1550: Jordan, *Young King* (1968), 211–13 and *Threshold* (1970), 242–4. Bonner was likewise imprisoned in 1549, but not deprived until 1550; Heath and Day were not deprived until 1551 (*ibid.*, 244–9). Bonner's servant William Seth and his chaplain William Chedsey were implicated in catholic book smuggling in 1551. Gardiner continued his opposition in print – *Explication of the true catholic faith* (1551) – in manuscript (attacking Hooper's Jonah sermons: SP 10) – and even perhaps in ballad form – *Their deeds in effect my life would have* (?1548), as suspected by the author of *A poor help*. See J.A. Muller, *Stephen Gardiner and the Tudor Reaction* (1926), chs 20–6. Richard Smith wrote in defence of tradition (*Divers truths*, 1547; *Of unwritten verities*, 1548), but was forced to recant in May 1547 and burn his books at Paul's Cross. His recantation was published: see E.A. Macek, 'Richard Smith: Tudor cleric in defence of traditional belief and practice,' *CHR* (1986): 383–402. Miles Hoggard was brought before the Council in December 1547 for giving the Sacrament unscriptural names in his answer to a protestant ballad, later answered by Robert Crowley in *The confutation of the mis-shapen answer* (1548); he also published a ballad in favour of free will: *A new treatise which sheweth the excellency of man's nature* (1550). Catholic 'libels' include *Ballad of little John Nobody* (BL Harl. MS 372); *The time hath been* (BL Add. MS 5832), cited in Jordan, *Threshold*. Took, 'Government and the printing trade', 177–8, describes a catholic book network centred on Rouen and London.

12 See MacCulloch, *Cranmer*, ch. 13.

13 Crowley, *Confutation of the mis-shapen answer*, sigs A2vo–4. Crowley also accused him of attending sermons, including Latimer's, to collect incriminating evidence, and of being an accessory to the burnings at Smithfield from Frith to Askew.

14 For the Gardiner and Bucer debate, see J.A. Muller, *Stephen Gardiner and the Tudor Reaction* (1926), 125 and ch. 18; C. Hopf, *Martin Bucer and the English Reformation* (Oxford, 1946), ch. 5. John Bale *The acts of the English votaries* (1546); see L. Fairfield, *John Bale, Mythmaker for the English Reformation* (West Lafayette, IN, 1976), 94–6. Bale used a scriptural argument, based on Numbers 30, in his *Apology against a rank papist*. John Ponet, *A defence of the marriage of priests* (1550), was answered by Thomas Martin when the controversy continued into Mary's reign.

15 For an indication of the effectiveness of the Henrician abolition of shrines and pilgrimages, even in a conservative part of the country, see R. Whiting, 'Abominable idols: images and image breaking under Henry VIII', *JEH* (1982): 30–47. For an overview of the speed with which the religious reforms were carried out, see Hutton, *Merry England*, ch. 3.

16 See J. Phillips, *The Reformation of Images: Destruction of Art in England, 1535–1660* (Berkeley and Los Angeles, 1973), chs 3 and 4; M. Aston, *England's Iconoclasts*, vol. 1: *Laws Against Images* (Oxford, 1988), 246–277.
17 The differences between Erasmus and Luther on this are summarised in S. Ozment, *The Age of Reform* (New Haven, CT, 1980), 302–9. For the humanist background to Zwingli and Calvin, see G. Potter, *Zwingli* (Cambridge, 1976), 25–7, 39–44, 65–6; and H. Höpfl, *The Christian Polity of John Calvin* (Cambridge, 1982) Ch. 1. Horton Davies, *Worship and Theology in England from Cranmer to Hooker 1534–1603* (Princeton, NJ, 1970), summarises the attitude of the Henrician and Edwardian reformers. For a key problem of interpretation, see B. Verkamp, *The Indifferent Mean: Adiaphorism in the English Reformation to 1554* (Athens, OH, 1977).
18 Best summarised in Cranmer, *A fruitful exhortation to the reading and knowledge of holy scripture*, in *Homilies* (1549), Book 1 sigs A3vo–A8.
19 Protestants tended not so much to discuss as to dismiss tradition, ensuring that argument was about scripture. Gilby doubted tradition on the grounds of false ministry of scripture (*Answer*, sig. Dd5vo); cf. John Mardeley, *A declaration of the power of God's Word concerning the holy Supper of the Lord* (1548), sigs A5vo–A8.
20 John Bale, *The latter examination of Anne Askew* (Wesel, 1547), PS 202; Bale also cites 2 Corinthians 6.
21 E.g. R.V., *The old faith of Great Britain and the new learning of England* (?1549), sig. C4; Mardeley, *Power of God's word*, sig. B3vo.
22 John Bale, *The image of both churches* (Antwerp, ?1545; London, 1548 and 1550), PS 622; cf. 'For of the Scripture can we make neither art nor science, no more than we can make an art or science of God's eternal wisdom.' Also Bale, *Rank papist* (1550); sig. D3.
23 Thomas Cranmer, *Answer to a crafty cavillation by Stephen Gardiner* (1551), PS1 254; John Hooper, *Answer to my Lord of Winchester's book* (Zurich, 1547), PS1 164; Phillip Nichols, *Copy of a letter sent to master Crispin* (1548), sigs B5–B5vo.
24 Both Richard Smith, *A brief treatise setting forth divers truths* (1547), and Stephen Gardiner, *A detection of the devil's sophistry* (1546), defend tradition at length; Smith modified his defence in the pamphlet *Of unwritten verities* (1548) along rather unconvincing Erastian lines. Cranmer was preparing a full-scale rebuttal of tradition, using arguments from scripture, reason and patristics; notes from his commonplace book were published in 1557 in a tract edited by 'E.P.' See P. Marshall, 'The debate over unwritten verities in early modern England', in B. Gordon (ed.) *Protestant History and Identity in Sixteenth Century Europe* (Aldershot, 1996).
25 Thomas Cranmer, *Defence of the true and catholic doctrine of the Sacrament* (1550), PS1 105; on variance as a sign of falsehood, disingenuously applied to catholics, see *Answer*, PS1 249.
26 George Joye, *Refutation of the bishop of Winchester's false articles* (1546), sigs B4–B4vo.
27 Cranmer, *Answer*, PS1 92.
28 Contempt was expressed for scholastic 'glosses'; the production of commentaries and scriptural study aids was an important part of protestant printed work: e.g. Lancelot Ridley's expositions of Pauline epistles (RSTC 21039–42); John Hooper, *Godly and most necessary annotations to the thirteenth chapter to the Romans* (Worcester, 1551); Anthony Gilby, *A commentary upon the prophet Micah* (1551), a polemical commentary. The 1547 *Injunctions* specified that each parish church should possess a copy of Erasmus's *Paraphrases*; J.K. Maconica, *English Humanists and Reformation Politics under Henry VIII and Edward VI* (Oxford, 1968), describes their translation, ch. 8; J. Booty, *The Godly Kingdom of Tudor England: Great Books of the English Reformation*

A religion of the Word

(Wilton, CT, 1981) ch. 2, sees them as central to an 'Erasmian' reform programme. Other study aids included John Marbecke, *Concordance* (1550) and, as a bridge between oral and literate cultures, William Samuel, *The abridgement of Gods's statutes* (1551), which includes a mnemonic device for remembering the verses based on the finger joints.

29 Hooper, *Answer*, PS1 111; cf. Bale, *Image*, PS 576, the deceivers condemned by prophecy.
30 Gilby, *Answer*, sigs Bb8–Bb8vo; Robert Crowley, *Confutation of the mis-shapen answer* (1548), sig. F8; John Hooper, *Funeral oration* (1549, 1550), PS1 562; *A report of Dr Redman's answers* (1551), sig. B3vo, affirms scriptural comfort in dying.
31 Bale, *Image*, PS 452–3.
32 John Hooper, *A declaration of Christ and his office* (Zurich, 1547), PS1 45–6.
33 For conservative accusations that protestants were 'carnal', see Gardiner, *Detection*, sigs A6–B3; Hoggard, *A new treatise*, sig. B2.
34 See Introduction, n. 9.
35 Hoggard, *A new treatise*; and see above, n. 11.
36 See above, n. 3. For the 'absorption' of the justification debate into the Sacrament debate, see e.g. Gilby, *Answer*, sigs X2vo–X3vo; Crowley, *Confutation of the mis-shapen answer*, sig. B5vo; Veron, *Five blasphemies*, sigs B4vo–B5.
37 For Cranmer's attempted 'ecumenical conference', see MacCulloch, *Cranmer*, 394–5, 501–2, 518–19; the *Consensio mutua in re sacramentaria ministrorum Tigurinae* between the various reformed protestant camps was published in England in 1552.
38 Crowley, *Confutation of the mis-shapen answer*, sig. D4. For further imagery of 'spiritual eyes', see *ibid.*, sigs A7vo, D7, E6vo; Gilby, *Answer*, sig. L8; and also the section 'Delusion', below, pp. 41–7. 'The eye of the soul' was a phrase used by Gardiner in *Detection* (sig. D1), and taken up by Gilby, who used it in exactly the opposite sense.
39 Gilby, *Answer*, sig. D2.
40 Anon., *The fall of the Romish church* (?1549), sig. A6; Hooper, *Answer*, PS1 156–7, declared that even Christ could not make his 'carnal audience' understand his spiritual meaning.
41 Crowley, *Confutation of the mis-shapen answer*, sig. E8.
42 Gilby, *Answer*, sigs T7–T7vo.
43 Edmund Guest, *Treatise against the privy Mass* (1548), sigs H7–H7vo.
44 Cranmer, *Defence*, PS1 42–3; Gilby, *Answer*, sigs Aa7–Aa7vo; Veron, *The five abominable blasphemies*, sig. B1; Anon., *The true judgement of a faithful Christian* (?1548), sigs A5–B3vo; Crowley, *Confutation of the mis-shapen answer*, sigs G1vo–G2.
45 Cranmer, *Defence*, PS1 39, and *Answer*, PS1 164.
46 John Bale, *The first examination of Anne Askew* (Wesel, 1546), PS1 155; Hooper, *Answer*, PS1, 151; Crowley, *Confutation of the mis-shapen answer*, sig. E2.
47 William Turner, *A new dialogue, wherein is contained the examination of the Mass* (1548), sig. F6vo; cf. Salesbury, *Battery of the pope's buttress*, who attacks the doctrine of the sacrifice of the Mass. Celia Hughes, 'Two sixteenth century northern protestants: John Bradford and William Turner', *Bulletin of the John Rylands Library* (1983): 132 suggests that Turner's dialogue is a translation of a work by Ochino. For Salesbury, see below, chapter 5, n. 52.
48 Gilby, *Answer*, sig. Q1vo.
49 John Ramsey, *A plaster for a galled horse* (1548), 3.
50 Gilby, *Answer*, sig. D7vo.
51 Robert Crowley, *The confutation of thirteen articles whereunto Nicholas Shaxton . . . subscribed* (1548), sig. K8, referred to Lutheran ideas about predestination. Crowley and Joye, in the latter's *Refutation of Gardiner* (sigs xlvii.vo–li.vo), were not concerned

The struggle against popery

with the complexities of the doctrine of assurance. See also Chapter 3, 'The Christian body', pp. 114–27.

52 Gilby, *Answer*, sig. C1.
53 Bale, *Image*, PS 290.
54 *Ibid.*, 531–2.
55 *Ibid.*, 254; Hooper, *Answer*, PS1 153; Joye, *Refutation*, sig. F7; Crowley, *Confutation of Shaxton's articles*, sigs B3, B6–6vo.
56 Bale, *Image*, PS 254–5.
57 Gilby, *Answer*, sig. T6vo; Crowley, *Confutation of the mis-shapen answer*. sig. A6vo.
58 Hooper, *Answer*, PS1 152.
59 Joye, *Refutation*, sigs Q3–3vo.
60 Nicholls, *Copy of a letter*, sigs B6–B8. Nicholls described any attempt to assert unscriptural articles of faith as 'Satanic'.
61 Thomas Cranmer, *Answer to Smith's preface* (1551) PS1 377.
62 See above; also Chapter 3 – 'The Christian body', pp. 114–27.
63 Augustine, *The City of God*.
64 Gilby, *Answer*, sig. T3vo, marginal note: 'The world doth always strive against the spirit.' See also 'The declaration of the true church', sigs I1–K2. See A. Ryrie, 'Problems of legitimacy and precedent in English protestantism', in B. Gordon (ed.) *Protestant History and Identity in Sixteenth Century Europe* (Aldershot, 1996).
65 Gilby, *Answer*, sigs H8–8vo.
66 *Ibid.*, sig. N4vo.
67 I.e. 'Delusion' (see pp. 41–7).
68 Gilby, *Answer*, sigs P2–P2vo, F8vo–G1.
69 Cranmer, *Answer*, PS1 172.
70 E.g. Bale, *Image*, PS 368 and 543; Nichols, *Copy of a letter*, sig. B7; Crowley, *Confutation of Shaxton's articles*, sigs G4–G4vo.
71 Bale, *Image*, PS 319, 353, 486, and *Acts of the English votaries*, 60–79: St Dunstan.
72 E.g. Gilby, *Answer*, xlviii.vo, cxiii.vo; Cranmer, *Answer to Smith's preface*, PS 377.
73 Turner, *A new dialogue*, sig. D7; William Kethe, *A ballad, declaring the fall of the whore of Babylon, entitled 'Tie thy mare, Tom boy'* (?1548), 9; John Ponet, *A defence of the marriage of priests* (1549), sigs A8–B7vo.
74 Nichols, *Copy of a letter*, sig. B4.
75 See K. Firth, *The Apocalyptic Tradition in Reformation Britain* (Oxford, 1979), chs 1 and 2; Fairfield, *John Bale*, ch. 3; P. Christianson, *Reformers and Babylon* (Toronto, 1978), ch. 1, perhaps overestimates Bale's immediate influence.
76 Bale, *Image*, PS, 514.
77 *Ibid.*, 405–6.
78 See below on 'Inversion', pp. 28–34.
79 Bale, *Image*, PS 251.
80 For inversion as a satirical method, see – pre-eminently – Erasmus, *The Praise of Folly*; S. Clark, 'Inversion, misrule and the meaning of witchcraft', *P&P* (1980): 98–127, especially 104–10.
81 See R. Scribner, *For the Sake of Simple Folk: Popular Propaganda for the German Reformation* (Cambridge, 1981), ch. 6, and Watt, *Cheap Print*, Part 2.
82 Stephen Gardiner, *A detection of the devil's sophistry*, sigs A2–A2vo.
83 E.g. Cranmer, *Answer*, PS1 337.
84 Phillip Gerrard, *A godly invective in defence of the gospel* (1547), sig. A4vo.
85 Cranmer, *Defence*, PS1 30.
86 Hooper, *Declaration of Christ*, PS1 66.

87 Isaiah 5:20; e.g. Bale, *Image*, PS 294.
88 Cranmer, *Answer*, PS1 185-6, cf. *ibid.*, 50.
89 Gilby, *Answer*, xxii, lxiii.
90 E.g. Guest, *Treatise against the privy Mass*, sigs D1-D3vo.
91 E.g. Cranmer, *Defence*, PS1 187.
92 Hooper, *Answer*, PS1 174; Bale, *Image*, PS 294; Anon., *A caveat for the Christians against the archpapist* (1548), where Gardiner is referred to as 'this subtle sophister and fraudulent counterfeiter of God's holy Word'.
93 Cranmer, *Defence*, PS1 243.
94 Hooper, *Answer*, PS1 216-17; he went on to describe examples of papal pronouncements that contradicted both each other and scripture.
95 *Ibid.*, 155.
96 Bale, *Image*, PS 420: the imagery of the sands of the sea, and the sea itself, out of which arises the apocalyptic beast.
97 Nicholls, *Copy of a letter*, sig. D8vo.
98 Bale, *Image*, PS 289-90 – an extreme statement partly justified by the conception of the true church in spiritual terms.
99 See below, 'Repression', pp. 47-51.
100 Cf. William Turner, *The rescuing of the Romish fox* ('Winchester', i.e. Bonn, 1545), sigs E7, G4; Bale, *Image*, PS 284; cf also Gilby, *Answer*, sigs Aa8-Aa8vo, on fasting; Bale, *Apology against a rank papist*, sig. E2, on vowed celibacy.
101 Gilby, *Answer*, lxxxii.
102 Joye, *Refutation*, sig. P7.vo5.
103 See below 'Dichotomy', pp. 21-8.
104 Cranmer, *Answer*, PS1 37.
105 Hooper, *Answer*, PS1 121.
106 *Ibid.*, 128.
107 *Ibid.*, 147.
108 Veron, *The five blasphemies*, sigs B5-B5vo.
109 Cranmer, *Answer*, PS 248.
110 *Ibid.*, 236.
111 *Ibid.*, 235; Guest, *Treatise against the privy Mass*, sig. H1; Crowley, *Confutation of Shaxton's articles*, sig. D6; Veron, *The five blasphemies*, sigs A5vo-A6; Gilby, *Answer*, sig. V6vo.
112 *Ibid.*, sigs T5vo, K6; cf. Hooper, *Answer*, PS1 164.
113 Cranmer, *Answer*, PS1 4, 57, 164.
114 Cf. Peter Moone, *A short treatise of certain things abused* (1548), sig. A2vo. For the Ipswich group of propagandists (Peter Moone, John Ramsey, Richard Argentine, John Oswen), see Dickens, *Notes and Queries* (1954): 513.
115 Cranmer, *Answer*, PS1 153.
116 See above, n. 32; also cf. R. Kyle, 'John Knox and the purification of religion: the intellectual aspects of his crusade against idolatry', *Archiv* (1986): 265-80.
117 Gilby, *Answer*, sigs R4, T5; Cf. Turner, *Rescuing*, sig. H4.
118 Hence Gerrard's view of the contrast brought about by the reformation, *A godly invective*, sig. C3vo.
119 Cf. Hooper, *Answer*, PS1 202-5; Turner, *Rescuing*, sigs. F3-H6.
120 Bale, *Apology against a rank papist*, sig. B3.
121 Gilby, *Answer*, sigs T8-V3; Bale, *Latter examination of Anne Askew*, PS 243-5.
122 Bale, *Image*, PS 496.
123 See above n. 80; also the anticlericalism in late mediaeval literature, notably in Geoffrey Chaucer's *The Canterbury Tales* and William Langland's *The Vision of Piers Plowman*.

The struggle against popery

Langland's anticlericalism was such that Crowley thought he was a Lollard, and hence part of the proto-protestant tradition – see Chapter 5, n. 36.
124 Bale, *Image*, PS 497.
125 For antagonism towards clerical charges for Easter Communion and marriage, see Crowley, *Confutation of the mis-shapen answer*, sig. D3vo; for clerical venality, sig. D5vo; Bale, *Image*, PS 430, 446–8; Lynne, *Beginning and ending of all popery*, 23, 34; for the sale of absolution, see Bale, *Apology against a rank papist*, sig. P6; for sale of Masses, see Gilby, *Answer*, sig. H7vo.
126 Kethe, 'Tie thy mare', 14.
127 For episcopal arrogance and 'lordliness', see Bale, *First examination of Anne Askew*, PS 173–4; cf. Gilby, *Answer*, sigs A8vo, Ee1vo; for increasingly arrogant papal claims, Bale, *Image*, PS 319.
128 Ramsey, *Plaster for a galled horse*, 6.
129 Bale, *Apology against a rank papist*, sig. P8vo.
130 Gilby, *Answer*, sig. Aa8 vo. 'Sweet suckets' and 'subtleties' were elaborate desserts.
131 See above, n. 14; D.M. Palliser, 'Popular reactions to the reformation', in F. Heal and R. O'Day (eds) *Church and Society in England: Henry VIII to James I* (1977), 42, gives the proportions of married clergy by 1553 as: London, 33 per cent; Essex, Suffolk, Norfolk, 26 per cent; Cambridgeshire, 20 per cent; Lincolnshire and Yorkshire, 10 per cent; and Lancashire 5 per cent. Bishops tended to marry partly as a statement of protestant affiliation, but this was less likely for lesser clergy. For the scandalous cases of Holgate and Ponet, see E. Carlson, *Marriage and the English Reformation* (Oxford and Cambridge, MA; 1994), 59; for clerical marriage, *ibid.*, 52–9; compare with H. Parish, *Clerical marriage and the English Reformation* (Aldershot, 2000), for a detailed survey of the polemic and further research on the reality.
132 E.g. John Bale, *Acts of the English votaries* (1548) part 1, 2ovo, where the Celtic saint Illtyd is described as 'a tyrant to marriage' because of his renunciation of his wife; Augustine's monks use their 'feigned chastity' to oust married priests from their livings (*ibid.*, 31). See Betteridge, *Tudor Histories*, ch. 2, for an analysis of Bale as interpreter.
133 Gilby, *Answer*, sig.Bb7vo; Joye, *Refutation*, sig. xii.vo; Anon., *The upcheering of the Mass* (1547); Ramsey, *Plaster for a galled horse*, 7; Kethe, 'Tie thy mare', 18.
134 John Ponet, *A defence of the marriage of priests* (1549), sig. D6vo.
135 Revelation 17–18.
136 E.g. the destruction of the nunnery-brothels of Saints Hildwitha and Osyth by both the plague and the Danes, in Bale, *English votaries*, 36vo–37; the discovery of Pope Joan, *ibid.*, 54vo; St Ebba's monastery for men and women at Coldingham destroyed by a 'wildfire', *ibid.*, 45vo.
137 See below, 'Repression', pp. 47–51.
138 As allegory, see the usurping claims and consequent punishment of the Whore of Babylon in Bale, *Image*, PS 508–11; as threat, see the end envisaged for Gardiner in Joye, *Refutation*, sigs G2vo–G3.
139 Bale, *First examination of Anne Askew*, PS 144; cf. Gilby, *Answer*, 18–18vo, asserts that the ecclesiastical hierarchy should be poor for the purity of the church.
140 Bale, *Image*, PS 296, 368, 436, 491; cf. Gilby, *Answer*, sig. I6vo.
141 Bale, *Image*, PS 420; cf. Gilby, *Answer*, sigs. I1vo–I2; Crowley, *Confutation of Shaxton's articles*, sig. B4vo.
142 Gilby, *Answer*, sig. F8vo, quoting Romans 8.
143 Bale, *Image*, part 3. See also Chapter 5, 'Divine judgement', pp. 193–7.
144 E.g. the 'harlot's faces' of those who shamelessly corrupt scripture (quoting Jeremiah 3:3), in Cranmer, *Answer*, 249; the power of Rome as the power of the Whore, in Bale,

A religion of the Word

      Image, PS 493–4; the prophetess Jezebel dominates Thyatira (*ibid.*, 283); the power of the courtesans Theodosia and Marozia over the tenth-century papacy, in Bale, *English votaries*, 63vo–64.

145 Gardiner as whoremaster (reference to the Southwark stews which were on land belonging to the bishop of Winchester), in Turner, *Rescuing*, sig. M1; Bale, *English votaries*, 29.

146 'J.M.', *A brief recantation of mistress Missa* (1548); Kethe, '*Tie thy mare*'; Anon., *The upcheering of the Mass*; Turner, *A new dialogue*; William Punt, *An inditement against mother Mass* (1548); Luke (?)Shepherd, *Pathos, or an inward passion of the pope for the loss of his daughter the Mass* (?1548). See also Veron, *Five blasphemies*, where he characterised the Mass as the 'adulterous Helen'. See also Parish, *Clerical Marriage*, ch. 7, for clerical celibacy and the Mass.

147 Lyndal Roper, 'Luther: sex, marriage and motherhood', *History Today* (1983), argued that the repression of brothels reflected the Lutheran elevation of marriage. While this is one side of the problem, it reduces the equally important ideological and eschatological humiliation of the Whore as a symbol of the purification of religion. This is a theme which is not only developed at length in Revelation (see Bale) but has powerful links with the Old Testament, both in history (the stories of Jezebel and Athaliah) and allegory/prophecy (especially Hosea). Idolatry, both for Old Testament prophets exhorting Israel to stay true to the purity of the covenant and for protestants who regarded popery as faithless innovation, was consistently characterised as 'spiritual fornication' or 'whoring after strange gods', encapsulating the ideas both of breaking faith and of contamination, while alluding to the different sexual codes implied both by pagan priestess/goddess cults and by catholic celibacy. The recurrent theme of adultery in Edwardian protestant writings indicated not so much a sudden plunge in moral standards as an increased sensitivity among protestants to sexual infidelity as a mirror of idolatry. see also Chapter 3, n. 144.

148 Bale, *Image*, and also *English votaries*. The papacy rose to dominance in the 'third age' and continued unthreatened to the end of the 'fifth age'. A more complex chronology than that of the seals of the apocalyptic angels was symbolised by the heads of the Beast. Bale interpreted the last head, which 'is not yet come', as the papacy, which was not in existence when Revelation was written. See Firth, *Apocalyptic Tradition*, ch. 2

149 See below, 'Repression', pp. 47–51.

150 'Antichrist' was shorthand for all things popish, rather than a specific identification with the papacy – though of course it included it. See e.g. Gilby, *Answer*, xlviii; Ramsey, *A plaster*, 5; *Fall of the Romish church*, sig. B4. Cf. P. Lake, 'The significance of the Elizabethan identification of the pope as Antichrist', *JEH* (1980) 31: 161–77.

151 Cf. especially German lay pamphleteers in the early reformation, who placed a much greater stress on lay ministry and emphasised the priesthood of all believers. See P. Russell, *Lay Theology in the Reformation* (Cambridge, 1986), 62–3, 71–3, 91–5. Cf. also Chapter 3, pp. 94–100.

152 Bale, *Image*, 637; Gilby, *Answer*, sig. Y7.

153 Cranmer, *Defence*, 161; cf. *Fall of Romish church*, sig. C2: refusal of papists to 'search the Scripture'.

154 Gerrard, *Godly invective*, sig. D4.

155 Eg, Gilby, Anthony, *Answer to the devilish detection of Stephen Gardiner* (1547) for Latin liturgy see sig. G8vo, for scholasticism see sig. T1.

156 See above, nn. 28, 89.

157 Cranmer, *Answer*, 335; Gilby, *Answer*, sig. K7; see also below, 'Delusion', pp. 41–7.

158 Hooper, *Answer*, PS1 214
159 Turner, *A new dialogue*, sigs B3vo–B4.
160 Cf. Gilby's defence of the protestants against the charges of arrogance and ignorance, *Answer*, sigs C6–6vo.
161 Gerrard, *Godly invective*, sig. C5.
162 *Ibid.*, sigs C7–C7vo.
163 *Ibid.*, sigs. D3vo–D4. For the 1536 and 1538 *Injunctions*, see MacCulloch, *Cranmer*, 166, 196, 226–9, 301.
164 Just as the law needed interpretation, so did scripture: a corrupt lawyer merely swindled his clients of lands and property, whereas corrupt theologians defrauded the unlearned of heaven. See Salesbury, *Battery*, sigs C1–C2.vo, D6–D7vo. Salesbury's was a classic statement of the humanist element in protestantism, i.e. that the diffusion of a literal understanding of scripture could result only in enlightenment.
165 I.e. original sin (*ibid.*, sig. C8).
166 *Recantation*, sig. A3vo.
167 For communion in one kind, see Turner, *Rescuing*, sigs I4.vo–I7; Gilby, *Answer*, sig. Aa7; Crowley, *Confutation of Shaxton's articles*, F4–F7vo; on priestly powers, see Guest, *Treatise against the privy Mass*, sigs E5–E6; Gilby, *Answer*, sigs. Dd7–Ee1; Veron, *Five blasphemies*, A5–A6vo; and on private Masses, see Guest, *Treatise against the privy Mass*, especially sigs K7vo–K8; Crowley, *Confutation of Shaxton's articles*, sigs F7vo–G3.
168 Veron, *Five blasphemies*, sig. B6.
169 See n. 167.
170 All translations: Bernadino Ochino, *A tragedy or dialogue of the unjust, usurped primacy of the bishop of Rome* (1549), tr. John Ponet; Walter Lynne (tr.) *The beginning and ending of all popery* (1548), from Osiander's edition of the Joachimist *Vaticinia sive prophetiae*; M. Flacius Illyricus, *Wonderful news of the death of Paul III* (?1552), tr. William Baldwin. see King, *English Reformation Literature*, 196–206, 371–87. For Edward's version of Ochino, see MacCulloch, *Tudor Church Militant*, 26–30.
171 E.g. Thomas Gibson, *A brief chronicle of the bishop of Rome's blessing* (1550, reprint of a supremacist tract of the ?1530s).
172 E.g. the conspiracy to make Canterbury not London the prime see, in Bale, *English votaries*, 26; the increasing power of Dunstan over king Edgar and the removal of married priests from cathedrals, *ibid.*, 67–74; cf. the 'politic silence' of conservatives on the papacy, in Bale, *First examination of Anne Askew*, PS 181.
173 E.g. Joye, *Refutation*, 'To the reader', iii; Gilby, *Answer*, xxviii, lxxiii.vo, sigs Y8–Y8vo; Anon., *A caveat for the Christians against the arch-papist*, 1548.
174 Samuel, *The practice*, sig. A4.
175 Cranmer, *Defence*, 353.
176 Hugh Latimer, *Third lenten court sermon* (1549), PS1 130.
177 See below, 'Inversion', pp. 28–34; also Chapter 5, 'Providence', pp. 178–80.
178 Nicholas Lesse, *The justification of man by faith only* (1548), tr. Melanchthon, sig. A6.
179 Gilby, *Answer*, sig. Cc5.
180 *Ibid.*, sigs T1–T2.
181 John Mardeley, *A short recital of certain holy doctors* (1548), sig. A1vo.
182 English protestants tended to ignore the divisions on the subject among their own ranks, while publicly attacking the Mass. However, they were well aware of confessional divisions; see above, n. 37, though evidence from Bullinger's correspondents should be used cautiously. They were after all trying to present the English reformation in continental terms.

183 Cranmer, *Answer*, 152
184 See Chapter 5, pp. 209–214.
185 Especially e.g. Veron, *Five blasphemies*, also Crowley, *Confutation of the mis-shapen answer*, sig. F6; Turner, *A new dialogue*, sigs. A6–A7vo.; *Fall of the Romish church*, sigs B4vo–B5; Gilby, *Answer*, sig. V4vo; Cranmer, *Defence*, 345.
186 See also below, 'Inversion', pp. 28–34.
187 *Ibid.*
188 Gilby, *Answer*, sigs M6vo–M7; Hooper, *Answer*, PS1 191–200.
189 Crowley, *Confutation of Shaxton's articles*, sig. E6.
190 Cranmer, *Answer*, 245, 301.
191 *Ibid.*, 87
192 *Ibid.*, 19
193 See Chapter 5, pp. 187–93.
194 Hooper, *Declaration of Christ*, PS1 43.
195 Gerrard, *Godly invective*, sig. C4.vo.
196 Turner, *A new dialogue*, sig. B3; cf. Gilby, *Answer*, sigs T5, V3: model of Israel's abandonment of God and consequent punishment. See Chapter 5, 'Divine judgement', pp. 187–93.
197 E.g. Gilby, *Answer*, sig. V7; Bale, *Rank papist*, sigs. N4, O8.
198 Romans 1:24–32.
199 Romans 1:29–30; cf. also 1 Corinthians 8, 10:14–22, and Acts 17. Though the bulk of the references used in this study are to Old Testament warnings against idolatry, Paul's antagonism to Roman idolatry should not be forgotten; see J.S. Coolidge, *The Pauline Renaissance: Puritanism and the Bible* (Oxford, 1970).
200 E.g. Bale, *Apology*, sig. P2; Ramsey, *A plaster*, 6–7, Luke Shepherd, *Philogamus* (?1548). See also n. 1, above.
201 Certain works by Bale 'could not with propriety be presented to the public; and the reprinting of the present portion of them must not be considered as indicating an approval of all he either said or did'. Henry Christmas, *Select works of bishop Bale*, PS, xi.
202 See below, 'Inversion', pp. 28–34.
203 See above, n. 147.
204 See below, 'Conspiracy', pp. 34–7. Cf. links between popery and rebellion in chapter 5, 'Resisting the Gospel', pp. 209–11. See Parish, *Clerical Marriage*, on celibacy, and on Antichrist and the Mass.
205 Bale, *Apology against a rank papist*, sig. B4vo.
206 *Ibid.*, sig. E2.
207 *Ibid.*, sig. B1; cf. Bale, *Image*, PS, 487.
208 Bale, *Apology against a rank papist*, sigs. D2–vo.
209 *Ibid.*, sig. N4vo.
210 *Ibid.*, sig. T1vo.
211 *Ibid.*, sig. G6.
212 Bale, *English votaries*, 78vo, 47; cf. Ponet, *Defence of the marriage of priests*, especially sigs. B7, C1–C7vo.
213 See below, 'Conspiracy' pp. 34–7 and 'Dichotomy', pp. 21–8.
214 Cranmer, *Defence*, 349: Mass invented 'for lucre'.
215 Cf. Bale, *Rank papist*, sig. P6: the disinheriting of heirs to pay for Masses.
216 E.g. Gilby, *Answer*, lxxxii; Nichols, *Copy of a letter*, sig. D8vo.
217 See above, 'Inversion' pp. 28–34.
218 Gilby, *Answer*, sig. Cc3; Hooper, *Answer*, PS1 184.

219 Bale, *Image*, PS 422–3, 459–60; cf. Gilby's refusal to call Gardiner 'lord', in *Answer*, sig. B3vo.
220 E.g. the power of Simon Magus over Nero, which Bale alleged led to the persecution of the early Christians, in *Image*, PS 445.
221 *Ibid.*, 361–2.
222 *Ibid.*, 282, 499.
223 Cf. Revelation 17.
224 Ramsey, *A plaster for a galled horse*, 3–4, 7; cf. Ponet, *Defence*, sig. C8vo.
225 See above, n. 170.
226 2 Thessalonians 2: the description of the coming of the 'Man of Sin', i.e. Antichrist, especially seen in those who rejected the Gospel (verses 10–11). This 'strong delusion' was both a providential sign of the Last Days, and, as such, a comfort to the elect. See also Chapter 5, pp. 193–7.
227 See below 'Conspiracy', pp. 34–7.
228 Thomas Becon, *The Castle of comfort* (1550), PS2 563–7.
229 See below, 'Inversion' pp. 28–34 and 'Disorder', pp. 37–41.
230 Bale, *Image*, PS 486–7.
231 *Ibid.*, 506; John Hooper, *An oversight and deliberation upon the holy prophet Jonah* (*fifth sermon*) (1550), PS1 526.
232 Bale, *English votaries*, *i.
233 John Hooper, *A funeral oration* (1549), PS1 569.
234 *Ibid.*, 570.
235 Crowley, *Confutation of Shaxton's articles*, sigs F2–F2vo.
236 *Fall of the Romish church*, sig. B7vo.
237 Cranmer, *Answer*, 260.
238 Gilby, *Answer*, sig. Y2; John Bale, *Answer to a papistical exhortation* (1548).
239 Gilby, *Answer*, sig. V7vo.
240 Bale, *Image*, PS 287.
241 Bale, *Rank papist*, sigs A8–A8vo.
242 See above, 'Dichotomy', pp. 21–8.
243 *Fall of the Romish church*, sigs A3, B7vo.
244 E.g. Gilby, *Answer*, sigs Dd2–Dd3.
245 'J.M.', *Recantation of mistress Missa*, sig. A2.vo; Ramsey, *Plaster for a galled horse*, 6; Guest, *Treatise against the privy Mass*, sig. K5.
246 See above, 'Conspiracy', pp. 34–7.
247 Bale, *Latter examination of Anne Askew*, PS 237; cf. John Mardeley, *A declaration of the power of God's Word* (1548), sig. B4vo; Lynne (tr.) *Beginning and ending of all popery*, 3.
248 Joye, *Refutation*, sigs G1vo–G2vo; Mardeley, *Power of God's Word*, sig. C8vo.
249 E.g. Cranmer, *Defence*, 130, 161; *Answer*, 133.
250 Gilby, *Answer*, sig. Aa5.
251 Cranmer, *Answer*, 293; see below, 'Repression', pp. 47–51.
252 *Ibid.*, 311.
253 Cranmer, *Defence*, 229.
254 Hooper, *Answer*, PS1 151–2.
255 E.g. Guest, *Against the privy Mass*, sig. A3.
256 Ponet, *Defence of the marriage of priests*, sigs A2vo–A3.
257 Guest, *Against the privy Mass*, sig. L6vo. See also Chapter 5, 'Resisting the gospel', pp. 211–14.
258 Joye, *Refutation*, sig. A3; Gilby, *Answer*, sigs D3vo, K2vo.
259 'R.V.', *The old faith of Great Britain and the new learning of England* (1549), sigs a8–a8vo.

260 Cf. Hooper, *Answer*, PS1 114, 152; Guest, *Against the privy Mass*, sigs B4vo–B5; Cranmer, *Defence*, 250, *Answer*, 254.

261 E.g. Gilby, *Answer*, sig. Bb3; Guest, *Treatise against the privy Mass*, sigs 3–4; Crowley, *Confutation of the mis-shapen answer*, sig. D5vo; *Fall of the Romish church*, sig. C4vo. See Keith Thomas, *Religion and the Decline of Magic: Studies in Popular Beliefs in Sixteenth and Seventeenth Century England*, 2nd edn (1973), ch. 3, for the effects of the reformation on popular beliefs; note that in this chapter very little pre-Elizabethan evidence is used.

262 E.g. Moone, *Short treatise*, sig. A2vo; *Fall of the Romish church*, sigs B4vo–B5; Anon., *An epistle exhortatory*, 6.

263 Crowley, *Confutation of Shaxton's articles*, sig. E8, and *Confutation of the mis-shapen answer*, sig. D8; Bale, *Acts of English votaries*, 40, 73, 75vo, and *Image*, PS 537; Moone, *Short treatise*, sig. A2vo; Anon., *An epistle exhortatory*, 6; (?)Luke Shepherd, *John Bon and master Parson*.

264 Gilby, *Answer*, sigs. N5vo–N6.

265 Cranmer, 'To the reader', in *Answer*, 7.

266 Bale, *Image*, PS 438; Veron, *Five blasphemies*, sigs A8–A8vo.

267 E.g. *Epistle exhortatory*, 1–2; *Fall of the Romish church*, sig. A3.

268 Crowley, *Confutation of the mis-shapen answer*, sig. A7vo; cf. Gilby's reinterpretation of Gardiner's phrase 'with the eye of the soul', in *Answer*, sig. L8.

269 See above, n. 38.

270 Turner, *A new dialogue*, sig. C3vo.

271 Cranmer, *Answer*, 61.

272 Gilby, *Answer*, sig. V3vo; *Epistle exhortatory*, 4.

273 Bale, *Image*, PS 376.

274 Cranmer, *Defence*, 229.

275 Joye, *Refutation*, sig. X5vo; Crowley, *Confutation of Shaxton's articles*, sigs A6–A8; 'R.V.', *Old faith of Great Britain*, sig. A5vo.

276 Gilby, *Answer*, sig. L7vo.

277 John Hooper, *A declaration of the ten holy commandments of almighty God* (Zurich, 1548, and London, 1550) PS1 317; Moone, *Short treatise*, sig. A2vo; Cranmer, *Answer*, 343.

278 Gilby, *Answer*, sigs Dd7vo–Ee2vo; cf. Bale, *Image*, PS 532.

279 Gilby, *Answer*, sig. I7vo.

280 Hooper, *Funeral oration*, PS1 569.

281 Moone, *Short treatise*, sigs A3–4.

282 Kethe, 'Tie thy Mare', 15–16, 20.

283 Bale, *Image*, PS 314–5.

284 Cranmer, *Defence*, 353; Samuel, *Practice*. Cf. John Bale, *King John*, Camden Society (1838).

285 Bale, *Latter examination of Anne Askew*, PS 213, 222–5, 243. Anne was interrogated in order to incriminate evangelicals at court. See Maria Dowling, 'The gospel and the court: reformation under Henry VIII', in P. Lake and M. Dowling (eds) *Protestantism and the National Church in Sixteenth Century England* (1987), 36–77, especially 65, 69–70.

286 See Introduction; also above, n. 5.

287 Joye, *Refutation*, sig. L6; cf. Gilby, *Answer*, sigs C5vo–C6, Ee5.

288 See works attacking Gardiner by Turner, Gilby, Hooper, Joye and Cranmer. It was easier to blame him than attack Henry VIII: see Glyn Redworth, 'A study in the formulation of policy: the genesis and evolution of the Act of Six Articles', *JEH*

(1986) 37: 42–67. See Ryrie, 'English evangelical reformers', ch. 1, for a further reassessment.
289 Gilby, *Answer*, sig. E6vo.
290 Crowley, *Confutation of Shaxton's articles*, sig. A8vo.
291 This was originally a term used by catholics of heretics; for protestant examples of this usage, see Bale, *Image*, PS 321; Mardeley, *Power of God's Word*, sig. C1.
292 Dickens, *English Reformation*, 263–5.
293 Gilby, *Answer*, sig. Y7.
294 Gerrard, *Godly invective*, sigs D1–D2.
295 Bale, *Image*, PS 441.
296 *Ibid.*, 427; cf. Thomas Lancaster, *The right and true understanding of the Supper of the Lord*, sig. B1.
297 Gilby, *Answer*, sig. S2vo.
298 *Ibid.*, sig. Y8vo.
299 Cranmer, *Defence*, 131–2.
300 E.g. Dunstan plunders the cathedrals under the pretext of enforcing celibacy (Bale, *English votaries*, 67); the Celtic saint Illtyd is labelled 'a tyrant to marriage', for repudiating, impoverishing and blinding his wife (*ibid.*, 20vo); Alphege forbids sexual relations to married couples in Lent (*ibid.*, 56vo).
301 Ponet, *Defence of the marriage of priests*, sigs C6–C6vo.
302 Nichols, *Copy of a letter*, sig. D3vo.
303 *Fall of the Romish church*, sig. C5vo.
304 On indoctrination by catechising, see *ibid.*, sig. C4; by auricular confession, Crowley, *Confutation of Shaxton's articles*, sigs H3–H8; control by the abuse of oaths, Hooper, *Ten commandments*, PS1 335; the laity went to church out of a sense of fear, which made them 'worse than the beasts', according to Guest, *Treatise against the privy Mass*, sig. K7.
305 E.g. Gilby, *Answer*, sigs C4vo–Cc8vo; Hooper, *Answer*, PS1 200–1; *A caveat for the Christians*, sig. B6vo.
306 Bale, *Image*, PS 482–3.
307 For hostility to marriage, see above, n. 132; for excessive profit from fees, etc., see above, n. 133.
308 Bale, *Image*, PS 425–6.
309 Gilby, *Answer*, sig. E6vo; cf. *ibid.*, sigs Aa7–Aa7vo;
310 Bale, *Image*, PS 555; Joye, *Refutation*, sig. L5.
311 His list of martyrs is as follows: 'Richard Hunne, Robert King, John Debenham, Nicholas Marsh, Thomas Saxie, Thomas Hitton, Thomas Bilney, Richard Byfield with Tewkesbury and Collins, William Leton, George Bainham, John Frith, John Lambert, William Tyndale, Robert Barnes with Gerrard and Jerome, and xvc more'. Punt, *A new dialogue*, sig. C4vo; cf. Bale, *Image*, PS 277, 393; Gilby, *Answer*, sig. T6vo.
312 Bale, *Image*, PS 392.
313 Gilby, *Answer*, sig. B6vo.
314 I.e. 'upholders of the gospel', not necessarily just protestants. See Maria Dowling, 'The gospel and the court', in Lake and Dowling (eds) *Protestantism and the National Church*, 36–40, for use of this terminology. Note the problems caused by Foxe's inclusive definition of membership of the pre-reformation 'true church'.
315 Bale, *Image*, PS 276, 326.
316 Crowley, *Confutation of the mis-shapen answer*, sig. A6vo.
317 Zechariah 13:9; e.g. Bale, *Image*, 604.

318 Cranmer, *Answer*, 14–15.
319 Bale, *Image*, PS 567.
320 See C. Davies, '"Poor persecuted little flock" or "commonwealth of Christians"? Edwardian protestant concepts of the church', in Lake and Dowling (eds) *Protestantism and the National Church*.
321 See Chapter 3.
322 See Chapter 4.
323 See Chapter 5.

Chapter 2

The threat of religious radicalism

INTRODUCTION

WRITING from London in June 1549, John Hooper described to Heinrich Bullinger how, when he preached, 'the anabaptists flock to the place, and give me much trouble with their opinions... How dangerously our England is afflicted by heresies of this kind, God only knows; I am unable indeed from sorrow of heart to express to you...'.[1] Hooper's anxiety was genuine enough, but his fears were, if not groundless, at least exaggerated. While there is evidence of unorthodox ideas at this time, there is very little to indicate that they were being expressed within the setting of organised 'gathered' congregations. If Joan Bocher did boast that 'a thousand in London were of her sect', that should not be taken as a literal fact, but as an indication of the religious ferment there.[2] Indeed, J.W. Martin has suggested that 'their diversity may be one of their most important characteristics'.[3] It appears that, far from being a national problem, protestant heterodoxy was commonest in London and the south-east, and even there an exceptional occasion like the Bocking conventicle of 1550 was a gathering of only about sixty people.[4]

However, as the opening description by Hooper indicates, the importance of 'anabaptists', or radicals, was out of all proportion to their numbers. That such people existed at all constituted a threat to both the social order and the establishment of religious uniformity in the reformed church. Thus the response of the authorities could only be a determined one. It resulted, at its most extreme, in the burning of two 'anabaptists': Joan Bocher, who denied that Christ took the flesh of the Virgin, was burned on 2 May 1550, after a year's imprisonment; and George van Paris, a Dutch immigrant, was burned on 27 April 1551 for denying Christ's divinity.[5] C.H. Smyth asserted that 'at least two-thirds of the martyrs who were burned by Queen Mary would almost undoubtedly, had Edward VI survived, have been burnt in the normal course by the Church of England'.[6] He may have exaggerated the figures, but he describes the temper of the reforming church fairly accurately.[7]

Action against the radical threat was taken in the courts, from the pulpit and in print. There were two Heresy Commissions, in 1549 and in 1551; the first presided over by Cranmer and six other bishops, the second increased to include twenty-five leading lawyers and other divines.[8] Hooper's 1549 preaching tour was accompanied by the publication of his *Incarnation of Christ*, a didactic tract attacking heterodox Christologies.[9] Nicholas Ridley was concerned at the activities of radicals in the diocese of London, particularly after the influx of refugees from the Netherlands in 1549. He wrote to Cheke in 1551 desiring preferment for a preacher who, 'for detecting and confuting of the anabaptists and papists in Essex, both by his preaching and by his writing, is enforced now to bear Christ's cross'.[10] William Turner, Somerset's physician, preached a series of sermons against anabaptism at Isleworth which were answered by the radical and court musician Robert Cooche. Turner replied in *A preservative or treacle against the poison of Pelagius* in 1551; it was dedicated to Hugh Latimer and had commendatory verses by leading protestants.[11] Jean Veron and Nicholas Lesse dedicated their translations of works by continental reformers on the theological issues raised by anabaptism to the lord protector, his wife and Sir John Gates in a bid for official approval.[12] The Privy Council was involved in the investigation of radical 'cells'. Joan Bocher pitted her wits against the combined intellectual forces of Cranmer, Ridley, Goodrich, Latimer, Lever, Whitehead and Hutchinson. It was the difficulty of converting her that in 1550 led Hutchinson to write his anti-heretical compendium *The image of God*.[13]

All this indicates how the whole weight of the establishment was set against these few dissidents – or rather against what they stood for. For if the threat of anabaptism was as serious as protestants presented it to be, why were there so few burnings and recantations? The impression of a disproportionate campaign is strengthened by comparing the reality of religious radicalism with its propaganda image. It is argued in what follows that the discrepancy between the image of anabaptism and its English reality was a significant element in the presentation of protestant ideology. In campaigning against 'anabaptism', Edwardian protestants were clearly using a sledgehammer to crack a nut – but it was vital to their credibility that they should be seen capable of wielding the sledgehammer.

WHO WERE THE RADICALS?

English religious radicals in this period can be divided into two groups: one group maintaining unorthodox Christologies, and the other upholding free will, rather than the predestinarian theology that was taking hold among orthodox protestants, as the key to the achievement of spiritual regeneration and visible godliness.[14] The doctrinal differences between these groups should not be allowed to obscure their similar experiences. All appear to have come to their heterodox views by way of personal Bible reading and discussion with like-minded acquaintances. Their degree of education varied; John Assheton (Proctor's 'Arian') and Robert Cooche both mentioned contemporary continental theologians, and Cooche had some knowledge of church history, while the learning of Henry Harte and John Champneys was solely Scriptural.[15] However, they were alike in their anticlericalism, their demand for godly living and their stress on Bible reading rather than the sacraments as the focus of Christian worship.[16]

That being said, the radicalism of the first type was obviously much easier to identify because of their unorthodoxy. Joan Bocher's connections with Lollard groups in Essex may be open to doubt, but she had been involved with Anne Askew in smuggling protestant literature to court in the 1540s.[17] Her views at this point seem to have been similar to Anne's: antagonism to images and ceremonies, and a memorialist view of the Sacrament. But Joan went further than her mentor, and taunted Cranmer: 'It was not long since you burned Anne Askew for a piece of bread, and yet came yourselves soon after to profess the same doctrine for which you burned her. And now, forsooth, you will needs burn me for a piece of flesh, and in the end you will come to believe this also, when you have read the Scriptures.'[18] The 'piece of flesh' in question was her conclusion that Christ did not take his humanity from the Virgin, but passed through her 'as light through glass'. Roger Hutchinson's account of her beliefs is more detailed: she did not deny the humanity of Jesus, but said that

> There is a natural and a corporeal seed, and there is a spiritual and a heavenly seed, as we may gather of St John, where he saith, 'The seed of God remaineth in him and he cannot sin.' And Christ is her seed; but he is become man of the seed of her faith and belief; of spiritual seed, not of natural seed; for her seed and flesh was sinful as the seed and flesh of others.[19]

This theory was very similar to the ideas of the Dutch spiritualist Melchior Hoffman, and Joan may well have come across it among Dutch exiles in London.[20] It is just as likely, though, that she drew her own conclusions from her own reading of the Bible, as did a more educated radical, John Assheton.

In 1549, John Proctor, a Kent schoolmaster of conservative views, published a detailed refutation of Assheton's deposition, thereby preserving it.[21] Assheton had opened with a sneer at reformed theologians: unlike his contemporaries, he did not obtain his opinions 'out of Sarcerius, Conradus Pellican and such garbages or rather sinks and gutters, but out of the sacred fountain'.[22] His

A religion of the Word

definition of true religion was impeccably protestant except that he extended the familiar protestant taunt of distorted reading of scripture to the whole range of his opponents, both catholic and protestant: 'I call that right faith which doth credit and believe that of God which the Scriptures do testify not in a few places, and the same depraved and distorted into wrong sense, but as ye will say "thoroughly" with one and the same perpetual tenor and consent.'[23] As Proctor was quick to point out, this resulted in a very partial view of scripture. 'Arian' was determined, however, to make sense in his own way of what he read. Contrasting the divine attributes of God with the descriptions of the human Jesus was to conclude that orthodox theology was illogical.[24] Claiming a literal view led him to make far from literal statements: 'the Word was made flesh', for instance, was explained as a personal revelation to Jesus of the divine will, of such intensity as to make him the 'image of God'.[25] He envisaged Christ as an exalted human being: 'Verily, that he was the most elect vessel, the organ or instrument of the divine mercy, a prophet and more than a prophet, the son of God but according to the spirit of sanctification, the first begotten but among many brothers &c.'[26]

Since faith, according to 'Arian', cannot contradict itself, he could dismiss as absurd the paradoxical biblical basis of Trinitarianism. Naturally, his use of 'reason' in the task of making sense of scripture was abhorrent to John Proctor, who blamed protestant policies for the existence of such lay rationalism.[27] He was not far off the mark here; had the 'Arian' been using the same language and approach to attack the Mass he would not have attracted the attention of the authorities. However, it was highly likely that he had learned his 'rationalism' from such protestant anti-Mass literature and preaching, in which 'reason' was aligned with 'true religion' against the 'blind faith' of belief in transubstantiation. In extending to Christology the protestant rejection of 'blind faith', he, like Joan Bocher, crossed the boundary-line of acceptable theological speculation.[28]

This was true also of the second group of religious radicals, though the heterodox element in their thinking was not made explicit in their published works, for obvious reasons. The tracts of Henry Hart and John Champneys were not openly subversive of the Edwardian reform of the church – indeed, both their language and their demands grew out of it.[29] A good example of this was their anticlericalism, in that they both employed deliberately vague language which conflated the papist tyranny of keeping the Bible from the laity with the new intellectual elitism of the protestant 'learned ministry'. Thus Champneys referred to the clergy indiscriminately as 'marked men', a term which fitted the apocalyptic tone of his tract, but one which conventional protestants would apply only to papists.[30] Hart described them as a conservative authority, whose demands for reform were limited by self-interest:

> Woe unto those bishops, pastors and lawyers of what name and place soever they be, which boast of power and authority to rule and govern other, and yet have no respect to their own souls ... [who say] 'Tush, we be well enough, for the holy laws, ceremonies and sacraments of God are remaining among us, and thereby are we known to be his people.'[31]

Hart demanded a sinless and unworldly ministry which would not delude either itself or the people into the practice of 'outward' religion. It is possible that he was hinting at some form of perfectionism, but his demand was couched in conventional evangelical language.[32] Champneys was more extreme, accusing the clergy of doing 'as much as lieth in them spiritually to murder all those souls to whom they have preached'. Unlike conventional protestants, he blamed preaching, rather than the lack of it, for the destruction of the flock, in that he clearly resented its use as a showcase for learning. To him, the difference between the reformed and unreformed clergy was merely one of style, not substance: 'they be as crafty as ever they were, disguising themselves with sophistical hypocrisy, either new or old, as fast as ever they did, and the Devil is as familiar with them as ever he was'.[33] Comparing himself to Elijah, who challenged the priests of Baal to a trial of sacrifice, Champneys dared the 'learned ministers' to a trial of preaching:

> If the compiler hereof, a poor layman and of small literature be not able by God's assistance only by the power of the Spirit of Christ, to show the Word of God written in the true literal sense, both for the clear discharge of his own conscience and conversation, and also of all other that be regenerate in Christ, let it be death unto him.[34]

The distinction between 'human doctrine' and the 'true literal sense' of divine inspiration in scripture recalled Hart's more developed concern with the spiritual illumination of the regenerate:

> Brethren, your minds are now lightened by grace and ye have now received the Spirit of God, which bringeth knowledge and a perfect willing obedient mind to do the will of God. But he who hath not the Spirit the same is none of his. Forasmuch as ye are partakers of the Holy Spirit and are born anew, ye are not now (my brethren) under the Law but under grace.[35]

This was not a declaration of antinomianism, but a plea for visible godliness: 'For many do hear, read and speak the holy Scriptures, (praised be God) and many desire to know much. But blessed and happy are ye which obey to that truth so that ye do thereafter, for the kingdom of God standeth not in words (as ye well know) but in power and working.'[36] Hart's conclusion was not that the regenerate could not sin, but rather that they should not mix with sinners.[37] His reasoning was based on 1 Corinthians 10:20 – he demanded that the regenerate should not be 'partakers of ... the table of devils'. This could have been a call for separation; and, indeed, some of the members of

A religion of the Word

the Bocking conventicle, where Hart's influence was apparently respected, had refused the communion 'for above two years'.[38] However, it was not an explicit command, and did not preclude outward conformity, especially in view of Hart's description of the illuminating nature of true faith:

> for true faith is lively and cannot be hid, neither may she in any wise dwell or abide alone, for she hath a great desire to many virtues. She accompanieth herself with God's wisdom and love. She is nourished daily with the bright sun of righteousness and the highest watereth her plants with the sweet showers of grace. Through perfect obedience to the will of God, she spreadeth forth her branches in due season, whereby she obtaineth a sure hope her fruits proceed from the tree of life.[39]

As an account of 'lively faith', this was uncontentious; the only possible criticism protestants could make of it would be that the struggle of the faithful against sin and the encounter with the law of God were matters dangerously underplayed in these tracts.

A similar reticence prevailed in Hart's approach to the doctrine of free will. In his tracts he merely mentioned that the godly consisted of 'all those who with a free heart do put themselves under the covenant of God to do his will...'. Champneys, Hart and Cooche were later to confront predestinarians like Bradford and Knox on this issue, but it does not appear to be developed in their writings at this point.[40] J.W. Martin has argued convincingly that to label Hart as the leader of a congregation of 'free-willers' is to misunderstand what was in reality a far less formal situation.[41]

What, then, is the significance of this brief survey of Edwardian radical ideas? As we have seen, heterodox ideas certainly were present, sometimes in a form so extreme that the authorities had to act. If the doctrinal differences are set aside, it is clear that both Arians and free-willers had the same origin: the confrontation of the unlearned but literate layman and his friends with the Bible.[42] What is more, Bible reading was taking place in the context of protestant propaganda pervaded both by antipopery and the dissociation from 'carnal gospellers', which threw the distinction between the minority of the godly and the rest into sharp relief. So too much should not be made of the hints of a call to separation in Hart's tracts.[43] The fact that the open Bible and their own writings and sermons were in large measure contributing to radical ideas and possible schisms clearly worried the reformers – and, worse, laid them open to catholic taunts. Thus Richard Smith, erstwhile regius professor of divinity at Oxford, saw heresy as the inevitable result of the 'open book':

> What folly and madness is it then to dispute and reason so much as Englishmen do, upon the articles of our faith. What brought Joan of Kent to her abominable heresy? Was it not over much reasoning upon God's Word and

measuring of it, and of God's power by her wit and natural reason? What hath brought many other men and women into divers heresies in England which are not yet known commonly? Was it not mistaking of the Scriptures and arrogant reasoning upon them?[44]

PROTESTANT IMAGES OF 'ANABAPTISM'

Protestant awareness that the 'open Bible' policy did entail pitfalls for the unwary will become apparent in the following study of protestant anti-anabaptist literature. The works produced fell into three categories: translations of works by continental reformers attacking anabaptist doctrines;[45] confutations of individual English religious radicals;[46] and more general theological treatises.[47] In addition, there was the defence by the unknown 'J.B.' against a slanderous charge of anabaptism.[48]

Nowhere in these tracts was there an attempt to meet or understand the kind of theological exploration that we have noted was fundamental to English religious radicalism. This should not come as a surprise, since lay access to the Bible had always been a central plank of the protestant platform. Instead, their authors found it necessary to characterise the radicals as alien to the protestant cause, and this was achieved most obviously by branding them as heretics. Discussion of heresy rather than just anabaptism broadened the terms of the debate; a narrow definition involving believers' baptism was thus avoided – which was useful, as the practice was no longer common by this time, even in Europe.[49] 'Anabaptist' in the literature under consideration could be used as a generally pejorative term as well as a specific criticism.[50] The wider connotations of heresy made it easy for protestants to invoke the associated problems of separatism and anarchy: disorder in doctrine was mirrored by the disruption of church and state. Such threatening behaviour released protestants from any need to deal with religious radicals on equal terms. They proceeded to characterise radicals as irrational to the point of insanity, and even to prove that, far from being radical protestants, they were papists in all but name. Further examination of these assertions will reveal how seriously protestants took what was more a paper tiger of their own making than a real threat to the stability of church and state.

Firstly, then, radicals as *heretics*. Both protestants and radicals believed in the proximity of the last days, but protestants applied the prophecies of heresy and division in the church (notably those found in 1 John 1, Matthew 24 and 2 Thessalonians) to the radicals.[51] The true Christian continuously struggled against heresy; according to Hooper, 'seeing as it was so in the apostles' time by the craft of the Devil, that men by the diversity of opinions troubled the truth of the gospel; which was and is done to prove the faithful'.[52] Defining the radicals as false prophets, who were so plausible that they could mislead even the elect, fulfilled a triple function: of identifying the reformed with the primitive church; of saving souls; and of providing evidence that the last days were at hand.[53]

While apostolicity was a priority, protestants also broadened their case with patristic references and patristic terms. Whether these were accurately applied or not, those using them confirmed their own orthodoxy.[54] Thus even in doggerel verse, Edmund Becke described Joan Bocher as a Marcionite. Polycarp had described Marcion as 'the Devil's eldest son'; Joan, by theological association, became in Becke's words 'the Devil's eldest daughter/ which lately was burnt'.[55] Proctor, coming from a more conservative standpoint, quoted the Athanasian creed in full at the end of his confutation of the contemporary 'Arian', and described in lurid detail Arius's career of treachery, lies and deceit, culminating in his repellent death. 'Such', he wrote, 'are the tabernacles of heretics'.[56] Hutchinson's treatise aimed to refute not only popery and anabaptism, but also 'our late Epicures ... Donatists ... Novatians ... and Sadducees'.[57] All the heresies in his index, current or not, were described in the present tense. Even though William Turner spent most of his treatise defending infant baptism, he referred to his opponent more often as a Pelagian than as an anabaptist. This was particularly significant in that he had first-hand knowledge of continental sectarianism, acquired during his exile in the 1540s.[58] The use of patristic 'labels' was also to be found in the translations of anti-anabaptist material by Calvin and Bullinger. If English protestants were copying the tactics of their continental mentors, they also shared their motives.[59]

The use of patristic 'labels' was further emphasised by comparative lack of reference to mediaeval heresies. Bullinger mentioned Catharism and the unorthodoxy of Peter Abelard, and Hooper in his *Godly confession* described the acute disruption caused by the flagellants.[60] Protestant reference to these heresies could only be limited: such an argument could backfire, linking them with antiheretical popish tyranny.[61] Moreover, heresies like Waldensianism and Lollardy already belonged to the history of proto-protestantism, so any hint that the radicals had much in common with these heresies could not be countenanced.[62]

By presenting the threat of religious radicalism as heresy, the reformers could claim the orthodox high ground from catholics who had accused them of negating the traditions of the church and opening the door to religious anarchy.[63] This accounted for the predominance of doctrinal discussion in anti-anabaptist propaganda. The things that radicals had in common with protestants – rejection of Rome, insistence on the scriptures as the source of all authority in the church, demands for a visible godliness – were thus all pushed aside as mere hypocritical godliness which succeeded in fooling only the 'simple folk'.[64]

However, given the evangelical and Christocentric nature of Edwardian reform, it is not surprising that Christological concerns were a priority. The doctrines that did come under scrutiny were those that undermined or contradicted the Pauline Christocentric views held by protestants. Only if Christ were God could the prophecy of Genesis that 'the seed of the Woman' should break the head of the serpent, setting mankind free from the bondage of sin, be fulfilled.[65] Conversely, Christ's humanity was not a contempt of his divinity, argued Hooper, 'but rather a certain argument of God's mercy (which passeth all his works) that he would not abhor to be partaker of our infirm nature'.[66] On the other hand, Proctor argued that denial of his divine nature was a denial both of the power of providence and of scriptural evidence.[67] Even in a tract which was taken up with discussion of primitive church practice, Turner's main point was a theological one: 'If they need none of Christ, he died not for them ... It is not too early nor too timely to carry the children by the prayers of the Church to Christ that he may heal them.'[68] To deny baptism to infants suggested that Christ's death redeemed us only from original sin. The extension of this doctrine into perfectionism (i.e. that once baptised and regenerate, a believer should not sin, for there would be no forgiveness for whoever did) threatened the nature of protestant piety, which was a discourse of sin, repentance and dependence on God's grace. Such an extreme version of the doctrine of justification by faith alone projected human restrictions onto the divine mercy. The result was either spiritual pride, forgetful of God's saving grace, or desperation as the daily evidence of spiritual corruption manifested itself in the conscience.[69] Protestants were more worried by this error of perfectionism than by antinomianism, despite the terrors that the latter could inspire. It seems likely that they perceived it as being the greater pastoral problem.[70]

The identification of heresies to be refuted was used by protestants as a useful opportunity to clarify their doctrinal position, even though they could not always invoke the Bible with the same ease here as they had done against popery, as the tortuous logic of the case for infant baptism showed.[71] On the next two charges, those of separation and sedition, protestants had to construct a more conjectural picture. The potency of rumour and implication as polemical devices meant that conjecture did not necessarily reduce the effectiveness of the propaganda,[72] but it did offer a clear contrast to the kind of careful refuting of specific doctrinal errors that we have seen so far. It must be noted that on these questions the most developed arguments were found in the translations of tracts by Bullinger and Calvin. Their experience of anabaptist thinking and practice (in separation from even reformed churches, and in opposition to oaths, fighting and magistrates) was gained at first hand. English radicalism offered nothing so developed or sophisticated,[73] yet English protestants took these characteristics for granted, perhaps because

A religion of the Word

the European experience provided the only available model for protestant sectarianism, and it was assumed that these were the forms it would take. The origin of this is to be found in the traditional model of heresy, in which schism and sedition were seen as the destructive result of spiritual error: the inward sickness of heresy in the souls of individuals would manifest itself in the world as a rejection of the established order.[74]

Firstly, *separatism*: the suspicion that religious radicals, as Hooper put it, 'despised and rejected the lawful ministry of the church'.[75] As we have seen, this does not appear to have taken on a particularly organised form in this period in England. But the 'heresy' of perfectionism opened the back door to separation, even if this only meant in practice absence from communion rather than from organised worship in a gathered church. Hutchinson pointed out that this was presumption: 'But thou art not godly minded but carnal, the servant of sin, if thou despise the ordinance of God and his commandment, who biddeth thee "Take and eat": and carnal and ungodly men do not receive the body of Christ, but the spiritual and godly.'[76] Absenteeism on the grounds that the minister was not truly godly was likewise given short shrift: 'Does God's mercy depend of the goodness of the minister? Then our faith cannot be steadfast and sure, but wavering and uncertain, forasmuch as no man can discern what is a good minister; for he that seemeth good may be an hypocrite.'[77]

The radical response to this would be that in the congregation of the godly, the spiritual knowledge provided by the presence of the Holy Spirit would be able to discern true godliness. Protestants could only shrug off this dart by refusing to acknowledge that the Holy Spirit could be present in radical congregations. Bullinger and Hutchinson passed on the catholic accusation that protestantism was naturally fissiparous, by applying it to the sects. These were mistaking a mere 'carnal affection' for the Holy Spirit, with the result that they quarrelled not only with the reformed church but with each other.[78] Indeed, Veron saw the destruction of the unity of the church as the prime aim of heretics: '[It is] the wicked and perverse nature' of false and seditious heretics [to] study for naught else but to divide and separate the church, to get unto themselves disciples, to scatter and dissipate the flock of Christ, to sow discord, to teach perverse things . . .'.[79] If there was no salvation outside the church, then the threat posed by the radicals of drawing people away from it was serious indeed. The authority of the reformed church was fragile enough without the possibility of the sects undermining it still further.[80]

The second danger, *sedition*, was that heretics, having rejected the authority of the church, would reject also the duty of obedience owed by the citizen to the state.[81] This was far more immediate a danger than the threat of separatism, particularly in the wake of the 1549 rebellions and the widespread unrest that accompanied them; it is clear, for instance, that the Council pursued its investigations of heretics in Kent with the possibility of seditious gatherings in mind.[82] 'They will have no magistrates nor judges on the earth', cried Latimer.[83] Veron was worried that the achievements of the reformers were endangered by such radicalism. Their activities were a perversion of the reformers' own insistence that preachers should speak out without respect of persons into a 'carnal and fleshly liberty'.[84] Such ideas endangered the security of the country, and both the bodies and the souls of those who expressed them.[85]

Just how destructive radicalism could be had been demonstrated in the disastrous events at Münster in 1535, but surprisingly little propagandist capital was made out of this. One exception was William Turner, who had experienced more extreme anabaptism whilst in exile and linked Robert Cooche's 'dishonesty' with it:

> I may a great deal be less ashamed of my poor and innocent infants, than ye may be to defend the doctrine of your seditious and murdering anabaptists, which destroyed the noble city of Münster in Westphalia, and rose up against the magistrates in Amsterdam, and Zwolle not far from Deventer, and were about to have destroyed Groningen in West Friesland. Let the innocents be mine still, and the factious catabaptists be yours![86]

'J.B.' denounced the 'breeding out' of the 'doctrine of the carnal kingdom of Christ' as a 'dreadful error' which caused 'great slander and hindrance of the true gospel of God'; the leaders of such chiliastic movements were to be regarded as 'Antichrist above all Antichrists, yea, above the Romish Antichrist'.[87] But considering the enormous propaganda value of these incidents, reformers did not make much of them, presumably because nothing so unsettling had taken place in England.

They seemed more worried by the prospect of radical political quietism, which could be equally subversive, if less dramatic. Hooper emphasised that the notions that no Christian should hold office and, furthermore, that in a truly Christian society, there would be no need for magistrates were fundamentally mistaken in two respects. They confused the office holder (who might be godly or ungodly) with the divinely ordained office; and they refused to acknowledge that even a Christian society contained sinners, who had to be restrained by the magistrate and the laws.[88] The anabaptist teaching thus gave the reformers another opportunity to focus on the doctrine of obedience.[89] But it also revealed a chink in the protestant armour. As Bullinger's 'seditious anabaptist' declared, Christ and the prophets had been called seditious in *their* day; he was content to follow them. When Latimer himself used similar words to defend his outspoken sermons, he did so, in part, ironically – Christ and the apostles were scrupulous in upholding the authority of the state. But irony alone could not wholly counteract conservative charges that protestantism was by its nature potentially seditious. By

A religion of the Word

directing the charge of sedition on to a radical 'fringe', protestants tried to deflect some of the fire, especially in the aftermath of the 1549 rebellions.[90]

At this point the argument ended and the abuse began. 'J.B.'s bitterness reflected the destruction of his reputation on a charge of anabaptism.[91] Jean Veron described heresy as a disease 'infecting the minds of rude and simple people with pernicious and detestable opinions'.[92] Becke saw it as a mental delusion inspired by Satan: 'He captivates our senses, so fond and fantastical/ That we doubt not to deem the day to be night.'[93] Nicholas Lesse was even more vicious, describing 'free-willers' as 'having in their heads the eyes of cockatrices, in their tongues the stings of adders, and in their stomachs the poison of toads...'.[94] Both Hooper and Turner referred to anabaptists as 'fantastical sprites', a description with connotations of supernatural madness.[95] The inspiration talked of by the radicals became at worst possession by evil spirits, at best a pathetic delusion or 'carnal affection'.[96] Turner, with characteristic heavy irony, declared that 'it is no material thing that we must fight withal, but ghostly, that is, a wood spirit...'.[97]

The last charge made by protestants against radicals – that they were papists without the pope – may seem to indicate that they themselves had begun to fall victim to delusion and irrationality. If it is assumed that papists and anabaptists were irreconcilably opposed extremes, then this might be the case. But this would be to dismiss as a mere parting shot a theme that reflected the evangelical nature of the Edwardian reformation. The key was the sense in which these extremes were represented as occupying common ground. Both, for instance, preached false doctrine, especially in their emphasis on a 'Pelagian' understanding of works and original sin.[98] Both presented a case based on a mangled and deliberately misinterpreted selection of texts.[99] Turner, after cornering Cooche into placing the burden of proof against infant baptism on the decisions of early church councils, crowed with delight that he had thereby fallen into a classic papist trap, for: 'Whosoever goeth about to confute Scripture with councils and men's decrees and his own arguments, prefereth councils and decrees before God and his Word and reckoneth himself better than God.'[100] He went on to balance his denunciation of anabaptism with an attack on the Mass. To deny infants the benefit of baptism while offering it to 'believers' was as bad as the priest offering the wine at Mass and then drinking it himself: both made a mockery of the rights of the congregation.[101] Veron and Becon described papists and anabaptists as false prophets; according to Becon they were both 'damnable sectaries'.[102] Latimer likened the separatism of the anabaptists to the retreat from the world of the monks who,

> forgetting this commandment of love and charity, ran away from their neighbours, like beasts and wild horses, that cannot abide the company of men. So

the anabaptists in our time, following their example, segregated themselves from the company of other men, and therefore God gave them *reprobum sensum*, that is, a pervert judgement.[103]

They may look completely different, was the moral, but their motivation and attitudes were identical, as were their destructive effects on the bonds of charity within society.

Understanding anabaptism and popery as aspects of the same phenomenon rather than different enemies of the reformed church, attacking it from opposite sides, fitted the protestant self-image very well. Far from fighting for a *via media* between these two extremes, they saw themselves as defending true religion against false. If the reformed church was the true church, any body outside it laying claim to that title had to be a member of Antichrist. Both papists and religious radicals were, to protestants, wolves in sheep's clothing: the only difference was, that to the newly reformed church (or, rather, its more gullible members), the sheep's disguise of the radical was the better fitting and the more convincing.

CONCLUSION

If one were to look for a dialogue between English protestants and religious radicals in Edward VI's reign, one would be disappointed. Furthermore, this propaganda battle had no such sense of engagement as the equivalent one with the catholics, which had such well-matched opponents as Gardiner and Hooper, or Smith and Cranmer. Instead, the reformers attacked a composite image, made up of the heretic, the schismatic, the rabble-rouser, the madman and the counterfeit papist. The defence of infant baptism against anabaptism balanced the defence of the Lord's Supper against the Mass, making a complete case for the two protestant sacraments. However, in terms of bulk of material, it was clear that English protestants realised that the main threat to the establishment of the reformed church came from conservative piety.[104] But by describing popery and radicalism not so much as right-wing and left-wing extremes but as aspects of an Antichristian conspiracy to subvert the true church, protestants completed the picture of themselves as definers and defenders of 'true religion'. The reformation was thus shown not just as a negative force which was solely concerned with destroying the religious practices of the past, but as a positive means of upholding the eternal truths of doctrinal orthodoxy. In the face of catholic charges that protestantism was fissiparous by nature, the defence of orthodoxy gave the reformers a useful opportunity to present a united front, both within England and abroad.[105]

The confident posture maintained by protestant writers in attacking religious radicalism was not, however, as strong as it appeared. Underneath it lurked a real uneasiness that unguided access to the Bible would have dangerous consequences. The 'unlearned simple folk' were easy prey for the plausible Bible piety of the 'uncalled' preacher.[106] As Veron sadly commented, heresy was commonest 'wheresoever the truth doth spring and beginneth to come abroad'.[107] Latimer, by contrast, blamed clerical neglect: decades of 'unpreaching prelates' had driven the people, hungry for the Word, to read the Bible for themselves and come to their own conclusions.[108] Either way, this was a blow to the notion that all men could read the scriptures and necessarily remain orthodox Christians. The salvation of souls was at stake, and the only solution would be the provision of a learned ministry. William Turner, for one, lost no time in pointing up the moral:

> Wherefore, if that we will have the church of Christ delivered from the enemies wherewith it is now besieged, we must provide not only livings for young scholars, that they may continue in this godly study, but also that the ripe and perfect soldiers may have sufficient livings that they need not for lack of livings to run unto their adversaries for better wages, to commit treason against us.[109]

Religious radicals did not have to be present in great numbers to arouse a propagandist response. The threat they presented had to be exaggerated: it was a small but necessary part of the protestant case. Radicalism presented an opportunity to defend orthodoxy in doctrine and 'right order' in church and state, and its presence demanded a learned ministry to defeat its arguments and combat its appeal. If such radicals had not existed, it would have been necessary to invent them, and that, to a great extent was what protestants did.[110] Encounters with real radicals certainly lay behind anti-anabaptist propaganda, but the image of heretical and seditious sects it conjured up was far more threatening than was the contemporary English reality.

NOTES

1 *Original letters*, PS1 Letter 33, 65–6. For my preferred term 'radical' to describe those who rejected both catholicism and protestant justification by faith and predestination, see G.H. Williams, *The Radical Reformation* (1962), xxv.
2 D.M. Loades, 'Anabaptism and English sectarianism in the mid-sixteenth century', *SCH* (1979), subsidia 2: *Reform and the Reformation*: 64.
3 J.W. Martin, 'English protestant separatism at its beginnings: Henry Hart and the free-will men', *SCJ* VII (1976): 55; see also Martin, 'The first that made separation from the reformed Church of England', *Archiv* (1986): 281–312. Champlin Burrage, *The Early English Dissenters (1550–1641)* (Cambridge, 1912), 2 vols, discusses the Kent group. I.B. Horst, *The Radical Brethren: Anabaptism and the English Reformation to 1558* (Niewkoop, 1972), overestimates the significance, spread and coherence of anabaptism in England.
4 C.J. Clements, 'The English radicals and their theology, 1535–65', unpublished PhD thesis, Cambridge University (1980). Martin gives a biographical list of religious

The threat of religious radicalism

radicals belonging to the free-willer group in *Archiv* (1986): 304–12, and points out that the Bocking 'conventicle' was not a gathered church but a religious discussion group. See *APC* III (1550–52), 198–9, 206–7.

5. D. Wilkins, *Concilia* (1737), iv, 44–5.
6. C.H. Smyth, *Cranmer and the Reformation Under Edward VI* (Cambridge, 1926; reprinted Greenwood, CT 1970), 3.
7. It is difficult to gauge the numbers of real 'radicals' among the Marian martyrs: Christopher Marsh summarises the debate in *Popular Religion in Sixteenth Century England* (1998), ch. 4.
8. Smyth, *Cranmer*, 196.
9. Hooper, John, *A lesson of the incarnation of Christ* (1549) PS2 1–18.
10. Letter from Ridley to Cheke, 23 July 1551, in *Works*, PS 331. The preacher referred to is unknown: see Jasper Ridley, *Nicholas Ridley. A Biography* (1957), 255. On the effect of the fear of radicalism both on Ridley's relations with the Strangers' churches and on their own internal affairs, see A. Pettegree, *Foreign Protestant Communities in Sixteenth Century London* (Oxford, 1986), ch. 2.
11. Clements, 'English radicals', 176. Commendatory verses, in William Turner's *A preservative or treacle against the poison of Pelagius* (1551), by Nicholas Grimald (to Latimer and Turner in Latin, to the anabaptist and the reader in English), Thomas Norton (in English, French and Latin – he also wrote down Turner's Isleworth sermon), Randall Hurlestone (in English), and Thomas Some and Thomas Becon (in Latin). Roger Hutchinson's *The image of God, or layman's book* (1550) was dedicated to Cranmer.
12. Jean Veron: translations of works by Henry Bullinger dedicated to protector Somerset, Sir John Gates, Sir Thomas Fleetwood; Nicholas Lesse: translations of Francis Lambert of Avignon and of Saint Augustine on predestination, both dedicated to Anne, duchess of Somerset, and Melanchthon on justification, to protector Somerset.
13. John Strype, *Ecclesiastical Memorials* (Oxford, 1822), vol. 1, part II: 335, fits with the defiant picture given in Roger Hutchinson, *The image of God, or layman's book*, PS 145–6. Edmund Becke also described her as 'the wayward virago that would not repent', in *A brief confutation of this most detestable and anabaptistical opinion* (1550), 1. John Davis stresses Lollard rather than Dutch influences on Joan in 'Joan of Kent, Lollardy and the English reformation', *JEH* (1982) 33: 225–33.
14. Joan Bocher, George van Paris, Michael Thombe and John Assheton upheld unorthodox Christological and anti-Trinitarian beliefs, but the two latter recanted; see John Strype, *Memorials of Archbishop Cranmer* (Oxford, 1848), 94–101. John Champneys recanted before the Commission of 1549 and was bound to do penance at Paul's Cross, to desist from preaching and unlicensed publishing, and to recall and destroy as many of his books as he could (*ibid.*, 92–4). Robert Cooche was not summoned, but debated free will and ceremonies with Jewel and Parkhurst (Burrage, *Early English Dissenters*, vol. II: 7–8). The members of the Bocking 'conventicle' were finally given bail, and told to resort to their ordinary for resolution of their religious problems (*ibid.*, 1–6). Thomas Cole later preached before Cranmer, repudiating the Kentish radicals' ideas: *A godly and fruitful sermon made at Maidstone* (1553); See Martin, *Archiv* (1986): 298–301; *APC* III: 199, 206–7. The main debate between 'free-willers' and predestinarians took place in the King's Bench prison, during Mary's reign, between Henry Harte and John Careless and John Bradford. See M.T. Pearse, 'Freewill, dissent and Henry Harte', *CH* (1989).
15. Assheton, Cooche and Cole were educated men – see John Proctor, *The fall of the late Arian* (1548), sig. E2vo; Robert Cooche, in Turner, *A preservative*, sigs B7vo–D1vo; Cole, *Maidstone sermon*. However, Henry Harte was suspicious of all learning except of

A religion of the Word

scripture (see *A godly new short treatise* (1548), sig. A5), and described learned men as 'the source of great errors' in *APC* III: 198; John Champneys, in *The harvest is at hand* (1548), sigs A6, D8-D8vo, was similarly antagonistic, but was won over by discussion with leading theologians and eventually was ordained (see MacCulloch, *Cranmer*, 424).

16 Cf. Martin, *Archiv* (1986), and Davis, *JEH* (1982).

17 See above, n. 13; Marsh, *Popular Religion*, ch. 4, notes similarities of outlook between the Lollards and later doctrinal dissenters in a more subtle way than Davis, *ibid.*

18 Strype, *Ecclesiastical Memorials*, vol. 1: 335; For the hagiography of Anne Askew, see John Bale, *Examinations of Anne Askew* (Wesel, 1546 and London, 1547), PS 136-248; L. Fairfield, 'John Bale and the development of protestant hagiography in England', *JEH* (1973): 145-60.

19 Hutchinson, *Image of God*, PS 146. This is a much more sophisticated argument than that describing Mary as 'a spice bag with the spice out', current in the 1520s and 1530s; see John Davis, *Heresy and the Reformation in the South-East of England, 1520-59* (1983), 37-8, 83.

20 *Ibid.*, 105; Horst, *Radical brethren*, 110. Melchiorite Christology is described more fully in Williams, *Radical Reformation*, 328-32.

21 Proctor, *Fall of the late Arian*, dedicated to princess Mary and comparing her qualities with those of the Virgin. Unusually, it has two woodcuts, of the Annunciation and the Nativity, probably re-used from an earlier devotional work. Proctor used the opportunity given by unorthodoxy for reproaching protestant reformers in similar ways to those of Richard Smith, *A confutation of 'A defence of the true and catholic doctrine of the Sacrament'* (1550). The 'Arian' of the title was probably John Ashton: see MacCulloch, *Cranmer*, 407.

22 Proctor, *Fall of the late Arian*, sig. E2vo. Though the 'Arian' was not an atheist, extracts from his confession, taken from Proctor's confutation, were found in the possession of Thomas Kyd and formed part of the evidence for the charges of atheism laid against Christopher Marlowe; see W. Dinsmore Briggs, 'On a document concerning Christopher Marlowe', in *Studies in Philology* (1923), xx. I owe this reference to Dr Michael Hunter.

23 Proctor, *Fall of the late Arian*, sig. E7vo; 'Arian's' rationalism could usefully be compared with Menocchio's: see C. Ginzburg, *The Cheese and the worms: the Cosmos of a Sixteenth Century Miller*, tr. J. and A. Tedeschi (London and Henley, 1980).

24 Proctor, *Fall of the late Arian*, sig. I2vo.

25 *Ibid.*, sig. P2.

26 *Ibid.*, sigs R5-R5vo.

27 For fears of the misuse of the free access to scripture, see *ibid.*, sigs A7vo-B1vo; for 'strange opinions', sig. C3vo; the attraction of novelty, sigs D5vo-D6; for attacks on the use of reason where it conflicts with faith, sigs G2-G3vo.

28 See Chapter 1, 'Dichotomy', above pp. 21-8.

29 Henry Harte, *A godly new short treatise instructing every person how they should trade their lives...* (1548), *A godly new exhortation to all that profess the Gospel...* (1549), *A consultory for all Christians* (Worcester, 1549); Champneys, *The harvest is at hand*.

30 See John Bale, *Image of both churches*, PS 445-7.

31 Harte, *A consultory*, sig. D7vo.

32 *Ibid.*, denunciation of the clergy under twelve headings, sigs C5vo-D7vo. See also Chapter 3, 'The good shepherd', pp. 94-100 and Chapter 5, 'Conclusion', p. 217.

33 Champneys, *Harvest*, sigs F2-F2vo. He accused the clergy of being 'clearly destitute of all true knowledge', sig. C8vo. See Chapter 1, 'Repression', pp. 47-51 and 'Delusion', pp. 41-47.

34 *Ibid.*, sigs D8–D8vo. Horst, *Radical brethren*, 112–15, discerned the influence of Hoffman and Joris in Champneys's views. When Champneys did penance, Coverdale preached the recantation sermon, but later he ordained him deacon; see Clements, 'English radicals', 85–6. Perhaps his heresy was less significant than his evident desire to preach. Cf. Chapter 3, n. 107.
35 Harte, *Godly new short treatise*, sig. A4; see 1 Corinthians 3.
36 *Ibid.*, sig. B1.
37 *Ibid.*, sig. B5; cf. Harte, *Consultory*, sig. G3vo: the godly associate only with the godly and not with 'flatterers'; also Thomas Cole's denunciation of Christians who associate only with those they call 'Brother' and 'Sister', *Maidstone sermon*, sig. D1vo.
38 APC III: 198–9, 206–7.
39 Harte, *Godly new short treatise*, sig. B6. For 'interior religion' and the evidence of 'Ledley's prayers', see Martin, *Archiv* (1986): 296–8.
40 *Ibid.*, sig. B1vo; see also above, n. 14. Anti-predestinarian ideas were refuted in Cole, *Maidstone sermon*, sigs B4–C5.
41 Martin, *SCJ* (1976): 72.
42 *Idem.*, *Archiv* (1986): 302–4; also above, nn. 13, 15.
43 See also Chapter 1, 'Dichotomy' pp. 21–8; Chapter 5, 'Pretending the gospel', pp. 204–9.
44 Smith, *A confutation*, 11. But heresy brought out a similar response in protestants: e.g. Becke, *A brief confutation*, 1.
45 See above, n. 12, for details of translations. The Veron translations were printed in Worcester by John Oswen, who also printed Harte's *Consultory*, including in it his royal patent. See also Anon. tr. of Jean Calvin, *A short instruction*. Horst's appendix on this (see *Radical brethren*, 185–9) is a rather doubtful theory.
46 Turner, *Preservative* – apparently unfinished because of the more pressing demands of his herbal. There was to have been a further volume on predestination and free will. Cf. refutations by Proctor, Becke, Cole and Hutchinson.
47 Hutchinson, *Image of God*; John Hooper, *A lesson of the incarnation of Christ* (1549), PS2. Additional references were made by Jean Veron, *Certain little treatises for the learning of the simple* (1548) – second section refuting anthropomorphism, sigs D1voff.; Anthony Gilby, 'A digression against the adversaries', in *A commentary upon the prophet Micah* (1551) sigs H5–I4vo, refuting Christological heresies; John Hooper attacked chiliastic and anti-authoritarian radical movements in *A godly confession and protestation of the Christian faith* (1550), PS2 73–5.
48 'J.B.', *A brief and plain declaration made . . . to satisfy . . . them that have judged me to be a favourer of the anabaptists* (?1547). The author of the tract remains unidentified.
49 Melchior Hoffman repudiated believers' baptism in 1539; under the influence of Menno Simons, the 'ban' was much more important in anabaptist thought and practice; see Williams, *Radical reformation*, 309, 394.
50 'Anabaptist' was always a pejorative term when used by opponents; see C.-P. Clasen, *Anabaptism: A Social History, 1525–1618* (Ithaca, NY, 1972), 13–14.
51 E.g. Hooper, *Incarnation of Christ*, PS2 3; see Veron's translation of Bullinger, *Wholesome antidote*, sigs A3vo–A4.
52 Hooper, *Incarnation of Christ*, PS2 4; cf. Veron's translation of Bullinger, *Wholesome antidote*, sigs A2vo–A3.
53 See Chapter 5, 'Divine judgement', pp. 193–7.
54 Cf. Chapter 5, n. 21.
55 Becke, *Brief confutation*, 1.
56 Proctor, *Fall of the late Arian*, sig. I2.

A religion of the Word

57 Hutchinson, *Image of God*, PS xv.
58 Turner, *Preservative*, sig. A3vo, lists 'Anabaptists, Adamites, Loykenists, Libertines, Schwenkfeldians, Libertines and the Spoylers' – Dutch sects of the 1540s; see also below, n. 86.
59 Calvin, *Short instruction*, sig. I6; Bullinger, *Wholesome antidote*, sigs F1vo, K5vo.
60 See Veron's translation of Bullinger, *Wholesome antidote*, sig. K5vo; John Hooper, *Godly confession* (1550), PS2.
61 See Chapter 1, 'Repression', pp. 47–51.
62 See M. Aston, *Lollards and Reformers: Images and Literacy in Late Mediaeval Religion* (1984), chs 7 and 8; also Chapter 5, 'Time as revelation', pp. 180–3.
63 E.g. Richard Smith, *A brief treatise setting forth divers truths* (1547), sigs R4vo–R5 and *Confutation of a defence*, sigs B1, B6vo–B7vo, G3; Stephen Gardiner, *A detection of the devil's sophistry* (1546), sigs K5–vo.
64 E.g. Turner, *Preservative*, sigs L2vo–L3; Cole, *Maidstone sermon*, sig. B4: the temptation of those 'living well but speaking evil'; see Veron's translation of Bullinger, *Wholesome antidote*, sigs A8–A8vo.
65 Hooper, *Incarnation of Christ*, PS2 6–12; Proctor, *Fall of the late Arian*, sig. G3; Becke, *Brief confutation*, 1–6.
66 Hooper, *Incarnation of Christ*, PS2 17.
67 Proctor, *Fall of the late Arian*, sig. G3vo.
68 Turner, *Preservative*, sig. M2.
69 Cole, *Maidstone sermon*, sigs C8vo–D1; cf. Calvin, *Short instruction*, sig. C8vo.
70 E.g. Cole above, n. 69; Joye claimed that perfectionist radicals thought that 'they need neither book written, nor external word, preachers, nor magistrates secular': *A contrary to (a certain man's) consultation* (?1549), sig. F5; cf. Hutchinson, *Image*, PS 113–14. See also n. 34.
71 See Turner, *Preservative*; also Veron's translation of Bullinger, *A most sure and strong defence*, and the anonymous translation of Calvin, *Short instruction*, sigs A8vo–B5.
72 For sedition and 'communism', see 'Piers Plowman', *Exhortation* (1550), sigs A2vo–A3vo; Robert Crowley, *The way to wealth* (1550), sigs A3–A3vo. For separation, see Cole, *Maidstone sermon*, sigs C5–C8; cf. above, n. 37.
73 Veron's translation of Bullinger, *Fruitful dialogue*; Anon. translation of Calvin, *A short instruction*.
74 See e.g. R.I. Moore, *The Origins of European Dissent* (1977), ch. 10, especially 281–2.
75 Hooper, *Godly confession*, PS2 76.
76 Hutchinson, *Image of God*, PS 44.
77 Ibid., 97; see also Chapter 3, n. 103.
78 E.g. Hutchinson, *Image of God*, PS 134. Cf. Chapter 1, 'Delusion', pp. 41–7.
79 Veron's translation of Bullinger, *Wholesome antidote*, sigs A2vo–A3.
80 See Horst, *Radical brethren*, 170–6. It could be claimed that as many as twelve articles were made against radical ideas.
81 See also Chapter 4, 'Obedience and its limitations', pp. 158–62.
82 See above, n. 14.
83 Hugh Latimer, *Fourth lenten Court sermon* (1549), PS1 151.
84 Veron's translation of Bullinger, *Fruitful dialogue*: dedication to Sir John Gates, sig. B4.
85 Ibid., sigs A2vo–B1vo.
86 Turner, *Preservative*, sigs F1vo–F2. For details of Turner's exile, see Hildebrandt, 'English protestant exiles', ch. 2. For the events at Münster, see Norman Cohn, *The Pursuit of the Millenium* (1978), ch. 13. English protestants did not make much use of this terrifying example, perhaps because it had ceased to be topical, since anabaptism

in the Low Countries had become much more introspective under the influence of Menno Simons and David Joris. See C. Krahn, *Dutch Anabaptism: Origin, Spread, Life and Thought, 1450–1600* (The Hague, 1968), ch. 6.
87 'J.B.', *A brief and plain declaration*, sig. B3.
88 Hooper, *Godly confession*, PS2 82–6; see also Chapter 4, 'Godly judgement: the role of the magistrate, pp. 146–58.
89 See Chapter 4, 'Obedience and its limitations', pp. 158–62.
90 *Ibid.*, Lesse thought it this aspect of anabaptism that made it more of a threat than popery. See Lesse's translation of Augustine, *A work of predestination*, sig. A4vo.
91 'J.B.', *A brief declaration*, sigs A1vo–A2; cf. sigs B7vo–B8vo. See also above, p. 77, Chapter 3, 'Preaching and the preacher', especially p. 92.
92 Veron's translation of Bullinger, *A wholesome antidote*, sigs A8–A8vo. Veron described heresy as poison 'overlaid with sugar and honey', *A sure and strong defence*, sig. A3; Turner described it as a 'venomous seed' in *A preservative*, sig. A3.
93 Becke, *Brief confutation*, 1. Cf. Nicholas Grimald 'To the reader' in Turner, *Preservative*: 'Now fostered is a madding malady/ In heads newfangled and bewitched thoughts,/ Refusing all good leeches remedy,/ ... sore disease of mind and brain fantastical ...' (sig. A6vo). see also Chapter 1, 'Delusion', pp. 41–7.
94 Lesse was vicious, describing free-willers as 'having in their heads the eyes of cockatrices, in their tongues the stings of adders, and in their stomachs the poison of toads', *Predestination*, sigs A2–A2vo. Proctor, *Fall of the late Arian*, sig. K6, called heresy a 'foul and prodigious monster'; Turner compared anabaptism to the Hydra, whose seven heads corresponded to seven sects: *A preservative*, sig. A3.
95 Cf. Veron's translation of Bullinger, *A sure and strong defence*, sig. A5, refers to 'fantastical and mad brains'.
96 Thomas Some described the radical reference to 'the Spirit' as 'a fanatic spirit, a brain-sick spirit, a seditious and malignant spirit': *Preface to second and subsequent court sermons of Hugh Latimer* (1549), PS1 106. Joye described them as possessed by the 'spirit of frenzy and hypocrisy' in *A contrary*, sigs F8vo–G. On mental and physical illness as emanations of the power of Satan, see Michael Macdonald, *Mystical Bedlam: Madness, Anxiety and Healing in Seventeenth Century England* (Cambridge, 1981), 173–217.
97 Turner, *A preservative*, sig. A3vo. Probably a pun on 'wood' meaning mad, or raging, and the 'natural' source of Cooche's thought; cf. sigs K1vo and K5.
98 Grimald, 'stout pelagians blows forth the last of antichristians ...', from 'To the reader', in Turner, *Preservative*, sig. A6vo. The linkage between popish and anabaptist 'Pelagianism' emerges also in Calvin, *A short instruction*, sig. A6; see also Chapter 1, 'Inversion', pp. 28–34.
99 See Chapter 1, 'Disorder', pp. 37–41.
100 Turner, *A preservative*, sig. E2, also sig. D7vo; he also referred to Cooche 'idolatrously' kneeling to receive communion (sigs D6vo–D7).
101 Turner, *Ibid.*, sig. I4vo, accused him of being 'a justiciary with the pope', sig. M5vo, and answering him 'very friarly', sig. E3.
102 See above, n. 51.
103 Hugh Latimer, *Sermon preached on the 5th Sunday after Epiphany* (Lincolnshire sermons) (1552), PS2 197.
104 There are six specifically anti-anabaptist tracts for this period and six relevant translations; compare with the more than forty antipapist tracts – see Chapter 1, n. 2.
105 Both Hooper and Ridley were concerned about the activities of anabaptists – Hooper shared Bullinger's concern (see above, n. 1); N. Ridley, *Works*, PS 331 (Letter to Cheke).

A religion of the Word

106 On simple folk as prey, see Turner, *A preservative*, sigs L2vo–L3; also Lesse's translation of Augustine, *Predestination*, sigs A2–A2vo.
107 Veron's translation of Bullinger, *Wholesome antidote*, sigs. A8–A8vo; Proctor, *Fall of the late Arian*, agreed with him for conservative reasons (sigs. A8–B1).
108 Latimer, *Fourth lenten Court sermon*, PS1 151–2.
109 Turner, *A preservative*, sig A4; Becke, *Brief confutation*, 6: 'And to 'stablish true doctrine, God send us good preachers.' See also Chapter 3, 'Preaching and the preacher', pp. 88–93.
110 Cf. the 'invention' of the 'Ranters' in the seventeenth century, as proposed by J.C. Davis, *Fear, Myth and History: The Ranters and the Historians* (Cambridge, 1986).

Chapter 3

The reform of the church

INTRODUCTION: REFORMATION BY THE WORD

CENTRAL to the protestant case for reform of the church was the supreme authority of the Bible. However much opinions varied in practice as to the nature and extent of that authority,[1] there was a propagandist consensus that scripture was the touchstone of reform. In this sense, Henry VIII's provision of the Bible in English was seen as almost a more important achievement than the break with Rome.[2] Edwardian protestants emphasised the biblical foundation for the Henrician attack on traditional piety.[3] Scripture, as the sole objective source of truth, had to be fundamental to reform.[4] As Cranmer wrote about the Sacrament, 'all doctrine concerning this matter . . . which is not grounded on God's Word, is of no necessity . . .'.[5] Faith could be founded only on scripture.[6] The life-giving nature of this truth was revealed in the identification of Christ the Word of God with the Bible.[7]

So salvation depended on access to the Bible – Bale described this as heaven being 'open'.[8] Thus the reformation was both the sum of a host of individual conversions and the means by which they could happen. Bible study was intended to increase the number of the godly rather than of theologians – 'the science of Scripture is practive, not speculative'.[9] It was not just an inward but a visible change of behaviour, bringing with it the desire to bear witness and change others.[10] In this sense an Erasmian theme of true virtue emerging from the Gospels, as comfort and discipline were brought to naturally wayward humans, was a strong strand in Edwardian reform.[11] The message was within everyone's grasp, so knowledge of the Bible was the key to Christian 'enfranchisement'.[12] The Bible was to become incarnate in its readers: 'And in reading of God's Word he most profiteth not always that is most ready in turning of the book, or in saying it without the book, but he that is most turned into it; that is most inspired with the Holy Ghost most

A religion of the Word

in his heart and life, altered and transformed into that thing which he readeth ...'.[13]

Such individual and personal transformations required the affirmative context of a church reformed on spiritual lines. In the Sacrament, for instance, Christ's words at the Last Supper were be taken 'for the steadfast groundwork of your building, for the direct line, the just square, the undeceivable compass ...'.[14] All things had to edify the church – 'the everlasting builder measureth all things concerning his church according to his undefiled scriptures, which are the right rule of faith and the rod of right order in his kingdom'.[15] Both doctrine and its defenders would be judged on the basis of their adherence to scripture.[16]

What, then, were the main areas to be changed if the church was to be aligned with biblical dictates? The fundamental priority was to transform the priesthood into a ministry of the Word: emphasis on preaching and the nature of its effects shaped protestant attitudes to the duties of the minister. The role of the preacher was the foundation of protestant clericalism, which will be seen at work both in criticism of inadequate clergy and in limiting lay activism. Though the minister could be a 'good shepherd' only if he was a conscientious preacher, wider pastoral relations, whether in the context of discussion about confession, excommunication or episcopacy, were also matters of concern. Traditional and humanist preoccupations with ignorance and corruption within the church, and a new concern about the economic power of the laity were all reflected in proposals for financial and economic reforms. The laity were, however, important not only as passive recipients of preaching and as sources of money and patronage: they constituted the *body* of the church, and with the end of a traditional ecclesiology centring on the progress of the church through purgatory to heaven, the visible church on earth became the focus of attention. The transformation of public worship focused on the Sacrament of Holy Communion. The Mass may have been buried, but the Lord's Supper required more than a rearrangement of the furniture to become part of the culture of the faithful.

THE MINISTRY OF THE WORD

Preaching and the preacher

The author of *The upcheering of the Mass* ironically made his conservative character declare: 'The Scripture hath nothing/ Whereby profit to bring/ But a little preaching/ With tattling and teaching.'[17] This was exactly what protestants intended: the Word had to be preached as well as read, for ideological as well as practical reasons. The collective act of listening to the Word being preached had important dramatic and transformative effects. The evangelical nature of the reform made it imperative to 'go into all the world and preach...'.[18] So as a consequence of God's will, preaching was still the prime means of achieving conversions. Latimer converted the idea of the catholic *scala coeli* by fitting it to the stages of salvation described in Romans 10:14.[19] Despite the impact both of printing itself and of official policy[20] in increasing the availability of the Bible, illiteracy still shut out vast numbers of potential converts;[21] preaching was still the best and safest way of reaching them. In the unguided discussion of such explosive doctrines as justification by faith alone or predestination, protestants feared the wider development of misunderstanding, which could lead to antinomianism, sectarianism or, at the very least, contention.[22]

Nevertheless, so anxious were protestants to avoid the charge that they idolised preaching, that some even denied that it had any inherent power to change people. Thus Hooper was able to state that 'the preaching of God's Word is of all things in this world the most necessary for the people', being the precondition for conversion, while paradoxically claiming 'Yet is the Word of God of no such efficacy. For the words can do nothing but signify the conscience of him that believed.'[23] Crowley agreed that preaching was necessary 'for the guidance of the elect'.[24] Since no one could tell who the elect were, it was imperative to preach to everyone in order to reach them. Latimer summed up the argument:

> But some will say now, 'What need we preachers then? God can save his elect without preachers.' A goodly reason! God can save my life without meat and drink; need I none therefore? God can save me from burning, if I were in the fire; shall I run into it therefore? No, no; I must keep the way that God hath ordained, and use the ordinary means that God hath assigned, and not seek new ways.[25]

The Word should be preached in season and out to all comers. Latimer even questioned the restriction of preaching to the pulpit – had not Christ preached to the crowds from a boat? It was, of course, worse to have ministers who could or would not preach at all, leaving even the pulpits empty and as useless 'as bells without clappers'.[26] Even *The Homilies* needed the support of frequent visitations to ensure that they were properly read, not 'hacked and chopped'. He emphasised that motivation for attendance at sermons did not matter: once listeners were present 'the preacher may chance to catch you on his hook'.[27]

The power of preaching could not only radically alter individual behaviour: it could transform the entire social order. Hooper's sermons on the book of Jonah during Lent 1550 went straight to the heart of the case for reform by evangelism.[28] Latimer agreed that the example of Nineveh showed that preaching was a potent force for change:

> They believed God's preacher, God's officer, God's minister, Jonah; and were converted from their sin. They believed that, as the preacher said, if they did not repent and amend their life, the city should be destroyed within forty days. This was a great fruit, for Jonah was but one man and he preached but one sermon, and it was but a short sermon neither, touching the number of words; and yet he turned all the whole city, great and small, rich and poor, king and all.[29]

Such 'great fruit' gave a challenge to England, as Hooper warned:

> But I rede both the king and the council to be admonished and to amend things amiss: if not the king of Nineveh with his people shall rise at the latter day and condemn both king and council to death, for they converted at the preaching of one man, yea at the preaching of a stranger; we have not only heard the same by the mouth of strangers but also by the mouth of our own countrymen, and that many times.[30]

The effectiveness of preaching could only be measured after the event, in the visible repentance of the listeners. As much depended on the quality of *their* response as on the preacher's skill.[31]

If protestants believed in the efficacy of preaching, they were also aware of the difficulties. Latimer compared the hostility met by preachers with the disbelief with which the people of Bethlehem responded to the news of the birth of Christ brought by the shepherds – clear evidence of ingratitude to God.[32] Hooper likened such people to Judas: 'Men associate themselves into the company of such as fear God, come unto the sermons to hear God's words and be nothing the better; they amend their life nothing at all. They say "It was a good sermon, the man spake well," but what availeth it that he spake well and the hearer to live ill?'[33] Latimer was outspoken about the lack of attention paid to both his own sermons and *The Homilies*; he was particularly irritated by 'talking and babbling' among his congregation.[34] Such hostility or indifference was compounded by the success of false preachers who appealed to corrupt human nature. As Hooper pointed out, God did not stop the false preachers or make their congregations deaf, but gave grace for them to hear the good, if they chose to do so. In this respect, the 'falsehoods' of Gardiner, which were felt to have achieved widespread acceptance, were comparable to those of the ten spies who threw the Israelites into desperation.[35]

And yet hostility to the truth was a necessary response. It is tempting to interpret this as justification for the failure both of preaching as a vehicle for reform and of the impracticability of the protestants' message. However, though a sense of frustration does emerge, its ideological message should also be borne in mind: that is, that the true church was validated by persecution. Hooper noted the preacher's dilemma in the example of Jonah:

The reform of the church

> Continually, whether it happen and come to pass that he speaketh, or come it not to pass, the preacher standeth in danger of obloquy and contempt. We may see an example hereof in Jonah, that preached by the Word of God the destruction of Nineveh, which if it had so come to pass they would have called Jonah a cruel tyrant and seeker of blood; and now that he seeth the city spared, he feareth lest he should be accounted a false prophet, not only among his own countrymen the Israelites, but also among the Gentiles, and then all his preaching should be taken for a mockery. This contempt sore feareth Jonah, and he is therewithal so troubled that he offendeth God grievously. I might accommodate the same fortune unto myself and others right well when we speak for a reformation of the Church, schools and policies. . . .[36]

More expansively, Gilby compared Latimer, Lever, Hooper, Becon and Horne to Jeremiah, whom Phassur tried to silence. Such persecution was doomed to failure, for 'when these are gone, other cometh of their ashes'.[37] Latimer likewise rejoiced that Isaiah, Elijah and even Christ himself were all 'called seditious' in their day.[38]

Saving souls was no easy task. The parable of the sower showed that even Christ himself converted only about a quarter of his hearers – 'And if he had no better luck that was preacher of all preachers, what shall we look for? Yet there was no lack in him, but in the ground; and so now there is no fault in preaching, the lack is in the people, that have stony hearts and thorny hearts.'[39] Many were called but few were chosen, and this should not dispirit the preacher. The remedy for ungodliness was the provision of more and better preaching. This claim reflected not a lack of imagination, but was consistent both with faith in the transforming power of the Gospel, and with the belief that the Word would always be resisted. It was significant that, in the context of his own difficulties in 1550, Hooper increased his demand for the government to listen to sermons from one a week[40] to one a day.[41] His demands – and indeed his own hyperactivity in this field – may have been exceptional,[42] but the point remained a sound one. However arduous the task was, it was only by means of a committed and forceful evangelism that England could be made into a godly commonwealth.

The evangelical imperative was amplified in Paul's letter to Titus, as Latimer pointed out.[43] Teaching the truth meant that he had to confute opposition, ensure that his flock understood their calling and duties, and wage war on sin. While the first two requirements demanded his verbal and rhetorical skills, the last raised the question of his authority.[44] First, however, he had to teach true doctrine.[45] Bale contrasted Moses's straightforward teaching with the 'fables and enchantments' of pharaoh's sorcerers and the 'witty speculations' of the Egyptians.[46] The 'Christian orator' not only preached the truth but convinced his flock.[47]

A religion of the Word

Since true doctrine was validated in struggle, the true preacher must 'confute the gainsayers'.[48] Cranmer saw this task as his priority:

> I know what account I shall make to him hereof at the last day, when every man shall answer for his vocation and receive for the same good or ill, according as he hath done. I know how Antichrist hath obscured the glory of God, and the true knowledge of his word overcasting the same with mists and clouds of error and ignorance through false glosses and interpretations. It pitieth me to see the simple and hungry folk of Christ led into corrupt pastures, to be carried blindfold they know not whither, and to be fed with poison instead of wholesome meats. And moved by duty, office and place, whereunto it has pleased God to call me, I give warning in his name unto all that profess Christ that they flee far from Babylon . . .[49]

Preaching and writing were the main methods of dealing with opposition,[50] though Roger Hutchinson advocated the use of a peripatetic ministry, apparently combining the episcopal visitation and the academic disputation, in which papists and anabaptists were to be examined in doctrine and forced to defend their views in open debate in front of the whole parish. 'By this means papists and others should best be overcome, and the people should learn more of one disputation than in ten sermons.'[51] Hutchinson was confident that the protestant preacher would convince his opponent of the truth by sheer force, though his academic approach would have had limited appeal.

Antichrist's wolves had scattered the Christian flock, and the preacher had to fight to deliver it. It was his duty to gather the flock that had been so 'miserably dissipated and separated' and ensure its health.[52] This meant more than merely teaching right doctrine. The minister had to lead his flock into an active godliness and a proper obedience to God.[53] He must make his flock awake from the 'sleep of sin' to a new life of obedience to God's will.[54] However keen he was to repudiate the 'Aaronic' ceremonial still required of the English priesthood, Hooper still valued the Levitical model, since Moses commended the law to them, 'to show it unto the whole multitude of the people, men, women, children and strangers, that they might hear it, learn it, fear the Lord God and observe his commandments'.[55]

He could only achieve this by ensuring that his message was applicable and accessible to everyone, in their various callings, with their varying needs, temptations and levels of understanding. Hutchinson's idea of the quasi-academic disputation would not have appealed to Latimer, who insisted that he sought 'more the profit of those which be ignorant than to please learned men'.[56] Since 'true doctrine' contained lessons for all men, the preacher would achieve more by tailoring his subject to fit the needs of his congregation – 'If he preach before a king, let his matter be concerning the office of a king; if before a bishop, then let him treat of bishoply duties and orders, and so forth in other matters, as time and audience shall require.'[57] These imperatives were echoed by Bale – 'tell every man his right office'[58] – and Hooper, who intended to use his Court sermons on Jonah to discourse 'on the duties of individuals'.[59]

Fitting subject matter to audience necessitated outspoken and hard-hitting criticism where appropriate, and indeed, Latimer noted gleefully that those who attacked him for being 'indiscreet' could not find fault with his doctrine. He could not apologise, for sin 'must be rebuked, sin must be plainly spoken against'.[60] The preacher was not to be a 'respecter of persons': 'Therefore you preachers, out with your swords and strike at the root. Speak out against covetousness and cry out upon it. Stand not ticking and toying at the branches nor at the boughs, for then there will new boughs and branches spring again of them; but strike at the root and fear not these giants of England...'.[61] His own reputation for plain speaking was eulogised in the Dedication to the 1549 edition of his sermons, in which Thomas Some declared that 'God... hath stirred up in him the bold spirit of Elijah...'.[62] So long as he preached the Gospel, the preacher had authority to criticise all levels of society. The fight of Christ with Satan was re-enacted in the faithful declaration of the Word by preachers. The Word 'valiantly battled' to save the elect.[63]

The message remained the same, though approaches varied, since '[u]nto each of them is given a diverse utterance of the Spirit to edify'.[64] Latimer likened the activity of preaching to that of the ploughman, on account both of their 'diversity of works' and of their 'labour' through all the seasons of the year:

> ... now casting them down with the law and with the threatenings of God for sin, now ridging them up again with the Gospel, and with the promises of God's favour: now weeding them by telling them their faults and making them forsake sin, now clotting them by breaking their stony hearts and by making them supplehearted, and by making them to have hearts of flesh, that is soft hearts and apt for doctrine to enter in...[65]

Faithfulness, diligence and persistence were required of the preacher, deriving from the love he should bear both to Christ and to his flock.[66] Indeed, according to Latimer, the clergy could well follow the example of the Devil in diligence – 'which every day and every hour, laboureth to sow cockle and darnel, that he may bring out of form and out of estimation and room, the institution of the Lord's Supper and Christ's cross...'[67] While good doctrine had to be backed up by the visitations of bishops,[68] and the influential position of noble chaplains,[69] there was no substitute for the preaching ministry in this fundamental work of reformation.

The good shepherd

Protestant clericalism?

Protestants invested a great deal of time and energy in explaining the need for preaching because preaching offered a solution to two key problems. The first, as we have seen, concerned the means by which the transformation of society could be achieved. The second was what was the positive role of the clergy, in the context of an anticlerical and antisacerdotal ideology? In answering the second question, protestants found themselves in difficulties. On the one hand, their polemic's background combined the destructive demystifying effect of the campaign against popery, and the spectre of radical sectarianism raised by an untutored, Bible-reading, lay piety.[70] On the other hand, they were faced by the practical problem of an inadequate ministry; here perennial clerical vices were combined with new problems brought about by protestant reforms.[71] However, the radical option of completely sweeping away the clergy was unthinkable.[72] It is also important to remember that most of the writers and preachers under consideration here were clerics of some kind: from bishops and the ex-religious to those newly ordained under protestant rites.[73]

So the problem of changing the clergyman from priest into minister, of building a new protestant clericalism out of the ashes of the old catholic priesthood, was as much a social and personal issue as an ideological one. It was solved by insisting that preaching was one of the highest of callings, since the preacher was responsible, both by preaching and by setting a prominent example of godliness in his own behaviour, for saving the nation's souls. The status of the minister depended on the diligence and zeal with which he carried out these tasks. But when facing the practical result of their demands they were less confident: they could neither approve the laity's taking matters into their own hands nor satisfactorily reconcile the directness of God's command to preach with the need for official sanction.

Reformers used exalted language in describing the office of the preacher. Bale, in the *Image of both churches*, interpreted the imagery of angels, stars and candlesticks in Revelation as describing the ministry as the bringer of light into the world.[74] Ministers were 'not the light itself but only instruments ordained to bear that light, for there is one light (i.e. Christ) for all'.[75] The official Catechism declared that the congregation should listen to the preacher as if listening to God himself.[76] Latimer described the preachers as 'treasurers' of God's Word or his 'ambassador[s]', explicitly making the comparison with high officers of state, and requiring similar respect and credit.[77] According to Philip Gerrard, 'the most glorious life that can be for a minister is to preach, and the shamefulest again is to be daintily nourished and live in idleness, for of this (witness all ancient writers) arise all other mischiefs'.[78]

As the model of Ezekiel's watchman showed, high authority carried high responsibility.[79] 'Our office therefore is to be diligent and circumspect for the people of God...', declared Hooper, 'lest they die, and their blood is required at our hands'.[80]

The preacher's task of leading his flock in obedience to God's commands required him to set an example of godly behaviour: he had to be a pattern as well as a director.[81] This was not so much a specifically protestant notion as a perennial motif in church reform. The royal *Injunctions* of 1547 specified that the clergy should not frequent alehouses, and should spend their time in studying scripture and in other 'honest occupations', setting an example to the community in the purity of their lives.[82] Foxe's contempt for those ministers who were 'asleep to sin', indulging themselves in drinking, dicing, whoring and brawling, contrasted vividly with his idealistic vision of a clergy whose personal godliness gave weight and authority to its censures.[83]

Foxe was describing a clergy that was nominally protestant, but clearly fell far short of reformist demands. It was assumed that 'true' ministers should have none of the vices of their predecessors. Crowley repudiated the 'consecrated priesthood' partly on account of the notoriety of their sins:

> Paul sayeth, that whoso coupleth himself with an harlot is the member of an harlot, and he that worketh vice is the servant of sin – then tell me, I pray you, whose minister he is, the member of an whore, the servant of sin and the minister of Christ? *Non coherent*... It is necessary they first be the members of Christ, then ministers... But your sacrificing priests are so far gone that their conversation declareth them to be the members of the devil and the ministers of Baal.[84]

Elsewhere Crowley, like Bale, described the ministry in terms of the star and candle imagery of Revelation; in the darkness of error they shed the light of true doctrine and the 'godly conversation of living'.[85]

The evangelical minister should live by a standard of biblical simplicity, rather than in 'popish' asceticism – Gilby was not alone in his suspicions that undue emphasis on the godliness of the clergy had led some of them to develop a 'feigned holiness' at the expense of preaching.[86] Hooper saw Jonah in his shack outside the walls of Nineveh as a pattern for the clergy: 'we see with what simplicity the good man was contented withal, and likewise how he himself was contented to labour to make his own couch. Our bishops and priests have all things prepared to their hands; God give them grace better to deserve it!'[87] Even Foxe, who wrote the most sustained attack on the depravity of the contemporary clergy, couched it in the language of classical Stoic virtue rather than 'holiness'.[88] Bale, acutely aware of the popular appeal of the austerities of the religious orders, pleaded for 'sobriety and temperance' – 'His ministration is great labour and no dignity; pain and not pride or arrogance; and having his food and raiment he ought to require no more.'[89]

A religion of the Word

Crowley saw the problem as one of recruitment, and exhorted the bishops to take responsibility:

> Let none have cure within thy see
> In whom any great vice doth reign
> For where misliving curates be
> The people are not good certain.[90]

Examples of the kind of behaviour that was seen as damaging were unsurprising. Latimer inveighed against extravagance in dress not only in females but in the clergy themselves:

> Here were a good place to speak against our clergymen which go so gallantly nowadays. I hear say that some of them wear velvet shoes and velvet slippers. Such fellows are more meet to dance the Morris-dance than to be admitted to preach. I pray God amend such worldly fellows; for else they be not meet to be preachers![91]

Gilby thought that their bad example was followed:

> It is your ambition and covetousness that maketh our lords, heads and governors to do so evil; you cannot worthily rebuke them being evil yourselves. Therefore our older master Christ, coming to reform the world, beginneth with the scribes and pharisees, the bishops and the priests and thundereth woe against them.[92]

Lever described these covetous clerics both as hirelings who neglected their flocks and as wolves who preyed on them – 'which by their evil example of living and worse doctrine do far more harm than they do good by their fair reading and saying of service'.[93]

Gilby went on to criticise a newly emergent form of clerical greed – the kind of dynasticism which was attendant on clerical marriage. It was this that made them the worst sort of 'covetous oppressor', as Micah had prophesied:[94]

> The bishops and priests do look over [England] as the devil doth look over Lincoln (as is the common proverb of that country), or else dare they never practise for purchasing other men's lands and houses to make their wives ladies and their sons lords. Yet can I praise the bishops of the popish Church for their cleanly conveyance of their matters, in regard of our protestants, which thus openly shame their profession.[95]

Crowley was more critical even than Gilby of the social pretensions of clergy wives, whose

> womanlike behaviour and motherlike housewifery ought to be a light to all women that dwell about you, but is so far otherwise that unless ye leave them lands to marry them withal, no man will set a pin by them when you be gone... I would not your wives be taken from you, but I would you should

The reform of the church

keep them to the furtherance of God's truth whereof ye profess to be teachers. Let your wives therefore put off their fine frocks and French hoods, and furnish themselves with all points of honest housewifery, and so let them be a help to your study and not a let.[96]

Another topical complaint was that of the clergy's desertion of the flock in time of pestilence. Latimer recalled it as a perennial problem, and reminded his audience how, in times past, the abandoning of plague-stricken towns by the secular clergy had allowed the friars access to plunder the flock.[97] Hooper wrote a homily on the great sweat of 1551–52, warning against desertion – 'and if they forsake their people in this plague time they be hirelings and no pastors and they flee from God's people into God's high indignation'.[98] The minister might no longer have to give the Last Rites, but he was responsible for trying to save souls until the last minute of life.

While protestants were passionately certain of the qualities which went to make the good shepherd, they were less convincing in facing the problem of what to do about the hireling. Here the metaphor of shepherd and flock showed its limitations: the safety of the flock depended wholly on the quality of its shepherd, but it was unthinkable that the laity should be able to discard an inadequate minister. Fear of anabaptism on the one hand and on the other an unwillingness to trust a conservative population, especially in the wake of the 1549 'stirs', prevented protestant divines from advocating the introduction of adequate institutional means whereby the laity could effectively assess or police their pastors.[99]

Instead, they fell back on what was an essentially traditional position. In canon law, the sacraments were not invalidated by the ministrations of a notoriously sinful priest, though the church authorities should discipline or remove him. The Forty-Two Articles similarly stressed the importance of maintaining order, stating that a minister's wickedness did not prevent the effectual operation of God's ordinances and that it was up to the church to discipline him.[100] The catholic emphasis on the sacraments had given way to a more general statement that (by implication) included preaching. So long as the minister 'sat in Moses' seat',[101] he must be listened to – 'Be he good or bad, God performeth the words spoken of him, not presuming beyond his commission. Does God's mercy depend on the goodness of the minister? Then our faith cannot be steadfast and sure, forasmuch as no man can discern who is a good minister, for he that seemeth good may be an hypocrite.'[102]

The limitations of this theory were revealed in practice. Latimer counselled a congregation troubled with an ungodly pastor not to vote with their feet, but to continue to attend church, to appeal to the authorities to replace him, and failing that to pray that God would either convert him or remove him. Clearly, even if the congregation could judge the worth of its pastor, it was not free to act on that judgement – to do so would have smacked of anabaptist insubordination.[103] On another occasion, however, despite insisting on the need for regular church attendance, he remained silent when confronted by the argument that the godly layman would be better to teach his family at home than endure the ministrations of an ignorant or ungodly pastor.[104] Crowley, too, advised reliance on the grace of God rather than lay activism:

> Do not as thou seest him do, but at thy first entrance into the church, lift up thine heart unto God, and desire of him that he will give thee his holy spirit to illumine and lighten the eyes of thine heart that thou mayest see and perceive the true meaning of all the Scriptures that thou shall hear read unto thee that day. And so shalt thou be sure that though thy curate be a devil and would not that any man should be the better for that which he readeth, yet thou shalt be edified and learn as much as shall be necessary for thy salvation.[105]

Given these restrictions, it was not surprising that, in view of the acute shortage of qualified preachers, godly laymen should want to be able to instruct their brethren. Philip Nichols clearly resented the fact that mere ordination rather than doctrinal soundness allowed priests to preach.[106] He apparently considered the ministry as the declaration of the Gospel by the godly:

> I do exhort you brethren beloved in the Lord Jesus Christ again and again, you chiefly that are sent by the spirit in your conscience to spy out the land of Canaan for your brethren: whether it be by preaching, reading, writing, exhorting or otherwise declaring unto the people the heavenly kingdom through the gospel of the Lord Jesus.[107]

Nichols described a highly informal ministry, but others expressed similar frustrations. Crowley threatened that Londoners would provide their own ministry if the present one continued to exact what he considered to be crypto-papist fees,[108] and in his confutation of Hoggard, he emphasised the potential of the diverse spiritual gifts with which God invested individual Christians.[109] Thomas Lancaster denounced the sects, but declared that the Lord's Supper should be ministered by 'him that is called of a Christian congregation, compelled through the Holy Ghost to come unto the Lord's vineyard or heavenly harvest, which is found without fault, according to the declaration of God's Word, both in his life and learning'.[110]

Such demands for an ideologically pure ministry, called directly from the people and untainted by association with a corrupt establishment, received strong support in the biblical accounts of the direct calling of the prophets and apostles. The prophetic impulse needed no official sanction. Thus Thomas Lever declared himself to be in the same relation to England as Christ was to Jerusalem, when he lamented that he wished to shelter her, as a hen gathers her chicks, 'with the same affection it behoveth the minister and preacher of

God, seeing intolerable vengeance hanging over England, to cry, to call and to give warning to the people ...'.[111]

The danger that these examples would be used to support the case for unlicensed preachers was appreciated by many divines, who felt caught between their duty to admonish the authorities and their position as officially sanctioned preachers. Latimer discussed the problem at length, in a sermon for (suitably enough) Saint Andrew's Day. The humble occupations in which the prophets and apostles laboured until God called them showed that God transcended social convention. The moral Latimer drew, however, was that none should seek spiritual office or promotion, but abide in his lawful occupation till the call came – presumably from the earthly powers, though he did not specify the means. He even cited the case of Uzzah, who was stricken by God for preventing the ark from stumbling, to show the punishment that awaited those who acted out of turn, from even the best of motives. Against this there were 'special vocations', such as Abraham's readiness to sacrifice Isaac, or the even more subversive and problematic case of Phineas, who slew the adulterers on the direct command of God, bypassing the judgement of the earthly powers.[112] Latimer constantly drew back from the anarchic potential of his examples, as the conclusion of his sermon showed: 'but for all that a man may not take upon him to preach God's Word except he be called unto it. When he doth it, he doth not well, although he have learning and wisdom to be a preacher; yet for all that he ought not to come himself without any lawful calling ...'.[113]

Latimer's conclusion attempted to reconcile the pressure from those who wanted to preach with the legal requirements that restricted entry into the preaching ministry. The 1547 royal *Injunctions* demanded that parish clergy preached sermons at least quarterly, and that they should not resist preachers with royal or episcopal licences, but that they should allow no-one else to preach.[114] This principle was confirmed in the 1553 *Articles*.[115] But some divines were more anxious to show that though they were licensed and indeed encouraged by the government, they retained their purity of motivation and message – Hooper made particular play of this.[116]

However, it was possible to tone down the anarchic potential of the direct calling, while retaining an ideal of purity, by insisting on the Pauline model of the pastor, whose abilities both in preaching and in godly living and learning were proven. Lancaster's charismatic minister was no exception to this rule,[117] and Peter Moone, Crowley and Peter Pickering all demanded like standards.[118] The fundamental point was that none of these writers or anyone else was prepared to take the bull by the horns and suggest a radical reorganisation of the church. Thus the problem of redefining the role of the clergy took place within an unquestioned structure. The constraints this structure imposed on reform were clear enough with regard to preaching; the

Pastoral problems and clerical powers

Despite the overwhelming importance of preaching in their vision of the godly minister's task, protestants retained a strong sense of the importance of his pastoral role. This has been noted in part in examining the insistence on the personal godliness of the minister, but it was in the workings of his relations with his congregation that the full implications of the protestant emphasis on preaching were felt. If preaching alienated his parishioners, how could the minister impose godly standards of behaviour on them? And how did the bishop's authority differ from the preacher's? Pastoral difficulties were clearly beginning to raise the thorny question of clerical powers, as an examination of the issues of confession, excommunication and episcopacy will show.

Although confession was still sanctioned by the first Edwardian *Prayer Book*, as a matter of individual conscience,[119] it was axiomatic to protestants that auricular confession was a burden to the conscience, an unnecessary barrier between the individual and God, which afforded opportunities for clerical malpractice.[120] However, there was also an awareness that it had provided a degree of personal contact between people and minister that was lost when the pulpit became the main source of communication between them. Different reformers approached this problem with varied solutions. Hooper, whose view of the sacraments as seals of faith necessitated evidence of their nature, thought that it was the duty of the minister to examine his parishioners individually before they took Communion, in order to 'ascertain the church that he is God's friend and reconciled in Christ'.[121] Other protestants were more circumspect: Crowley hoped that spiritual exhortation on an individual basis would replace formal compulsory auricular confession,[122] as did the author of *The recantation of Jack Lent* – 'I will that all troubled consciences resort unto a discreet and learned counsellor, to have and receive at his hand as by an instrument to comfortable absolution of the spirit, by hearing of the great and ready mercies of God towards repentant hearts rehearsed unto them.'[123]

Perhaps unsurprisingly, since he was of the older generation of protestants, it was Latimer who betrayed the greatest anxiety about the alienation created by the protestant hostility to confession. Though he stressed that absolution could be given collectively only from 'the open pulpit', he pointed out that godly ministers could also give private and personal comfort. The problem was to find ministers who understood this modification of their traditional role. He was well aware that auricular confession had been open to abuse,

The reform of the church

but clearly valued the opportunity for personal contact it had offered.[124] As he said:

> But to speak of right and true confession, I would to God it were kept in England, for it is a good thing. And those which find themselves grieved in conscience might go to a learned man and there fetch of him comfort of the Word of God, and so come to a quiet conscience, which is better and more to be regarded than all the riches of the world. And surely it grieveth me much that such confessions are not kept in England, &c.[125]

Did the '&c' hide a degree of nostalgia for the old ways that his Swiss servant and editor Augustine Bernher discreetly obliterated? Both Latimer's age and the fact that he referred to the problem several times make this a possibility.

An alternative to this tentative support for individual spiritual counsel, and one which was compatible with 'pulpit exhortation', was advocated by Foxe. He favoured the idea of a ministry which was loving and forgiving of human weakness rather than being distant and severe. Such an attitude would be more in line with the New Testament values which Foxe thought had been abandoned by protestants' over-compensating for the potential licentiousness that misinterpretation of their doctrine of justification might arouse. Christ had come into the world to save sinners; did not his rebuke of 'the sons of thunder', James and John, and his attitude to the woman taken in adultery, prove that he was replacing Old Testament violence with New Testament forgiveness and charity?[126] Ministers should open the church to the sinful and weak, rather than seeming to intend their exclusion and alienation. They should be healers of wounded consciences and the forgiving fathers of wayward children.[127] Forgiveness and repentance rather that death and retribution should be preached; the sword of the Word should be wielded against sin rather than sinners.[128] But Foxe's was a lone voice pleading for charity. Joye defended the prevailing consensus that the good of the commonwealth was more important than sensitivity to the sinner's plight, and censured Foxe for theological unsoundness.[129] Though Foxe was not alone in worrying that the pulpit was having an alienating effect, he was distinctly unusual in pleading for greater understanding of and charity towards individuals. Most protestants were determined that their repudiation of auricular confession and penance should not be seen as permitting sinful behaviour.

The only other way of purging the church of at least the flagrant sinners was to impose strong moral discipline, culminating if necessary in the use of excommunication. However, to most protestants this sanction smacked of popish tyranny.[130] The royal supremacy had humbled clerical power, and emphasised the separation of the spheres of governance of church and state. Thus Gilby insisted that the clerical hierarchy had been corrupted by power – the early (pre-papal) bishops of Rome had been God's ministers not his

A religion of the Word

makers, shepherds not lords, and teachers not masters.[131] Similarly Hooper attacked Gardiner for his 'unsuitable' legal background and his involvement in affairs of state. He went on to explain the argument for separate spheres:

> [E]very commonwealth ought to have but two governors, God and the prince, the one to make a law for the soul, the other for the body: all the king's officers to be ministers of the law made to the conservation of the commonwealth, and the bishops to be ministers in the Church of the law that is prescribed by God.[132]

But this begged the question of the extent of sanctions open to the clergy in ministering God's law.[133] By contrast, the doctrine of the priesthood of all believers emphasised the levelling of differences between clergy and laity: Latimer declared that '[w]hosoever cometh asking the Father remedy in his necessity for Christ's sake he offereth up as acceptable a sacrifice as any bishop can do'; indeed, 'a poor woman in the belfry' in this way 'hath as good authority to offer up this sacrifice as hath the bishop in his *pontificalibus*'.[134] The only difference between clergy and laity in relation to the Sacrament was one of ministration.[135] In matters of faith all Christians were equal: 'But all other Christian men have the spirit of God, then are all other Christian men spiritual men. Then must ye either take me for no Christian man, or else grant that I am a spiritual judge.'[136]

Nevertheless, firmly though they believed in the humbling of clerical pretensions, protestants retained the imagery of the spiritual sword and the keys by which to distinguish clergy from laity. The spiritual sword was defined as the Word, and very few protestants took things further than that. Latimer explained the extent of this 'spiritual magistracy':

> Our office is to teach every man the way to heaven, and whosoever will not follow, but liveth still in sin and wickedness, him we ought to strike and not to spare. Like as John Baptist did, when he said to the great and proud King Herod, *'non licet tibi . . .'*. Other people that have not this vocation, may exhort everyone his neighbour to leave sins; but we have the sword, we are authorised to strike them with God's Word.[137]

He seems to have had in mind a licence to admonish all levels of society, from the prince downwards, rather than a jurisdictional or binding power.[138] On the power of the keys, Cranmer, comparing ministers of the Gospel with civil magistrates in terms of power and honourable estate, asked: 'how much more are they to be esteemed, that be the ministers of Christ's words and sacraments, and have to them committed the keys of heaven, to let in and shut out by the ministration of his Word and gospel?'[139] Becon put it negatively: non-preachers had no binding powers.[140] Hutchinson described the keys as symbols of the two Testaments: 'Their forgiving and loosing is to declare the sweet and comfortable promises that are made through Jesus

Christ in God's book to such as be penitent, and their binding and retaining is to preach the law, which causes anger to such as be impenitent.'[141]

Hooper, in reaction to papal claims, declared that the minister's role was simply to explain that only Christ could bind or loose.[142] Inconsistently, though, he demanded the restoration of excommunication, describing it as 'an act politic and civil' which maintained order in the church.[143]

Even this limited definition of the nature of the binding powers of the clergy could create controversy. A perceived increase in adultery and divorce troubled many divines,[144] and raised the question of appropriate punishment for an offence that blurred the boundaries between sin and crime, public and private, civil and ecclesiastical jurisdictions. Foxe and Joye clashed violently on the subject. Joye interpreted the spiritual sword as the right of ministers to demand the full implementation of the Mosaic law by the civil authorities.[145] To Foxe this was tantamount to trespassing on the civil jurisdiction – he defined the spiritual sword as waging war on sin rather than on sinners.[146] Joye, like Hutchinson, argued that the Word did not control those who did not listen; the sword was ordained by God to repress unrepentant sinners and prevent them from endangering others.[147] In response to this Foxe honed his definition of the spiritual sword to include powers of discipline, and demanded the restoration of a reformed method of excommunication.[148] The demands of the controversy had forced him into advocating something that hitherto had been considered one of popery's main abuses, which he had to take into account.[149] Foxe and Joye's controversy was unusual, given the limitations observed by other protestants,[150] but it indicated the way in which the Edwardian reformation was growing away from its Henrician roots.

In general, protestants handled the problem of clerical powers either by attacking what they considered to be catholic usurpations or by restricting themselves to a fairly uncontentious definition of the significance of preaching. This latter solution maintained to some extent the distinction between clergy and laity, while the tentative demands for the restoration of excommunication shows that there was a degree of anxiety that the message was not getting through from preaching alone.

The limitations of the debate about clerical powers were almost as marked in discussion of episcopacy – an unresolved issue which would eventually prove a major source of conflict. Foxe (alone) hinted that levelling sentiments were being expressed;[151] no one developed a positive *iure divino* argument in this climate of debate. An attempt was made to distinguish terms: 'prelate', with its connotations of lordliness, political power, personal extravagance and reluctance to preach, was contrasted with 'bishop', which could refer to the apostolic model of the letters to Timothy and Titus.[152] 'Lordliness' was being humbled by the policy of ruthlessly stripping episcopal estates, against which there was no appeal. Henrician policy was being followed with a vengeance even if the profits did not always go into the royal purse. Even radical protestants had to be circumspect once in office – which is perhaps one of the main reasons Latimer did not wish to return to a diocese. As the crucial question of ordination was not discussed, the resulting ideal was little different from that of the ideal minister. Hooper, who was the one influential protestant whose radicalism might have led him to attack episcopacy, instead restricted his objections to the vestiges of popery that he saw in vestments and in swearing by the saints during ordination.[153] But he went on to become almost a model 'apostolic' bishop – one who defended the office not in writing but in action. His tireless preaching and visitations, and his careful observance of charity, showed his determination to be a builder of the church.[154] However, when protestants wrote that the authority of bishops was given to them to edify and not to destroy, it was Gardiner's capacity for destruction and not Hooper's for edification that they had in mind.[155]

The result was that bishops were only distinguished from ministers by the size of their flocks. Joye wrote that bishops should be like the apostles, leading their flocks in 'the right way both in true doctrine, preaching and also in example of godly living'.[156] They were the 'hands and eyes' of the flock, and when they were misused to become 'slanderous and false pointing hands' and 'cruel eyes' Christ commanded them to be cast out of the body. Gilby wrote that the bishops' authority was intrinsic not to the office itself, but to the doctrine they preached as 'prophets and preachers of the heavenly mysteries and the disciples and scholars of Christ.'[157] The good bishop should preach with deep fervour in order to 'stir up this heavy slackness within us'.[158] Latimer's description of the preacher in the *Sermon on the plough* was directed at bishops as well as the ordinary clerics. Hooper described Christ as the model bishop who taught 'the people, which was the chiefest part of a bishop's office, and most diligently and straightly commanded by God'.[159] Elsewhere he wrote that a bishop's office was not to legislate or spend time on ceremonies, but to educate the people, ensuring that they understood how to pray 'in spirit and truth', daily and weekly expounding the fundamentals of creed, ten commandments and Lord's Prayer, and making certain that their faith was based on understanding and obedience to 'the whole Word of God'.[160]

However, if a distinction had to be made between bishop and minister, it lay in the supervisory aspect of the bishop's role. Hooper's model bishop could not examine his flock individually in person, but the size of his diocese should be limited by a degree of personal contact – it should be no bigger than one in which 'ten diligent learned men' could examine all the parishioners once a year.[161] Joye described the bishop as 'a diligent superintendent, watcher over Christ's flock, to feed them with the pure Word of God . . . to see that none want this ghostly food, nor perish for lack thereof . . .'.[162] Strictures on episcopal extravagance were an attempt to realign the priorities of the bishops to the financing of a proper preaching ministry.[163] Crowley's advice to the bishop was to ensure that his parish clergy were godly preachers with decent livings, and also take special care that the young were educated 'in God's truth', for he was responsible for all the souls lost through his negligence.[164] Lever placed more emphasis than other protestants on the bishop's responsibility for organising charity. It was to the shame of the London city fathers that no provision was made for the honest poor or for the punishment of 'dissembling caitiffs', but the appointment of a 'good overseer' should put matters to rights.[165] It is perhaps no coincidence that organised charity was one of Ridley's prime concerns and achievements.[166]

The ideal that emerges is of a bishop concerned above all with the welfare of his diocesan flock. His office was not a worldly dignity but one of special service. If he was to carry out his responsibilities for preaching and charity effectively, both by personal example and as an overseer of the parish clergy, he would have plenty to fill his time without taking on additional offices of state. Hooper deplored this mediaeval inheritance on the grounds that 'no man can serve two masters': if a bishop was 'so necessary for the court that in civil causes and giving of good counsel he cannot be spared, let him use that vocation and leave the other, for it is not possible that he should do both well'.[167] Latimer was more specific in his targets: he declared it was 'to England's shame' (cf. 1 Cor. 6:5) that bishops should fill high offices,[168] for 'I would fain know who controlleth the devil at home in his parish while he controlleth the mint? If the apostles might not leave the office of preaching to the deacons, shall one leave it for minting?'[169]

However, this position of clearly demarcated duties and spheres was not so inflexible as it might at first appear. Crowley did not appear to disapprove of bishops serving as royal advisers so long as they remained uncorrupted by the desire for worldly advancement and power. If a bishop was careful, his position would enable 'godliness' to influence government policy.[170] Hooper managed to marry his own position of political influence with the theoretical separation of the offices of magistrate and minister:

> [T]he king's office is enough for a king, and the bishop's office enough for a bishop. Let them do the best they can, and study each of them in their office. But let the king take heed he be able to judge whether the bishop do true service to God in his vocation, by the Word of God, and let the bishop do the same.[171]

The duty of counsel thus became the duty of admonition. Though bishops should not hold government office, since to do so was contrary to the apostolic model, as preachers they were bound to speak out on temporal and political matters of policy and justice. So Hooper attended the House of Lords

A religion of the Word

frequently, as well as giving outspoken sermons at Court.[172] After all, how could the commonwealth be made godly, if the ministry, represented and headed by the bishops, failed to take part in the political process?

Thus the 'good shepherd', whatever level he occupied in the clerical hierarchy, was to watch over his flock, feeding its members with the Word and guiding them by his own example of godly living. While this ideal solved the problem of providing a basis for respect of the clergy, at least in theory, it did not face the problem of the nature and extent of clerical powers, of which protestants were well aware but which they tended to play down. However, these theoretical problems were peripheral compared to the practical task of achieving such a worthy ministry, especially at a time when clerical morale was unsurprisingly low. Three areas were in urgent need of reformation: the education of the preaching ministry; the financing of the church and the laity's part in it; and clerical corruption. It is to these questions that we must now turn, before tackling the broader question of the church as a Christian body.

THE NEED FOR FURTHER REFORMATION

The provision of a learned ministry

The ideal of reform by evangelism threw the shortcomings of the contemporary clergy into sharp relief. As a 'religion of the Word', protestantism had to be served by a literate, preferably university-trained, ministry. Not that the idea of using the universities as seminaries of godly learning was by any means new: conservative humanists like John Fisher had achieved far more, thirty years previously, than the new protestant generation.[173] Indeed, this was a source of frustration to many university-educated protestants who were afraid that, far from building on earlier achievements, the political elite was either plundering or else allowing them to decay, while purporting to uphold the Gospel. Instead of using the monastic wealth released by the dissolution to invest massively in education and charity, this elite had selfishly spent it on itself. Hence what was new was not the preoccupation with education, but the bitterness that opportunities to provide for it were being squandered, by a supposedly enlightened elite.[174]

Well-known proponents of educational investment included Hugh Latimer and Thomas Lever, but Thomas Ruddoke also emphasised it in his plan for 'the livings of ministers'. Latimer lamented that poor men's sons could not afford to study, while the sons of the rich, who were driving them out, were not highly motivated divinity students – sentiments echoed by Thomas Ruddoke.[175] Such changes would 'pinch at the office of preaching', and erode learning, making it difficult to withstand popery.[176] If only people would endow education with as much zeal as they had once 'bestowed ungodly' on

The reform of the church

private Masses and 'purgatory matters'. But instead of enlightenment he saw only greed:

> Every man scrapeth and getteth together for this bodily house, but the soul-health is neglected. Schools are not maintained; scholars have not exhibition; the preaching office decayeth. Men provide lands and riches for their children, but this most necessary office they for the most part neglect. Very few there be that help poor scholars; that set their children to school to learn the word of God, and to make a provision for the age to come. This notwithstanding is the only way to salvation.[177]

God had stirred up the magistrates to extirpate popery, but they now needed to look forward and direct their energies to educational provision.[178] Providing preaching for the future would 'hallow God's name' just as much as would hearing sermons in the present;[179] and the endowment of education was thus a practical way of furthering the advancement of the kingdom of God.[180]

Lever's critique was less nostalgic and more pointed than Latimer's:[181]

> Your majesty hath had given and received by act of Parliament colleges, chantries and guilds for many good considerations and especially as appeareth in the same act for erecting of grammar schools, to the education of youth in virtue and godliness, to the further augmenting of the universities and better provision for the poor and needy. But now many grammar schools, and much charitable provision for the poor, be taken, sold and made away, to the great slander of you and your laws, to the utter discomfort of the poor, to the grievous offence of the people, to the most miserable drowning of youth in ignorance and sore decay of the universities.[182]

While a good start had been made at Cambridge with the foundation of the regius professorships and of Trinity College, Lever alleged that since then the university had been decayed by 200 students.[183] He gave a heart-rending description of the dedication and devotion to study of the divinity students, who were not wearied by study but beset by worries that they would not be able to afford to continue their way of life as 'the living saints which serve God taking great pains in abstinence, study, labour and diligence, both with watching and prayer'.[184]

Declining education and an inheritance of uneducated clergy meant that there would be a large proportion of 'unlearned pastors' in the ministry for some time to come. Latimer struck out at the employment of ex-monks and chantry priests merely to save their pensions – 'Christ bought souls with his blood, and will ye sell them for gold or silver?'[185] But he still refused to countenance the right of a congregation to dismiss a curate who was alleged to be 'an ass-head, a dodipole, a lack-Latin and can do nothing';[186] the congregation's only redress was to be achieved by complaining to the authorities or prayer. Hooper's emphasis was more ideological:[187]

Although there be diversity of gifts and knowledge among men, some know more and some know less, and if he that knoweth least, teach Christ after the holy Scriptures, he is to be accepted; and he that knoweth most, and teacheth Christ contrary or [in] any other ways than holy Scriptures teach, is to be refused.[188]

More important than learning was true witness 'as records and testimonies, ministers and servants of God's Word and God's sacraments unto the which they should neither add, diminish nor change anything'.[189]

Crowley took a line that was more positive than Latimer's and more practical than Hooper's. Both uneducated and educated clerics had lessons to learn. The unlearned priest should make himself worthy of the ministry by giving up his bad habits,[190] repudiating popery and doing some elementary teaching – as it was assumed that he was literate.[191] The educated minister was cautioned to live perfectly, so that his learning should not offend people; he should not traffic in benefices, or use his position to advance his career; above all, he should be charitable.[192] If radical financial measures were not forthcoming to provide a supply of educated ministers, then it was necessary to make the best of those who were already in the ministry, even though they were far from ideal.

The redistribution of wealth in the church: sacrilege and patronage

Given the strong element of anticlericalism in protestant propaganda, particularly the attacks on clerical venality and episcopal extravagance, the problem of adequately financing the ministry was not an easy one for protestants to confront. As Latimer observed: 'We of the clergy have had too much, but that is taken away, and now we have too little.'[193] Meanwhile, as in the more specialised case of education,[194] there was a strong sense that the laity, both in government and privately, had simply used the reformation to enrich themselves rather than reinvesting in the church to support 'true religion'. Wholesale secularisation could not be condoned by protestants, but the cautiousness of their clericalism, as we have seen in other areas,[195] prevented them from espousing radical alternatives in ecclesiastical finance and organisation. They were hampered both by an unreformed church structure and by the force of their own attacks on clerical wealth.

The limitations imposed by antipopery showed especially where the financing of the ordinary parochial clergy was concerned. Edmund Guest thought it in accordance with biblical practice that there was 'a livelihood to be due and payable to the gospel preachers of their auditors, for their evangelical preachment'.[196] This of course was quite different from payment for saying Mass, for 'by Paul's doctrine, to serve the altar and to preach be sundry and severable offices and ministries'.[197] Crowley attacked the superfluous crypto-papist fees for officiating at weddings, purifications and funerals. He asked that parliament should

> set such an order in this and such other things that either we may have ministers found upon the tenths that we pay yearly to the churches, otherwise that it may be lawful for us to do such ministries ourselves, and not to be thus constrained to feed a sort of carrion crows which are never so merry as when we lament the loss of our friends.[198]

In view of the attack on popish 'pharisaical' practices, the Old Testament basis of tithes proved somewhat embarrassing. Latimer advanced no less than three counter-arguments to support the payment of tithes: that they constituted an act of 'godly usury', or a loan which God would repay with blessings; that they fulfilled the Pauline injunction that provision should be made for the ministry; and that they were ordered by the law of the land.[199]

The urgency of the problem of payment may reflect the fact that many of those stressing it were themselves preachers.[200] Thus Thomas Becon preferred to praise the good pastor rather than criticise the clergy in his *Flower of godly prayers*. He asked: 'If the preachers sow unto their parishioners spiritual things, is it a great thing if they reap their carnal things?'[201] Moreover, 'God's ordinance' of payment needed supplementing by charity like that offered to the apostles by Lydia. Elijah, Jeremiah and Christ had relied on such charity,[202] but this degree of insecurity was especially scandalous when the church was riddled with non-preaching pluralists.[203] The worthy minister should have both the respect and the financial support of his parishioners, a combination to which Latimer referred as 'a double honour'.[204] Though they should not profit from such a vocation, he urged that preachers should be properly maintained – 'Great is their business and therefore great should be their hire. They have great labours and therefore they ought to have good livings that they may commodiously feed their flock.'[205] He hoped that the foreign divines who came to England were being well paid, for 'the realm would prosper in receiving of them'.[206] 'Feeding the flock' meant charity as well as preaching. Instead of campaigning for the revival of the primitive church office of deacons,[207] protestants suggested that ministers should be responsible for redistributing a proportion of tithes as poor relief and hospitality.[208] Concern for poor relief made Crowley attack impropriations:

> Ye had the tithes
> Of men's increase
> That should have fed
> My flock and me
> But you made your
> Selves well at ease
> And took no thought
> For poverty.[209]

A religion of the Word

Thus tithes should be paid willingly, especially by the rich: '"Bring every tithe into my barn," saith the Lord, "that there may be meat in my house." The parsonage . . . is God's house, and tithes are paid unto them that they should have meat in their houses to nourish and comfort the poor . . .'.[210] The exact detail of what proportion of tithe was for poor relief and what for supporting the ministry (in itself seen as an act of charity) was left vague. Rather, a sense of anxiety emerges that the apostolic nature of the ministry was an excuse to allow preachers to live off thin air.[211] The practical consideration of finance balanced the idealism of the preoccupation with the spiritual necessity of preaching, and emphasised the fact that preachers had not left society but were playing a crucial role within it, which had to be paid for somehow. This social aspect emerged in the context of concern about the problems of poverty and disorder: both by preaching and distributing charity, the minister struggled to combat these threats.[212] However, no one put forward a coherent scheme of reorganisation – their fire tended to be deflected by lay greed. The laity had profited from the church after the dissolutions without comparably increasing their responsibilities, which suggested that avarice and indifference, even posing as anticlericalism, did not differentiate between a reformed ministry and a popish priesthood. Thomas Ruddoke complained bitterly that the new impropriators covered up their reluctance to fulfil their obligations to the parochial clergy by criticising clerical insufficiency, by protesting that tithes were part of the law abrogated by Christ and were therefore a matter of conscience only, or, most disingenuously of all, by pleading poverty.[213]

Protestant disappointment that the proceeds of the dissolutions were not being ploughed back into the church was clear. Crowley mused on the ruins of the monasteries:

> O Lord (thought I then)
> What occasion was here
> To provide for learning
> And make poverty cheer
> The lands and the jewels
> That hereby were had
> Would have found godly preachers
> Which might well have led
> The people aright
> That now go astray
> And have fed the poor
> That famish every day . . .[214]

Such greed was tantamount to sacrilege. This was the greatest theft of all, as Hooper showed in his *Declaration of the ten commandments* – 'it is an horrible offence to take these goods away from the godly use they be appointed to'.

The reform of the church

This new form of sacrilege was comparable in seriousness with the old pluralism.[215] Lever denounced the London merchants who bought benefices and did not supply ministers – 'A mischievous mart of merchandise is this, and yet now so commonly used that thereby shepherds be turned into thieves, dogs into wolves, and the poor flock of Christ, redeemed with his precious blood, most miserably pilled and spoiled, yea, cruelly devoured.'[216] Philip Nichols described those who snatched the spoils of the old religion as Israelites who wanted to conquer Canaan without God's help.[217] It damaged the reputation of the reformation and the aristocracy.[218] Crowley assumed that 'all the world seeth and all godly hearts lament' the greed which 'raked together' farms and benefices;[219] and Lever denounced the nobles who profited from the dissolutions as 'Judases' who claimed for the poor the ointment with which Christ was anointed, while intending only their own profit.[220]

The denunciation of aristocratic sacrilege was not just a matter of clerical outrage. More positively, the critical role the lay patron should play in saving souls was being delineated. 'The office of the patron is to have a care, a zeal, a vigilant eye for souls' health, and to provide for his churches, that he is patron of, that they might be taught in God's Word.'[221] The responsibility of patronage was 'a great charge, a great burden before God', not just a new asset to litigate about.[222] Such stress on responsibility accounts for the bitterness of Lever's description of the nobles as 'Judases'. On all counts the new patrons were failing to provide for the flock: there were those who were too lazy to care who was installed, those who covetously 'hired a Sir John Lack-Latin which shall say service so that the people be nothing edified', and who and raked off the profit,[223] and worst of all those who sold benefices, or gave them 'to your servants for their service, for keeping of hounds or hawks, for making of your gardens'.[224]

The finances of the church had not been reformed, but had merely changed hands. Monastic impropriations were a case in point. Latimer insisted that impropriations impoverished the clergy because 'all the great gain goeth another way'.[225] Lever made the point even more forcefully:

> The first part of reformation is to restore and give again all such things as have been wrongfully taken and abused. Surely the abbeys did wrongfully take and abuse nothing so much as the impropriations of benefices. Nothing is so papistical as impropriations of benefices be, they be the pope's darlings and paramours . . .[226]

As God made the covetous nobles 'vessels of wrath' to destroy the greed of the abbeys, so they had the opportunity of becoming 'vessels of honour' by repudiating impropriations.[227]

The transference of monastic wealth to private gain meant that sacrilege was compounded by idolatry:

A religion of the Word

> Yet one sort making this most godly and glorious fact to serve their lucre and gain to the slander of such a notable enterprise, have seemed to change the kind of idolatry, making the muck which they found heaped about those idols to be their God. So that they may be worthily be called idolaters, so long as they have it, keep it and set so much store [there]by.[228]

Gilby recommended that the monastic spoils should be made 'anathema',[229] but that 'lands [and] possessions' should support the reformation.[230] Anxiety that the assets of the church were being stripped and that this was a dangerous state of affairs were all the preachers could communicate. Coherent solutions took second place to the bewailing of greed. As Hutchinson commented:

> O living God this is a strange kind of surgery, a strange reformation, to sweep things away and make that private which was common! Well! David said that God will make them like unto Sisera and Jabin, like unto Oreb and Zeeb, which have the houses of God in possession; he will root out their generation utterly.[231]

Corruption within the church

While much of their attention was devoted to the new roles of the laity, protestants did not neglect clerical shortcomings. Both institutional problems and political circumstances gave cause for concern: pluralism and non-residence were perennial problems, while 'unpreaching prelates' and flattery reflected the centrality of preaching.[232] Pluralism was the most pressing of these problems; a traditional complaint, but one made more urgent both by falling clerical recruitment and by the need for a better distribution of preachers. The royal *Injunctions* specified that there should be a learned minister in every cure, or at least a competent curate.[233] Protestants were quick to point out how far short the church fell of this ideal. Pluralism was built into the system of both church and state. Clerics took on 'secular' office, and were rewarded with multiple benefices. Hutchinson regarded this as illogical – 'They give them benefice upon benefice but they will not suffer them to come at their parishes, to preach . . .'.[234] Noble and episcopal chaplains were also singled out as offenders, whose self-interest made them 'dumb dogs, choked with benefices so that ye be not able to open your mouths to bark against pluralities, impropriations, buying of advowsons, nor against any evil abuse of the clergy's livings'.[235] Pluralist clergy deceived themselves if they thought it possible to serve all their cures; and their absence brought 'inequity amongst the people'.[236]

It was, however, easier to criticise pluralism than solve the problem. Crowley offered to help pluralists 'satisfy the consciences of them that be offended at your doings herein . . .' if they could defend themselves by scripture, knowing full well that this would be unlikely.[237] Lever declared that pluralism was 'robbery by warrant' which the king was forced to support because of the self-interest of the pluralists. However, only the king could cut through the system and redistribute office and benefices so that good preachers were spread more evenly about the realm.[238] Crowley fictionalised the appeal to royal justice in *One-and-thirty epigrams*: the king feels remorse and resolves to make a start by dealing with a notorious pluralist:

> 'But tell me, Master Doctor,
> Will you have your benefices still?'
> 'If your grace will do me right,' (quoth he)
> 'I must have them my life time.'
> 'So shalt thou,' (quoth the king)
> 'For tomorrow, by prime,
> God willing, thy body
> Shall be divided and sent
> To each benefice a piece
> To make thee resident.'[239]

A Solomonic solution, but scarcely a practicable one.

Shortages through absenteeism were exacerbated by 'unpreaching prelates'. Lever thought that even the use of curates was inexcusable: if the curate was good then he should be beneficed; if not, he merely emphasised the prelate's greed. The call of other duties in government was also a mere veil for greed.[240] Latimer saw refusal to preach as a deliberate policy to bring about dissension and the return of popery. Such men were the 'salt that hath lost its savour' (Matt. 5). They should all be made 'quondams': 'Out with them; cast them out of their office. What should they do with cures, that will not look them [to] it?'[241] Latimer's own 'quondamship', however, was something he appeared to be proud of, as a symbol that he had withdrawn from the establishment of a corrupt church.[242]

Refusal to preach demonstrated both a lack of support for the reformation and an unworthiness of it. Active support of corruption was almost as bad, especially in those who were well placed to advance the interests of the reform. Instead they preferred to protect themselves, flattering the nobility that things were going well, in much the same way as had the 400 false prophets.[243] Flattery by these men, especially noble chaplains, allowed the reformation to be hijacked by the greed of 'carnal gospellers':

> And as for their chaplains, which do chop with them their benefices and give a whole year's rent ere they enter, or greater gain peradventure, and so long as my lord and they can agree of covenants or that my lord will get them more promotions, they will tell my lord he may hawk, he may hunt, he may bowl, he may play at the ball, and what he will, so he do stop their mouths with somewhat all is well, and it please your grace, but against their poor brethren which have nothing to give them they are cruel and devouring wolves...[244]

A religion of the Word

Greed and careerism were corrupters of clergy as well as of laity: the antagonism felt by Gilby and Latimer towards such people reflected their personal reluctance to become part of a corrupt system. The denunciation of human greed and inadequacy reflected frustration with the lack of radical change. Apart from appeals to the consciences of the king and the Council, they were in no position to develop a coherent programme.

Until now, we have concentrated on discussing the ways in which the church could be made a more effective proselytising institution. The laity have played a largely passive part, as the receivers of doctrine preached. In the absence of an adequate minister their only recourse was to prayer and to complaint through the 'proper channels'. Indeed, when these failed, the laity's apparent willingness to vote with their feet, when combined with the great economic power over the church which the lay ruling class now enjoyed, gave protestants cause for concern. However, in protestant thought the laity did have an important and positive role. After all, they constituted the body of the church, newly liberated from popery, and now able to enjoy the benefits of the Gospel, the sacraments and the liturgy in their own tongue. But the 'true church' in the context of antipopery was seen as a persecuted minority. How did the visible established church relate to this uncompromising model?

THE CHRISTIAN BODY

The visible church

The nature of the church in its visible earthly form was a problem that Edwardian protestants tended not to discuss.[245] Definitions centred on a hierarchical or jurisdictional approach, or on a narrow understanding of apostolic succession, had obviously been precluded by the attack on popery; definitions centring on the purity and autonomy of particular congregations were likewise precluded by fear of anabaptism.[246] Here protestants fell back on their legacy of opposition, in stressing that the true church consisted of the godly, or even the elect, known only to God, scattered in both time and space and unrecognised by the world except to be persecuted.[247] It seemed that the 'true' church had more in common with the 'invisible' church than with the institutional structures of even reformed churches on earth. However, the visible church had to contain the truth, otherwise it would be a worthless and corrupt earthly form.

Instances where polemical circumstances allowed protestants to get round this problem merely served to highlight the difficulty. Thus, in Bale's definition the true church was unknown to the world,[248] but in his description of Christ's millennial rule, in which the church on earth was to achieve its truest form, he described a protestant church, with the minister preaching to congregations of the godly, who read the scriptures, mortified the flesh and participated in the Lord's Supper, as well as being persecuted.[249] The millennial setting did not require Bale to prescribe the means whereby the church would consist only of the godly. Hooper similarly brushed aside this problem in his discussion of baptism, which he defined as the confirmation of God's promise to the faithful, when he was thanked 'for the acceptation of this christened person into the commonwealth of his saved people; remembering that only those be appertaining to God that be thus called openly into the visible Church and congregation . . .'.[250]

Most writers, in keeping with both their suspicion of human institutions and their aspirations towards membership of the invisible church, seemed content to leave the tension unresolved. Thus Veron declared:

> The Church therefore, although outwardly it is taken for the congregation of all them that customarily come together to preach and hear the gospel of Jesu Christ and also to minister and receive the sacraments instituted by him whether they have the true faith or not: yet not withstanding the true Church is the congregation of them only which do believe truly in Jesus Christ, and have indeed his holy spirit in them.[251]

Veron equated the true church with the invisible church,[252] and he concluded: 'Wherefore he that is without true faith in Christ Jesu, and hath any wrinkle of infidelity in his uncircumcised heart, though outwardly he seemeth to be the chief member of the Church, yet notwithstanding he cannot be a true member of it.'[253]

Only one valid claim to true status was left to the visible church – its support for the gospel.[254] The assent of both faithful and unfaithful to the truth of Bible gave authority to the church, but 'that authority is not granted unto the congregation to any liberty against the word of God, but to obedience towards God and his Scriptures. A power I say, is given unto the Church, but not so free as many men make it. It is circumscribed within certain limits and bounds.'[255] The church could only bind within the limits of teaching the remission of sin through faith in Christ; it must serve Christ through obedience to his word: 'Let us therefore remember we are men: not authors but witnesses of the Scriptures, not heads but members of the Church, not masters but ministers and servants of our Lord Jesus Christ.'[256] Cranmer was even more explicit: to him, the visible church was only true insofar as it was a treasury of God's Word, like the register of wills, whose task was to keep it and see that it was fulfilled.

> For if the Church proceed further to make any new articles of faith, besides the Scripture, or contrary to the Scripture, or direct not the form of life according to the same, then it is not the pillar of truth, nor the Church of Christ, but

A religion of the Word

the synagogue of Satan, and the temple of Antichrist, which both erreth itself and bringeth into error as many as do follow it.[257]

At the same time he upheld the identification of the true church as a small minority, the body of God's elect which was the 'pillar of truth'.[258]

Increasingly therefore, protestants looked to the New Testament for models of the visible church. Hooper set the reformed churches the standard of the seven churches of Asia: like them, the reformed churches should preach the complete and simple Word of God, allow no idolatry or images, and cast out 'lukewarmness' in favour of zealous faith.[259] In this way it became possible (and increasingly necessary) to assign 'marks' or distinctive outward features of true status to the visible church.[260] Only at the end of Edward's reign, however, did the Forty-Two Articles define the visible church, and even then the definition was at its most basic: 'The visible Church of Christ is a congregation of faithful men in the which the pure word of God is preached and the sacraments be duly ministered, according to Christ's ordinances in all things that of necessity are requisite to the same.'[261] It added that the visible churches of Jerusalem, Antioch, Alexandria and Rome had erred in living and in faith because they betrayed their function as the witness to, and keeper of, scripture.[262] The official Catechism, however went into more, and significant, detail, adding two extra 'marks':

> The marks therefore of this Church are first pure preaching of the gospel, then brotherly love, out of which as members of all one body springeth good will of each to other; thirdly upright and uncorrupted use of the Lord's sacraments according to the ordinance of the gospel, last of all brotherly correction and excommunication or banishing those out of the Church that will not amend their lives. This mark the holy fathers termed discipline...[263]

Such a church (unlike that of Cranmer's earlier definition) was 'the pillar of truth', which possessed the power of binding and loosing, 'so that whosoever believeth the gospel preached in this Church, he shall be saved, but whoso believeth not, he shall be damned'.[264] The inclusion of discipline as a mark of the church showed that the baseline of a general adherence to scripture was beginning to be considered imprecise if not inadequate, even in official quarters. Ponet in 1553 did not have to observe Hooper's restraint of 1551, when he stated that 'these two marks, the true preaching of God's word and right use of the sacraments, declare what and where the true Church is', so that everyone should attend despite the possible absence of discipline, 'for no Church as touching this part can be absolutely perfect'.[265]

However, the purification of the church by a revived discipline remained a distant prospect, despite Cranmer's ongoing project for the reformation of ecclesiastical law.[266] In any case, acceptance of the impurity of the visible church was not necessarily a polemical weakness. True, it acknowledged that the visible church in England was a mere approximation to the ideal outlined in scripture. But by emphasising the mixed nature of the church, protestants were accepting a reality which they found both in the Gospels and in contemporary hostility to the reformation. Latimer showed that the effect of even Christ's preaching was random – 'the preaching is likened to a fisher's net, that taketh good fish and bad, and draweth all to the shore'.[267] Elsewhere he categorised the members of the visible church as an ungodly majority – rejecters of the Gospel, or the unrepentant hardened sinners, or fairweather or worldly Christians – and the minority of the faithful who hear and keep God's Word (the four seeds).[268]

Acceptance of the mixed nature of the church had various effects. Foxe realised that it would make imposing excommunication difficult, though not a practical impossibility.[269] Joye's more conventional response to the fact that the 'holy church' would only be completely free of sin after Doomsday was to give the magistrates the responsibility of imposing excommunication.[270] Yet another response – one which did not exclude the possibility of either excommunication or intervention by the magistrate, but which was the most persuasive argument in the context of an undeveloped church discipline and an indifferent magistracy – was to let the Sacrament of Holy Communion do the sifting process, on a purely internal, spiritual basis. The doctrine of 'spiritual eating' was corroborated by the assumption that only the faithful truly communicated. Thus frequent Communion both affirmed the faith of the godly and sealed the damnation of the unfaithful.[271] As the author of the *Song of the Lord's Supper* put it:

> The cause also, together we have gathered
> And why Christ's flock, the Supper oft should be eating,
> Because Christ's Church is like a fisher repleting
> His ship with all kinds of fish: whereof bad be some
> That the weak may taste joy, and the stubborn threatening
> To be cast out in the fire when the Lord doth come.[272]

This view of the Sacrament retained the insistence that the saving faith of an individual was crucial to his membership of the true/invisible church, while preserving for the visible church its important role as the provider of the Word and the sacraments which nurtured faith.

Concentration on the church's performance in that role and the changes needed to make it more effective obviously led to disproportionate attention being given to the clergy's role in the church.[273] But, however vital was the provision of a preaching ministry that would understand and propagate the 'true use of the Lord's Supper', such a ministry did not constitute the church. In the protestant mind a church was always a congregation,[274] and it is to this that we must now turn to complete our picture of the visible church.

A religion of the Word

The congregation and public worship

Paradoxically, given this definition of the visible church, protestant interest in the function of the congregation, especially in public worship, was somewhat limited. While this is perfectly consistent with the early reformation emphasis on faith, it is surely remarkable that a reign which produced two prayer books should leave them to speak largely for themselves.[275] With the exception of the sacrament, corporate public worship and prayer went undefended,[276] in contrast to the major debates occasioned by the vernacular scripture in the 1520s. Even the Forty-Two Articles managed only a lukewarm definition of the second *Prayer Book* – it was to be commended to the people as 'godly and in no point repugnant to the wholesome doctrine of the gospel, but agreeable thereto, furthering and beautifying the same not a little . . .'.[277] Protestant attitudes to public worship and the congregation were constrained chiefly by two considerations: on the one hand, the assumption that what mattered was the quality of an individual's faith;[278] and, on the other, a paramount concern for order, especially in view of the hostility to the 1549 *Prayer Book*.[279] The first consideration tended to atomise the congregation into a series of private experiences, rather than value its collective contribution.[280] The second was intensified by awareness of the opportunities for contention in the newly reformed church, and had the effect of restricting the congregation to a passive role.

After all, the prime duty of the congregation's members was that of being good listeners, especially to sermons.[281] The Catechism described the purpose of 'Sabbath exercises' as: 'First to hear the learning of the gospel, then the pure and natural use of the ceremonies and sacraments; last of all prayer made unto God by Christ . . .'.[282] Being passive recipients was not a role without responsibility – Hooper, for one, insisted that 'the science of the Scriptures is practive and not speculative; it requireth a doer and not a hearer only'.[283] Nor was it an unworthy part to play – Latimer praised the devotion of the common people in flocking to hear the Word of God as always outranking that of the clergy.[284]

Yet even here the demands of individual faith soon overrode any impulse to discuss the role of the congregation in positive terms. In preparation for Communion, Hooper emphasised above all the importance of the individual's response to the Word, especially as proclaimed in the sermon. He feared that the 'conscience destitute of God's fear, passeth not a deal of the Word, is moved neither with fear nor with love, but contemneth both God and his Word . . .'.[285]

The high premium protestantism placed on an individual's response to scripture made the visible act of worship the least important part of his or her activities. Of the greatest importance was the inward, intensely personal, spiritual experience of worship through private prayer. Based on a strong relationship to God, an individual's outward worship was largely expressed outside the church, in behaviour in the world. The public act of worship was thus only valuable as an expression of, and an inducement to, the godly life. True worship was spiritual, as the attack on idolatry revealed. Guest declared: 'so we being as pilgrims in this world exiled as [it] were from heaven, our Jerusalem and native country where God dwelleth, must honour and pray unto him always as resident in that heavenly Jerusalem, and not elsewhere'.[286] Such spiritual worship was an attitude of mind and a way of life even more than a type of devotion, according to Gilby; indeed, without godliness worship was a blasphemy. Godly people were filled with a childlike fear of God's majesty; they were frightened of displeasing him, but were also

> prompt and ready, like obedient children, to express in our living, judgement and mercy, the two special properties and greatest show of his image which appeareth unto his creatures ... Then if we do bring unto God as for his honour and worship sacrifices, offerings or whatsoever it be without the love of God, what do we do but declare ourselves detestable hypocrites, dissembling to love him whom we do not love, to honour him whom we dishonour, and to worship him, who by us is blasphemed.[287]

Similarly the Catechism focused attention on the cultivation of the godliness of the individual soul – 'For first let us labour to root out froward and corrupt lusts, and afterward plant holy and fit conditions for Christian hearts. Which if they be watered and fatted with the dew of God's Word and nourished with the warmth of the Holy Ghost, they shall bring forth doubtless the most plentiful fruit of immortality and blessed life ...'.[288] Hooper's aim of educated scriptural piety for all[289] attacked even reformed practices when they became mechanistic and self-fulfilling. What mattered was a way of life. He described the people's duty as consisting in giving worship and prayer to God, service to their king, love to their neighbour and time for the study of scripture, exclaiming: 'Away, away! I pray you with this opinion, that thinketh a man to owe no more to himself for religion than to learn by rote the Creed, the Ten Commandments and the Pater Noster.'[290] Becon showed how spiritual self-development should work in its social context. The duties of charity and witness were indicated in Christ's command to 'occupy till I come': '... which straightly chargeth me not only to occupy myself privately in virtuous studies and godly exercises, but also openly that his holy and glorious congregation may be edified and brought to the true and perfect knowledge of his most godly will', though Becon here was referring to individual witness rather than congregational worship.[291]

A slightly less individualistic view could be seen in the advocacy of the godly household. This was more a 'cellular' view than a fully collective one, since it still depended on the activity and sense of responsiblity of the head of

A religion of the Word

the household.[292] Latimer fought nostalgia for the 'religious houses' (i.e. monastic communities) among his flock by advocating the lay household as their true replacement. It was not religious houses that had been dissolved but places of idleness and hypocrisy; true religious houses were still active, as lay households living together in the fear of God and who devoted considerable time to charitable works.[293]

Latimer's ideal drew heavily on pre-reformation lay piety,[294] but Hooper's more militant ideal drew on his experience of Bullinger's circle in Zurich. He saw the household almost as a little church, with its head having almost the responsibility of a minister:

> Of what degree soever he be, he should cause his family and children to read some part of the Bible for their erudition, to know God. Likewise he should constrain them to pray unto God for the promotion of his holy Word, and for the preservation of the governors of the commonwealth, so that no day should pass without prayer and augmentation of knowledge in the religion of Christ.[295]

Given that the individual and his household were envisaged as the starting-point for worship, protestants still were left with the problem of justifying public worship. To do this adequately they were forced to fall back on the need for order, whether based on the law of God or that of man. The ideal of order not only necessitated Sunday worship but contradicted popular interpretations of the Sabbath rest. Latimer admonished his hearers that 'there be some which think that this day is ordained only for feasting, drinking, or gaming or such foolishness; but they be much deceived: this day was appointed of God that we should hear his Word, and learn his laws and so serve him.'[296] Latimer's concern that the traditional pastimes and recreations should give way to 'God's ordinance' echoed that of the *Injunctions*, where that ordinance was reinforced by the authority of the king. The Sabbath was henceforth to be spent not in games or riot, but in hearing the Word, praying, charity and sick visiting, or participating in Communion.[297]

Hooper thought that it was necessary to enforce the Sabbath as the Israelites did, because God 'appointed the seventh to exercise the ceremonies of the Church, which are instituted for the preservation of the ministries of the Church; as to use common prayer, hear the sermon, use the blessed supper of the Lord and give alms.'[298] However, he did allow the element of recreation to have its place, albeit in the form of gathering spiritual strength. Even this rest from worldly tasks should be an exercise of Christian patriarchy: servants for instance should not be forced to do domestic tasks on Sundays, but they must be made to go to church; an effort must be made to convert guests, and other charitable works should be done. Even participation in communion was seen by Roger Hutchinson as obedience to God's command to 'Take and eat'.[299]

Latimer made church attendance essentially a matter of good order and obedience, taking as his model Mary's journey to Jerusalem to keep the feast:

> I fear, this journey of hers will condemn a great many of us, which will not go out of the door to hear God's Word. Therefore learn here, first, to love and embrace God's Word: secondly, to follow all good orders, thirdly to be content to go with thy neighbours every holy-day to the church; for it is a good and godly order, and God will have it so.[300]

Only one of the writers under consideration here successfully united the divergent strands of individual piety and public worship – Edmund Allen in his 1551 *Catechism*. Allen saw the Sabbath as constituting a unity of interior and exterior worship, of private individual and public corporate cultivation of the spirit. Thus during the Sabbath the Christian's duty was to advance the Gospel by his own witness or by listening to preaching, he should be present 'at the communion prayers ... endeavouring himself to pray devoutly and earnestly as well for his own private as for the common necessities of Christ's universal Church'.[301] He should receive the Sacrament, give alms to the poor and see that he sets an example of virtue. Against those who thought church-going contradicted Christ's command to pray in secret, he argued that Christ was not opposed to public worship as he too prayed in the temple.[302] Indeed, those who deliberately stayed away from church should be excommunicated: 'the Lord gave commandment in his law that their souls should be rooted out and taken from among his people men who forsake and refuse the common congregation and other godly ordinances'.[303] Allen's insistence that public worship was necessary was aimed at those who over-emphasised that strand of protestant spirituality which saw the believer's spiritual life as best developed either within himself/herself or in the world, rather than by worship in church. His insistence was backed not only by the invocation of the law of God but by a sense of the value of congregational meeting and worship.

However, the issue of the value or distinctive contribution of corporate prayer was by no means developed. That is not to say that prayer was not discussed – it was simply seen as a matter for individuals. Thus in discussing the Lord's Prayer, Latimer did not mention its congregational use but instead emphasised its relevance at all times as the basis of a prayerful life: 'let us at all times call upon him, and glorify his name in all our livings'.[304] The thrust of his argument was to attack the mechanistic use of this prayer: prayers, especially the Lord's Prayer, should be said 'considerately with great devotion' and understanding,[305] but he did not differentiate between the public and private use of prayer.[306] Similarly the Catechism, which extolled the accessibility of the Lord's Prayer, since 'specially it belongeth equally to all and is as necessary for the lewd as the learned',[307] had nothing to say about its distinctive place in public worship.[308]

It is possible that, having presented the sermon and the Sacrament as the main reason for a congregation to gather together, protestants saw no other need to justify public worship, or indeed had any real interest in what took place there, provided it was not an act of superstition or idolatry.[309] This being said, it is interesting that one of the most uncompromising protestants, Anthony Gilby, should provide a rare instance of positive writing about congregational worship. He saw the Mass as damagingly exclusive, centring as it did on the priest and the Host, and demanded instead a service that included as many people as possible for the greater glory of God:

> Oh blind guides you ought to wish that the name of God and the special work of his mercies in the death of his son Christ might be most largely renowned, praised and sanctified in the congregation, not only by the mouths of sucklings and babes, by the lowest, by the highest, by the smallest, by the greatest, but if it were possible, that the very stones should burst forth his praise.[310]

Gilby's positive view of the congregation underpinned his support for a vernacular liturgy, which would undermine support for the Mass because ordinary people would be able to understand. The warmth with which he regarded congregational worship was shown by his testimony that he 'dwelt for seven years in a place without sermons' but congregational thanksgiving for the death of Christ was as good – 'and generally to give thanks together, in comeliness and order, that by the multitude thus praising and giving thanks the honour of God may be amplified and we the better resemble that heavenly Jerusalem where they do incessantly sing praise, crying with one voice, *sanctus sanctus sanctus* . . .'.[311] Such worship was both a public profession of faith and an inward thanksgiving, comparable to the celebrations of the children of Israel in Deuteronomy 26, when they acknowledged the promised land before the priest. It must be remembered, however, that both of these statements referred not to the regular performance of morning and evening prayer, but to worship in the context of the Lord's Supper. In the Sacrament the congregation played its most significant part, and this deserves separate consideration.

The body of Christ: the Sacrament and the congregation

The part played by congregation members in the celebration of the Lord's Supper was more than that of passive recipients, since their presence and participation was a vital component of the Sacrament. Protestants were concerned that the celebration of the Lord's Supper should fall neither into the trap of excessive devotion nor into a contempt for a 'bare sign'.[312] So concerned was he that people were ignorant of its importance to their spiritual welfare that Latimer risked mocking the doctrine of obedience:

> If there were a proclamation made in this town that whosoever would come unto the church at such an hour, and there go to the communion with the curate, should have a testoon; when such a proclamation were made I think, truly, all the town would come and celebrate the communion to get a testoon: but they will not come to receive the body and blood of Christ, the food and nourishment of their souls, to the augmentation and strength of their faith![313]

The aim of many tracts on the Lord's Supper was thus not only to differentiate it from the Mass, but to show how necessary it was to spiritual welfare and how vital a part was played by the congregation.[314]

The presence of the congregation was necessary in the Sacrament to reenact the role of the disciples, as in the Last Supper. As Hooper put it:

> The best manner and most godly way to celebrate this supper is to preach the death of Christ unto the Church, and the redemption of man, as Christ did at his supper and there to have common prayers, as Christ prayed with his disciples; then to repeat the last words of the supper, and with the same to break the bread and distribute the wine unto the whole Church, then, giving thanks to God, depart in peace.[315]

The other major reason for emphasising the part played by the congregation was antagonism to private Masses. Turner, citing Luke 22 and 1 Cor. 11, concluded: 'Then doth not only bread and wine and the words of consecration said by a priest make the Supper of the Lord, except the remembrance of Christ's death and the presence of Christ's Church be annexed also thereunto.'[316] Allen further attacked private Masses on the grounds that communion required a congregation as a symbolic necessity.[317] 'For the Church was not ordained that one should be sundered and divided from another, but that we should all come together, and that if any were divided they should there be united and joined in one. And that is signified by the coming and assembling together.'[318]

Allen had defined sacraments as symbolic occasions integral to the functioning of the church:

> They are holy visible actions and exterior exercises instituted, ordained and appointed of almighty God to be used in his Church and congregation of the faithful, to represent unto them after a most lively sort his heavenly gracious benefits that they might thereby be confirmed in the faith and excited and stirred up to mutual love one toward another.[319]

Not only were sacraments seals and witnesses to strengthen faith and admonitions of Christian duty: they should be 'tokens' of separation from 'all other false sects', which would allow the congregation to 'show and declare by them their service, reverence and obedience toward God and so may provoke others also through their example unto the true religion and service of God'.[320]

A religion of the Word

Thus the Sacrament was not only a symbol of the uniqueness and faith of the church, but was essential to both the spiritual nourishment and growth of its members, and to its growth as a body both in faith and numbers. Cranmer described how the act of eating the bread and wine was paralleled by a process of spiritual nourishment and growth in the faith of the believer:

> But when such men for their more comfort and confirmation of eternal life, given unto them by Christ's death, come unto the Lord's holy table, then as before they fed spiritually upon Christ, so now they feed corporeally also upon the sacramental bread: by which sacramental feeding in Christ's promises, their former spiritual feeding is increased and they grow and wax continually more strong in Christ, until at the last they shall come to the full measure and perfection in Christ.[321]

As believers took the Sacrament they testified to their fellows in the congregation to their mutual membership of the body of Christ: 'And we eat Christ in this fashion as oft as we join the outward signs of bread and wine, that is to say, the sacrament of the Holy Communion with our faith and inward belief, receiving a visible testimony of our inward belief in the face of the congregation.'[322] Such a public statement required careful examination of the individual conscience prior to communion. If a person felt fleshly and lacking in faith, he should wait for grace:

> But if he perceive by his faith that he is knit wholly to Christ and that he is a lively member of him, let him then go forward and eat of this bread and drink of this cup to his most heavenly comfort. And let him say to himself on this wise when he goeth to receive the communion. I go now to make a solemn profession before God and his congregation of my faith, and to receive that comfortable sacrament and mystical pledge that Christ hath appointed.[323]

The experience was one not only of the strengthening of personal faith but of increasing charity and mutuality among the participants in the Supper. Cranmer argued that the experience of hearing of Christ's love for mankind in the context of a symbolic meal eaten with friends could not fail to increase charity:

> For we see by daily experience that eating and drinking together maketh friends, and continueth friendship; much more then ought the table of Christ to move us to do so. Wild beasts and birds be made gentle by giving them meat and drink: why then should not Christian men wax meek and gentle with this heavenly meat of Christ? Hereunto we be stirred and moved as well by the bread and wine in this holy supper, as by the words of the holy scripture recited in the same. Wherefore, whose heart soever this holy sacrament, communion and supper of Christ will not kindle with love unto his neighbours, and cause him to put out of his heart all envy, hatred and malice, and to grave in the same all amity, friendship and concord, he deceiveth himself if he think that he hath the spirit of Christ dwelling within him.[324]

Thomas Lancaster was even more lyrical in his praise of the mutuality celebrated in communion, especially among the godly:

> Oh what [a] glorious banquet is this wherein the hungry soul, the inward man receiveth that invisible bread and heavenly food which is Christ Jesus. O glorious congregation, wherein are no shameful songs nor unprofitable words, save only brotherly instruction and giving thanks to our saviour Jesus Christ. O glorious congregation, where no wanton eyes are casting here and there but all bent to the help and comfort of thy poor brethren. O gloricus congregation, where men use not to drink, dance or play, but where men are drunk in the wisdom of God, there shall the soul be joyful in the Holy Ghost, playing and dancing before the Lord.[325]

However, membership of this 'glorious congregation' entailed also responsibilities. Jean Veron insisted on perpetual mutual vigilance to ensure that the Communion presence was maintained among the godly, to see that their faith was 'lively' (Eph. 2; Gal. 5), especially by obedience, charity and fellowship. It was assumed that godliness entailed wearing a 'livery' of righteous behaviour that could be judged by one's fellows.[326]

Given the presence of Christ in the faithful, assured and nourished by frequent communion,[327] Cranmer envisaged the consolidation and growth of the reformation as taking place quietly and yet inexorably among the people. The Lord's Supper could not fail to attract potential converts, for 'Christ said that he that eateth me shall attain everlasting life':

> Wherefore whosoever doth not contemn the everlasting life, how can he but highly esteem this sacrament? How can he but embrace it as a sure pledge of his salvation? And when he seeth godly people devoutly receive the same, how can he but be desirous oftentimes to receive it with them? Surely no man that well understandeth and diligently weigheth these things, can be without a great desire to come to his holy supper.[328]

The Sacrament was assurance enough for the humble godly; its peaceful, unhindered repetition would in time transform the life of the church.

At the same time as witnessing to the growth of the church as a body of faithful people, the Sacrament witnessed to the church's corporate unity. Indeed, the organic unity of the church was symbolised by Christ's choice of bread and wine:[329] 'But in saying this is my body: he intended to declare unto his faithful disciples (and in them to us) the mystery of his Church and congregation, which is of many made one, even as the bread is of many grains and the wine of many grapes . . .'.[330] Christian unity transcended the bounds of the national church. As the Catechism put it:

> For God, throughout all coasts of the world hath them that worship him. Which though they be far scattered asunder, by diverse distance of countries,

and dominions, yet are their members most nearly joined of that same body whereof Christ is the head, and have one spirit, faith, sacraments, prayers, forgiveness of sins, and heavenly bliss common among them all, and be so knit with the body of love, that they endeavour themselves in nothing more than each to help the other, and to build together in Christ.[331]

The sacramental imagery of the body of Christ provided a weighty counterbalance to the atomising, centrifugal effects of protestant ideology. Neither novelty nor the need for obedience to an imposed order outweighed the need to present Christian unity as something with a positive organic value.[332] Nor was it simply a reaction to the recent division in Christendom, for there could be no unity with popery or with the sects.[333] Rather, it recognised the impact of religious change within local communities and congregations. As a 'religion of the Word', protestantism was prone to bring with it argument and division. While Latimer railed against the indifference that followed religious change,[334] his superiors saw contention as a far more worrying problem. The advent of English Bibles and translations of Erasmus's *Paraphrases* to the parishes in 1547 was accompanied by a stern warning to refrain from theological disputes; the minister should 'charitably exhort' and 'straightly charge and command' that 'in the reading thereof no man to reason or contend, but quietly to hear the reader'.[335]

The *Injunctions* represented an official anxiety about order, but in *The Homilies* that same fear of contention was presented as sorrow that the fabric of Christian unity was being destroyed. The author attacked in particular those who 'delight to propound certain questions, not so much pertaining to edification as to vainglory and ostentation' and whose arguments end in a fight. Religious questions were becoming an excuse for name-calling and faction – the author cited Paul's outrage at the division in the church of Corinth, and lamented:

> Oh how the Church is divided. Oh how the cities be cut and mangled. Oh how the coat of Christ, that was without seam, is all to-rent and torn. Oh body mystical of Christ, where is that holy and happy unity out of the which whosoever is, he is not in Christ? If one member be pulled from another, where is the body? If the body be drawn from the head, where is the life of the body?[336]

Thomas Lancaster, however, did not mourn so much as exhort his flock to unity:

> So may there be no strife nor debate in the congregation of God. They must all speak one thing, there must be no dissension among them having one heart, one soul, one mind and one meaning. There may be no strife in the faith, but in meekness of mind every man esteem other better than himself, to the praise of God and to the loving and faithful service of all the children of God.[337]

Was this thought control or charity in operation? Lancaster would have seen the two as part of the same phenomenon, that special unity which was found in godly congregations, which was the aim of the primitive church, and which Cranmer hoped would be the lasting achievement of the reformation of the Sacrament.

CONCLUSION

Discovering exactly what English protestants in the circumstances of Edward VI's reign meant by 'the church' is a somewhat tantalising process. On the one hand, it seemed that the only church of importance was the invisible body of Christ, a principle springing partly from the doctrine of predestination, but perhaps more, in this polemical context, from a revulsion to the oppressively worldly edifice of the popish church. On the other, protestants were faced with a visible national church that was clearly failing to fulfil the demands they made of it as an instrument of proselytising and edification. While the nature of worship had been transformed, and the clergy was no longer a priesthood, much of the institutional structure of the English church remained unreformed – corruption, pluralism and inadequate clerical training and finance still dogged it. Where the structure had changed, as in the expansion of lay patronage, things had clearly not improved; the world was still exploiting the church as it had done under popery, only this time the wolves were lay rather than ecclesiastical.

And yet, despite all this, protestants shrank from a wholesale reform of the church, to align its government with the theological imperatives of predestination. Not only would the practical implications of such an upheaval have been unnerving, especially in a situation where protestants were anxious to align themselves with order and stability, but it would have meant reconsidering the role of the prince and the supremacy, neither of which Edwardian protestants were prepared to question. Hence the uneven picture of the church that resulted, consisting of a very developed idea of the exalted role of the preaching ministry and a much less developed view of the nature of the Christian congregation, both of them held back by the practical inadequacies of incomplete reform.

However, this imbalance is partly rectified if the Christian commonwealth is considered. This was where the central problem of authority was faced, and where the workings of the body of Christ were displayed. True religion depended on right order if it was to flourish, and the godly prince was ultimately responsible for that order. Only he could wield the sword of temporal power against sin and popery, as directed by the preaching ministry. Revulsion to the idea of clerical hierarchy led to ample support for the social hierarchy of vocation, whose smooth working was the glory of the godly

A religion of the Word

commonwealth. Unlike popish clerical oppression, the 'godly order' functioned by balancing the obligations of obedience with justice and charity. These obligations were the sinews of the Christian body, binding it together and enabling it to act, transforming the rather static image that has emerged thus far.

NOTES

1. E.g. the vestments controversy between Hooper and Ridley, or the 'Black rubric' on kneeling to receive the Sacrament, which arose from Knox's opposition to Cranmer; see J. Primus, *The Vestments Controversy* (Kampen, 1960), chs 1–4; J. Opie, 'The anglicizing of John Hooper', *Archiv* (1968): 150–75; MacCulloch, *Cranmer*, 526–30. Cranmer protested that the authentic position in which to receive the communion would be reclining, which was clearly ridiculous, SP 10: 15, 15. This moderation did not prevent him upholding scriptural literalism against Gardiner; see Chapter 1 'Dichotomy', pp. 21–8.
2. E.g. Gerrard, *Godly invective*, sig. D3vo; Lynne, *The beginning and ending of all popery*, 4; see also E. Hageman, 'John Foxe's Henry VIII as "Justicia"', *SCJ* (1979): 35–42; King, *English Reformation Literature*, 188–95.
3. See Chapter 1, 'Dichotomy' pp. 21–8. Dickens, *The English Reformation*, 183–96, emphasises the centrality of the Bible to the establishment of an 'Anglican' tradition, using evidence mainly from Foxe.
4. Compare Cranmer, *Defence*, PS1 254; with Hooper, *Answer to Gardiner*, PS1 164.
5. Cranmer, *Defence*, PS1 30; cf. 'the sword proceeding from Christ's mouth', Bale, *Image*, PS 557.
6. Cf. 'Faith is not a light opinion grounded upon man, but a firm persuasion and constant assurance stablished in the scripture, Heb. ix', Hooper, *Answer*, PS1 221.
7. Nicholls, *Copy of a letter*, sigs B1, C7–D3; Gerrard, *Invective*, sig. B2vo.
8. Bale, *Image*, PS 546, but also it closes heaven to the unfaithful, *ibid.*, 389–90. See below, n. 247 on predestination.
9. John Hooper, *A declaration of Christ and his office* (Zurich, 1547), PS1 95; cf. Hooper, *Answer*, PS1 110–11.
10. Bale, *Image*, PS 376.
11. Moses insists that none should be exempted from obedience to the law: Gilby, *Answer*, sigs Bb8–vo.
12. Hooper, *Answer*, PS1 214; the Christian soldiers/militia attack the stronghold of the Whore, preparing themselves by godly living: Kethe *'Tie thy mare, Tom boy'*, 3–5; Christian citizenship is described in Turner, *Examination of the Mass* (1548), sigs A2–A2vo.
13. Thomas Cranmer, 'A fruitful exhortation to the reading and knowledge of holy Scripture', *Homilies* (1547; repr. 1549), sig. B1vo; cf. his Preface to the *Great Bible*, PS2 120.
14. Ramsey, *A plaster for a galled horse*, sig. B8.
15. Bale, *Image*, PS 600.
16. *Ibid.*; cf. Hooper, *Answer*, PS1 138–9.
17. Anon., *The upcheering of the Mass*.
18. Mark 16:15; Matt. 28:19.
19. Hugh Latimer, *Second lenten sermon preached before Edward VI* (1549), PS1 123; Latimer, *Sixth lenten Court sermon*, PS1 200; *On the parable of a king that married his son*, in *Certain sermons preached in Lincolnshire* (1552), PS1 470.

20 See above, n. 3; Sources and methodology, n. 27.
21 See David Cressy, *Literacy and the Social Order: Reading and Writing in Tudor and Stuart England* (Cambridge, 1980), especially chs 1–3.
22 See Redman's opinion that justification by faith alone was correct but should not be 'taught the people, lest they be negligent to do good works': Anon., *A report of Master Doctor Redman's answers to questions propounded him before his death* (1551), sig. B3. Cf. Latimer on predestination, *Sermon for Septuagesima Sunday* (1552), PS2 204. see also Chapter 2 and below, 'The Christian body', pp. 122–7.
23 Hooper, *Answer*, PS1 205–6. The analogy between the efficacy of the Word and that of the Sacrament is not an exact one, but Hooper's Zwinglian sacramental theology helps to explain it.
24 Crowley, *A confutation of Shaxton's articles*, sigs K4vo–K5.
25 Hugh Latimer, *Sermon preached at Stamford* (1550), PS1 306; cf. God saves 'through the foolishness of preaching...', Latimer, *On the parable of the king that married his son (Lincolnshire sermons)*, PS1 471.
26 The bishop was angry that the bells lacked clappers so that his arrival in the town could not be announced by ringing, but failed to notice that the pulpit had lacked preachers for over twenty years: Latimer, *Sixth lenten Court sermon*, PS1 207.
27 Ibid., 201–2; *Second lenten Court sermon*, PS1 121.
28 See Chapter 5, 'Judgement', pp. 187–93.
29 Hugh Latimer, *A most faithful sermon preached before the king...* (1550), PS1 240. Latimer used Nineveh in conscious reference to Hooper's sermons during that Lent; see also Thomas Lever, *Sermon preached the third Sunday in Lent* (1550), sig. C6.
30 John Hooper, *Jonah* (seventh sermon), PS1 558.
31 See below, 'The Congregation and public worship', pp. 118–19.
32 Latimer, *On Christmas Day* and *On St Stephen's Day*, PS2 92 and 107 (Lincolnshire sermons).
33 Hooper, *Answer*, PS1 178.
34 Latimer, *Second lenten Court sermon*, PS1 121–2; cf. inattentiveness to his own preaching at court: *Sixth lenten Court sermon*, PS1 203–4.
35 Hooper, *Answer*, PS1 103–4.
36 Hooper, *Jonah* (seventh sermon), PS1 548–9.
37 Anthony Gilby, *A commentary upon the prophet Micah* (1551), sig. E3vo.
38 Latimer, *Third lenten Court sermon*, Christ: PS1 134; Isaiah: PS1 137; Elijah: *A most faithful sermon*, PS1 249–50.
39 Latimer, *Fourth lenten Court sermon*, PS1 155.
40 Hooper, *Jonah* (seventh sermon), PS1 558.
41 'Exercise and diligence bringeth credit unto religion, whether it be true or false...': John Hooper, *A godly confession and protestation of the Christian faith*, PS2 79–80.
42 Anne Hooper expressed her concern that Hooper was seriously overworking: *Original letters*, Letter 49, Anne Hooper to Henry Bullinger, 3 April 1551, PS 108.
43 Titus 1:9; e.g. Latimer, *Third lenten Court sermon*, PS1 129.
44 See below 'The good shepherd', pp. 94–106.
45 Hugh Latimer, *Sermon on the plough* (1548), PS1 59. The first three sermons in this series are not extant; their subject was true doctrine – 'the seed' – and might well have clarified Latimer's ideas on the Sacrament.
46 Bale, *Rank papist*, sig. T6vo; cf. Nicholas Lesse, *The justification of man by faith only*, tr. Melanchthon (1550), sig. A5; Hooper, *on Jonah* (fourth sermon), PS1 501.
47 Latimer, *Third lenten Court sermon*, PS1 129–31.
48 Ibid., PS1 130.

A religion of the Word

49 Cranmer, Preface to *Defence*, PS1 6.
50 Bale, *Image*, PS 456–7.
51 Hutchinson, *Image of God*, PS 201–2.
52 Hooper, *Answer*, PS1 184; cf. Robert Crowley, *The opening of the words of the prophet Joel* (1546; printed 1567), sigs C5–E2: Crowley used an extended metaphor of sheep diseases to describe the effect on society of the years of 'hireling shepherds'.
53 Latimer, *On the parable of a king that married his son*, in (*Lincolnshire sermons*), PS1 456.
54 John Hooper, *Godly and most necessary annotations in the thirteenth chapter to the Romans* (Worcester, 1551), PS2 113.
55 John Hooper, *A declaration of the ten holy commandments of almighty God* (Zurich, 1548; London, 1550), PS1 280.
56 Hugh Latimer, *Second sermon on the Lord's Prayer* (1552), PS1 341; cf. Gilby, *Answer*, sigs. F7vo–F8.
57 Latimer, *First lenten Court sermon*, PS1 87.
58 Bale, *Image*, PS 553.
59 *Original letters*, Letter 38, Hooper to Bullinger, 5 February 1550, PS 75.
60 Latimer, *A most faithful sermon*, PS1 241.
61 *Ibid.*, 247.
62 Thomas Some, Dedication to the duchess of Suffolk of Latimer's *Sermons preached before Edward VI in Lent 1550*, PS1 111.
63 Bale, *Image*, PS 516, 547.
64 *Ibid.*, 458.
65 Latimer, *Sermon on the plough*, PS1 61–2.
66 Hutchinson, *Image of God*, PS 103–4.
67 Latimer, *Sermon on the plough*, PS1 72.
68 Latimer, *Second lenten Court sermon*, PS1 122 – but the king had to ensure that the bishops were not negligent in the visitation of their dioceses.
69 Latimer, *Fourth sermon on the Lord's Prayer*, PS1 381.
70 See Chapter 1, 'Inversion' pp. 28–34 and 'Delusion', pp. 41–7; Chapter 2.
71 Notably the marriage of priests, see below, ns 95, 96, 97 and Chapter 1, n. 131; also economic problems, see below, and F. Heal 'Economic problems of the clergy', in F. Heal and R. O'Day (eds) *Church and Society in England: Henry VIII to James 1* (1977).
72 Cf. the hostile reaction to the early Quakers' lack of a clergy.
73 Of the fifty-two named protestant authors in this study, 13 were ex-religious or ordained priests, 8 were ordained as ministers or were licensed preachers, of whom 6 were bishops. A further 10 were clergy, but it is not known when they were ordained; 6 were of unknown occupation. See Appendix for further details.
74 For the minister as the 'angel of the rising sun', see Bale, *Image*, PS 332; the 'seven angels', *ibid.*, 341; the 'angel warning of the Last Judgement', *ibid.*, 456–7; the 'seven stars', *ibid.*, 270; the 'two witnesses', *ibid.*, 388.
75 The ministers as 'candlesticks', *ibid.*, 388.
76 ?John Ponet, *A short Catechism or plain instruction* (1553), sig. H4.
77 For the ministers as 'treasurers of God's Word', see Latimer, *Lincolnshire sermons*, PS 461; as 'ambassadors', *Second sermon on the Lord's Prayer*, PS1 349. Latimer preferred to remain free to preach rather than be a bishop again; see A. Chester, *Hugh Latimer, Apostle to the English* (Philadelphia, PA, 1954).
78 Gerrard, *Godly invective*, sig. C6vo.
79 Ezekiel 33; see e.g. Gilby, *Answer*, sig. Cc3; Latimer, *Twenty-third Sunday after Trinity* (*Lincolnshire sermons*), PS1 524.

80 Hooper, *Annotations on Romans 13*, PS2 95; in *An homily to be read in time of pestilence* (Worcester, 1553), PS2 159, Hooper cites Ezekiel 33:8–9. Both these works were dedicated to the clergy of his diocese.
81 See above, 'Preaching and the preacher', pp. 88–93.
82 *Injunctions given by the king's majesty* (1547), item 8
83 On ungodly clergy, see John Foxe, *De censura* (1551), sigs A6–A6vo, D5vo; on godly clergy, see *ibid.*, sig. C8vo.
84 Robert Crowley, *Confutation of the mis-shapen answer* (1548), sig. D2vo.
85 See above; also Crowley, *Confutation of Shaxton's articles*, sig. G3.
86 Gilby, *Answer*, sig. B3vo; Anon., *Fall of the Romish church* (?1549), sig. C4; John Ponet, *Defence of the marriage of priests* (1549), sig. A2vo.
87 Hooper, *Jonah*, PS1 552; cf. Gilby, *Answer*, sig. I4; cites Mat. 10, total renunciation of apostles; also Latimer, *Sermon on the plough*, PS1, 66.
88 Foxe, *De censura*, sig. D1.
89 Bale, *Image*, PS 569; cf. *ibid.*, 388.
90 Robert Crowley, *The voice of the last trumpet, blown by the seventh angel* (1550), sig. B5vo.
91 Latimer, *On the Gospel for the third Sunday in Advent* (Lincolnshire sermons), PS2 83.
92 Gilby, *On Micah*, sig. D1.
93 Thomas Lever, *A sermon preached the third Sunday in Lent before the king's majesty and his honourable Council* (1550), sig. B6vo.
94 Micah 2:1–2.
95 Gilby, *On Micah*, sigs C8vo–D1. Parish, *Clerical Marriage*, 219–22, suggests that in reality, the position of married clergy tended to be economically insecure.
96 Robert Crowley, *The way to wealth* (1550), sig. A8vo; cf. 1 Tim. 3.
97 Latimer, *Sixth sermon on the Lord's Prayer*, PS1 416.
98 Hooper, *Homily on the pestilence*, PS2 168.
99 Cf. the detailed disciplinary procedures set up by the Stranger churches, described in John à Lasco, *Toute la forme et manière du ministère ecclesiastique* (Emden, 1556) 221vo–243vo.
100 *Articles agreed upon in the convocation and published by the king's majesty* (1553), in *The two liturgies . . . of Edward VI*, PS 533: article 27. See also Spalding, *The Reformation of the Ecclesiastical Laws of England, 1552* (Kirksville, MO, 1992).
101 I.e. taught the law of God.
102 Hutchinson, *Image of God*, PS 97.
103 Latimer, *Stamford sermon* (1550), PS1 304–5.
104 Latimer, *First Sunday after Epiphany* (Lincolnshire sermons), PS2 156–7; see also below, 'The Congregation and public worship', pp. 118–22.
105 Crowley, *The way to wealth*, sig. B2.
106 See above, Sources and methodology, n. 21
107 Phillip Nichols, *A Godly new story of twelve men . . . sent to spy out the land of Canaan* (1548), sigs G1–G1vo. Cf. John Champney's challenge to the clergy cited in Chapter 2, n. 34; contrast with the official *Copy of a letter sent to all those preachers which the king's majesty hath licensed to preach* (1548), sigs A2–A3vo.
108 Robert Crowley, *An information and petition against the oppressors of the poor commons of this realm* (1548), sigs B4vo–B5. See also below, 'The need for further reformation', pp. 106–14.
109 Crowley, *Confutation of the mis-shapen answer*, sigs D1vo–D2; cf. 1 Cor. 12:27–8.
110 Thomas Lancaster, *The right and true understanding of the supper of the Lord* (1550), sig. D1vo. see below, 'The body of Christ', pp. 122–7.

111 Thomas Lever, *A sermon preached the third Sunday in Lent before the king's majesty* (1550), sigs A4–A4vo.
112 Latimer, *On the Gospel for St Andrew's Day* (Lincolnshire sermons), PS2 23–43; see Matthew 4:18–20, 2 Samuel 6:6–8, Numbers 25:6–9, Genesis 21.
113 Latimer, *Lincolnshire sermons*, PS2 38.
114 Royal *Injunctions*, items 2 and 10; see also *Letter to licensed preachers* (see n. 107).
115 *Liturgies*, PS 532: article 24. This does not specify exactly who should 'call' ministers; though we assume it refers to royal and episcopal authority, it does not rule out an active lay patronage, or even a presbyterian system.
116 Hooper, *Jonah* (third sermon), PS1 468.
117 See note 110.
118 Moone, *Short treatise*, sig. B3; Crowley, *Confutation of the mis-shapen answer*, sig. D2; Peter Pickering, *A mirror or glass for all spiritual ministers to behold themselves in* (1551), sigs A3–A4.
119 *Liturgies*, PS 82 (1549); cf. *ibid*., 274 (1552).
120 Confession was a much more important polemical issue in the early German reformation; see S. Ozment, *The Reformation in the cities: The Apeal of Protestantism to Sixteenth Century Germany and Switzerland* (New Haven, CT, 1975), 49–56.
121 Hooper, *Answer*, PS1 147; see John Bossy, *Christianity in the West, 1400–1700* (Oxford, 1985), 126–40, for an illuminating comparison between reformed 'discipline' and Tridentine spiritual direction.
122 Crowley thought that 'wounded consciences' needed an 'expert and learned physician', who would give them scriptural solace, rather than annual confession to 'such blind apothecaries as do neither know simple from compound nor medicine from poison', *Confutation of Shaxton's articles*, sigs H8–H8vo.
123 Anon., *Recantation of Jack Lent*, sig. A5vo.
124 Latimer, *Sixth sermon on the Lord's Prayer*, PS1 423; *The Epistle for the first Sunday in Advent* (Lincolnshire sermons), PS2 13.
125 Latimer, *The third Sunday after Epiphany*, in *ibid*., PS2 180.
126 On Christ rebuking the 'sons of thunder', see John Foxe, *De non plectendis morte adulteris* (1548), sig. C2; on his treatment of the adulteress, *ibid*., sig. B6vo; telling Peter to forgive seventy times seven, *ibid*., sig. B6vo.
127 On pastors as healers, *ibid*., sig. B5vo; as loving fathers, *ibid*., sig. A6.
128 *Ibid*., sig. B4vo.
129 For an attack on Foxe's testamentary theology, see George Joye, *A contrary to (a certain man's) consultation: that adulterers ought to be punished with death* (?1549), sigs C8vo–D3vo, E1vo–E3; Joye accuses Foxe of antinomianism and perfectionism, *ibid*., sigs E8, F5, F8vo; and popery, *ibid*., sigs C2vo, E8vo.
130 See Chapter 1, 'Repression', pp. 47–51.
131 Gilby, *Answer*, sigs I7vo–I8.
132 Hooper, *Answer*, PS1 142.
133 See Davies and Facey, 'A reformation dilemma', *JEH* (1988), and R. Houlbrooke, *Church Courts and the People during the English Reformation 1520–1570* (Oxford, 1979).
134 Latimer, *Fourth lenten Court sermon*, PS1 167–8.
135 Cranmer, *Defence*, PS1 350; cf. Hutchinson, *Image of God*, PS 50.
136 Turner, *A new dialogue*, sig. B6.
137 Latimer, *The Epistle for the twenty-first Sunday after Trinity* (Lincolnshire sermons), PS1 506; cf. *First lenten Court sermon*, PS1 86.
138 Perhaps the more important point was that the clergy were freed from the need to 'respect persons', unlike the laity.

139 Cranmer, *Defence*, PS1 350.
140 Thomas Becon, *The castle of comfort*, PS2 566.
141 Hutchinson, *Image of God*, PS 96.
142 Hooper, *Declaration of Christ*, PS 21–2; Hutchinson, *Image of God*, PS 100.
143 'There is no Church can be governed without this discipline, for whereas it is not, there we see no godliness at all, but carnal liberty and vicious life...': Hooper, *Answer*, PS1 183.
144 See Carlson, *Marriage*, 82–5. The perception among protestants of a disturbing increase in adultery and divorce was a more political one than perhaps it seems on first reading: partly perhaps an oblique reference to Henry VIII's matrimonial problems, partly a rebuke to aristocratic scandals, notably the divorce of William Parr, earl of Northampton. It raised the question of the enforcement of the Mosaic law, perhaps more than any other social issue; the failure of Cranmer's reform of canon law halted developments here. Coverdale's translation of Henry Bullinger's *The Christian state of matrimony* (1543) ran to several editions. It influenced Thomas Becon's *Homily against whoredom and adultery*, and the controversy between Foxe and Joye on discipline; see R.B. Bond, '"Dark deeds darkly answered": Thomas Becon's *Homily against whoredom and adultery*, its contexts and its affiliations with three Shakespearean plays', *SCJ* (1985): 191–205; Davies and Facey, 'A reformation dilemma', 40–2. Hooper took a very radical line, insisting that 'innocent' women as well as men in a divorce case should be allowed to remarry: *Declaration of the ten commandments*, PS 374–87, cf. 269–70 (Preface to the 1550 edition). For sexual misconduct as a mirror of disorder and false religion, see Chapter 1, nn. 144–7, and the debate over clerical celibacy, *ibid.*, nn. 14, 131. Endemic syphilis was a new and predominantly urban disease. The stews had been officially closed down in 1546, but as Latimer pointed out, that just moved the problem elsewhere – *Third lenten Court sermon*, 133–4; see also M. Pelling, 'Appearance and reality: barber–surgeons, the body and disease', in A.L. Beier and R. Finlay, *London 1500–1700: The Making of the Metropolis* (1986). (I owe this reference to Dr Pauline Croft.) Brigden, *London and the Reformation* (Oxford and New York, 1989), 472 notes a rise in adultery cases in London at this time.
145 Joye, *A contrary*, sigs D2–D7, D8vo; Davies and Facey, 'A reformation dilemma', 37–50.
146 Foxe, *De non plectendis adulteris*, sig. B4vo.
147 Joye, *A contrary*, sig. A7
148 Foxe, *De censura*, sigs A6–A6vo.
149 *Ibid.*, sigs A2, D4–D5.
150 E.g. Latimer, *First lenten Court sermon*, PS1 85–6; cf. Davies and Facey, 'Reformation dilemma', 42–3.
151 Foxe, *De censura*, sig. E7vo.
152 E.g. Gilby, *Answer*, sig. I3vo; also 'To the bishops', *ibid.*, sigs Aa3–Aa5.
153 Hooper, *Jonah* (third sermon), PS1 479; see Primus, *Vestments controversy*, ch. 1.
154 See F.D. Price, 'Gloucester diocese under Bishop Hooper', *Transactions of Bristol and Gloucestershire Archaeological Society* (1938): 51–151, and S. Thompson, 'The pastoral work of the English and Welsh bishops, 1500–58', unpublished DPhil thesis, Oxford University (1984), 171.
155 Cf. Gilby, *Answer*, sig. B6vo; George Joye, *The refutation of the bishop of Winchester's dark declaration of his false articles* (1546), sigs B1–B3. Gardiner was a convenient scapegoat for government policy in the mid-1540s; see Redworth, *In Defence of the Church Catholic: The Life of Stephen Gardiner* (Oxford, 1990).
156 Joye, *Refutation*, sigs E7–7vo.
157 Gilby, *Answer*, sig. Y8vo.

158 Ibid., sigs R3vo–R4.
159 Hooper, *Declaration of Christ*, PS 19, citing 'all the books of Moses and the prophets', Christ's command to Peter (John 21) and Paul's commands in Acts 20.
160 Hooper, *Answer*, PS1 143–5.
161 Ibid., 146.
162 Joye, *Refutation*, sig. M4vo.
163 See below 'The need for further reformation', pp. 106–14. See also F. Heal, *Of Prelates and Princes: A Study of the Economic and Social Position of the Tudor Episcopate* (Cambridge, 1980), chs 7–8.
164 Crowley, *Voice of the last trumpet*, sig. B5vo.
165 Lever, *Sermon preached at Court*, sigs D5–D6.
166 See J. Ridley, *Nicholas Ridley. A Biography* (1957), 285–8; for a general survey of episcopal charity and bequests, see Thompson, 'Pastoral work', 192–220.
167 Hooper, *Declaration of the ten commandments*, PS1 398.
168 E.g. Latimer, *Sermon on the plough*, PS1 67–8.
169 Ibid., 68.
170 Crowley, *Voice of the last trumpet*, sig. B6.
171 Hooper, *Jonah (fifth sermon)*, PS1 507.
172 Price, 'Gloucester diocese', 51–151.
173 See J. Simon, *Education and Society in Tudor England* (Cambridge, 1979), ch. 2; cf. Malcom Underwood, 'John Fisher and the promotion of learning', in B. Bradshaw and E. Duffy (eds) *Humanism, Reform and the Reformation: The Career of Bishop John Fisher* (Cambridge, 1989).
174 Ibid., part II.
175 Latimer, *Fifth lenten Court sermon*, PS1 179, and *Sixth lenten Court sermon*, PS1 203; cf. Thomas Ruddoke, *A remembrance for the maintenance of the living of ministers* (1551), sigs B3–B3vo. See Simon, *Education and Society*, ch. 10; P. Carter, 'Clerical polemic in defence of ministers' maintenance during the English reformation', *JEH* (1998): 239–42, develops the debate about the distinction between the right to maintenance and the merits of the minister.
176 Latimer, *Fifth lenten Court sermon*, PS1 178–9; cf. Latimer, *A most faithful sermon*, PS1 269.
177 Ibid., 291.
178 Latimer, *Sixth sermon on the Lord's Prayer*, PS1 418.
179 Latimer, *Second sermon on the Lord's Prayer*, PS1 349.
180 Latimer, *Third sermon on the Lord's Prayer*, PS1 358.
181 Thomas Lever was educated at St John's and became its master in 1551.
182 Lever, *Sermon preached at Court*, sig. E1vo. The example he cited was Sedbergh school; for details see Simon, *Education and Society*, 228.
183 Thomas Lever, *Sermon preached at Paul's Cross* (1550), sigs E1vo–E2; see Jane Dawson, 'The foundation of Christ Church, Oxford and Trinity College, Cambridge in 1546', *BIHR* (1984): 208–15.
184 Lever, *Sermon preached at Paul's Cross*, sigs E2–3; for protestant 'new monastics', see Thomas Sampson's *Life of Bradford*, prefaced to the 1574 edition of two of his sermons, PS1 29–37; or Simon, *Education and Society*, 264, for Thomas Cartwright (matriculated at St John's in 1547).
185 Latimer, *Second lenten Court sermon*, PS1 123. For the employment of monks, see D Knowles, *The Religious Orders in England* (Cambridge, 1961), vol. 3: 402–17; and for chantry priests, see Simon, *Education and Society*, ch. 9.

186 Latimer, *Sermon preached at Stamford*, PS1 304; cf. *Epistle for the twenty-first Sunday after Trinity* (Lincolnshire sermons), PS1 503. Cf. Ruddoke, *A remembrance*, sig. C2vo. See also below, 'Good shepherd', pp. 94–100.
187 Hooper, *Declaration of the ten commandments*, PS1 326.
188 Hooper, *Godly confession*, PS2 90.
189 Ibid., 91.
190 See above, 'Protestant clericalism?', pp. 94–100.
191 Crowley, *Voice of the last trumpet*, sig. B2.
192 Ibid., B5–B5vo.
193 Latimer, *First lenten Court sermon*, PS1 101.
194 See above, and Introduction, 'Whatever happened to social conscience?' pp. 6–8.
195 See above, 'Protestant clericalism?', pp. 94–100.
196 Guest, *Treatise against the privy Mass*, sig. G5.
197 Ibid., sig. G5vo.
198 Robert Crowley, *An information and petition against the oppressors of the poor commons of this realm* (1548), sigs B4vo–B5. A Latin version of this tract was also published in 1548.
199 Latimer, *Sermon preached at Stamford*, PS1 303–4; cf. Ruddoke, *A remembrance*, sigs C1–C7 – he does not flinch from using the Levitical injunctions – also 1 Cor. 9.
200 Especially those who were themselves preachers – see above, n. 73.
201 Thomas Becon, *The flower of godly prayers*, PS3 37.
202 Thomas Becon, Preface, *The fortress of the faithful*, PS2 585–6.
203 Ibid., 587.
204 Latimer, *Fourth lenten Court sermon*, PS1 153.
205 Latimer, *Sermon on the plough*, PS1 62.
206 Latimer, *Third lenten Court sermon*, PS1 141.
207 Cf. Calvin's difficulties with instituting poor relief through deacons: W.G. Naphy 'Calvin and Geneva', in A. Pettegree (ed.) *The Reformation World* (2000), 314–15, 320.
208 Becon, *Jewel of joy*, PS2 432.
209 Robert Crowley, *Pleasure and pain* (1551), sig. B4.
210 Becon, Preface, *Fortress of the faithful*, PS2 590–1.
211 Cf. P. Carter, 'Clerical polemic in defence of ministers' maintenance during the English reformation', *JEH* (1998).
212 See Chapter 4, 'Social bonds', pp. 162–7; Chapter 5, 'Pretending the gospel', pp. 200–9.
213 Ruddoke, *A remembrance*, sig. B7vo.
214 Robert Crowley, *One-and-thirty epigrams* (1550), sig. A5.
215 Hooper, *Declaration of the ten commandments*, PS1 395. It is difficult to square the plunder of the church with a thriving pre-reformation piety: see J. Scarisbrick, *The Reformation and the English People* (Oxford, 1984), ch. 5, and Duffy, *The Stripping of the Altars* (compare Parts 1 and 2). Hence the problem of the 'compliance conundrum'.
216 Lever, *A fruitful sermon*, sig. B4vo.
217 Nichols, *A godly new story*, sigs E5–F2 – the reference is to Numbers 13–14.
218 See Chapter 5, 'Pretending the gospel', pp. 200–9.
219 Crowley, *Way to wealth*, sig. B5.
220 Cf. Lever, *Sermon preached at Court*, sigs C8–C8vo.
221 Latimer, *Sermon preached at Stamford*, PS1 290; cf. Hooper, *Jonah*, PS1 508.
222 Latimer, *On the Gospel for St Andrew's Day* (Lincolnshire sermons), PS2 28–9; cf. Lever, *Sermon preached at Paul's Cross*, sigs C3vo–C4.

A religion of the Word

223 Latimer, *On the Gospel for St Andrew's Day* (*Lincolnshire sermons*), PS2 28.
224 Latimer, *Sermon preached at Stamford*, PS1 290; cf. Richard Tracy, *A supplication to... Henry VIII* (Antwerp, 1544), sigs A8vo–B1; Robert Crowley, *Pleasure and pain, heaven and hell* (1551), sigs C2ff.
225 Latimer, *First sermon before Edward VI*, PS1 101.
226 Since profiting from impropriations was spiritual fornication, the profiteers should be destroyed, just as Phineas had killed the adulterers; Lever, *Sermon preached at Paul's Cross*, sig. E6; see Chapter 5, 'Pretending the gospel', pp. 200–9.
227 Lever, *Sermon preached at Paul's Cross*, sig. E7.
228 Anthony Gilby, *A commentary upon the prophet Micah* (1551), sig. A6vo.
229 Cf. Joshua 7:1–26, Deuteronomy 7:25–6.
230 Gilby, *On Micah*, sig. H3.
231 Hutchinson, *Image of God*, PS 203, citing Psalm 83:9–12.; see below, pp. 112ff. Chapter 5, 'Pretending the gospel', pp. 200–9.
232 See above, 'The ministry of the Word', pp. 88–94.
233 *Injunctions given by the king's majesty* (1547), sigs a4–a4vo.
234 Hutchinson, *Image of God*, PS 105.
235 Lever, *Sermon preached at Paul's Cross*, sigs D2–D2vo.
236 *Ibid.*, sig. D4vo.
237 Crowley, *Way to wealth*, sig. B1.
238 Lever, *Sermon preached at Court*, sig. D1vo.
239 Crowley, *One-and-thirty epigrams*, sigs C4–C4vo.
240 Lever, *A Fruitful sermon preached at St Paul's in the shrouds* (1550) sigs B5–B6.
241 Latimer, *Fourth lenten Court sermon*, PS1 154. See MacCulloch, *Tudor Church Militant*, 59.
242 Cf. Bale, *Image*, 510 – the resignations of Latimer and Shaxton.
243 Gilby, *On Micah*, sig. E8, citing 1 Kings 22.
244 *Ibid.*, sigs F3–F3vo; cf. Ruddoke, *A remembrance*, sigs B1–B1vo, for the influence of patrons over their ministers, quoting Isaiah 30:59. For conflicting pressures on a noble chaplain, see *Original letters*, Letter 130, James Haddon to Henry Bullinger, August 1552, PS 281–8.
245 The 'visible church' is a somewhat anachronistic term, used here for the purposes of clarity. This was a later development in England, a feature of the conformist–puritan rather than the catholic–protestant debate: see P. Lake, *Anglican and Puritan? Presbyterianism and English Conformist Thought from Whitgift to Hooker* (1988); and below n. 278.
246 See Chapter 2.
247 See Chapter 1, 'Dichotomy', pp. 21–8; Davies, 'Poor persecuted little flock...', 79–87. Edwardian protestants were predestinarian but it was not the key issue that it later became; see R.T. Kendall, *Calvin and English Calvinism to 1649* (Oxford, 1979). The problems it posed were a matter of pastoral concern (see above, n. 22), and the case of Spiera who died despairing of his salvation was referred to by Latimer and Martyr. Ochino published twenty-five sermons about it. It was debated with catholics (Joye, *Refutation of Gardiner* (1546), xlviii.vo–li; Crowley, *Confutation of Shaxton's articles*, sigs I1–K8) and radicals – see Chapter 2, n. 14. Bartholemew Traheron was concerned that Bullinger did not agree with Calvin on the problem (*Original letters*, PS 324–7). Hooper's Preface to the *Declaration of the ten commandments* has been read as evidence of his 'Arminian' approach, but this is anachronistic – he was more concerned with the convenant than with predestination here (PS1 255–68).
248 Bale, *Image*, PS 570.

249 *Ibid.*, 567–9.
250 Hooper, *Answer*, PS1 131; cf. Latimer – 'all within the ship of Christ's Church saved', *Fourth Sunday after Epiphany* (*Lincolnshire sermons*), PS2 182.
251 Jean Veron, *Certain little treatises... for the erudition and learning of the simple and ignorant people* (1548), sigs B6vo–B7.
252 *Ibid.*, Christ the head, the immaculate spouse: Ephesians 4:15–6, 5:23–32; the body of Christ: 1 Corinthians 12:12–28; the holy city, the new Jerusalem: Isaiah 60.
253 *Ibid.*, sig. B8.
254 See above, 'Reformation by the Word', pp. 87–8 and chapter 1, 'Dichotomy', pp. 21–8.
255 Veron, *Certain little treatises*, sigs C3–C3vo.
256 *Ibid.*, sig. C8. See above, 'Preaching and the preacher', pp. 88–94.
257 Cranmer, *Answer to Smith's preface*, PS1 377.
258 *Ibid.*, 377–8.
259 Hooper, *Declaration of Christ*, PS1 29–30.
260 Especially after the revision of the first *Prayer Book*, as part of the drive to consolidate the reform of the church.
261 *Liturgies*, article 20, PS 531.
262 *Ibid.*
263 Ponet, *A short catechism*, sigs G1vo–G3.
264 *Ibid.* For problems caused by the earlier Catechism (a translation of Justus Jonas) see MacCulloch, *Cranmer*, 386–92.
265 Hooper, *Godly confession*, PS2 87; cf. Hooper, *Declaration of Christ*, PS1 81–2: church not defined by apostolic succession or human traditions.
266 For reasons noted above; see 'Good shepherd', pp. 94–106 and Chapter 5, 'Godly magistrate', pp. 146–58. See also Spalding, *Reformation of Ecclesiastical Laws*.
267 Latimer, *Sermon preached at Stamford*, PS1 285.
268 Latimer, *Sexagesima Sunday* (*Lincolnshire sermons*), PS2 210–15.
269 Foxe, *De censura*, ch. 8.
270 Joye, *A contrary*, sig. E3vo.
271 Cranmer, *Answer*, 71.
272 'E.T.', *Here beginneth a song of the Lord's Supper* (1550), sig. B3; 'E.T.' also believed in the excommunication of notorious sinners. See also Davies, 'Poor persecuted little flock...', 91–2.
273 See above, 'The ministry of the Word', pp. 88–94.
274 For Tyndale's translation of *ecclesia*, see A. Ferguson, *Clio Unbound: Perception of the Social and Cultural Past in Renaissance England* (Durham, NC, 1979). 154.
275 For the preface to the 1549 *Prayer Book*, see *Liturgies*, PS 17–9; for 1552 Preface, *ibid.*, 193–9. Divine Service was principally a vehicle for the reading of the whole Bible for the edification both of clergy and laity; the variety and complexity of the old services and the use of Latin prevented this. There is no defence of the necessity or efficacy of corporate prayer and worship – it seems to be taken for granted, nor is there an attack on extempore prayer, which seems to have been a development of later puritanism; both of these emerged in late Elizabethan–Jacobean debates. See especially Hooker, cited in Lake, *Anglican and Puritan?*, 169–73, and J. Booty, 'Communion and commonweal: the Book of Common Prayer', in Booty (ed.) *Godly Kingdom*, 139–219.
276 Which raised a range of issues – see end of this section.
277 *Liturgies*, article 35, PS 535–6.
278 E.g. The description of how the Lord's Supper should be received in Hooper, *Jonah* (*sixth sermon*), PS1 535–7. There was not much discussion of a presbyterian system:

see Edmund Allen, *A Catechism, that is to say a Christian instruction*, 2nd edn (1551), sigs L8–M3; also above, 'Clerical powers', pp. 100–6. Cf. Patrick Collinson, *The Elizabethan Puritan Movement* (1967), 101–8.
279 See John Cheke, *The hurt of sedition* (1549), sig. A6; also Chapter 4, Introduction, pp. 140–6.
280 Cf. John Bossy, 'The Mass as a social institution', *P&P* 100 (1983): 29–61; E. Mason, 'The role of the English parishioner, 1100–1500', *JEH* (1976): 17–29.
281 See Chapter 4 – Introduction, pp. 140–6.
282 (?)Ponet, *Short Catechism*, sig. G7.
283 Hooper, *Declaration of Christ*, PS1 95.
284 Latimer, *Sixth lenten Court sermon*, PS1 199–200: Christ the carrion and the eagles.
285 Hooper, *Answer*, PS1 178.
286 Guest, *Treatise against the privy Mass*, sig. H2; Daniel 6:10.
287 Gilby, *On Micah*, sigs L8vo, M3vo.
288 (?)Ponet, *Short Catechism*, sig. K4.
289 'But it is the office of every man to know the manner of speech in the Scripture, and to judge according to the meaning of the words, and not as they sound only...' Hooper, *Answer*, PS1 210.
290 Hooper, *Godly confession*, PS2 92: the duty of 'due labour' both in daily prayer and work. Cf. S. Brigden, 'Religion and social obligation', *P&P* (1984).
291 Becon, *Jewel of joy*, PS2 418.
292 For the religious responsibilities of the head of the household, see R. Houlbrook, *The English Family, 1450–1700* (1984), 111–14, 167–71.
293 Latimer, *Fifth sermon on the Lord's Prayer*, PS1 391–2.
294 See Tudor, 'English devotional literature', 217–20; M. Todd, 'Humanists, puritans and the spiritualised household', *CH* (1980): 18–34.
295 Hooper, *Declaration of Christ*, PS1 32–3.
296 Latimer, *On the parable of a king that married his son (Lincolnshire sermons)*, PS1 471.
297 *Injunctions*, sig. C1vo.
298 Hooper, *Declaration of the ten commandments*, PS1 341.
299 Hutchinson, *Image of God*, PS 42–4; Hooper, *Declaration of the ten commandments*, PS1 338–41.
300 Latimer, *Lincolnshire sermons*, PS2 156.
301 Allen, *A Catechism*, sig. C3vo.
302 Ibid., sig. C4.
303 Ibid., sig. C6vo.
304 Latimer, *Seventh sermon on the Lord's Prayer*, PS1 445.
305 Latimer, *First sermon on the Lord's Prayer*, PS1 328–9.
306 This could be a problem of survival, as a reference to a past sermon on the diversity of public (common) and private prayer (preached in 1551?) seems to indicate (ibid., 326).
307 Ponet, *Short Catechism*, sig. H6vo.
308 For changing uses of the Catechism, see P. Tudor, 'Religious instruction for children and adolescents in the early English reformation', *JEH* (1984): 391–413.
309 See above, 'Preaching and the preacher', pp. 88–94. also below.
310 Gilby, *Answer*, sigs R3vo–R4.
311 Ibid., sig. R4vo.
312 E.g. Veron, *Godly sayings*, sig. A6vo.
313 Latimer, *On the parable of a king that married his son (Lincolnshire sermons)*, PS1 459.
314 Especially Guest, *Treatise against the privy Mass*; Ponet, *A notable sermon*; Lancaster, *The right and true understanding*; 'E.T.', *Song of the Lord's Supper*.

315 Hooper, *Declaration of Christ*, PS 61.
316 Turner, *A new dialogue*, sig. C5.
317 Cites Chrysostom on 1 Cor. 11.
318 Allen, *Catechism*, sig. K5vo.
319 *Ibid.*, sig. I5vo.
320 *Ibid.*, sig. I6vo.
321 Cranmer, *Answer*, PS1 71; cf. E.T., *Song of Lord's Supper*, sigs A4vo–B1.
322 John Ponet, *A notable sermon concerning the right use of the Lord's Supper* (1550) sigs C7–C7vo.
323 *Ibid.*, sigs D1–D1vo.
324 Cranmer, *Defence*, PS1 42–3.
325 Lancaster, *Right and true understanding*, sigs C8vo–D1.
326 Veron, Epilogue, *Godly sayings*, sigs G4vo–G5.
327 Cranmer, *Defence*, PS1 42–4.
328 *Ibid.*
329 Crowley, *Confutation of the mis-shapen answer*, sig. D4.
330 Augustine's interpretation of the 'bread of many grains' was heavily quoted; see *ibid.*, sigs C7, A2vo, B5; cf. Veron, *Godly sayings*, sig. C3; Mardely, *Power of God's word*, sig. B7vo. Presumably unknown to these writers, Cyprian used it first, though it derives from Paul. Thanks to Prof. Diarmaid MacCulloch for pointing this out.
331 Ponet, *Short Catechism*, sig. G5–vo.
332 See Chapter 4, Introduction, pp. 140–6.
333 See Chapter 1, n. 37.
334 See above, nn. 300, 313.
335 *Injunctions*, sig. B1; cf. stress on suppression of dissent during a time of changing policy on worship, in parts 7, 19, 23, 25, 27, 33.
336 *Homilies*, 'Against contention and brawling', sig. Y3; cf. Veron, *Godly sayings*, sigs A8–A8vo and Cranmer, homily *Of salvation*, sig. E3vo.
337 Lancaster, *Right and true understanding*, sig. C3vo, citing 1 Cor. 1, Phil. 2.

Chapter 4

The godly commonwealth

INTRODUCTION: MODELS OF ORDER IN THE COMMONWEALTH

True order was the corollary of true religion: the one could not exist without the other. The traditional models of society were those of the cosmos, the family and the body, the latter two microcosms of the first, and these models dominated the subject. Protestants were not original in this respect, nor did belief in salvation by faith alone mean that they were socially egalitarian. However, they did stress the interdependence and mutuality involved in maintaining the 'true' order in society.[1] The homily *Of obedience* set out their idea of the cosmological hierarchy clearly, and it is worth quoting at length:

> Almighty God hath created and appointed all things, in heaven and earth, and waters, in a most excellent and perfect order. In heaven he hath appointed distinct orders and states of archangels and angels. In earth he hath assigned kings, princes, with other governors under them all in good and necessary order. The water above is kept and raineth down in due time and season. The sun, moon, stars, rainbow, thunder, lightning, clouds and all birds of the air, do keep their order. The earth, trees, seeds, plants, herbs, corn, grass, and all manner of beasts, keep them in their order. All the parts of the whole year, as winter, summer, months, nights and days continue in their order. All kinds of fishes in the sea, rivers and waters, with all fountains, springs, yea the seas themselves, keep their comely course and order. And man himself also, hath all his parts, both within and without, as soul, heart, mind, memory, understanding, reason, speech, with all and singular corporal members of his body in a profitable, necessary and pleasant order. Every degree of people in their vocation, calling and office, hath appointed to them their duty and order.[2]

The careful layering of this text shows how firmly the political[3] and social[4] orders were embedded within the natural order, whose consistent functioning and pattern were a perennial lesson to mankind of the necessity of obedience to God[5]. Disruption of order in the state thus had cosmological and theological repercussions.

There was nothing new in this, but that was the point. It was essential to a regime that changed so much to present itself as defending the created order.[6] For the danger of disorder was ever present, in the shape of papal power, as the supremacist rhetoric of the homily showed: 'For where there is no right order there reigneth all abuse, carnal liberty, enormity, sin, and Babylonical confusion.'[7] The thunder of the Henrician conservatives, that their defence of the Mass was a defence of true order, was stolen by the protestants, in the context of a reforming government.[8]

However, many protestants preferred the intimacy of analogies for order that were less than cosmic in scale. Bale, dedicating the second edition of *The acts of the English votaries* to Edward VI, described the office of the king as patriarchal, founded by God the Father, 'which had an everlasting monarchy before the world's constitution, and on the earth by his special gift it took success in man'.[9] Hooper described the fifth commandment (Honour thy father and mother) as the foundation of government. It began the second table of the law, which 'prescribed how, and by what means, one man may live with one another in peace and unity in this civil life . . .'.[10] The king was to the commonwealth as the father of a family: that is, the representative of God in nourishing virtue and true religion, and punishing vice.[11] As in the patriarchal family, the monarchy should bind the commonwealth together in love:[12] 'the best life of obedient subjects is one to behave himself to another, as though they were brethren under the king their father'.[13] But a subject's deference to his social superiors and the harmony he enjoyed with his neighbours were not the only lessons of patriarchy.[14] It could also be used to preach social responsibility to magistrates: the sins of oppression committed by the powerful against their 'children' were a particularly unnatural outrage.[15]

The next stage down in the microcosm, the image of the body, allowed more emphasis on the functioning of the constituent parts of the commonwealth. Not only the church but the commonwealth itself was analogous to the body of Christ, each member playing his allotted part to the greater glory of the head who was Christ.[16] The fact that the body analogy applied to both church and commonwealth allowed the boundaries between them to be blurred or overridden. The Christian magistrate was responsible for seeing that the body was nourished with the Word and with justice.[17] These should make it function harmoniously, accepting the inherent inequalities that existed between the parts. Anticipating the argument that the example of the primitive church, where all was held in common, should impel the reformers to demand the levelling of social distinctions, Lever replied with Paul's own antiegalitarianism: 'And they that would have like quantity of everything to be given to every man intending thereby to make all alike do utterly destroy the congregation, the mystical body of Christ, whereas there must needs be divers members in divers places, having divers duties.'[18] Thomas Lancaster exhorted the congregation to 'let love be among you without dissimulation, and every man abide in the same state wherein he is called, no other wise than to the edifying of the body of Christ, which is his congregation'.[19] There was a degree of evenhandedness about the insistence that the body of Christ should be edified and not destroyed, either by levelling radicalism or by individual ambition.[20] Social mobility was regarded as destructive, so that the only way in which the body could grow was through charity. Thus Lever, in the same sermon in which he denounced 'communism', also declared that toleration of too wide a disparity between rich and poor was a mockery of the body of Christ. It was unseemly for the upper part of the body to be clad in silks and velvets while the lower parts were scantily clothed in rags.[21]

The harmonious functioning of the Christian body was dependent upon the health of its individual parts. This accounted for the preoccupation with vocation and duty in protestant propaganda.[22] The litany of social groups, professions, trades and members of households, recurred with almost monotonous frequency in both devotional and homiletic literature.[23] Crowley's *Voice of the last trumpet*, a collection of verses 'calling all estates of men to the right path of their vocation ... which if they learn and follow, all shall be well and nothing amiss', exemplified the theme.[24] The title gave this theme a new urgency – the imminence of the last judgement should intensify personal efforts to ensure social well-being, while the righting of social iniquity could safely be left to the judgement of God.[25] Sanctification could thus be achieved not only by dramatic witness, in extreme circumstances, but by daily striving to fulfil the prayer that 'every man in his vocation may do the work whereunto God hath called him'.[26] The submission of all vocations to the service and glory of God would channel the energy of ambition and discontent into the formation of a Christian society.[27]

However, the cosmic and organic analogies for true order were only part of the story. While the metaphors of the body and the family may have served to illustrate the general functioning of society, they were less useful tools for discussion of political questions about the nature of nationhood and kingship. For instruction in these matters, protestants turned to the Old Testament.[28] The ambiguity inherent in the choice of Israel as a model reflected the preoccupations of the preachers. Both England and Israel had been 'chosen' by God to receive his special favour, but both nations constantly strayed from the path of righteousness required by the covenant.[29] Within both nations the nature of royal leadership was crucial to the strength of the covenant. The prophets had to remind them of this fact, so protestants seized the opportunity of the royal minority to set out their ideal of biblical kingship.

The godly commonwealth

The ultimate model of godly magistracy of course was Moses,[30] who had delivered the children of Israel from the bondage of Egypt and who took the final decision in matters of worship, overriding the authority of Aaron.[31] According to Hooper, the foundation of Israel itself prescribed the order of precedence in the state: first came God as manifested in his Word and the celestial signs of the pillars of fire and cloud, which gave visible proof to the Israelites of God's care for them; then came Moses, supreme commander and prince under God; then Aaron and the priests; the inferior magistrates; and finally the children of Israel. Moses's solution of the dispute over the celebration of Pesah was used by Hooper to advocate a solution which pointed to the royal supremacy.

> This declareth that no general council, no provincial assembly, no bishops of any realm or province may charge the subjects thereof with any law or ceremony, otherwise than the prince of the land by the word of God can give account to be good and godly. For the people are committed unto the prince to sustain the right of them all, and not only to defend their bodies but also their souls ...[32]

Archetypal godly magistrate though he undoubtedly was, Moses was not a king, and this limited his usefulness in the discussion of kingship.[33] More seriously, the institution of kingship showed how the Israelites' lack of faith caused a deterioration in the polity of Israel. In contrast to Reginald Pole's use of this evidence to cast doubt on kingship, Latimer used it against the Israelites' faithlessness:

> They would have a king of their own swing, and of their own election, as though they passed not of God. In another point there was pride; they would be like the heathen, and judged under kings as they were. Thirdly, they offended God because they asked a king to the injury and wrong of good father Samuel, to depose him; so this was a wrong towards Samuel.[34]

A monarchy was instituted in Israel because of the anarchy prevailing in the final years of the Judges, a situation which was paralleled in England when the king failed to 'have all [e]states set in order to do their office'.[35] God, not the Israelites, set the terms of their monarchy: 'their king should be such a one as he himself would choose them'.[36] The covenant had to be safeguarded from the waywardness of the Israelites.

God's 'conditions' of kingship, as set out in Deuteronomy 17, applied to all kings. In Edward VI, England had a monarch who fitted these requirements in some respects (i.e. nationality, legitimacy), but who was too young to receive anything but exhortation to conform in the future to others (i.e. marriage, governing).[37] The first condition was that the king should not be a foreigner. This was vital to preserve the covenant, to prevent an inevitable change of religion. Latimer placed heavy emphasis on the need for loyalty to

143

A religion of the Word

Edward, who fulfilled this first condition by being 'our own brother, both by nativity and godly religion'.[38] Such loyalty was especially necessary when the succession was indirect:

> Oh what a plague were it, that a strange king, of a strange land, and of a strange religion, should reign over us! Where now we be governed in the true religion, he should extirpate and pluck away altogether; and then plant again all abomination and popery. God keep such a king from us! Well, the King's Grace hath sisters, my lady Mary and my lady Elizabeth, which by succession and course are inheritors to the crown, who if they should marry with strangers, what should ensue?[39]

The only chance of averting this disaster would be for the people to 'repent and amend', thus demonstrating their loyalty to the king and 'true religion' at the same time.

If the thought of an unstable succession was designed to send a *frisson* of anxiety through his Court audience, the other conditions Latimer set out were more outrageous since they imposed limitations on the king's own behaviour. He should not 'prepare unto himself too many horses', for instance; this was a warning against placing undue reliance on economic and military power. 'I do not intend to speak against the strength, policy and provision of a king; but against excess, and vain trust that kings have in themselves more than in the living God . . .'.[40] The 'honour of a king' was thus limited by God; he should have enough to maintain his state, but not so that his subjects were oppressed.[41]

Secondly, he should take care that he married not for lust, riches, policy or 'enlarging of dominions',[42] but that he took the considered advice of 'all estates' and chose a wife from the 'household of faith', to safeguard true religion and set a good example of sexual morality.[43] Here were not only obvious critical references to Henry VIII's extravagance, wars and marital escapades, but admonitions to Somerset and his pursuit of war with Scotland and the Scottish match. What is more, they were blatant invasions of the prerogative – it is not surprising that a courtier described these sermons as seditious.

The most important condition, however, was that 'the king should write out the book of the law'.[44] It was this which made the king the chief guardian of 'true religion'. The king's emblems were the sword and the book, symbolising both God-given power and rule by the law of God.[45] Bale pointed out that it had been many years before God allowed Israel to have a king.[46] 'But when it was once determinately granted them, what was more earnestly required of [i.e. by] God in that magnificent ministration than were the necessary affairs of religion?'[47] God's law constituted the chief limitation on the king's actions. As Hooper put it: 'They must lead the people and themselves by the law, and

The godly commonwealth

not against the law; to be ministers of the law, and not masters over the law.'[48] Within the law of God, the king's power over his subjects was complete, but the law itself made the prime task of the king the guardianship of 'true religion' and right order.[49] The king must be learned in scripture, in order to exercise proper leadership over the church,[50] and govern the realm in godliness, 'for if the king is well ordered, the realm is well ordered'.[51]

The king was seen as God's instrument or minister for the governing of his people.[52] Even ungodly kings fulfilled this function, for they were sent as a punishment for the sins of the people.[53] In the context of a protestant government, however, protestants preferred to fall back on the distinction between the office and the man,[54] rather than draw out the fullest implications of the limited view of monarchy described previously.[55] As Hooper declared: 'Truly, be the ruler himself never so evil, yet the laws, judgements, punishments and statutes made for the punishment of evil and the defence of the good, be the very work of God; for the magistrates be the keepers of discipline and peace.'[56]

The defence of order was thus the defence of true religion. Church and state were in this sense indistinguishable; it was the 'commonwealth of Christians' rather than the 'national church' that protestants described when discussing the national and corporate aims of reform.[57] Crowley used the model of the primitive church to demand ecclesiastical and social reform – indeed the latter validated the former:

> And this reformation had, no doubt the majesty of God shall so appear in all your decrees, that none so wicked a creature shall be found so bold as once to open his mouth against the order that you shall take in all matters of religion. Yea, the very enemies of David shall do homage unto Solomon for his wisdom. All the kings christened shall learn at you to reform their Churches. You shall be even the light of the world.[58]

Similarly, 'Piers Plowman's' *Exhortation to parliament* hoped that God would send the king such

> zeal and strength to make, set forth and cause to be kept such good politic laws and statutes as this realm may be thereby replenished with justice, equity and wealth, that in all regions whereas it shall be reported how that we of this realm have expelled all vain traditions of men, and received the true religion of Christ, that there also it may be said how that we have received thereto fruitful blessing of God, promised unto the followers of his Word.[59]

True order entailed the establishment of true religion and justice under a godly king and magistracy, enabling the nation to seek salvation as individuals in charity with their neighbours. In campaigning for the regulation of all social relations by God's law, protestants bound the idea of the Christian body to that of the nation, the godly commonwealth, avoiding defining who

A religion of the Word

constituted 'the godly' – of whose numbers they were not entirely sure. To achieve true order, both magistrates and subjects had to understand their own vocations. The remainder of this chapter examines in more detail, firstly, the vocation of the magistrate to uphold the gospel and execute judgment; secondly, the extent of the subject's obedience; and, finally, the bonds of justice and charity which held the godly commonwealth together.

GODLY JUDGEMENT: THE ROLE OF THE MAGISTRATE

The godly magistrate was the lynchpin of the Christian commonwealth. Though the spiritual transformation of society depended on individual responses to the Word, only the magistrate had the power to take action against the forces which prevented its freedom, that is popery and sin, whether in institutional or individual form. With power came responsibility, as the homily *Of obedience* stated: 'Let us pray that they may rightly use their sword and authority for the maintenance and defence of the catholic faith, contained in Holy Scriptures, and of their good and honest subjects, and for the fear and punishment of the evil and vicious people.'[60] 'The magistrate' primarily meant the king, and most of the material used in this section was addressed to him. However, because of Edward's minority this often assumed or included reference to the lord protector or the Privy Council, or it could be used fairly loosely to mean judge, justice of the peace, or member of parliament, or nobleman, depending on the context. Whatever his formal status, it was vital that the magistrate was committed to reform. Supremacist rhetoric had been transformed into protestant zeal.

For the reformation was of necessity a political act imposed from above. Though the true church, in the sense of the godly, had always existed, their 'leavening action' within society was not hailed as the reformation itself. This was an independent process which was helped by the institutional reformation, but would have happened anyway, over an indefinite period.[61] The creation of a Christian commonwealth, however, was a political process, one which protestants hoped they could mould by their now open influence at court. The new king was young and teachable; his uncle the lord protector was sympathetic to protestantism; Cranmer's evangelical commitment was clear. All of these developments gave protestants confidence at the beginning of the reign. Even when the motivation of the nobles was dubious, protestants continued to hope that they could change things, since in the last resort the king was still young. Thus political reality shaped the ideals of godly magistracy with which protestants exhorted the king, the nobility and parliament.[62]

True order could only be restored by the magistrate exercising godly judgement. Particular qualities of character and specific abilities were considered necessary to fit him for this task of reformation, but it should begin with his personal commitment to the gospel. The first task of godly judgement was the destruction of idolatry, to make way for true worship, that is to say, the destruction of popery. Next, in conjunction with the church, the much broader task of fighting sin must be embarked upon. The overall aim of the godly magistrate was to reflect divine justice on earth.

The characteristics of the godly magistrate

According to the homily *Of obedience*, kings were powers ordained by God and the law was to the benefit of the godly, so that it was imperative that the authorities should 'apply themselves to knowledge and wisdom . . .'.[63] God needed to endow the 'powers that be' with suitable qualities to maintain the 'beautiful order' that existed in England.[64] Gerrard hoped that the Holy Spirit would inspire Edward VI 'earnestly to promote the gospel of Christ to the maintenance of true religion and virtue';[65] such zeal would be rewarded by peace and prosperity at home and a strong reputation abroad.[66] Latimer proposed a similar list of qualities for all officers of state:

> Holy Scripture qualifieth the officers, and showeth what manner of men they should be, and of what qualities: *viros fortes* some translations have, *viros sapientes* 'wise men'; the English translation hath it very well, 'men of activity', that have stomachs to do their office, they must not be milksops nor white-livered knights; they must be wise, hearty, hardy, men of a good stomach. Secondarily, he qualifieth them with a fear of God: he saith they must be *timentes deum*, 'fearing God'. For if he fear God, he shall be no briber, no perverter of judgement, faithful. Thirdly they must be chosen officers *in quibus est veritas*, 'in whom is truth'; if he say it, it shall be done. Fourthly *qui oderunt avaritiam*, 'hating covetousness' far from it, he will not come near it that hateth it. It is not he that will give five hundred pound for an office.[67]

Such combative activities would harness Old Testament righteousness to good governance, to purge the corruption of the unreformed commonwealth. Bale's image of the godly magistrate, however, contrasted with the tyrants of the false church: 'as the chosen, holy and well-beloved of God, [they should] take upon them a tender pity, kindness, lowliness, softness, swift, forgiving, with other fruits of the Spirit, acknowledging always Christ for their only wisdom, righteousness and redemption . . .'.[68]

Faithfulness and wisdom were the two qualities most sought after in the magistrate. Old Testament exemplars were easy to find. David was cited as the 'good shepherd' of Israel, whose care for his subjects was a model of faithfulness. Nichols singled out Joshua and Caleb, faithfully bringing the people the truth about the promised land.[69] Latimer related the stories of Moses at the Red Sea, of Joshua and Achan, and of Jehosophat and the Assyrians as examples of the trust that leaders should place in God's deliverance.[70] The

A religion of the Word

wisdom of Solomon was another obvious model: Latimer concluded from the story of his judgement that 'it is wisdom and godly knowledge that causeth a king to be feared'. The protestant gentleman in the *Dialogue between a gentleman and a priest* confidently assumed that Edward VI, despite his youth, was as wise as Solomon.[71]

However, these were all religiously neutral qualities to which all Christian kings should aspire; they only became significant in a context which aligned good governance with the Gospel.

Upholding the Gospel

In order to support the Gospel, the magistrate needed a close personal knowledge of scripture, which he would put into practice in his daily life.[72] Edward's youth made emphasis of the scriptural side of his education a controversial issue, which Latimer thought needed defending against the conflicting demands of aristocratic pastime.[73] The new king should build on his father's interest in the Bible, and reject his extravagant lifestyle. Lever warned that the king should take more pleasure in executing justice than in hawking and hunting, and more pleasure in edifying the church than in building fine palaces, thus implicitly rebuking Henry VIII and Somerset, both of whom spent considerable sums on building.[74]

Gilby prayed that Edward's witness to the Gospel should be unequivocal, lest his enemies asked '"Where is his God?" "What religion hath he professed?"'[75] A backward glance at Henry VIII's idiosyncratic religious policy, as well as a nod sideways at the hesitations of the new regime, were implied here. Gerrard was more confident; he rejoiced that the combination of Bible-reading king and Bible-reading people would lead to the proper functioning of the realm in perfect duty.[76] Thus the king must not only provide English Bibles, but also ensure that the Gospel was 'diligently and sincerely preached'.[77] Latimer reminded his noisy audience at Court of the king's good example in this respect: 'This place was prepared for banqueting of the body, and his majesty hath made it a place for the comfort of the soul, and to have the word of God preached in it; showing thereby that he would have all his subjects at it, if it might be possible.'[78] For listening to the Word was only the beginning: the godly magistrate not only took its lessons to heart himself, but ensured that his subjects did likewise.[79]

The godly noble had a similar responsibility as a patron of the Gospel, as evidence from dedications shows.[80] 'Your lordship's hearty good will and unfeigned favour both towards the setting forth of the glorious gospel of our saviour Christ, and also the promoting of the true professors and faithful preachers of the same is more known than it needeth here to be rehearsed', declared Becon of Sir Francis Russell.[81] Nichols described his patron Sir

Peter Carew as the 'harbour' in the hostile west for 'Christian ships' such as himself, and even more extravagantly as 'the whale sent to succour Jonah'.[82] Verbal support for the Gospel was praiseworthy, but extending charity to hardpressed gospellers was seen as a much more substantial act of witness.[83]

The need to appeal to the aristocracy did not prevent protestants from taking the humanist line that true nobility consisted not in birth but in godly learning and virtue. Hooper gave a classic account of noble virtue decayed:

> In time past men were accounted noble for virtue and justice; such as had done some noble act, either in peace, in governing the commonwealth or in war for the defence of his country and the heads thereof. They were born no gentlemen, but made gentlemen for their noble and virtuous acts. The nobility nowadays is degenerate. It applieth no study to follow the wisdom, learning and virtues of their [sic] predecessors, but thinketh it enough to have the name, without effect.[84]

Such degeneracy should cancel their privileges, since God's Word alone should be the standard by which nobility and government should be judged. The point was that both merit and protestant commitment were more important than noble lineage,[85] a tenet which could be applied to the mobility offered by the Tudor Court, in opposition to protestant hostility to the mobility of greed.[86] It also offered ladies as much scope as gentlemen in the role of protestant patron: Katherine Parr, Anne Stanhope (Somerset's wife), Mary Fitzroy (duchess of Richmond) and Katherine Brandon (duchess of Suffolk) were some of the most important patrons of protestant learning in this period.[87]

Godly, noble households should influence their social inferiors as examples of protestant living. But, again, degeneracy was much in evidence. Noble frivolity was suspiciously reminiscent of Rome; their newly built gorgeous palaces and their penchant for conspicuous consumption reeked of a similar worldly corruption. Even their devotions were suspect: they

> have not spared to spend much riches in nourishing many idle singing men to bleat in their chapels, thinking to do God an high sacrifice, and to pipe down their meat, and whistle them asleep, but they have not spent any part of their substance to find a learned man in their houses to preach the word of God, to haste them to virtue and to dissuade them from vice.[88]

Rectifying this by employing a protestant chaplain was not enough – a personal conversion had to ensue. James Haddon's fruitless attempts to stop the Dorsets from gambling showed that status and culture were not always amenable to reform from within the household.[89]

The high expectations that protestants had of the nobility for both personal patronage and political support were heightened by the king's minority. Political instability made it imperative to maintain links with whoever was in power in order to keep protestantism at the centre of politics. Hooper's easy transference from the household of Somerset to the favour of Northumberland[90] and the assiduity with which the Dorsets were cultivated[91] were cases in point. There were material advantages to be had from association with the Court; protestants were coming in from the chill of exile in the late 1540s.[92] Following the tradition of the previous generation of humanists, they sought either livelihoods as tutors, secretaries or chaplains within noble households, or benefices within their gift. William Turner's letters to Cecil in pursuit of patronage showed that it could be a very frustrating waiting game.[93] Personal gain was an important bonus, and was a significant factor in determining the recipient of dedications, but the ideological basis of the relationship came first, however disingenuously it was expressed. For the chief point of noble virtue in protestant eyes was the nobility's support of the reformation.

Fighting popery

The magistrate bore the sword, according to 1 Peter 2:14, 'for the punishment of evildoers and the praise of them that do well'. This was glossed as the repression of popery and the comfort of the godly.[94] Hence Bale distinguished between kings and emperors who protected the church (Constantine, Theodosius, Edmund, Oswald) and those who merely supported popery,[95] and described the protestant 'saint' Anne Askew as pleading to have her cause judged by the king, 'to put them in remembrance of their office concerning the sword, which they ought not vainly to minister (Rom. 13) . . .'.[96] The ascendancy of the false church would be halted with an end to the persecution of the godly,[97] but retribution would follow. Gilby and Hooper both threatened the king with the vengeance of God if he failed to punish 'Romish traitors' like Gardiner.[98] Becon urged the magistrate to 'banish all false religion and idolatry, to punish, yea, and if they will not turn, to kill the preachers and maintainers of false doctrine'.[99] The author of *The song of the Lord's Supper* prayed that God would

> Help our magistrates to destroy
> That pestilent cage of foul birds and wicked fry
> Let them (O God) with Michael's strength them consume
> That even over foul sprites they may have victory,
> To defend the Lord's memory, till he come.[100]

The king's fight against popery was not, however, principally a matter of attacking individual papists, but one of destroying the structure of idolatrous worship. The Old Testament models cited by protestants were carefully chosen.[101] Kings should follow the example of Moses in delivering the people[102] and Hezekiah, who 'prepared the temple, purified the sanctuary, purged the Levites, reformed the priests, restored again the true religion of

Judah, provided for the ministers and offered up sacrifice unto the Lord'.[103] Significantly, the idol pulled down by Hezekiah was the brazen serpent set up by Moses in obedience to God;[104] like the Mass, it was at first legitimate, but had become an idol through ignorance and superstition. The author of *The old faith of Great Britain* concluded that Hezekiah's action showed kings that they should disregard custom and put God's commands first.[105] Latimer put a sharper edge on the well-known example of Josiah: 'Josiah began, and made an alteration in his childhood; he turned all upside down, he would suffer no idolatry to stand. Therefore you must not take it for a general rule, that the son must ever walk in his father's ways.'[106] Here was implicit criticism of Henry VIII's conservatism, though as a reformer he too had been hailed as the new Josiah, even in grossest old age.[107] Josiah's significance was thus less as a young king, than as a reformer who 'removed all false doctrine and idolatry out of the Church, and restored the book of the law in to the Temple, bound himself and all his subjects to honour and obey God only, as that book taught'.[108]

The duty of extirpating popery was incumbent on all magistrates, not just the king, especially in a period of royal minority.[109] When Veron praised Sir John Yorke as 'a valiant champion of the Lord' against the kingdom of Antichrist,[110] and when Nichols commended Sir Peter Carew's 'manifold labours and daily travail ... to have the verity known, to banish lying and cloaked holiness, to have the Lord truly worshipped and to root out idolatry',[111] they both hoped that their patrons and other aristocrats would continue to struggle against popery, whether privately or publicly. Bale's call to action was more apocalyptic: 'Be not now slack in your offices as in the blind time, but throw forth that wretched bond-woman with her daughter the Romish Church with her whorishness. No point of nobility were it, nor yet of learned worthiness, to be as ye have been of late years, still servant slaves to a most filthy whore ...'.[112] Hooper gave a practical suggestion for the exercise of the magistrates' authority against popery:

> It were well then, that it might please the magistrates to turn the altars into tables, according to the first institution of Christ, to take away the false persuasion of the people they have of sacrifices to be done upon the altars; for as long as the altars remain, both the ignorant people and the ignorant and evil-persuaded priest, will dream always of sacrifice.[113]

Order remained paramount – such a drastic step could not be taken by the mob.[114] Significantly, one of the earliest altars to be removed in London was from St Paul's, on the instructions of bishop Ridley.[115]

Protestants saw the extirpation of popery as the most pressing task faced by the new regime, which explains the threatening tone they adopted in their exhortations.[116] 'Look you thereto with earnestness', Bale charged Edward VI,

A religion of the Word

'for nothing will be at the Latter Day more straightly required of you ...' than removing the 'rags of popery' left behind by his father.[117] Bale (like others before 1549) was referring chiefly to the Mass. When the 1549 *Prayer Book* and Ordinal did not go far enough, Hooper gave warning that the Devil would do all in his power to ensure that the reformation remained incomplete, resulting in a 'mixed and mingled religion'. 'Christ cannot abide to have the leaven of the Pharisees mingled with his sweet flour', he warned; even in the face of opposition the king should 'remove and take away all the monuments, tokens, and leavings of papistry: for as long as any of them remain, there remaineth also occasion of relapse unto the abolished superstition of Antichrist'.[118] The ensuing controversy over vestments posed the question of whether purity in religious externals was more important than obedience. It seemed that the magistrate's ability to achieve such purity, with the speed and thoroughness for which some protestants had hoped, was, after all, debatable.[119]

Popery was increasingly identified with sin,[120] though at this stage it is still worth distinguishing between the two. The beginning of Edward's reign was the early days of the reformation in protestant eyes; the programme of the later puritans to refine aspects of the prayer book was fine-tuning by comparison. On the whole, the destruction of popery was treated as a separate issue from the struggle with sin at this stage. This being understood, the magistrate's more comprehensive task of fighting sin must now be examined.

Fighting sin and executing judgement

The two swords

In the Christian commonwealth, the Word had overall supremacy; in symbolic terms, the book took priority over both temporal and spiritual swords.[121] In his Lent sermons at Court in 1549, Latimer explained their resulting relationship:

> For in this world God hath two swords, the one is a temporal sword, the other a spiritual. The temporal sword resteth in the hands of kings, magistrates and rulers, under Him; whereunto all subjects, as well the clergy as the laity be subject, and punishable for any offence contrary to the same book. The spiritual sword is in the hands of the ministers and preachers, whereunto all kings, magistrates and rulers ought to be obedient; that is, to hear and follow, so long as the ministers sit in Christ's chair; that is, speaking out of Christ's book.[122]

Since both powers were subject to the Bible, the scriptural basis of the reformation was doubly ensured.[123] No-one suggested that the supremacy of the Word gave the king a sacerdotal role, but his government was theocratic in that protestants insisted that he must be learned in and obedient to scripture.[124]

The supremacy of scripture balanced the power of the sword. As Lever put it: 'Is not every Christian commonwealth the fold of Christ's sheep, the house of his family? Be not then all officers in a Christian commonwealth named by God's word shepherds of the fold, and stewards of the family of Christ?'[125]

However the jurisdiction of the magistrate differed from that of the minister. Broadly speaking the magistrate presided over the realm of externals, while the minister was responsible for the internal spiritual world. Thus, as Hooper declared: 'For though a civil law and punishment cannot change the heresies of the mind, neither the desire that men have to do evil, yet when they break forth against the honour of God, and trouble the commonwealth, they should be punished.'[126] This was why the magistrate should punish 'religious' sins such as blasphemy and adultery in the same way as he would 'secular' ones like sedition.[127] Only the magistrate had the power of life and death, and it was his task to maintain order among those untransformed by the preaching of the Word. Latimer explained the problem in expounding the parable of the field of wheat:[128]

> God hath appointed the magistrate to punish the wicked ... If he is a thief, an adulterer or a whoremonger, away with him. But when our Saviour saith 'Let them grow', he speaketh not of the civil magistrates, for it is their duty to pull them out; but he signifieth that there will be such wickedness for [i.e. despite] all the magistrates, and teacheth that the ecclesiastical power is ordained, not to pull out the wicked with the sword but only to admonish them with the Word of God.[129]

Or, as Joye more succinctly put it, 'the sword is ordained to repress what the Word cannot refrain' – the prevalence of blatant wickedness showed that many did not listen to the Word.[130]

The problem with this was that it assumed the godliness of the magistrate, and thus his willingness to use his powers against all sins, not just those that showed themselves as 'secular' crimes. The commonwealth had to be *visibly* godly. Adultery was a case in point: hitherto this had been a matter for the church, but the implementation of the Mosaic law called for the godly magistrate to impose the death penalty. Foxe, in *De non plectendis morte adulteris*, also basing his argument on the strict separation of spheres, came to radically different conclusions. He thought that preachers, presiding over the spiritual and internal sphere, had no right to insist that magistrates should re-enact the Mosaic law. If the magistrates wished to do so that was their affair and they should not be resisted:[131] *Quicquid licet magistratibus, externae reipublicae, aut apud illos expedit, non expedit continuo apud ecclesiastas ecclesiae spirituales.*[132] His view of the relation between law and Gospel led him to reprove preachers who advocated bloodshed rather than charity.[133] Even after Joye had taken up the cudgels against him, Foxe insisted that the solution to manifest wickedness was not to be found in the implementation of the Mosaic law. In *De censura*, however, he changed his tactics, advocating a revived discipline to deal with offences that were not yet defined as secular crimes.[134] The aim of the state was outward tranquillity; to maintain it, the state waged war on criminals rather than crime; the aim of the church was the salvation of the soul, so it waged war on sin with the sword of the Word, both in external discipline as well as internal repentance. Foxe was exceptional in lacking confidence in the godliness of the magistrate, and he did not think that exhortation could make much difference.[135]

The godly magistrate as a mirror of divine justice

God had ordained the temporal sword to deal out on earth justice which would, however imperfectly, reflect heavenly judgement. Even in the case of tyrants this was true, in the sense that they were God's scourge sent to punish the sins of the people. The godly magistrate, however, reflected a more rounded picture of heavenly judgement. He dealt justice righteously and personally, meting out retribution where it was deserved, but at the same time being merciful and accessible to the humblest of his subjects. In effect, he embodied the ideals of the Old Testament prophets, as revealed in both their criticisms of the kings of Israel and Judah and their prophecies of the divine justice that would govern the Messianic kingdom in the future.[136]

If the righteousness of God was imputed to believers by faith, the righteousness of the magistrate was implanted in the nation by his personal activity.[137] God's justice was the key to eternal salvation; the magistrate's justice led to a well-ordered society which allowed people to labour in their vocations both as Christians and as individuals in the world. Hooper's analysis of God's justice was reminiscent of the power of the sword:

> To obtain the first end of his justice, as many as be not utterly wicked, and may be helped, partly with threatenings, partly with promises, he allureth and provoketh them to amendment of life. The other part of his justice rewardeth the obedience of the good, and punisheth the disobedience and contempt of the ill. These two justice[s] the elders call *correctivam* and *retributivam* (Jonah 2, Matt. 25).[138]

Conversely, he elsewhere described the duties of the magistrate in soteriological terms. It was 'the nature and condition of every godly magistrate that would, if God would, and the law, all men to be saved'.[139] In carrying out his duties, he had a salvific effect on the nation:

> God would him to be a wealth and salvation of the people, to defend just causes, and to condemn such as be unjust; to remove false and superstitious religion and to plant true and godly religion; to maintain such as profit the Church and flock of Christ and to remove such as hinder and deceive them.[140]

Hooper envisaged the ship of state threatened by a moral crisis as dire as the storm brought down by Jonah's disobedience on the ship bound for Tarshish. Only by inquiring meticulously into the lives of his subjects, as Jonah's captain had done, could the king discover and punish the 'Jonahs' whose disobedience brought down God's anger on England.[141] It was his duty to make personally sure that others were doing theirs.

Though Hooper addressed the example of the ship's captain to the young king, that did not preclude his officers from sharing the same objectives. Indeed a good king could impose righteousness on his people by appointing like-minded lesser magistrates. The law could only be enforced with their help, whether it was the law of God,[142] 'good statutes' that prevented oppression,[143] or even that governing excommunication.[144] So Becon prayed that God would 'give him grace not only in his own person godly and justly to rule, but also to appoint such magistrates under him as may be likewise affected both toward thy holy word and toward the commonweal';[145] and Gerrard hoped that the new king would promote the Gospel by appointing justices in every town who would do justice without fear or favour and end the oppression of the poor.[146] The radicalism of this suggestion was less striking than it appears – both of these writers had in mind the example of Jehosophat, who had taken just such action when he came to govern Judah.[147]

Contrary to what protestants saw as corrupt contemporary practice, magistrates should be appointed on grounds of merit and fitness for the task,[148] and not granted office as a favour, or be allowed to buy it.[149] They were the 'eyes of the commonweal', vigilant for its welfare rather than their own personal benefit.[150] They should watch to see that sin did not settle in their own hearts, and would then be able to punish it in others.[151] Such altruism was diluted when crisis struck, as Cranmer and Cheke's certainty that the rebels opposed those who were fittest to rule over them showed.[152]

However, office itself still gave great opportunity for corruption, whether by bribery or by the more general abuse of power. Edward VI's reign saw an unprecedented opportunity for the corrupt conveyancing of crown lands, and was marked by scandals such as that of Sir William Sharington's fraudulent activities at the Bristol Mint.[153] Latimer was particularly concerned with the problem of official corruption; indeed, he 'marvelled that any rulers and great magistrates can be saved'.[154] Corruption had destroyed the rule of the Judges in Israel, the pristine polity designed by God for his people,[155] forcing Samuel to make restitution for his sons' iniquity.[156] Latimer appealed for corrupt officials to make similar restitution of their ill-gotten gains.[157] Lever appealed to the king to be vigilant lest any 'Judases' among the nobility profited from his redistribution of church wealth, instead of acting as his stewards, like the apostles in the story of the loaves and fishes.[158] The prevalence of unpreaching prelates and corrupt justices made England, according to Latimer, seem uncomfortably like Israel in the anarchic last days of the Judges, when 'every man did that which seemed right in his own eyes'. His conclusion cast a cold light on the royal minority: 'To suffer this is as much as to say "There is no king in England".'[159]

The converse of this was the sweeping retribution in which the godly prince would purge the commonwealth of sinners. This was the universal obligation of all kings, not just those leaders of chosen nations who had to fulfil the covenant. This was why Hooper selected the example of the king of Nineveh. Not only was the king a pagan, but as Hooper pointed out we are not told how his proclamation of repentance related to previous or future behaviour, which intensified the arbitrariness of the example. The conclusion Hooper came to was that 'it is the king's offices and the peers' of the realm to purge their commonwealth from false religion by public and open proclamations. So did Nebuchadnezzar, Darius, and Cyrus, kings of most notable fame: therefore Christ calleth the princes the nurses of the Church.'[160] The godly prince should let nothing deflect him in this process of retribution; while he must not 'punish the innocent...' (as the kings of Israel who murdered the prophets had done), he should take care 'that he absolve not him that God condemneth, and commandeth to be punished, for gain, affection, good intention or else for any foolish and preposterous pity, for in so doing Saul lost his kingdom...'.[161] Subjects should not rail against this, but realise that 'it is not the magistrate that putteth them to execution, but God, whose ministers they be; and ought to save such as God's word saveth, and damn those that God's word damneth'.[162]

This purge should include all those who failed to do their duties, as well as more conventional criminals.[163] Nichols singled out those 'gospellers' who had a bad reputation for breaking the commandments and committing the seven deadly sins as prime targets: 'Look to it (O ye magistrates) for right sharp judgement shall be done on those that be in authority, and it pertaineth to your charge as well to maintain Christ's doctrine in punishing the wicked living as to destroy idolatry in abolishing false preaching.' If it had been possible previously to legislate against the reading of scripture, then surely it was possible to legislate against sin, now that the Gospel could be openly professed.[164] The impracticability and unrealistic nature of the task did not deter protestants from setting it: as Lever said, magistrates should not be discouraged by their own frailty or by the great numbers of offenders, since they were in authority by God's grace which would sustain them in the task.[165] Only the zeal of the magistrate could cause an immediate improvement in the outward godliness of the nation.

To strike terror into the hearts of the wicked was, however, only half of the magistrate's task. To complete it the magistrate had to 'promote the good'. This was not just a matter of making religious reforms in the narrowest

The godly commonwealth

sense, but one of actively promoting social well-being. Thus Becon prayed for the magistrates to be benevolent patriarchs:

> Grant that they may rule justly, seek judgement, deliver the oppressed, defend the fatherless, comfort the widow, favour good letters, maintain schools, nourish learned men, promote such as be godly and virtuous, and without any ungodly advancing of themselves, live among their people as a loving father among his natural children, seeking their quiet and wealth.[166]

Crowley put even more emphasis on this merciful and benevolent role: he had to defend the oppressed, and ensure that offices were not sold, or the flock devoured or ravaged by unnecessary foreign war (presumably like the recent French and Scottish campaigns).[167] He should even have outright sympathy for the predicament of poor criminals:

> Consider what extreme need is
> And how force may the weak compel
> And how fortune doth hit and miss
> When the intent was to do well . . .[168]

He should be like Daniel not pharoah, a model judge not a tyrant. Latimer pleaded for informal accessibility to justice for the poor, alluding to his own experience.[169] He praised an unnamed noble who heard suits personally every day from early in the morning, and cited the good example of Christian III of Denmark.[170] Edward should do the same, sitting in Council twice a week, so that the poor could petition him with some chance of success.[171] The godly magistrate should show the same kind of mercy to the poor as did God, to whom the poor prayed when they failed to obtain justice on earth, for: 'He saith, he will hear the tears of poor women when he goeth on visitation. For their sake he will hurt the judge, be he never so high. *Deus transfert regna*. He will for widows' sakes change realms, bring them into temptation, pluck the judges' skins over their heads.'[172] To ignore the cry of the poor would be to ignore the gospel; it was sin not poverty that should be punished.[173]

The godly magistrate was thus the antithesis of the popish tyrant. He ensured that the commonwealth was governed by the law of God rather than by human tradition, ensuring that his subjects lived according to the Word, and fulfilling his own scriptural obligations to punish the wicked and defend the good. Just retribution for sin would replace the repression of the godly. The magistrate was not only the destroyer of popery, but the reformer of the whole of society. Such an exalted ideal was bound to be disappointed, as the demands of worldly policy and elite self-interest came into conflict with those of godly principle. Unsurprisingly, criticism followed hard on the heels of exhortation.

But this is to anticipate. If the godly magistrate was obliged to execute God's law, the godly subject was bound to obey him. Only on such an understanding

A religion of the Word

could true order be founded, so the nature of true obedience now demands attention.

OBEDIENCE AND ITS LIMITATIONS: THE DUTY OF THE SUBJECT

Ever since Tyndale, English protestantism had always emphasised the doctrine of Christian obedience. The key texts of Proverbs 8, Romans 13:1–7, and 1 Peter 2:13–16 were expounded literally; obedience to the higher powers had to be complete for the sake of conscience. The radicalism of Colet's humanist exegesis, explaining the apostle's words in the context of a hostile Roman empire, and, by implication, reducing their relevance in the context of a Christian state, had been forgotten.[174] The royal supremacy had made obedience an issue of the foremost political importance; a protestant regime merely served to bind protestants more tightly to the supremacist mast. In England, declared the homily *Of obedience*, God had provided his people with good order and godly government, for which they should be thankful.[175] Resistance to the 'powers that be' constituted resistance to God himself; private vengeance was forbidden; no one was exempt from the duty of obedience.[176]

Even when the actions of the magistrate seemed unjust, and his exactions onerous, he should not be resisted. Those who begrudged paying their taxes, according to Latimer, would not be able to recover their loss, and those who evaded them were thieves and perjurers.[177] Excessive taxes were a plague for sin, and moreover a specific punishment for unwillingness to pay taxes, so they should be suffered accordingly:

> [I]f the king should require of thee an unjust request, yet art thou bound to pay it, and not to resist and rebel against the king. The king, indeed, is in peril of his soul for asking of an unjust request; and God will in his due time reckon with him for it: but thou must obey thy king and not take upon thee to judge him.[178]

Elsewhere he attacked those who disobeyed out of ignorance of the law,[179] or who thought they could dispense with apparently trivial laws (e.g. on fast-days, gaming, clothing); or who thought that only the king's authority mattered and consequently ignored that of lesser magistrates.[180] In all these outward matters all magistrates had the authority of God. Disobedience not only mocked God, but gave occasion to the wicked to slander and blaspheme his Word.[181]

If tax evasion and ignoring social regulations were thought to be acts of resistance, the act of rebellion itself was an outrageous sin. The events of 1549 intensified the insistence that Christian subjects had no resort in oppression but to prayer. In line with the homily *Of obedience* Crowley declared that rebellion was a sign of reprobation, caused by ingratitude to providence and displayed in turning to idolatrous worship. Prayer and repentance were the only remedies in this situation: 'If thou wilt therefore that God shall deliver thee or thy children from the tyranny of them that oppress thee, lament thine old sins, and endeavour amendment of life.'[182] Latimer, Cranmer and Cheke all described how rebellion was only the beginning of disorder, destroying the peace of innocent individuals, disrupting the local economy and damaging the unity of the commonwealth.[183] God had not called the rebels to take leadership upon themselves.[184] God and the nation rejected them and defeat was inevitable:

> Thus if you do not think truly with yourselves that God is angry with you for your rebellion, the king's sword drawn to defend his country, the cry of the poor to God against ye, the readiness of the honest in armour to vanquish ye, your death to be at hand, which ye cannot escape, having God against ye as he promiseth in [his] Word, the king's power to overthrow ye gathered in the field, the commonwealth to beat ye down with stripes and with curses, the shame of your mischief to blemish ye for ever.[185]

Such was Cheke's somewhat hysterical conclusion to his tract *The hurt of sedition*.[186]

Protestants were united in denouncing the rebels, whose sin could never be justified even if their grievances could.[187] While the state was following a protestant policy, outrage and defensiveness were the only possible responses to anything that threatened it. However, protestant views on Christian obedience were not as absolute as all this seems to indicate. Though no one countenanced active or political resistance at this stage, it was accepted that in the case of a subject being commanded to do something contrary to the law of God, it was his duty to obey God rather than his human superior. 'Passive resistance' was a very significant limitation of obedience, because protestants were all too aware of the fragility of the reformation and the real possibility of the reimposition of catholic worship. At home the direction of policy was at the mercy of successive *coups*,[188] and the succession was by no means assured.[189] Abroad, the German states languished under the Interim.[190] Nor was passive resistance a tenet espoused only by a few mavericks – it was officially sanctioned in the homily *Of obedience*.

Almost half of the homily was concerned with the problem of lawful disobedience. Part three was a diatribe against the 'usurped power' of the pope: in this case none of the texts forbidding rebellion applied, as scripture demanded only that kings be obeyed and not popes. Resistance to the papacy was justifiable, and though this was intended chiefly to justify the king's action in breaking with Rome, it omitted to limit resistance to princes. Indeed, in the context of popery, the vocation of 'God's people to be patient and of

A religion of the Word

the suffering side'[191] was specifically modified: 'Yet let us believe undoubtedly (good Christian people) that we may not obey kings, magistrates or any other (though they be our own fathers) if they would command us to do anything contrary to God's commandments. In such a case we ought to say with the apostles, "We must obey rather God than man." Acts 5.29.'[192] It must be stressed that this was not a call to active political resistance; nor is there any whiff of the invocation of individual or collective rights. But in the context of an official statement, which opened with a paean to order,[193] did not the idea that disobedience was a duty in certain circumstances carry within it dangerous potential?

The key to the limitation of both the obedience of the subject and the power of the magistrate was the place of the law of God. Hooper, the most consistent advocate of the theme of limited obedience, stated in his *Declaration of the ten commandments* that the superior powers should be given 'no more, neither no less honour nor reverence, than the Word of God commandeth'. As the story of the twelve spies showed, 'such magistrates as persuade the people by God's Word should be believed and obeyed, the other not. In the cause of conscience there must only God be heard (Acts 5, Matt. 10) or else the people shall fail of a right faith.'[194] Under popery however, God's Word was 'not heard', salvation was endangered and patriarchal order overturned:[195]

> For in case they instigate their subjects to the transgression of God's laws, we must obey neither them, neither their laws; they be not then our fathers, but rather strangers, that would draw us from the obedience of God, which is our very father. It is not decent that their authority should be above and God's authority under. For as man's authority dependeth of God's, so should it bring men and lead men to God.[196]

The magistrate who ordered God's laws to be broken thus repudiated his office and broke the ties of duty binding his subjects to him. Hooper was not countenancing rebellion, but he made resistance a necessity. In his *Godly confession*, written to justify his stance during the vestments' controversy, he took pains to distance himself from 'seditious anabaptists' and emphasised the duty of obedience, but likened his position to the lonely stand of Joseph in Egypt and of Daniel in Babylon.[197] More radically, he included contravention of the law of nature as justifying disobedience, citing the example of the Egyptian midwives' refusal to carry out pharaoh's command to kill all the male children of the Israelites.[198]

Hooper was exceptional in putting these principles into practice and endangering his career during the vestments' controversy. But other protestants also made a point of limiting obedience.[199] Thomas Becon and Edmund Allen both used catechismal works to expound the principle,[200] and Allen explained how the office of the magistrate had distinct boundaries:[201]

The godly commonwealth

Doubtless they have power and authority over body, possessions, goods, life and whatsoever pertaineth unto the state of this transitory world. All which we ought obediently to submit to them without any manner grudging or murmuring. But if they go beyond this, and will take upon them to rule also over the soul and conscience of man (which is the peculiar regiment and possession of God only) and to command us anything that is expressly against God's Word, then we ought to say with the apostles, 'We must obey God rather than man.'[202]

Turner explicitly linked this idea of the breaking of bounds with the imposition of catholicism: 'But if he would go beyond his bounds, that is, if he would command men to believe that thing to be a worshipping of God which is either unspoken of in the written Word of God, or contrary unto the same Word, or if he should forbid this Word or any part of it, we are not bound to obey him in this case.'[203] Christians, on the basis of 1 Corinthians 2:16 and Galatians 1:8, should refuse to submit to any doctrine which was not 'of Christ'.[204] Daniel, the three children in the furnace, and the apostles Peter and John had all refused to submit to false worship. The moral of these examples was clear: 'the Mass is contrary unto the Scripture, therefore though the magistrates should command us to believe that it were of God, we are not bound in this case to obey them'.[205]

The 'scripture test' for obedience serves as a useful reminder that however much the magistrate was to be trusted as God's instrument, ultimately the reformation could only be achieved by the Word. Thus Hooper denied that political power alone could achieve anything without the support of God, as the failure of the league between Israel and Egypt showed.[206] Bale described even the achievement of the supremacy as a hollow victory: 'For unto kings hath not God given it to subdue these beasts. Only is it reserved to the victory of his living Word.'[207] Gilby cited the example of the influence of Arius over the emperor Constantius as evidence that kings were far from infallible in theological matters. The Word of God was the test of allegiance; obedience was truly a matter of conscience.[208] Protestants' consciousness of themselves as a 'persecuted little flock' gave the idea of limited obedience even more weight.[209] In the context of a protestant regime, rebellion could only be abhorrent, but if a catholic government were to reimpose traditional worship, the ideological line separating a withdrawal of obedience from an act of resistance would become very hazy. In this context, it is worth remembering that the disobedience of Peter and John, cited in several writers' works from the homily downwards, was the text on which the Marian exile Christopher Goodman based the sermons that became his radical call to resistance – *How superior powers ought to be obeyed of their subjects*.[210]

The ungodly magistrate threatened true order far more than did the legitimate disobedience of the godly subject to him. This balance of obligations that was needed to achieve true order was far from being an explicit contract,

A religion of the Word

but it contained the germ of the idea. Of course, the end result added up to an acceptance of the status quo, a presentation of society as a changeless hierarchy, seen at its most eloquent in the opening passage of the *Exhortation to good order and obedience*. Moreover, the political survival of protestantism necessitated the presentation of the Edwardian regime as a godly one until credibility reached its absolute breaking-point. But the conservative appearance of protestant notions of order should not be allowed to mask the radical implications of their conception of duty, which placed the service of God above all worldly considerations. This required true order, consisting of godly magistrates and obedient subjects bound together in justice and charity. These qualities were just as important as obedience in shaping the idea of the godly commonwealth. So it is to these social bonds that we must now turn.

THE SOCIAL BONDS: JUSTICE AND CHARITY

The ideal social order that has been described so far appeared to be static and changeless, a regime in which the prime duty of the superior powers was to govern and that of the subjects was to work hard in their callings and obey their superiors. However, such a view ignores the disruptive effect of sin, against which a constant struggle had to be waged in both the public and private arenas. Clearly, only individual repentance and faith could combat sin effectively, but such faith was made manifest in society by the presence and activity of *justice* and *charity*. These were the bonds linking each individual to his neighbour, and each social group to the whole. They prevented society from being atomised or divided; they expressed mutuality, which obedience alone did not. Justice and charity were linked to provide a vision of harmony and unity, which allowed for criticism but pre-empted radical 'anabaptist' interpretations of the Gospel.[211] It was a vision which reflected both the law, giving each his due,[212] and the Gospel, loving one another.[213]

Thus justice and charity could be discerned working in a number of different but overlapping planes or categories: charity could be described as operating within society, expressing the informal goodwill that bound one Christian to another across social boundaries, while justice was applied formally, from without, when sin disrupted the public peace; at the same time charity could itself be described in terms of justice, and vice versa.

Charity

Charity was the bond which distinguished the Christian commonwealth from all others. Ideally, it should regulate all dealings involving Christians. Thus Hooper described Paul's injunction 'owe nothing to any man, but love one another' (Rom. 13:8) as the summary of the whole of that chapter, a precept which transcended even the theme of obedience:

> As though he had said, 'What needeth it to write much of duties, contracts, of buyings, lendings and such other like things. Let charity be the rule of all these things; unto the which if the subject submit himself, he will use his higher power none otherwise than he would be used himself, if he were an higher power; the higher power the subject none otherwise than though he were a subject himself. Whatsoever thing agreeth with charity is good; whatsoever agreeth not with charity is evil.'[214]

A more limited application of charity was in almsgiving, or the exercise of Christian stewardship. Latimer, Lever and Crowley all regarded this as fundamental to a reformed society, even though it was a traditional theme; it was their insistence on charity that fuelled their sermons and tracts, not a distinctive 'commonwealth' ideology. The place of charity in society was expressed most fully in Latimer's *Sermons on the Lord's Prayer*. The quietist nature of Latimer's 'radicalism' was indicated by his statement that the great leveller of Christian society was the Lord's Prayer, which was common to all. Regardless of degree, all asked that God would 'Give us this day our daily bread', that is, the necessities of life: firstly, true religion (the food of the soul); secondly, bodily sustenance.[215] This said something about the relative unimportance of social status:

> And here we be admonished of our estate and condition, what we be, namely, beggars. For we ask bread: of whom? Marry, of God. What are we then? Marry, beggars: the greatest lords and ladies in England are but beggars before God. Seeing then that we all are beggars, why should we then disdain and despise poor men?[216]

The use of 'us' was significant:

> For because God is not my God alone, he is a common God. And here we be admonished to be friendly, loving and charitable to one another: for what God giveth, I cannot say 'This is my own'; but I must say 'This is ours'. . . Therefore when God sendeth unto me much, it is not mine, but ours; it is not given unto me alone, but I must help my poor neighbours withal.[217]

Charity thus provided a rationale for almsgiving which had nothing to do with merit or 'works' righteousness'.[218] Furthermore, though Latimer disapproved of usury, he used it metaphorically to explain the dynamic relationship between spiritual and worldly blessings. God permitted inequality in order to provide opportunity for practical charity: 'If every man were rich, then no man would do anything: therefore God maketh some rich and some poor.'[219] Inequality necessitated reciprocity, and the spiritual debt of the rich always outweighed their capacity for material giving: 'And truly the poor man doth more for the rich man in taking things of him, than the rich doth for the poor in giving them. For the rich giveth but only worldly goods, but the poor giveth him by the promise of God all felicity' [Marginal note: Few rich men will believe this].[220]

Justice

Latimer's choice of subject matter led him to emphasise charity;[221] others were more concerned with justice. Hooper's *Declaration of the ten commandments* described the law of God as the foundation of the commonwealth, the first table prescribing the correct honouring of God, the second 'how and by what means one man may live with another in peace and unity in this civil life . . .'.[222] Justice was thus vital to social harmony.

The ten commandments were more perfect than the classical descriptions of the ideal state, and abiding by them was the only way to preserve the commonwealth. Israel and Rome had both disregarded the second table, and doing so resulted in the internal strife which destroyed them. The law was not specific to time and place, but was universal:

> No manner of person is excluded from the league: whereby we know, as God's mercy is common for all men, which is the first part of the condition expressed in the league; so alike is the obedience towards the law required of all men, especially of such as be the governors of the people in the ministry of the Church, or else in the governance of the commonwealth.[223]

True justice could only prevail when the law of God was supreme. This was fundamental to Israel's covenant.[224] In a rare instance, Crowley related the law (in more general terms) to predestination, as necessary for the preservation of the 'lambs':

> By the princes and public ministers are the laws administered to the advancement of God's glory, whether the laws be wicked or godly. For by the administration of the godly laws, the wicked are plagued, and by the wicked laws, the godly are chastised and scourged that they may have the more cause to run unto their shepherd Christ for succour.[225]

However, the main discussion centred on the implementation of 'the godly laws' to 'plague the wicked'[226] Here the godly magistrate was seen regulating and purging society so that it could function in security and tranquillity.[227] Latimer summarised the difference between justice and charity in accordance with the categories discussed so far, relating justice to the public role of the magistrates and charity to private individuals: 'But this seemeth now as though malefactors ought not to be put to death, because God requireth mercy. Sir, you must understand that God requireth private mercy; so that private men one shall forgive unto the other; but it is another matter with the magistrates.'[228]

This was in line with the homily *Of charity* which reconciled the duty to love one's enemies with the execution of justice in similar style on malefactors. Both magistrate and minister should execute their offices diligently 'to impugn the kingdom of the devil ... Else they love neither God, nor they whom they govern, if (for lack of correction) they wilfully suffer God to be offended and those whom they govern to perish.'[229] Even when justice and charity were related to the separate spheres of public and private life, they were closely linked (justice being a result of love of God and country). It is thus worth considering them as interlinked concepts (*just* charity and *charitable* justice) to show the internal dynamics of the godly commonwealth at work.

Just charity

Charity was not simply a result of Christian love and equality under God. Similar results could be achieved by defining charity in terms of justice and duty. This was the result of treating justice as distributive rather than retributive,[230] and it emerges from a consideration of duties. For instance: 'Further the parents ought to do justice towards their children, to bring them up in godliness and virtue; to correct them when they do naught; likewise the children ought to be obedient unto their parents, and be willing to do according unto their commandment'[231] – and so on from servant up to king. Such a definition made a specific kind of charity incumbent on the rich and powerful, whose duty it was to see that the poor had justice. He attacked those who 'will not hear poor men's causes, nor defend them from wrong and oppression of the rich and mighty. Such proud men despise the Lord's Prayer; they should be as careful for their brethren as for themselves.'[232] This 'charitable duty' of providing access to justice was reciprocation for the support given by the obedient poor.[233]

Hooper also recognised that distributive justice was as important as the retributive variety. He saw it as the prime lesson of the eighth commandment: 'And in so doing we resemble the master of this law, God almighty, that abhorreth all injustice and loveth equity and right.'[234] Such equity was the foundation of Christian stewardship, 'Therefore to abuse them [i.e. riches] is not only a loss of the goods, but also injuries unto the dispensation of God, who willeth the rich to give gladly and with thanks unto the poor, the poor to receive religiously ... with thanksgiving ... .'[235] The exercise of charity was thus not just a sign of trust in and thanksgiving to providence, but an enacting of justice. 'Theft' was defined by Hooper as selfishness: anyone who withheld or withdrew the rights of others was guilty of it. He included ministers

A religion of the Word

who withheld spiritual food from their flocks, both by refusal to preach and by insisting on the Mass; those who sacrilegiously despoiled the church of its goods; nobles who made parks for animals at the expense of the poor; those who failed to give counsel or admonition; gamblers and plagiarisers; those who looted in war and cheated, by usury, in peace; even those who robbed others of their livelihoods by practising more than one trade or craft.[236]

The extension of this argument was the New Testament conclusion that charity fulfils the law:

> By this rule men may know whether they have charity or not: for in case we diminish the goods of our neighbours, whether they be of his body, or of his soul, or else of his possessions, honour, place, or dignity; or if we increase not these goods towards all men, if we may, there is no charity in us. Or else if we diminish not their evils and troubles as we may; either if we do the evils in any sort by ourselves or by other, we have no charity in us.[237]

Therefore injustice happened because people lacked charity, which was dependent on their faith. Or to put it another way, as Latimer did, justice was the chief expression of charity: 'Finally one neighbour ought to have justice with another; that is, to give him what pertaineth unto him; not to deceive him in anything, but to love him and to make much of him.'[238] There was thus an urgent social need for repentance and the faith that resulted in charity; the nature of the commonwealth would be transformed by it. 'True religion' could at last be seen in action, as the mainspring of a just society.

Charitable justice

Justice and charity linked each person together in their rightful place within the Christian body. When sin or crime disrupted or damaged that body, justice and charity were enacted as punishment. Here there was less of a consensus. The question was whether justice and charity were opposing principles that moderated each other, or different aspects of the same phenomenon, so that external retributive justice could also be a species of charity.

Both Latimer and the homily *Of charity* had anticipated the argument that the gospel enjoined charity and mercy, not destruction, towards sinners.[239] Foxe and Joye's dispute on adultery encapsulated this debate: Foxe's plea for charity seemed to follow exactly the kind of argument that the homily refuted. Severe judgement was not necessarily what God wanted, since the Gospel taught that sinners were those whom God most wanted to save – *Tantum interest inter dei iudicium et hominum*.[240] To agitate for the Levitical punishment of death for adultery was not becoming to Christians, who should be guided by the whole Word of God.[241] The coming of Christ had moderated the effect of the law *ut iam usu exerceant, non damnent, vigore, regant non obligent, pungant non occidant christianos...*[242] Christ and the apostles showed us that charity should be extended to the sinner, to encourage him or her to repentance. Destroying Christian liberty by bringing back the burden of the law was what the papists did.[243] Magistrates who followed the advice of those preachers demanding the enactment of the Mosaic code were being authoritarian rather than Christian.

More conventionally, however, Joye thought Foxe (despite his protestations to the contrary) was aligning himself with antinomian and licentious radicals, especially in his testamentary theology.[244] Jesus had not abrogated but confirmed the law (excepting the ceremonial law), extending its application to the gentiles. The 'law of love' that preserved members of the Christian body was a constant feature of the law of God:

> [W]herefore every law that beareth this love in itself is the everlasting will of God made by the same spirit, which is one and the same of both the testaments, and must needs stand firm and inviolable according to his own saying by his prophet, 'Lord thy judgements are equal, firm, fast and just. And all thy judgements shall endure for ever' (Psalms 18, 118).[245]

Malefactors harmed Christian society by evil example as well as by their deeds; thus wickedness spread from one diseased 'limb' into the whole 'body' like putrefaction. Thus justice was in itself an act of charity since it limited damage to others. Therefore to associate justice with human severity and not with charity showed a basic misunderstanding of the latter:

> Is it not expedient, yea, and necessary that such common malefactors be taken out of the commonweal. Greater is the charity that extendeth her to many, than to one man or woman, and which extendeth herself to the preservation and tranquillity of the whole Church and commonweal than it which is but a fond, foolish pity to save an adulterer or a murderer which hurteth the whole commonalty, which once delivered, continuing in his mischief and wickedness increaseth his crimes unto the great hurt of many.[246]

Foxe was forced, by the pressure put by this argument on his own, to advocate excommunication in his next tract. Joye's conclusion, that the corporate good should take precedence over individual interests, was in line with the themes of sermons by Lever, Latimer and Hooper and tracts by Crowley, and it would not have been rejected by less theologically committed writers.[247] But this should not obscure the fact that the controversy centred on Biblical theology. Foxe, in opening up a debate on the relationship between justice and charity, showed that the dialectic between law and gospel was as important as social and economic questions in generating discussion about the nature of the godly commonwealth.

CONCLUSION

The attainment of true order was for protestants the fundamental aim of the reformation. At the beginning of Edward's reign the prospects for achieving this aim seemed fair. The spiritual tyranny of the papacy had been largely overthrown by the establishment of the royal supremacy: the first prerequisite for true order, that the commonwealth was to be ruled by its rightful prince, had been fulfilled. Continuation of the anticatholic policy was not always certain,[248] though protestants applauded every step in that direction as a step nearer to the establishment of 'true religion' and prayed for the steps to break into a run. But the other prerequisites (that the magistrate should fight sin, that the subject should understand what it meant to be truly obedient, that both should strive after justice and charity) were far from being achieved, and seemed less and less likely to be so as the reign went on. The social and political criticism that resulted from this disappointment is one of the most well-known aspects of this period. This is not part of a separate 'commonwealth' ideology, but arises from an evangelical understanding of true order and also of time, providence and judgement, which are the subjects of the next chapter.

NOTES

1 See Tawney, *Religion and the Rise of Capitalism*, 149.
2 'An exhortation concerning good order and obedience to rulers and magistrates', *Homilies*, sig. R3.
3 *Ibid.*, lines 4–5.
4 *Ibid.*, lines 17–18.
5 John Hooper, *A declaration of Christ and his office* (Zurich, 1547), PS1 45.
6 The natural order is conceived in Aristotelian terms as developed by medieval writers like Fortescue or Raimond Sebond. Cf. Sir Thomas Elyot's 1531 *The Book Named the Governor*, ed. Foster Watson (1907), 3–7: 'where there is any lack of order needs must be perpetual conflict ... whereof ensueth universal dissolution'.
7 'Exhortation concerning good order and obedience,' *Homilies*, sig. R3vo; see also Chapter 1, 'Disorder', pp. 37–41.
8 I.e. Gardiner; see P. Janelle, *Obedience in Church and State* (Cambridge, 1930).
9 Bale, *English votaries*, Part 1, *i–*ii.
10 Hooper, *Declaration of the ten commandments*, PS1 351.
11 Cf. *ibid.*, 355; Thomas Becon, *Flower of godly prayers* (1550), PS3 21.
12 See below, 'The social bonds', pp. 162–7.
13 John Cheke, *The hurt of sedition, how grievous it is to the commonwealth* (1549), sig. F6vo.
14 Especially in the context of the 1549 rebellions; see e.g. Cheke, *ibid.*, passim.
15 Anthony Gilby, *A commentary upon the prophet Micah*, sigs E6–E6vo.
16 1 Corinthians 12, Ephesians 4:11–16. In this sense, the Christian body appears to be equivalent to the nation. For predestination see also Chapter 3, n. 247. See also D.G. Hale, *The Body Politic* (The Hague, 1971), for the Henrician background to the political imagery of the body, especially in Thomas Elyot and Thomas Starkey, 48–68.

The godly commonwealth

17 See below, 'Godly judgement', pp. 146–58; also Chapter 3, 'Introduction', pp. 87–8.
18 Thomas Lever, *A fruitful sermon made in Paul's church* (1550), sigs B2vo–B3; cf. 'Piers Plowman', *Exhortation unto the lords, knights and burgesses of the parliament house* (?1550), sigs A2vo–A3vo.
19 Lancaster, *True understanding of the Supper of the Lord*, sig. C5; see also Chapter 3, – 'The Christian body', pp. 114–27.
20 See Chapter 1; Chapter 5, 'Pretending the gospel', pp. 200–9.
21 Lever, *A fruitful sermon*, sig. E2; cf. Hugh Latimer, *A most faithful sermon* (1550), PS1 249: '... they in Christ are equal with you ...'; see below, 'The social bonds', pp. 162–7.
22 E.g. Status/occupational groups listed in Becon, *Flower of godly prayers*; a similar concern with individual status and occupation groups was displayed in sermons by John Hooper, *Jonah* (1550), PS1 456–7, 459–61, 465–84; cf. Hugh Latimer, *Sermons on the Lord's Prayer* (1552), PS1 349–52, 359; *Epistle for the twenty-third Sunday after Trinity* (*Lincolnshire sermons*), PS1 517; PS2 34, 214–15.
23 Cf. the Edwardian primer, *Liturgies*, PS 454–67.
24 Robert Crowley, Titlepage, *The voice of the last trumpet, blown by the seventh angel* (1549).
25 See Chapter 5, 'Divine judgement', pp. 162–7.
26 Latimer, *Second sermon on the Lord's Prayer*, PS1 349.
27 Both ambition and discontent were very specific accusations relating to the political situation in Edward's reign. Conservatives blamed the reformation for both of them, see Chapter 5, 'The ungodly commonwealth', pp. 187–97.
28 Hooper was exceptional, in *A declaration of Christ and his office*, 78–86, in using the model of Christ's kingship. See also below, 'Godly judgement', pp. 146–58; Chapter 5, 'Assumptions', pp. 178–97.
29 The theme of the covenant seems chiefly to have meant an identification of England with Israel, the archetypal chosen yet straying nation: D. Stoute, 'The origins and early development of the reformed idea of the covenant', unpublished PhD thesis, Cambridge University (1979); but see also J.G. Moller, 'The beginnings of puritan covenant theology', *JEH* (1963): 46–67; M. McGiffert, 'William Tyndale's conception of covenant,' *JEH* (1981): 167–84; J.H. Primus, 'The role of the covenant doctrine in the puritanism of John Hooper', *NAK* (1967–8): 182–96.
30 E.g. Hooper, *Answer to Gardiner*, 141; Latimer, *Third lenten Court sermon*, 143.
31 Bale, *Rank papist*, sig. A7; Joye, *A contrary*, sigs G2vo–G3.
32 Hooper, *Answer to Gardiner*, PS1 140–1, citing Numbers 9 and 11.
33 See P.D. Avis, 'Moses and the magistrate', *JEH* (1975).
34 Latimer, *Fifth lenten Court sermon*, PS1 187–8; he was referring to Pole's *Pro ecclesiasticae unitatis defensione* (Rome, 1537).
35 *Ibid.*, 193.
36 Latimer, *First lenten Court sermon*, PS1 89.
37 See Chapter 5, 'The royal minority', pp. 198–200.
38 Latimer, *First lenten Court sermon*, 91; cf. his patriotic paean on Edward VI's birth, Letter to Cromwell, 19 October 1537, PS2 385.
39 *Ibid.*; see Chapter 5, 'The royal minority', pp. 198–200.
40 Latimer, *First lenten Court sermon*, 92.
41 Cf. *ibid.*, 99.
42 Latimer was not only attacking aristocratic marriage patterns in general, but implicitly criticising Henry VIII's marriages and Somerset's pursuit of the marriage of Edward VI and Mary, queen of Scots.

A religion of the Word

43 Ibid., 94–5; cf. *A most faithful sermon*, 243; see Chapter 5, pp. 198–200.
44 See below, 'Godly judgement', pp. 146–58.
45 Cf. Latimer, *First lenten Court sermon*, PS1 85–6. For the royal iconography of the sword and the book, see King, *English Reformation Literature*, 188–96; Roy Strong, 'Edward VI and the pope: a Tudor antipapal allegory and its setting', *Journal of the Warburg and Courtauld Institutes* (1960): 311–13. This painting has been given a detailed, though still uncertain, interpretation by Margaret Aston, who dates it to the late 1560s: *The King's Bedpost: Reformation and Iconography in a Tudor Group Portrait* (Cambridge, 1993).
46 See above, n. 34.
47 Bale, *Rank papist*, sig. A2.
48 Hooper, *Declaration of the ten commandments*, PS1 362–3.
49 Mardeley, *Power of God's Word*, sig. A4vo.
50 The magistrate should only legislate for the commonwealth in accordance with the law of God, but in the church only the law of God should prevail, according to Hooper, *Declaration of Christ*, PS1 93. Elsewhere he insisted on the separation of powers, e.g. *Answer*, PS1 142.
51 Latimer, *Second lenten Court sermon*, PS1 120.
52 Bale, *Acts of the English votaries*, *i–ii.vo, cited above; for Hooper's view of the victory at Pinkie, see *Declaration of Christ*, PS1 xiii.
53 See above; also Chapter 5, 'Temporal judgement' pp. 187–93.
54 Hooper, *Declaration of the ten commandments*, PS1 358; *Annotations on Romans 13*, PS2 104.
55 See below, 'Obedience and its limitations', pp. 158–62.
56 Hooper, *A godly confession and protestation of the Christian faith* (1550), PS2 81.
57 Church and state are given separate chapters in this book only for the sake of convenience; see Davies, '"Poor persecuted little flock"', 78–102.
58 Robert Crowley, *An information and petition against the oppressors of the poor commons of this realm* (?1548), sig. B6vo.
59 'Piers Plowman's' *Exhortation*, sig. A1vo.
60 'Exhortation to good order and obedience', *Homilies*, sigs T2vo–T3.
61 See M. Dowling, 'The Gospel and the Court', in Lake and Dowling (eds) *Protestantism and the National Church*, 36–77; the Henrician understanding of 'godly leaven' was far more circumspect than the militant ideal of later puritanism.
62 See C. Haigh, 'The recent historiography of the English reformation', *HJ* (1982): 995–1007, updated in N. Tyacke (ed.) *England's Long Reformation 1500–1800* (1998), especially the Introduction.
63 'Exhortation to good order and obedience', *Homilies*, sigs R4–R4vo.
64 Ibid., sig. T2vo.
65 Phillip Gerrard, *A godly invective in defence of the gospel* (1547), sig. aii.vo.
66 Ibid., sigs D8vo, E6vo.
67 Latimer, *Fifth lenten Court sermon*, PS1 185–6; cf. Becon, *Flower of godly prayers*, PS3 20–1.
68 The new Jerusalem, in Bale, *Image*, PS 603.
69 Lever, *A sermon preached the third Sunday in Lent*, sig. B4vo; cf. Nichols, *A godly new story*. See C. Bradshaw, 'David or Josiah? Old Testament kings as exemplars in Edwardian religious polemic', in Gordon (ed.) *Protestant History*, vol. 2.
70 Latimer, *Third lenten Court sermon*, PS 143–4.
71 Latimer, *Second lenten Court sermon*, PS 126; cf. Anon., *A dialogue between a gentleman and a priest* (1547), sig. A4.

The godly commonwealth

72 See above, pp. 140–6.
73 Latimer, *Second lenten Court sermon*, PS 120–1.
74 Lever, *Sermon preached the third Sunday in Lent*, sig. C6-vo.
75 Gilby, *On Micah*, sig. O7.
76 Gerrard, *Godly invective*, sig. E1; see above, pp. 140–6.
77 See the *Copy of a letter sent to all preachers*, for 'godly order' of preaching. Cf. the praise of the king for setting forth the Word of God, in e.g. 'R.V.', *The old faith of Great Britain*, sig. C4; Lynne, *Beginning and end of all popery*, 4; Anon., *The true judgement of a faithful Christian*, sig. B3vo.
78 Latimer, *Sixth lenten Court sermon*, PS1 204.
79 Hooper, *Jonah (sixth sermon)*, PS1 539–42.
80 It is tempting to use dedications as clear evidence of patronage, cf. King, *English Reformation Literature*, 103–13. However, a distinction must be made between commissioned works and books offered to a potential patron in the hope of attracting his/her attention. As the latter category is extremely rare in Edwardian printed material, dedications can only be used to indicate the dedicatees' religious commitment rather than anything more substantial. See F.B. Williams, *Index of dedications* (1962).
81 Thomas Becon, *The Christian knight*, PS2 624–5: Dedication to Sir Francis Russell.
82 Nichols, *Copy of a letter*, sig. A4.
83 Veron, Dedication to Sir John Yorke of *Godly sayings*, sig. B1vo; William Salesbury, Dedication to Sir Richard Rich of *Battery of the pope's buttress*, sigs A2–A2vo.
84 Hooper, *Declaration of the ten commandments*, PS 363.
85 Thomas Becon, *The governance of virtue* (1547), PS1 398–9: Dedication to Somerset's daughter, lady Jane Seymour; cf. Becon, *Flower of godly prayers*, PS3 24: prayer for gentlemen.
86 Clearly all this conflicts with the 'aristocratic' conservative ideology (notably in its justification of office holding) prevailing in the 1540s. See also Chapter 5, 'Pretending the gospel', pp. 200–9.
87 Marriage and widowhood empowered Anne Stanhope, Katherine Brandon, Katherine Parr and Mary Fitzroy to act as significant evangelical patrons in their own right. See J.N. King, 'Patronage and piety: the influence of Katharine Parr', in M.P. Hannay (ed.) *Silent But For the Word: Tudor Women as Patrons, Translators and Writers of religious works* (Kent, OH, 1985), 43–60. For a different view of Katharine Parr's influence, see M. Dowling, 'The Gospel and the Court', 59–71. A detailed account of her piety is to be found in Tudor, *English Devotional Literature*, 58–90.
88 Becon, *Jewel of joy*, PS2 429.
89 James Haddon to Henry Bullinger, Letter 130, August 1552, *Original letters*, PS1 281–8.
90 Hooper made the transition of patronage apparently more easily than he did from exile to home: see J. Opie, 'The anglicising of John Hooper', *Archiv* (1968): 150–75; cf. Pettegree, *Foreign Protestant Communities*, ch. 1.
91 For the courting of the Greys, see *Original letters*, Letters 126 and 127 (John Aylmer); 130 and 131 (James Haddon); 187, 189, 191, 192, 203, 204 and 205 (John ab Ulmis).
92 See E. Hildebrandt, 'English protestant exiles', chs 1, 2, 4–6. Thomas Becon is perhaps the best-known example of a protestant who combined recantation and internal exile; see D.S. Bailey, *Thomas Becon* (1952), chs 2–5. See Ryrie, 'Evangelicals', chs 2 and 4.
93 E.g. Turner's letter to Cecil in SP 10: 11, 14; cf. the peregrinations of humanist scholars in search of patronage in M. Dowling, *Humanism in the Age of Henry VIII* (1986), ch. 5.
94 See Chapter 1.

95 Bale, *Image*, PS 612–3.
96 Bale, *Latter examination of Anne Askew*, PS 216–17.
97 Nichols, *Copy of a letter*, sig. F9vo.
98 Gilby, *Answer to Gardiner* (1547) sigs Y8–Y8vo; Hooper, *Answer to Gardiner*, PS1 140; Bale, *Frantic papist*, sig. A6vo. Although the leading conservative bishops had all been deprived and/or imprisoned by the end of Edward VI's reign, only the Second Act of Uniformity enforced worship.
99 Thomas Becon, *The principles of the Christian religion* (1550), PS2 511–15; cf. Lancaster, *Right and true understanding*, sigs B2–B2vo. The Privy Chamber was noted by several protestants as a key point of contact, e.g. Samuel, *The practice*; Gilby, *On Micah*, sigs B1–B1vo; Latimer, *First lenten Court sermon*, PS1 98. See also D. Starkey, 'Court and government', in C. Coleman and D. Starkey (eds) *Revolution Reassessed: Revisions in the History of Tudor Government and Administration* (Oxford, 1986), 29–58; D. Hoak, 'The king's Privy Chamber, 1547–53', in D.J. Guth and J.W. McKenna (eds) *Tudor Rule and Revolution: Essays for G.R. Elton from His American Friends* (Cambridge, 1982), 87–108.
100 'E.T.', *Here beginneth a song of the Lord's Supper* (1550), sig. B3vo.
101 E.g. Nichols's identification of Henry VIII as the Moses who brought England to the verge of the promised land and who destroyed the idols (golden calf) of monastic shrines, and Edward VI as the Josiah who would restore the temple, in *Godly new story*, sigs B6vo, E4 – i.e. they did not necessarily choose the obvious roles of Moses as lawgiver and Josiah as destroyer of idols and renewer of covenant.
102 Bale, *Rank papist*, sig. A7; see above, Introduction to this chapter.
103 *Ibid.*, sig. A3.
104 Moses set up the brazen serpent at God's command; all who looked on it in faith were cured of the bites of the plague of fiery serpents (Numbers 21:4–9). It was pulled down by king Hezekiah, as it had degenerated into an idol (2 Kings 18:4).
105 'R.V.', *Old faith*, sig. b1.
106 Latimer, *Fifth lenten Court sermon*, PS1 177.
107 See Arthur Kelton, *A commendation of Welshmen* (1546); Thomas Becon, *A pleasant new nosegay* (1542–4) PS1 191.
108 Hooper, *Answer*, PS1 201; Becon, *Flower of godly prayers*, PS3 3–4; see also above, Introduction to this chapter.
109 E.g. Moone's prayer in *A short treatise of certain things abused*, sig. B2vo; Veron claims not to 'run before' the king and Council, in *Five blasphemies in the Mass*, sigs a2–a3.
110 Veron, *Godly sayings*, sig. B1vo. Sir John Yorke was treasurer of the Southwark Mint, sherriff of London, and master of woods south of the Trent.
111 Nichols, *Copy of a letter*, sigs A3–A3vo.
112 Bale, *Acts of the English votaries*.
113 Hooper, *Jonah (fourth sermon)*, PS1 488; cf. William Punt's view that preaching alone was not enough: the magistrate had to root out and destroy idolatry; see *A new dialogue called the inditement of Mother Mass* (?1548), sigs A3vo–A4.
114 J. Phillips, *The Reformation of Images: Destruction of Art in England, 1535–1660* (Berkeley and Los Angeles, CA, 1973), ch. 4; and Aston, *England's Iconoclasts*, vol. 1: 246–77. For comparable material, see G. Potter, *Zwingli* (Cambridge, 1976), 140–1.
115 Ridley removed altars in London in May 1550, less than a month after becoming bishop – see Dickens, *English Reformation*, 339–40; but Cranmer's visitors in the diocese of Norwich removed the first altars in late winter 1550; see MacCulloch, *Cranmer*, 458. Thanks to Prof. MacCulloch for pointing this out.
116 Cf. Veron, *Five blasphemies*, sigs a2–a3.

117 Bale, *Acts of the English votaries*, sig. A7.
118 See Chapter 5, 'Conclusion', pp. 214-19.
119 Hooper, 'The epistle', in *Jonah*, PS1 438. A modification of Pettegree's account (*Foreign Protestant Communities*, 30-7) of Hooper's struggle is in MacCulloch, *Cranmer*, 477-84.
120 See above, Chapter 1; and Chapter 5, 'The ungodly commonwealth', pp. 197-214.
121 See above, Introduction to this chapter.
122 Latimer, *First lenten Court sermon*, PS1 85-6.
123 See Chapter 3, 'The good Shepherd', pp. 94-106.
124 See above, Introduction; 'Godly judgement,' pp. 146ff.
125 Thomas Lever, *Sermon preached at Paul's Cross*, sig. C4.
126 Hooper, *Godly confession*, PS2 87.
127 Demands that justice should be based on the Mosaic law were made notably by Hooper, *Jonah* (third sermon), PS1 476, and *Declaration of the ten commandments*, PS1 282; and by Joye, in *A contrary*. Latimer also demanded it at the same time as asking for the return of excommunication, which is more revealing of his anxiety than any consistency of argument; see *A most faithful sermon*, PS1 258.
128 Matt. 13:24-30.
129 Latimer, *Fifth Sunday after Epiphany* (Lincolnshire sermons), PS2 195-6.
130 Joye, *Answer*, sig. A7.
131 Foxe, *De non plectendis morte adulteris*, sig. A4vo; marginal note: *magistratibus non resistendum*.
132 *Ibid.*, sigs C3-C3vo.
133 *Ibid.*, sig. A5.
134 See Chapter 3, 'Good Shepherd', pp. 94-106.
135 See Chapter 5, 'Conclusion', pp. 214-19.
136 See Chapter 5, 'Divine judgement', pp. 187-93.
137 Becon, *Flower of godly prayers*, PS3 21.
138 Hooper, *Declaration of the ten commandments*, PS1 265-6.
139 The mariners attempt to save Jonah before casting him away; see Hooper, *Jonah* (third sermon), PS1 472.
140 Hooper, *Annotations on Romans 13*, PS2 107.
141 Hooper, *Jonah* (third sermon), PS1 465-9.
142 Joye, *A contrary*, sigs A3-A5.
143 Crowley, *Voice of the last trumpet*, sig. C8vo.
144 Foxe, *De censura*, sig. E2.
145 Becon, *Flower of godly prayers*, PS3 19.
146 Gerrard, *Godly invective*, sig. b5vo; cf. Hooper, 'The epistle', in *Jonah*, PS1 441.
147 2 Chronicles 17:7-9.
148 See above, 'Godly judgement', pp. 152-4.
149 Latimer, *Fifth lenten Court sermon*, PS1 186.
150 Thomas Becon, *Fortress of the faithful* (1550), PS2 599.
151 Nichols, *A godly new story*, sigs C1-1vo.
152 See Chapter 5, 'Resisting the gospel', pp. 209-11.
153 On official corruption, see J. Hurstfield, 'Corruption and reform under Edward VI and Mary: the example of wardship', *EHR* (1953): 22-36; on Sharington, see Jordan, *Young King*, 382-5; on the distribution of land to the Seymour faction, see Miller, 'Henry VIII's unwritten will', 87-105. See also Introduction, pp. 10-13.
154 Latimer, *First lenten Court sermon*, PS1 98, was quoting St John Chrysostom. Latimer, *Fourth lenten Court sermon*, PS1 158-9.

155 See above, Introduction, pp. 143–5.
156 Latimer, *Fifth lenten Court sermon*, PS1 192; cf. examples of both biblical and pagan incorruptibility: Anon., *The praise and commendation of such as sought commonwealths* (?1549), sigs A8–B2.
157 Chester, *Latimer*, 165–6.
158 John 6:5–14 was the text of Lever's sermon: *Sermon preached the third Sunday in Lent*, sig. D8.
159 Latimer, *Fifth lenten Court sermon*, PS1 193; see Chapter 5, pp. 198–200.
160 Hooper, *Jonah* (sixth sermon), PS1 541–2.
161 *Ibid.*, 474–5; cf. *Annotation on Romans 13*, PS2 108.
162 Hooper, *Jonah* (fourth sermon), PS1 495; see above, pp. 152–8.
163 *Ibid.*, 480–4.
164 Nichols, *Godly new story*, sigs B8vo–C2vo.
165 Lever, *Sermon preached at Paul's Cross*, sig. A8.
166 Becon, *Flower of godly prayers*, PS3 21.
167 Crowley, *Voice of the last trumpet*, sigs C8–D1vo.
168 *Ibid.*, sig. C8; but it was as important for the magistrate to use the balance as the sword: sig. C7vo.
169 Latimer, *Second lenten Court sermon*, PS1 127.
170 Latimer, *A most faithful sermon*, PS1 254–5; perhaps an example of Coverdale's influence? He had been in exile in Denmark, and published *The order that the church in Denmark doth use* in 1549; note also the reference in the same sermon to his work in the diocese of Exeter during bishop Vesey's absence.
171 *Ibid.*, 274–5; Cf. *Second lenten Court sermon*, PS1 126–8, Hooper, *Annotation on Romans 13*, PS2 106.
172 Latimer, *Third lenten Court sermon*, PS1 146; the story of Cambyses and the judge's skin also quoted by Hooper, *Jonah* (third sermon), PS1 483. Hoak showed the minimal interest of the Council in poor relief, in *The King's Council*, 216–7; contrast with Somerset's personal activity in the Court of Requests, in Jordan, *Young King*, 363–5.
173 For the prophets' concern for widows and orphans as the most vulnerable members of society, see e.g. Isaiah 1:17 and Jeremiah 5:28. For Tudor problems, see P. Slack, 'Social policy and the constraints of government, 1547–58', in Loach and Tittler (eds) *Mid-Tudor Polity*, 94–115. Further background is given in the Introduction, 'Whatever happened to social conscience?', pp. 6–8.
174 Colet's comment on Romans 13 is summarised in Q.R.D. Skinner, *The Foundations of Modern Political Thought* (Cambridge, 1978), vol. 1: 209–10. On Tyndale and obedience, see especially E.G. Rupp, *Studies in the Making of the English Protestant Tradition* (Cambridge, 1966), 73–88; more recently, S. Greenblatt has noted that Tyndale's obedience is more like submission, and could be reversed in specific circumstances: *Renaissance Self-Fashioning from More to Shakespeare* (Chicago, IL, 1980), 99–114.
175 *Homily of Obedience* (1549) sig. R3vo.
176 *Ibid.*, sigs R4–R4vo.
177 Latimer, *Sermon preached at Stamford* (1550) PS1 300.
178 *Ibid.*
179 Latimer, *Fourth Sermon on the Lord's Prayer*, (preached at Grimsthorpe, 1552) PS1 371.
180 *Ibid.*, 372–3.
181 *Ibid.*, 374
182 Crowley, Robert, *The way to wealth* (1550) sig. A6vo–A7.

183 Latimer, *Fourth Sermon on the Lord's Prayer*, PS1 376; Cranmer, (with Peter Martyr) *Sermon on rebellion* (1549) PS2, 193–4; Cheke, John, *The hurt of sedition* (1549) esp. sigs C5–E7.
184 Cheke, *Hurt of sedition*, sigs A3–A3vo.
185 Ibid., sigs H4–H4vo.
186 See also Chapter 5, 'Resisting the gospel', pp. 209–11. Cf. the 1530s tracts on obedience written in the wake of the Pilgrimage of Grace, notably those of Richard Morison.
187 See Introduction, 'The "commonwealth men": reality or illusion?', p. 6.
188 Religious policy in Edward's reign was not unequivocally protestant; see Elton, *Reform and Reformation*, chs 15 and 16, and MacCulloch, *Tudor Church Militant*, ch. 2. See also Chapter 5, 'The royal minority', pp. 198–200 and 'Pretending the gospel', pp. 200–9.
189 See Introduction, pp. 8–13 and Chapter 5, 'The royal minority', pp. 198–200.
190 This was the settlement imposed on the Lutherans by Charles V after their defeat at the battle of Mühlberg in 1547.
191 'Exhortation to good order and obedience', *Homilies*, sig. S2.
192 Ibid., sig. S4. see Rupp, *Studies*, ch. 5.
193 See above, Introduction to this chapter, especially n. 2.
194 Hooper, *Declaration of the ten commandments*, PS1 288.
195 See above, Introduction to this chapter.
196 Hooper, *Declaration of the ten commandments*, PS1 359, see also Chapter 1, 'Inversion', pp. 28–34.
197 Hooper, *Godly confession*, PS2 76–87.
198 Hooper, *Annotations on Romans 13*, PS2 103.
199 E.g. Latimer, *Third lenten Court sermon*, PS1 148; Latimer, *Fourth sermon on the Lord's Prayer*, PS1 371.
200 Thomas Becon, *Principles of the Christian religion* (1550), PS2 515.
201 See Skinner, *Foundations*, vol. 2: ch. 7. This the foundation of the private law theory of resistance used by the Lutherans and also by Ponet and Goodman. Allen and Turner (see below) go only halfway to stating this case, as befits subjects not immediately faced with the need to justify resistance, but it is significant that they got that far, probably as a result of encountering such arguments in exile.
202 Edmund Allen, *A Catechism, that is to say a Christian instruction* (1551), sig. D4vo.
203 Turner, *A new dialogue*, sigs E1vo–E2.
204 Ibid., sigs E2–E3.
205 Ibid., sig. E3.
206 Hooper, *Declaration of the ten commandments*, PS 309, referring to Isaiah 30–1.
207 Bale, *Image*, PS 365.
208 See above, pp. 160–2 and Conclusion, p. 233.
209 See Davies, 'Edwardian protestant concepts of the church', and also Chapter 1.
210 See Skinner, *Foundations*, vol. 2: ch. 7. For a detailed account of Goodman's thought, see Jane Dawson, 'The early career of Christopher Goodman and his place in the development of English protestant thought', unpublished PhD thesis, University of Durham (1978).
211 See White, *Social criticism*, and Chapter 2.
212 Especially in Hooper, from his commentary on the ten commandments; see below.
213 Especially in Latimer's, sermons on the Lord's Prayer; see below.
214 Hooper, *Annotations on Romans 13*, PS2 111: since many people do not know what charity is, it is not surprising they fail in their Christian duty.
215 Latimer, *Fifth sermon on the Lord's Prayer*, PS1 390–7.

A religion of the Word

216 Ibid., 397.
217 Ibid., 398.
218 For the change in charitable emphasis, from the Mass to organised works of social relief in both protestant and catholic countries, see J. Bossy, *Christianity in the West, 1400–1700* (Oxford, 1985), 143–9.
219 Latimer, *Fifth sermon on the Lord's Prayer*, PS1 399.
220 Ibid., 411.
221 Though the emphasis is on charity here, Latimer's court sermons were mainly about justice. See above, 'Godly judgement', and Chapter 5, 'Pretending the Gospel', pp. 200–9.
222 Hooper, *Declaration of the ten commandments*, PS1 351.
223 Ibid., 415, in answer to those who protested that the nobility (on grounds of privilege) and the young (on grounds of age) should be exempt from obeying the ten commandments, which were only a matter for priests.
224 See above, n. 29.
225 Crowley, *Confutation of Shaxton's articles*, sigs K4vo–K5.
226 In particular, the problems of adultery – see Joye, *A contrary*, sig. A7 – and tithes – see Thomas Ruddoke, *A remembrance*, sig. C5vo. The pressure for secular legislation also sprang from a gospel understanding of charity – see e.g. Lever, *Sermon preached the third Sunday in Lent*, sig. E1vo, on the Chantries Act; Crowley, *Information and petition*, on the need for parliamentary reform of abuses in church and society; Latimer, *A most faithful sermon*, PS1 248–9, on enclosure legislation.
227 See above, 'Godly judgement', pp. 152–8.
228 Latimer, *Gospel for All Saints (Lincolnshire sermons)*, PS1 484.
229 *Homilies*, 'Of Christian love and charity', sig. L3vo.
230 Latimer, *Epistle for the twenty-first Sunday after Trinity (Lincolnshire sermons)*, PS1 503; context of 'armour of God', Ephesians 6:10–12.
231 Latimer, ibid.
232 Latimer, *First sermon on the Lord's prayer*, PS1 339.
233 Latimer, *Third lenten Court sermon*, PS1 148–9.
234 Hooper, *Declaration of the ten commandments*, PS1 387.
235 Ibid., 388.
236 Ibid., 387–404.
237 Hooper, *Annotation on Romans 13*, PS2 112.
238 Latimer, *Epistle for the twenty-first Sunday after Trinity (Lincolnshire sermons)*, PS1 504.
239 See above, nn. 228, 229.
240 Foxe, *De non plectendis morte adulteris*, sig. A8.
241 Ibid., sigs B2vo–B3.
242 Ibid., sigs A7vo–B3vo, B8–C1vo.
243 Ibid., sig. A8vo.
244 Joye, *A contrary*, sigs F5–G1.
245 Ibid., sig. A5vo.
246 Ibid., sigs G5–5vo.
247 See Skinner, *Foundations*, vol. 1: 221–8; see above, A note on the term 'protestant', and Introduction, 'The "commonwealth men"', p. 6.
248 See above, n. 188.

Chapter 5

Signs of the times: hope and fear in the Edwardian reformation

INTRODUCTION

THE mid-Tudor period was for a long time regarded as a somewhat disastrous interlude, consisting of political instability, religious extremism and social and economic crisis.[1] Recently, historians have found more positive things to say about it,[2] suggesting that 'the distance between the Cromwellian achievement on the one hand and the reign of Gloriana on the other seems rather shorter than has been supposed'.[3] A significant part of the evidence for 'crisis', though, is what contemporaries thought about their own times. By surveying protestant views of Edward VI's reign this chapter aims to re-evaluate part of that evidence – evidence that has often been misused to give a picture of unmitigated gloom.[4]

While the evidence for pessimism in Edwardian protestant propaganda far outweighs that for optimism, we can only make sense of both in the light of assumptions about providence and prophecy. Both the passing of time and the nature of events were seen as providential revelations of God's will. Events were explained as manifestations indicating variously the confirmation of prophecies, the culmination of a pattern discernible in the past and a warning of events to come. God's judgement was imminent, whether in the form of plague and punishment, or at the end of time, at the last judgement. This did not mean that interpretations were always consistent; only Bale set out to show in detail that historical evidence could be found to fit his understanding of the Apocalypse.[5] But although Bale was unusual in this respect, his general assumptions that prophecy was the key to comprehending the contemporary world, and that he was living in the 'last days', were not. In what follows, assumptions about the relationship between providence, history, prophecy and judgement will provide a context for an examination of the evidence for optimism and pessimism.

ASSUMPTIONS

Understanding times past, present and to come

Providence: the master of time and the source of prophecy

The doctrine of providence allowed protestants to bridge the gap between an eternal and inscrutable God, on the one hand, and change and development in human history, on the other. It was one of the aspects of God which made him accessible to human understanding. As Cranmer explained in relation to the Sacrament:

> All man's works be done in succession of time (for a carpenter cannot build a house in a day), but God in one moment could make both heaven and earth: so that God worketh without delay of time such things as in us require leisure and time. And yet God hath tempered his speech so to us in Holy Scripture that he speaketh of himself in such words as be usual to us, or else could we speak here and learn nothing of God.[6]

The same principle lay behind protestant explanation of history as a revelation of God's will. Time itself was the creature of providence: the passage of time was not what changed things, but what revealed changes. The belief that providence determined the timing of events had a significant impact on attitudes to those events. A pattern and purpose could be discerned in events which otherwise might seem random and contradictory: 'Thus may all men (considering the works of God) judge without wavering, that all his works are perfect, firm, stable and unchangeable, and he worketh every one in due season, and when need is. So that a man needeth not to say this is worse than that, for in due season they are all pleasant and good.'[7] This was both reassuring and polemically advantageous, imbuing with divine purpose and meaning both the protracted domination of Christendom by popery and the relatively recent events of the reformation, and linking them with the biblical histories and prophecies.

The idea of providential purpose was essential to resolve the paradox that the Gospel was apparently not always victorious, but waned and waxed in strength. The fulfilment of providence's purpose was synonymous with the eventual victory of the Gospel; and the evil of popery was allowed to persist so that the glory of the resurgent Gospel would shine all the more brightly. The perfection of God's works was described by Gilby as a resolution of opposites:

> He hath always made two against two, and everything is well done in his due time. First darkness then light. First night, then day. First sin then grace. First wrath then mercy. First blindness then knowledge. First error then truth. For what worthy cause could we have had to renown and praise the grace and mercy of God if there had been no sin felt or wrath deserved or feared?[8]

Signs of the times: hope and fear

Both the persecution of the godly and their growing ability to discern the corruption of popery were explained in this way as providential. They were necessary stages towards fulfilment, which included both giving the persecutors the opportunity to repent and revealing the extent of their evil.[9] Gardiner, like '[Thomas]More and other mockers', was trying God's patience by 'wading into this secret work of God, with such lewd oppression and derision'. Even the clerical monopoly of scripture had its providential purpose: theologians were 'smeared with the black coals of their helly doctrine, that their souls should never be clear again', while the poor were forbidden access to the Bible and fobbed off with saints' lives, but this allowed their consciences to remain 'like a white wall, ready to receive all truth of God's holy Word'.[10] As maintainers of error and persecutors, the prelates were the 'seed of Cain'. But their monopoly of scripture would lead to destruction: 'For God hath caused the pharisees before them and our bishops following to keep these jewels for our use and profit, and for their own confusion, that by the same books which they kept and whereupon they boasted, they should be openly convinced and overcome.'[11]

Providential purpose explained past repression and justified the reformation. Thus Bale explained that the keeping of ill-advised vows was to put human will before the will of God not only in a theological but in a historical sense, since 'the change of things by his secret providence dischargeth the necessity of the oath . . .'.[12] But neither Bale nor the author of *A dialogue between a gentleman and a priest* saw any contradiction between trusting to providence and forwarding his own purposes, especially the reform of the Sacrament:

> I say unto you, until the time that God hath appointed no man shall redress it. For it is his business, therefore let him alone with it. For when all men hath wrestled, some true, some false, he will show the truth all his pleasure. Yet let all faithful men that love God's word unfainedly be doing still till the Lord come to judgement. Either with pen and ink, or with mouth and tongue, or both. For no doubt this abuse shall be reformed when the time that God hath appointed is come.[13]

While God alone knew when the Mass would be abolished, activism was the duty of the faithful. Even the imperfections of the reformation could be given a providential rationale. Thus Hooper explained the Lutheran doctrine of the Sacrament as an error allowed by God in the time of reformation – 'lest man should too much glory in himself'.[14] Human error merely emphasised the perfection of God, and encouraged people to seek it as revealed only in scripture, not in human interpretation.

Just as God had ordained both the rise and fall of the true and false churches, so he knew when their struggle would culminate. The last days were imminent but it was impossible for humans to pin-point the exact date

A religion of the Word

of judgement day. Again this was all part of providence's intent, allowing both Saint Paul and Gilby to believe that they were living in the last days without accusing God of indefinite delay: 'And the Lord is not slow in coming as the unwise do think him. But patient towards us, not willing any to perish but to receive all to repentance.'[15] In the end, he would shorten the time for the sake of the elect. 'Necessary is it that both good and bad know it; the faithful to be ascertained that their final redemption is at hand, the unfaithful to have knowledge that their judgement is not far off, that they may repent and be saved.'[16] The providential purpose of revelation was thus intimately linked with that of salvation.

This was particularly evident in relation to the understanding of prophecy, in which God revealed his will to humanity. Admonition by the prophets, whether biblical or otherwise, was preliminary to judgement of the false church. This was not a simple matter of cause and effect, but both were part of the divine plan. 'Mark in this process past the nature of God's eternal decree for this age of his Church: first it sheweth, then it condemneth the cursed synagogue of the devil. In signification whereof the true preachers of our time have manifestly opened her wickedness unto all the world, whereupon her utter destruction must shortly follow.'[17] Under the guidance of providence, time revealed the truth of prophecy only at significant moments. Walter Lynne described both the making and the rediscovery of mediaeval prophetic pictures showing the rise and fall of the papacy in providential terms:

> Whereby it is manifest that the fathers of ancient time saw in the papacy the thing they durst not utter, either by words or writing, but trusting that the time would come when men might be bold to speak it, they did in the meantime keep it in painting or portraiture, that such as could conjecture might gather knowledge thereby, and that the thing might remain till such time as God hath appointed it to be declared both in writing and in words.[18]

The human voice of the preacher, be he Old Testament prophet or protestant divine, was irrelevant; what mattered was that God was speaking through him.[19] 'Thus have we here in this prophet [i.e. Micah] wholesome doctrine for all ages. For the spirit of God seeth from time to time continually our iniquities, and striveth evermore there against.'[20] The insistence that prophecies were relevant and God-given was intensified by the belief that the passage of time, as shown in history and controlled by providence, revealed them to be true.

Time as revelation

With the exception of Bale, Edwardian reformists did not centre their arguments on history. The detailed minutiae of proving the existence of the

Signs of the times: hope and fear

precursor of protestantism in the 'first six hundred years' of the Church's existence was a debate yet to come.[21] This did not prevent history being used more generally as a polemical weapon, especially to show God's care for the true church, and to provide evidence of the antichristian conspiracy. History may have taken second place to the scriptures, but to protestant polemicists it provided a much-needed source of continuity. They used it to expound theological and polemical rather than moral lessons.[22] History showed that God allowed the passage of time to reveal what the world, the flesh and Satan worked to obscure. Thus the hallowed traditions of conservative piety were shown to be relatively recent inventions of the papacy, intended only to increase its worldly power. Conversely, several writers took the nationalistic line that there was a true church in England which maintained the ways of the primitive church until it was displaced by an invading, alien and tyrannical popery.[23]

If 'everything had its due season',[24] then the present was the time for the exposure of popery.[25] Protestants laid claim to the past by representing the primitive church as a 'golden age' from which the church under popery had declined: the 'new learning' was not protestantism but popery, 'new' in comparison with 'the old learning of God's word'.[26] 'As to their anciency, be sure to take Christ for thy guide, who was before all', warned Gilby.[27] This principle allowed the discussion of the theology and liturgy of the Mass to be packed with historical point-scoring. Gilby dated the central doctrine of transubstantiation not to the Last Supper, but to AD 1000 – a date full of eschatological significance, since it was then that 'Satan was loosed'.[28] Hooper saw continuity not in the Mass – 'but a yesterday's bird'[29] – but in the breaking of bread, and blamed the corruption of the Lord's Supper on the growth of monasticism and papal power. He dated private Masses from the reign of Louis the Pious, and transubstantiation (officially) from the Fourth Lateran Council.[30] Scriptural and patristic doctrine suffered great damage in the 'Dark Ages', but even so the 'legalising' of transubstantiation was only achieved with great difficulty, with the help of the friars, 'the self soldiers of Antichrist', in the thirteenth century.[31] John Mardely was less chronologically accurate: the Mass, he wrote, was 'not known in the Church of the faithful (as Bede saith) which was fourscore and ten years after the death of Gregory, then such masking was not known till monkery of Benedict's rule came in . . .'.[32] Bale described vowed celibacy as an invention of the papacy after Phocas, intended to increase clerical power by means of 'feigned holiness' and miracles.[33]

All this resulted in the oppression rather than the extinction of the true church: 'In the meantime, many godly men were sore afflicted in their conscience, yet durst not declare their grief, partly for fear, partly because that sophistry had blinded part of their judgements.'[34] But just as the power of

A religion of the Word

Antichrist was at its height, God raised up men to reveal the truth, starting with John Wyclif and going on to Luther and the continental reformers, so that by Edward VI's reign 'children know the ungodliness' of the Mass 'and may see it plainly to be naught...'. The choice of John Wyclif as the forerunner of the reformation showed the nationalistic element in the English protestant use of history.[35] Crowley's re-publication, with his own annotations, of *Piers Plowman*, was a deliberate attempt to foster the idea that protestantism was not a new foreign doctrine but had indigenous antecedents.[36] These later-mediaeval 'ancestors', however, might seem to be embarrassingly 'recent' in an argument which was intended to prove that popery not protestantism was 'new doctrine'. Perhaps this charge also accounted for protestant interest in the early history of Britain.

Bale's *Acts of the English votaries* was by far the most detailed exploration of this theme.[37] It was also the most complex, since it attempted to tie in the monastic chronicles to the apocalyptic chronology that he had outlined in the *Image of both churches*.[38] Bale saw the history of the church in England as a microcosm of the universal church in overall pattern, yet as having a unique contribution to make. Thus he asserted that Britain first received Christianity 'at the very spring or first going forth of the gospel, when the Church was most perfect and had most strength of the Holy Ghost'.[39] Yet heresy too was also present from the earliest times; Pelagius, whom Bale described as a 'monk of Bangor', linked a theology emphasising free will and monasticism.[40] However ambivalent he was to Celtic monasticism,[41] he emphasised that the first major threat to 'pure' Christianity in Britain was Augustine's mission to convert the Saxons, for with this England came under the aegis of the pope for the first time.[42]

Bale was not always entirely positive about the British church; he saw monastic celibacy as the source of corruption in the church, and he deplored the extreme asceticism of the Celtic saints.[43] Yet he admired the fortitude and learning with which Aidan, Hilda, Firmin and Colman defended the British church against Rome in the Easter controversy.[44] Elsewhere he likened Anne Askew to her British forebears Alban, for martyrdom, and Hilda, for 'openly disput[ing] in [scripture] against the superstitions of certain bishops'.[45]

It was almost certainly Bale's case for the significance of the history of the early British church that influenced other protestants.[46] Gilby thus traced the early church in Britain from Joseph of Arimathea, through Gildas 'who instructed the ploughmen of Kent and other countries [i.e. counties] of whom we have the monuments', to Robert Grosseteste, who 'did rebuke the world of blind judgement' and, last, 'the great clerk, John Wyclif, that wrote so many godly books'.[47] The author of *The old faith of Great Britain and the new learning of England* traced the Gospel in England, as Bale had done, to the time of king Lucius:[48] 'And thus we see the first faith received in this realm to be taught according to the Gospel. For at that time were few ceremonies used by the Christians other than were contained in the Gospel.'[49] The corruption of the church in England came with Augustine, 'unsent for' from Rome, 'and thus was the new learning brought into this realm of which we see much yet remaining in the Church at this present day, although the Britons at that time would in no wise receive [it] . . .'.[50] Like Bale he used the example of the slaughter of the monks of Bangor as evidence of the treachery and tyranny with which the 'new learning' of Rome was imposed on England.[51] William Salesbury contributed to the celibacy debate by publishing a case extract from the law of the Welsh king Hywel the Good to prove that secular clergy at least could marry in the Celtic church.[52]

Protestant interest in the early history of the British church, like the more conventional 'proof' that popery was a relatively recent development, had a specific polemical purpose. It gave England a unique claim to an important place in the wider primitive church, and thus gave English protestants an 'ancestry' that did not depend on recent developments on the continent. However nationalistic the results were, the intent was to show that protestantism was the resurgent form of a 'pure' primitive Christianity, and not a new development. History was, in any case, no more than the second line of defence, providing 'proof' that providence was faithful to his promises. Prophecy, which God gave to his people to understand their times, was a far more flexible polemical tool. Unlike history, it was not merely retrospective, but could be used to link past, present and future.

Prophecy

Prophecy was seen as a direct communication between God and his people, a merciful warning of future judgement which gave the opportunity to change the ways of the present. As a a link between the eternal and the temporal, it was as relevant to contemporary times as it was to the times in which it was made. This was dramatically announced by Gilby in the introduction to his commentary on Micah:

> We do need no new prophets. We do need no more prophecies. We do need no more miracles, signs or tokens, which now do live in these latter days, if we will call old things to memory; neither if we will not believe the old history reported by Moses and the terrible threatenings of the prophets could we believe, if the greatest miracles of raising the dead to speak amongst us were wrought in our days (as Christ our saviour saith to the rich glutton). Wherefore suffer me, I beseech thee, to renew old things written by this prophet Micah, the most earnest rebuker of vice in this time, and the most diligent watchman to warn of both good and evil, for to come upon his people, and if so be that the words of this old truth do chafe your old sores in this perilous time, wherein

> all old evils seem to have disguised themselves with new vizors, rather suffer them, to be ripped to the hard core, than to spurn impudently against the prick, to strive against the stream. For the time is at hand by the unchangeable appointment of the everliving Lord and most mighty judge, when every man shall be tried and judged, approved or refused by the thoughts of his heart, by the words of his mouth, and by the fruits of his own imaginations.[53]

Gilby maintained a strong sense throughout his commentary of the historical reality and context of Micah's prophecy, pointing out to the reader the political circumstances in Israel and Judah to which he referred.[54] At the same time his interpretation used Micah's words to shape his own critique of English society and politics. The format of the commentary enabled him to ride these two horses at once with great facility, but it was an approach that also shaped Latimer's use of Isaiah in his Court sermons of 1549 and Hooper's sermons on Jonah.[55] Gilby's reference to the consensus that contemporary times were the 'latter days' coincided with the eschatological element in Micah's prophecy, which was probably why he chose him.[56] Eschatology was not the only reason why prophets should be studied, but it did intensify their message. Gilby's commentary, with its intertwined strands of history, social comment and eschatology, showed very clearly how prophecy could be used to interpret past, present and future time.

The assumption that prophecy was God's will translated into temporal terminology for the good of his people had three main implications. One was that prophecy would sooner or later be fulfilled, since God was always faithful to his promise. This was particularly obvious in the description of the reformation as a fulfilment of prophecy. The second implication was that prophets were sent as an act of mercy to direct the people in a time of disorder and disintegration, by both warning them of impending crisis and offering them a way of averting it. It was thus dangerous to ignore prophecy, but history showed that many people did so. This brings us to the final implication, that there was a certain predictability about the responses that prophecy evoked.

Examples of the use of prophecy to emphasise the validity of the protestant case in doctrinal debate are manifold. Phillip Nichols cited Jerome's commentary on Nahum that the people would turn to the scriptures of their own accord, for lack of true teachers, before the second coming, remarking gleefully to his conservative opponent canon Crispin: 'Mark well this prophecy, for surely it biteth.'[57] Various writers noted the warnings of Christ and the apostles about false prophets,[58] linking the doctrines of transubstantiation and the Real Presence with the warning that the false prophets would point out multiple 'Christs' to the people.[59] The doctrine of the sacrifice of Christ on the cross in the Mass was reviled in the words of Isaiah and Malachi, in which God declared that he took no pleasure in the burnt offerings of the priests.[60] Crowley threatened the ranks of poorly educated lower clergy (especially chantry priests) with the prophecy of the destruction of the ignorant priesthood:[61] 'declare if you can that these drone bees that swarm so thick in every church be not the priests that the prophets speak of . . .'.[62] Evidence of the increase of Antichrist's power was to be found by Bale and Lynne in mediaeval Joachimite prophecy, as well as in the Bible.[63] The working out of events in history confirmed the truth of prophecy and hence the faithfulness of providence. Hence Bale described the 'text' of Revelation as 'a light to the chronicles and not the chronicles to the text',[64] admitting that he selected and interpreted historical evidence to fit the demands of his interpretation of scripture.

The second point raised by prophecy, that it was uttered in a time of crisis to warn the people of God's anger at their sin, was made more forcibly, as it related powerfully to the self-image of protestant publicists as prophets.[65] This providential role of the preachers was set out in the homily *Of declining from God*, which declared that they were sent as part of the 'gentle monition and communication' of God to his people before he finally abandoned them to his wrath.[66] The bitter message of the prophets was paradoxically evidence of God's mercy: 'such compassion hath he over our manifold weaknesses that he premonishes us of his most terrible plagues to call us back by fear if love will not do it . . .'.[67]

Prophecy was an index of crisis: Bale described how, in the divided kingdom of Israel, 'as the false worshippings or execrable idolatries began to increase by the devilishness of false priests, God raised up the prophets, with an earnestness to rebuke them and again to renew the heavenly doctrine of governance'.[68] Similarly Gilby emphasised the relevance of the historical crisis in which Micah wrote his prophecy – the idolatrous divided kingdoms of Judah and Samaria on the brink of destruction by the Assyrians: 'Of whomsoever it is spoken, we must mark for what cause it is spoken; to teach us that sin is the cause of the destruction to all kingdoms. The trust in chariots, in horses, in walled cities and strongholds, in enchantments and idols are the cause of God's wrath, indignation and heavy displeasure.'[69] Protestants both cited Old Testament prophets and identified with them, bringing the message of judgement to a nation which was oblivious of the extent of corruption within and the resulting imminence of disaster.[70]

The danger of not heeding prophecy was often emphasised by preachers who were highly conscious of the fact that most prophecies fell on deaf ears. The likelihood of a poor response was a prophetic tradition which protestants found very useful.[71] Becon described the woe that befell England for not listening to her own prophets, among whom he numbered Gildas, whose warnings were followed by the Saxon invasions; Wyclif, whose persecution and death was followed by the murder of Richard II, the loss of the French lands in the Hundred Years' War, and the Wars of the Roses; and more recently Tyndale, Frith and Bilney, whose unheeded preaching and murder heralded the present troubles.[72] Hooper referred to the Old Testament accounts of Israel and Judah's relations with the prophets, to show how 'the contempt of God's word was the occasion of the loss of these realms'.[73] The lack of response was shown by the propensity of the Israelites (and, by implication, of the English) to blame precisely the wrong people for the destruction. Ahab had asked Elijah 'Art thou he that troubleth Israel?' in the same way that the reformers found themselves now blamed for unrest, and the Israelites, in spite of being admonished by Jeremiah to turn to God, had preferred to base their prosperity on the worship of the 'Queen of Heaven', just like religious conservatives in England.[74] Gilby compared the fate of the papists to those of Cain, pharaoh and Herod, since like them, they 'suffer[ed] all the words of Christ, his prophets and apostles concerning the wrath of God in the latter days to be spoken in vain'.[75] Bale, however, explained this vanity in providential terms:

> Such is the nature of God's wisdom that though it be not in glorious words, fine painted terms nor in persuasible reasons of man's wit, but in plain simple speaking; yet can it not be known of the worldly-wise. The sweet dew thereof will not be received of them in the aforesaid days of prophecy; but he that is blind shall be blind still.[76]

While the unresponsiveness of the ungodly justified their punishment, the godly who did heed the warnings would not be exempt from punishment either, but would come to less harm: 'Much less harm felt they of Antiochus Ephiphanes that had read Daniel's prophecy afore, and marked it, than they which knew it not when that tyrant came upon them.'[77] If this sounded like cold comfort, it should be remembered that, because of the sinfulness of humanity, prophecy was always more useful as a key to understanding events than as a mechanism for altering their course. Hence Bale described Revelation as setting out the 'image of both churches ... to the merciful forewarning of the Lord's elect',[78] who would understand that the allegory revealed unalterable truths. The fact that the wicked never listened to prophecy and were consequently destroyed should not worry the godly, who should wait patiently 'and pray unto God that it will please him to revenge the shed blood of his saints, and shortly to deliver us of these cruel tyrants'.[79]

As a threat of disaster, prophecy both increased protestant anxiety about the present and helped them to engender anxiety in their audience. Paradoxically, by providing insight into future events and a framework for understanding the present it also increased their confidence. This both moderated their pessimism and helped to account for the urgency of their demands for reformation and repentance. Whether as a means of exposing popery, defending the reformation or adding weight to their social criticisms, protestants used prophecy as evidence on which to base their claims and issue their challenges. Rejection did not prevent them speaking out, but instead helped to confirm the faithfulness of their message.

The inevitability of divine judgement

The prophetic theme which protestants found most congenial was that of judgement. They were confident that it was imminent, whether it took the form of temporal plague and punishment, or the last judgement at the end of time. Indeed, it was not always clear where the one ended and the other began – and perhaps that was intentional, a way of heightening the sense of threat and urgency.[80] The blurring of boundaries between the temporal and the eschatological reflected the uncertainty surrounding England's commitment to the Gospel, and, within that context, the extent and role of the godly. The distinction between the two forms of divine judgement could, however, be made on the grounds of finality: temporal punishment, however likely, was theoretically avertable, while the last judgement was not. Nevertheless, whatever form the judgement took, it had the effect of concentrating attention on the present in terms of the immediate future.

Temporal judgement: plague and punishment

In his mercy, God always gave his people the chance of repentance, however deserving of immediate retribution were their sins. The pattern of God's 'visitations' was outlined in the homily *Of declining from God*. The first visitation was that of the Word, always insistent on the need for repentance.[81] But the people all too often showed the fact that they were 'declining from God' by their preference for idolatry, their lack of faith and their neglect of the commandments. The second visitation took place in two stages: God first turned his 'terrible countenance' towards them, in the shape of famine, disease and war, and if this failed to impress on them the seriousness of their offences, he turned away: 'But when he withdraweth from us his Word, the right doctrine of Christ, his gracious assistance and aid (which is ever joined to his Word) and leaveth us to our own wit, to our own will and strength, he declareth then that he beginneth to forsake us.'[82] Punishment by plagues was thus followed by abandonment to sin: 'he will let us alone and suffer us to bring forth even such fruit as we will, to bring forth brambles, briars and thorns, all naughtiness, all vice and that so abundantly that they shall clean overgrow us, suffocate, strangle and utterly destroy us'.[83] The pattern of the dual visitation by God was essential to the protestant understanding of the directions that the reformation was taking in England, and

A religion of the Word

had taken in Germany where protestantism was languishing under the terms of the Interim.[84] Latimer warned that England had received the first visitation of preaching and a 'noble King'; if the English did not show their gratitude by the sincerity of their repentance, it was only a matter of time before the second visitation of God's vengeance would take place.[85] He reminded his Court audience of what had happened in Germany; it

> was visited twenty years with God's Word, but they did not earnestly embrace it, but made a mingle-mangle and a hotch-potch of it – I cannot tell what, partly popery, partly true religion, mingled together ... God seeing that they would not come unto his Word, now he visited them in the second time of his visitation, with his wrath: for the taking away of God's Word is a manifest token of his wrath.[86]

Gilby compared the situation of England with both Old Testament Jerusalem and contemporary Germany:

> Hear by now England, and all those people whom God hath specially called in these our times by the light of his gospel hath great cause to tremble and fear God his secret judgement, considering that we have not so many promises as had Jerusalem and their fall was for their unthankfulness and forgetfulness of their duties towards God, as appeareth by our prophet. What shall we then look for, like fall with the Germans? Nay, much worse and much sorer, because we will not yet be warned.[87]

The pattern of the dual visitation accurately reflected the anxiety of Edwardian protestants: if England did not accept the reformation, which was God's first visitation, then the second visitation, when he took his Word away, would be seen in the reimposition of popery.

The critical nature of the people's response, made the reformation a conditional one, but did it imply that England was bound by a covenant? Even though the exact nature of the covenant between God and England was never explicitly expounded, various covenants between God and Israel were invoked in the discussion of kingship.[88] Most significantly for Edward, one of the first acts of the young king Josiah was to renew the covenant.[89] In more general respects, England was understood to be comparable to Israel:

> As God forsook the children of Israel for sin so will he do us. They were elected to be his people with this condition *'si audiendo audieris vocem meam, et custodieris pactum meum, eritis mihi in peculium de cunctis populis'* (Exod. 19). He that favoured not the Israelites but took cruel vengeance upon them because they walked not in their vocation will do and doth daily the same to us (Rom. 11).[90]

The English behaved ungratefully in the same way that the children of Israel did after God had delivered them from Egyptian slavery:

Signs of the times: hope and fear

> All this not withstanding (I say) for every trifle they murmured and grudged, wishing themselves again in Egypt, even despising the voice of the Lord their God, and made them other gods, and served the gods of the nations, or went a-whoring after their own inventions: for which the Lord plagued them often, very sore.[91]

God had promised that he would lead the English to the 'Canaan' of reformed religion, but by hankering after the 'Egyptian fleshpots' of popery and blaming the gospel for the increase of sin they risked the plague of abandonment by God. It might be even more catastrophic than the invasion and occupation of Israel had been – Gilby thought it would be, because the sins of England were far worse.[92] A more narrowly theological line was taken by Joye, who dealt with the covenant in the wider sense of the relations between the two testaments:[93]

> So that the name of Old and New Testaments springeth not out of the substance of the covenant but are of certain accidentary added considerations which were put for certain sundry seasons, places, persons and diversity of nations to be at last changed. Without which additions the substance of the covenant itself ever abode and abideth to the world's end . . .[94]

As a nation which claimed to be Christian, England was bound by the covenant of the law, and risked God's anger in flouting it.[95]

But destruction was not visited upon Israel only, but on foreign (i.e. pagan) nations and the world in general. The covenant was not therefore necessarily implied by notions of plague and punishment. Hooper pointed this out in his sermons on Jonah, comparing the pagan Nineveh's prompt response to Jonah's preaching against the response of both Israel and England: 'Their obedience to the Word of God condemneth both the Jews and us of obstinacy and malice.'[96] Hooper concluded that it was easier to convince 'infidels' of the need for repentance than those who were used to the idolatry and half-belief of either Israel or Rome.[97] God's mercy and destruction extended to all nations:

> [H]e premonisheth and forewarneth of his scourge to come, by his prophets, apostles and preachers, and willeth the world to amend. In case they do so, he will turn his ire from them; if they will not, no remedy but utter destruction; as ye may read Genesis 7 of the flood, Genesis 19 of Sodom, Exodus 14 of Pharaoh.[98]

Latimer compared London unfavourably with the city of Nebo in Moab – again a pagan nation – which 'was much reproved for idolatry, supersition, pride, avarice, cruelty, tyranny, and for hardness of heart, and for these sins was plagued of God and destroyed'.[99] Nebo would have repented had she had as many warnings as London:[100] 'Repent therefore, repent London, and remember the same God liveth now that punished Nebo, even the same God and none other; and he will punish sin as well now as he did then; and he will punish the iniquity of London as well he did then of Nebo.'[101] London was comparable with Nineveh and Nebo in wealth, relative size, and opportunity for vice and iniquity, as well as being the focus of protestant preaching activity.[102]

The model of the punishment of the foreign nations (Nineveh and Nebo) prefigured the destruction accompanying the last judgement:[103]

> He came many times; first in the time of Noah when he preached, but he found little faith. He came also when Lot preached, when he destroyed Sodom and Gomorrah, but he found no faith. And to be short, he shall come at the Latter Day, but he shall find a little faith. And I ween the day be not far off...[104]

As Christ had prophesied, the final destruction would happen when everyone was immersed in worldly concerns.[105] The crucial issue was rejection of the Word, rather than the breaking of the covenant. What was more, the rejection of the Word by corrupt human nature made punishment almost inevitable: 'No man can abide to have his faults rebuked by the law, but hateth his admonitors, and would that there were neither God neither law, so that he might, unpunished, satisfy his pleasure.'[106] Wilful refusal to listen of necessity incurred God's anger: 'Sin is now as odious to God as ever it was, and with more grievous plagues are they worthy to be punished which know now his will, and will not obey it.'[107]

Evidence that the gospel was being rejected increased the anxiety that had accompanied its return in the form of God's first visitation. The activities of papists, anabaptists and carnal gospellers made Becon describe Edward's reign as more a time of 'sadness' than of 'gladness'.[108] Hutchinson warned that

> we shall instead of the comfortable promises of God be destroyed and overwhelmed with terrible plagues, which he threateneth to the breakers of his law, as dearth, war, dissension, uproars, insurrections, pestilence, strange diseases etc. We have a taste of these curses already; God hath bent his bow and let slip some of his arrows which be his plagues, long since amongst us; we may perceive by that which has chanced, what touch he will keep with us hereafter, and what is like to follow.[109]

Such pessimism saw current events either as plagues in their own right or as indications of future plagues.[110] The epidemic of the sweating sickness of 1551 was explained by Hooper as England's punishment for ignoring calls to repent, the negligence of the ministry in making such calls and of the magistracy in punishing sin. Indeed, the sweating sickness was itself 'an extraordinary magistrate' appointed by God 'to reform and punish the mother of all mischief, sin, and contempt of God's holy Word'.[111] The extreme virulence of this pestilence was in itself a sign of the intensity of God's wrath – it struck so rapidly that sinners had no time to repent.[112] The relationship between dearth, poverty and rebellion was explained in terms of multiple plagues, though the order of cause and effect varied with the sympathies of the writer. Thus Becon described dearth and food shortage as a plague for idolatry and popery and as a cause of the further plague of rebellion,[113] while Cheke showed that the scourge of rebellion not only incurred just human punishment but both caused and was punished by famine and disease.[114] Crowley explained rebellion as the result of misery, greed and popishness among the commons and of the irresponsibility of their hireling pastors.[115] The immediacy of plague and punishment made protestants see the Edwardian reformation not as the end of the beginning but as the beginning of the end.

Speculation on the nature of future plagues increased the sense of threat. The return of popery was the most immediate likelihood;[116] evidence of the precariousness of the protestant achievement was reinforced by prophetic inevitability. Thus Richard Finch interpreted 1 Tim. 4 and 2 Thess. 2 by asserting that false prophets were sent by God because the people would not believe the true ones: 'But amongst all plagues of God, this is the greatest, that he taketh away his Word from the people, and suffereth them to be fed with lies, and Canterbury tales or fables.'[117] The plague was completed by the addition of false miracles and the legalising of false doctrine, all demanded by the ungodly people.[118] Lever drew back from uttering outright sedition when he threatened invasion: 'I do not mean the men, in whom there is some mercy, but the most cruel vices of these thy enemies, being without all pity, as the covetousness of Scotland, the pride of France, the hypocrisy of Rome and the idolatry of the Turks.'[119] Alternatively, God might punish the persecution of the preachers by sending a tyrant, like Nebuchadnezzar or Titus.[120]

The only chance of averting such punishment was national repentance. Even after advocating various social and economic measures to alleviate distress 'Piers Plowman' ended his *Exhortation* to parliament with a call to repentance: 'Yet I would not say that any man should think it possible by any worldly policy to defend this realm from utter destruction, except we amend our sinful living. For if God be determined to plague us for our offences, what can worldly policy prevail to the contrary?'[121] Gilby thought that the sweating sickness and war with Scotland were fatherly corrections sent by God before he finally abandoned the English to their enemies.[122] The wrath of God was not to be resisted by the 'worldly policy' of allying with antichristian nations, but by repentance. He urged the government to beware of the flattery of 'the French or Scottish lady' – pointed references to Northumberland's policy of peace with France and to Mary of Guise.[123]

God's mercy was England's only hope of survival, as Lever pointed out: 'Tell all England, high and low, rich and poor, that they, everyone, prowling for themselves, be servants unto mammon, enemies unto God, disturbers of common wealth, and destroyers of themselves. And for all this, let them know that I have no pleasure in the death of a sinner.'[124] However, the delaying of his vengeance was an important sign of his mercy.[125] Present plagues were sent by God acting not as 'a tyrant or butcher' but as a father 'that most dearly loveth us, which would not that we should be destroyed, but that we should correct our manners, amend and obtain health and salvation'.[126] Hooper chose the example of Nineveh precisely because repentance led to a happy outcome – and a happy end to the sermon. England should follow the example of the Ninevites, in fasting and prayer, and above all faith, for as the king of Nineveh proclaimed: ' "Who can tell whether God will turn from the fury of his wrath, that we perish not?" We may here learn to put away despair and trust to the Lord's mercy although he threaten never so much our destruction.'[127]

The concentration of attention on the depravity of the nation left something of a gap where the godly were concerned. Unlike the Marian exiles, they could not regard themselves as a self-defining group set apart from the rest of the nation. Their ability to act as a 'saving remnant' was therefore invoked by protestants even less than were theories about the covenant. They could not decide even whether the godly would be protected from the national plagues, or whether they were to be 'chastened' by them. But the conservative conclusion that social unrest punished the gospellers for espousing the 'new learning' did begin to draw attention to their role. Cheke accused conservatives of making the wrong causal link[128] – they were like the Jews who thought that God punished them for allowing Jeremiah to prophesy, or the pagans who thought that persecution of Christians resulted in fair weather:

> Such fancies lighted now in papists' and irreligious men's heads, and join things by chance happening together, and concludeth the one to be the cause of the other, and then delighteth in true worshippers' hurt, because they judge cursedly good to be bad, and therefore rejoiceth in the punishment of the godly.[129]

Even though on first sight it appeared that God had abandoned them, providence always looked after his own, as the story of Joseph showed – 'although the plague of famine be cast upon any realm and the wicked thereof perish for hunger, yet will God so provide for them that fear him and call upon his holy name that they shall want no good thing'.[130] Hutchinson's sermons *On oppression, affliction and patience* (unpublished) asserted that the oppressed were favoured by God who would not try them beyond endurance if they bore their troubles patiently. Hutchinson discussed problems of poverty, sickness and social oppression, familiar in other more reformist works, in this very passive context. God's people were tried by humbling them, like Jonah in the whale or 'gold in the furnace',[131] and indeed the innocent were often the first to suffer, like the two sons of the duchess of Suffolk, 'the hope, honour and comeliness of that house', who were victims of the sweating sickness.[132] However, the trust that the godly would not suffer in vain was extended to include even their eventual vindication: '[B]ut yet it is not so necessary that the same should continue in oppressing the offenders and the innocent together. For so shall they also deserve the Lord's wrath and in the end be plagued by some other that God shall stir up to revenge the innocent sort.'[133]

The message to 'the innocent sort' was one of patient suffering and waiting for God to revenge them. Because there was no developed sense of the part the godly could play as a 'saving remnant', their fate received very little attention. The important thing was to warn of impending disaster. If the godly were at all a self-selecting group it was as prophets and preachers, who may have felt 'persecuted' but were certainly not playing only a passive part in events. The idea of the dual visitation by God did not involve the kind of 'theological opportunism' that would be developed by the Marian exiles to bridge the gap between a covenanted nation and a predestined elect minority, since the covenant was not vital to its construction. Instead, it dramatised both protestant publicists into prophets, and social disorder into signs of God's wrath, in an attempt to accelerate the pace of change and infuse it with spiritual intensity. Crucially, plague and punishment could be averted if only the nation heeded the warnings of the prophets and repented. But just as imminent was a judgement that could not be averted, a judgement which came at the end of the world.

Eschatology: the last days at hand

It is now no longer assumed that belief in the proximity of the last days was the preserve only of fanatical millenarian movements, resulting in the kind of chiliastic upheaval experienced in the German reformation at Münster. Belief in the imminent end of the world was commonplace, and it significantly modified the attitude of many protestants to their own times.[134] It meant that their social criticisms and their perceptions of the recent history of the reformation were charged with eschatological significance, for they saw the world not as slowly changing and progressing but as hurtling to its final doom. Time itself was running out; disorder and oppression were both symptoms of this and would be cured by it. Eschatological prediction extended, rather than excluded, the idea of temporal plague and punishment. Both of these types of judgement increased the urgency of calls for repentance, and maximised the sense of threat and anxiety which protestants hoped would galvanise change for the better, whilst explaining and rationalising evidence of change for the worse.

At this stage, however, complex calculations to pinpoint the exact date of the last judgement were rare. Bale was the only writer to tackle the problem at any length, drawing heavily on continental theorists.[135] Whatever the method, the result was always that the last days were almost exactly contemporary. Gilby's calculations in his commentary on Micah went into some detail: he used the 'rabbinical' chronology of the 'six ages', in which there were 1,655 years from the creation to the flood, 793 years from the flood to the deliverance from Egypt, 480 years from Egypt to the building of Solomon's temple, 419 years from the temple to the Babylonian captivity, and 623 years from then to the reign of the Messiah. The reign of the Messiah was, aptly enough for the publication of Gilby's commentary, 1551 years, but even he felt it necessary to warn that time in God's eyes did not have the same value as it did in those of humans.[136] Latimer was less specific:

> How can we be so foolish to set so much by this world, knowing that it shall endure but a little while? For we know by Scripture and all learned men affirm the same, that the world was meant to endure six thousand years. Now of the six thousand be passed already five thousand five hundred and fifty-two, and yet this time which is left shall be shortened for the elect's sake, as Christ himself witnesseth.[137]

The three reasons most often given for suggesting that the last judgement was imminent were that the reformation heralded the defeat of Antichrist, that the true church was undergoing its final persecution, and that the social order was disintegrating at an alarming rate. By schematising history so that the reformation coincided with the final struggle of the last days, recent events were invested with meaning, as the culmination of a divine plan. Bale showed this by carefully organising the 'layers' of chronology and allegory in his commentary. Since it was agreed that the last days were times of struggle, Bale was easily able to juggle the idea of a powerful Antichrist with that of a resurgent true church.[138] Thus for instance, the 'ten horns' which make war on the Whore of Babylon were interpreted as the princes, bishops and reformers in England and the continent who 'shall hate the Whore. Her abominations once known by the gospel preaching, they shall abhor her laws, despise her authority and condemn her customs. They shall defeat her of those lands and possessions which now she unjustly holdeth.'[139] The cataclysmic events of the age of the sixth seal, which began with the death of Wyclif, saw both Antichrist at his most belligerent and the resurgence of the Gospel, with the 'sealing' of the godly.[140] It was mirrored by the age of the sixth trumpet, when 'the antichrists' lost many of their profits from piety, were defeated by the princes and 'raged' against the godly in consequence.[141]

Signs of the times: hope and fear

His view of the eschatological position of the late Henrician period was slightly ambiguous: as a time of struggle it belonged to the sixth age, but as a time of revelation of the gospel, when the church would grow in comparative security before the last battle, it belonged to the seventh age. 'God hath raised some godly persons now by whom many things are opened that aforetime were hid, except it were a few poor souls in corners...'.[142] The scriptures in the seventh age would be opened again – 'Everywhere shall the truth be open as well by writing as by words, and as well by books as by preachings.'[143] Enough of this had already happened, (despite the censorship of religious books) by the late 1540s in England, and certainly in Europe, for the advent of the seventh age to have begun. Had not Bale elsewhere referred to Luther as 'the very trumpet of this latter age of Christ's Church'?[144]

Other writers assumed that signs of reform were signs of the last days, without giving a detailed chronology to explain their assumption. Gilby saw the improved scholarship of the humanists as a providential sign of the last days: 'Why then may it not be that he hath sent these godly gifts, his worthy instruments for to reveal open and declare the hid mysteries of his Word which he said should flow like a water stream in these latter days that they should know him from the lowest to the highest.'[145] Likewise Crowley welcomed the translation of scripture: 'God, who hath in these our days (the latter days of this world) most plenteously poured out of his spirit upon those little ones that the world taketh for his excrements, revealing unto them those mysteries which he hath hidden from the wise and prudent of this world....'.[146] Thomas Lancaster described Edward VI's purgation of the church as the final 'enterprise' of overthrowing the kingdom of Antichrist. 'And without doubt the time is (by God's providence and your grace's) that Babylon hath in this realm such a fall that it shall not after this time at any time be repaired.'[147]

This triumphant tone was modified by the knowledge that the vindication of the true church would only take place after a struggle. Though there was an improvement in its condition now that the gospel was preached openly, the consequent revelation of Antichrist made these 'perilous times'.[148] The rage of the 'Antichrists' against 'the spiritual Israel' was according to Gilby providentially necessary; their eventual defeat would increase God's glory.[149] Bale interpreted the promise 'Behold, I come shortly' similarly: 'Of this admonition may the faithful sort be glad, being here in adversity, considering their deliverance is at hand and their crown of immortality not far off.'[150] Indeed the last judgement would occur when the power of Babylon was at its height:

> For now are their mischiefs at the full. Now are they most curious in their fashions and feedings, most covetous in their compassings most vain in their studies, and most cruel in their doings. For with them it shall be (saith Christ) as it was in the days of Noah and Lot; they shall build and banquet, ruffle and riot, buy and sell and plant for their pleasures; and suddenly as a

snare shall that terrible day light upon them unawares, as did death on the covetous jurer.[151]

Bale's description of the last days referred interchangeably to both popery and worldliness. The lust for both power and pleasure that it described was the exact opposite of the kind of godly order envisaged by the protestant ideal society.[152] The chaotic disintegration of society on all sides was interpreted as the final revelation of Antichrist.[153] Hooper roused his flock with the trumpet of God's Word from the deathly sleep of sin,[154] as likewise Crowley's *Voice of the last trumpet, blown by the seventh angel* was intended to emphasise the message that now was the last chance that all estates would be given to repent.[155]

The last days were marked by a complete breakdown of charity and social order.[156] Gilby compared Micah's 'desolate land' of the last days with his own vision of Edward VI's England, inhabited by those who sought only fleshly delights; by those who 'make themselves mighty men of great fame, riches and renown, imagining how to beguile our young king and to pill and poll his poor commons' (a sharply direct criticism of the Privy Council and leading courtiers); by parasitic clerics who failed to rebuke sinners, and finally by the 'scattered sheep of these despised commoners' who wandered out of the paths of righteousness in their search for succour and relief.[157] Everyone hated one another:

> And because in our perilous times there are so many Cainites it is no marvel though [i.e. that] every man be afraid of his brother, no man trusteth another. The nobles feareth the commons, the commons trusteth not the nobility. These are the last days wherein iniquity doth abound, love is lost, charity quenched, faith and trust are driven forth of man's company.[158]

Finch described the 1549 resistance and rebellion in apocalyptic terms: 'May not a man manifestly behold in them the monstrous beast that fighteth against the Lamb and Word of God?'[159] Crowley, commenting on Joel, described the church of the last days as a neglected flock, allowed by their hireling shepherd to wander at will, with the result that they caught diseases and suffered from hunger in poor pastures, or were lost for ever.[160]

Eschatological disorder, while predominantly seen in society, was mirrored in the heavens and in the hearts of the godly. Latimer and Gilby both noted recent portents,[161] but Latimer placed more weight on the evidence of fear and anxiety among the godly: ' "And the people shall be at their wits end through despair." Men shall be wondrous fearful, they shall pine away for fear: and no doubt they shall be good men which shall be thus troubled with such a fear of this day; for you know the worldlings care not for that day . . .'.[162] He thought that many had been 'vexed and turmoiled with such fear' of late: had not he personally ministered to Bilney's despair, and had not Martin

Luther himself written that 'he hath been sometimes in such an agony of spirit that he felt nothing but trembling and fearfulness'?[163]

The anxiety and foreboding described so vividly here was not unmitigated, however. The last days also meant that there was a sense of expectation, of hope of fulfilment, when the elect would inherit the kingdom and justice would be restored in Zion. This was the fulfilling of the covenant, which would 'make us which were not his people to be accepted as his people, and then shall it most perfectly be fulfilled in the end, when there shall be but one shepherd and one fold'.[164] The expression of Gilby's hopes was shaped by Micah's words; nearer home, others telescoped their hopes for social reform with the relief of oppression brought by the last judgement. Crowley hoped that if the 'evil humours' afflicting the body politic were not cured soon, which would show either the ineffectuality of the government or the incurable sickness of the body, the last judgement would happen speedily, to bring permanent relief. Latimer pleaded for the lowering of rents (and, by implication, other injustices) seeing hope only in the king's majority and the 'general accounting day . . . the dreadful day of judgement I mean, which shall make an end of all these calamities and miseries'.[165] Later he referred to the last judgement as the 'final parliament of the world' when 'reformations of all things shall be had' so that the faithful should 'desire it even from the bottom of their hearts'.[166] By this time he had withdrawn from active exhortation of the government, but he had not lost hope that society could be changed through preaching. Eschatological expectation was neither an excuse to preach revolution nor a call to purely personal reformation and pious introversion. It could be used to press for change in society, since the time was short, but equally it explained why change was so difficult to bring about. Evidence of the extent of that difficulty was to be found on every side, when protestants contemplated the ungodliness of the English commonwealth.

THE UNGODLY COMMONWEALTH

When protestant divines and publicists considered the state of England during Edward's reign, they saw signs of imminent judgement on every side. The godly commonwealth was an ideal which was winsomely simple to propound, but depressingly difficult to achieve. The corruption of human nature and the malice of Satan were its ancient enemies, and it seemed that just as the specific circumstances of Edward's reign appeared right for its inauguration, so they also tended to lay open the way for these enemies to flourish as never before. The royal minority may have allowed a political 'thaw' favouring protestantism, but protestants were well aware of how temporary it might prove. The climate of political instability in the court was reflected in

A religion of the Word

the uncertainty and change that characterised the nation. Instead of the ordered calm of the godly commonwealth protestants saw only disorder and injustice throughout English society. England had been offered the Gospel by the mercy of God, but appeared to be rejecting it, which left open the way for the second visitation of God's wrath. The ruling classes were rejecting the Gospel by the subtle means of pretending to uphold it; their hypocrisy in doing so was comparable to that which characterised popery. The commons rejected the Gospel by openly resisting it, either in rebellion or intractable refusal to abandon the 'old ways'. Popery, it seemed, was not so easily eliminated from the hearts of the English – as Gilby wrote, these were 'perilous time[s], in which all old evils seemed to have disguised themselves with new visors . . .'.[167] Repentance and restitution offered a way forward, but it seemed that God's determination to punish England's ingratitude had already begun to show itself. A closer look at these three areas – the royal minority, the ruling classes 'pretending the Gospel' and the commons resisting it – will reveal the 'siege mentality' of Edwardian protestantism at its most exposed.

The royal minority

The great advantage offered by the royal minority was that it allowed protestants to make the king in their own image, and thus to say things which could not with impunity be said either to Henry VIII or Elizabeth.[168] However, since their ability to make such prescriptive statements depended on the balance of political power remaining tilted in their favour, their advocacy of 'royal' reforms took on a somewhat disingenuous if not an embarrassed air. Their defensiveness was particularly exposed by the conservative view that Edward's youth invalidated his religious reforms.[169] Thus Latimer answered the text 'Woe be to the land where the king is a child' with 'Blessed be the land where there is a noble king'. Edward's nobility and godliness were reflected in those of his Council. Such conservative opposition was 'worse than the Jews' who may have been notoriously 'stiff-necked' but who never disobeyed their king on grounds of age.[170] He cited the story of the threats to king David's authority from his own sons in his old age or 'second childhood' to prove his point, unfortunately giving more of an impression of the danger of having a king who was not fully in control than of the validity of his government.[171] Hooper was even more dismissive of the critics – the king should not be troubled by them, since the policy of reform was upheld by scripture.[172] Bale defended the king against the comments of 'a frantic papist' – a Hampshire neighbour who had declared that the 'poor child' did not realise what was being perpetrated in his name, so that when he grew up he would undoubtedly restore the old religion and 'hang up a hundred of such heretic knaves'. Bale retorted that the king was not 'poor' but richly endowed

Signs of the times: hope and fear

with godly learning and counsel. Isaiah's prophecy referred to kings sent to punish the disobedience of the people, 'governors that are dissolute, rash, wanton and careless, yea, men inexpert and unexercised in princely affairs, and men which will not your commonwealth, but follow their own lusts'.[173] The Council's policy confirmed the king's own godly zeal:[174] 'If Christ be in the midst when two or three private men be collected in his name ... he is much more among the faithful council of so virtuous a king'.[175]

If protestants were quick to jump to the defence of the young king, they were also well aware of the problems. Latimer was particularly anxious about the safety of the succession. The survival of the king himself was crucial, and he exhorted the people to play their part in ensuring it by repentance and prayer, both in the *Sermon of the plough* of 1548 and the first of his *Sermons preached at Court in Lent, 1549*: 'God hath given us a deliverer, a natural king; let us seek no stranger of another nation; no hypocrite which shall bring in again all papistry, hypocrisy and idolatry; no diabolical minister which shall maintain all evil works and devilish exercises.'[176] The prosperity of the kingdom and the long life of the king depended on the people's acceptance of the 'liberty of the Gospel'. If he did survive, the next most important problem was that of marriage and the succession. Solomon, he warned was 'a meek king, who so continued, until he came into the company of strange women'.[177] Marriage to the wrong person would jeopardise the commitment to the Gospel of both the king and his heirs. Latimer did not need to remind his audience of the way Henry VIII's religious policy was closely bound up with his marital adventures.

Meanwhile, the most pressing problem was one which Latimer only faced up to in his farewell to the Court of 1550 – that the weakness of the king gave power to the wrong people.

> For where the king is within age, they that have governance about the king have much liberty to live voluptuously and licentiously; and not be in fear how they govern, as they would be if the king were of full age; and then commonly they govern not well. But yet Josiah and one or two more, though they were children, yet had their realms well governed, and reigned prosperously; and yet the saying *vae terrae cujus rex puer est* is nevertheless true for all that.[178]

For even the godly young Josiah did not present a model of unmitigated success. He had been killed prematurely in battle, admittedly not as a punishment for his reforms, but because his people would not support them, and thus 'God would not let him see the captivity that he brought upon the Israelites'.[179] In his short life time he had faced great opposition for his reforming zeal, as Edward did.[180] It was not surprising that Gilby prayed that God would have pity on the young king and preserve him from his enemies, for England's sins warranted a scourge rather than such a godly ruler.

199

A religion of the Word

> Under whom in his most weak and tender age thou hast caused to shine forth the clear light of this gospel, which hath beat down the idols and idolatrous altars throughout his realm. Whereby amongst the papists, Turks and Jews thou hast made the Britons to be bruited. Howbeit all this thou so wrought under a young child, that the glory might come wholly unto thee and to no man mortal.[181]

In this account the reformation took place almost despite the young Josiah, and thus remained a purely providential act. It seemed that, despite his disclaimers, Gilby did not believe the age of miracles was entirely over. If the minority offered the opportunity for protestantism to take a hold, it also heightened their sense that their advantage was only a temporary one.

Pretending the Gospel: the ruling classes

An ambitious and oppressive aristocracy

The most obvious result of the royal minority was that the nobility was the focus of attention. As the king's guardians and councillors, they were at the centre of the political stage, and the achievement of the reformation depended on their good will and actions.[182] The combination of dependence on the nobility for the achievement of protestant hopes and an exalted ideal of godly magistracy could not hold out against the realities of Court factions and worldly opportunism. It was too dangerous for protestants to name names, but it is significant that their criticisms, however generalised, were shrillest at periods of political instability. Moreover, the obliqueness of many of their references should not be allowed to detract from the sharpness of the criticism; the protestant preachers' audience, especially at Court, where many of the sermons on which this chapter draws were preached, was in a position to understand or guess at the references. The estrangement between Court and preachers in the latter part of Northumberland's rule has been noted by Collinson,[183] and it seems clear that many protestants were unconvinced by his sincerity in their cause.[184] However, this should not throw too a rosy light on their relations with Somerset.[185] The first burst of criticism came with his fall, in 1550, by which time it was clear that the reformation was neither unopposed nor complete enough for many tastes, but even Latimer's 1549 sermons should not be read as obsequious propaganda for Somerset's rule.[186] The sense of betrayal among protestants and their outrage at aristocratic cynicism and insincerity were at their most intense in the retrospective view from Mary's reign,[187] but the signs of disenchantment were a feature of Edward's reign.

Order, as it was described in the last chapter,[188] depended heavily on the idea of vocation as a means of reinforcing the status quo. 'First walk in thy vocation/ And do not seek thy lot to change/ For through wicked ambition/ Many men's fortune hath been strange' warned Crowley's *Last trumpet*.[189] If vocation cast society in bronze, ambition was the acid which corroded its face. It was a temptation to which the elite was particulary prone, since office and promotion were within their reach. It was not that office should be unnattainable, but that it should be bestowed for merit and not sought after. Latimer used the apostles as the guiding example:

> Well, Andrew, Peter, James and John, were not ambitious, they tarried in their calling, so I wish that every man would follow their examples, and tarry for their vocation, and not thrust themselves in until they be called of God. For, no doubt, vocation hath no fellow; for he that cometh by the calling of God to an office he may be sure that his adversaries shall not prevail against him, as long as he doth the office of his calling.[190]

But his audience was not willing to wait for God's call.

The problem was that ambitiousness was socially acceptable. Crowley sighed that it was regarded as a crime in ancient Rome, and punished with exile, but in England men with only one office were despised.[191] Instead of being defined by virtue, it seemed that nobility was based on the wealth and prestige that rewarded ambitiousness. This attitude was rooted in humanist social criticism; the difference was that protestants saw ambitiousness as a direct threat to their ideal of godly magistracy.[192] Bernard Gilpin exhorted the Court to remember that in the kingdom of heaven the first should be last, which should encourage the nobles to embrace virtue, especially humility, remembering who exalted them; but the signs were that this would not happen: 'But as dignity goeth nowadays, climb who may climb most highest, every man exalteth himself and tarrieth not the calling of God; humility is taken for no keeper but for an utter enemy unto nobility.'[193] His anecdote of the man who blasphemously denied Luke 14:11 and was struck down, was not enough to change the social climate:

> I fear me a great number are in England at this day, which, though in words they deny not this sentence of Christ, yet inwardly they can scarce digest it, else certainly they would never seek so ambitiously to advance themselves, to climb by their own might uncalled, never seeking the public weal, but rather the destruction thereof, for their private wealth and lucre, which causeth us to have so many evil magistrates.[194]

The most explicit 'by name' denunciation of an ambitious noble was of Thomas Seymour by Latimer. The dividing line between ambition and treason was a tenuous one, as the story of Solomon and the treason of Adonijah showed.[195] But Thomas Seymour gambled and lost, which made Latimer's denunciations problematic. At the time Latimer was accused of being a mouthpiece for Somerset, and while he denied it[196] his protestations do ring rather false, especially on the defence of Seymour's dubiously legal attainder. However, if he was acting as a propagandist, he did so on his own terms, and they were to depict Seymour as the antithesis of godly nobility. Here was one who openly rejoiced in ungodliness and attempted to gain control over the king in order to prevent him being brought up 'like a ward' in godly learning. His death was outwardly brave but his persistent plotting showed that he did not even die in charity.[197] In life his presumptuous lack of the fear of God was confirmed by his reputation for immorality and his conspicuous absence from the household prayers instituted by his wife, the godly queen–dowager Katherine Parr.[198] His ambitiousness above all made him a symbol of ungodliness and disobedience, one who 'wrestled with his calling' – 'he shall be Lot's wife to me as long as I live'.[199]

Seymour's ambitiousness had resulted in treasonable plotting, and he met with his reward, but noble faction continued to be admonished, even if names were not mentioned. Gilby likened Edward to Hezekiah, whose personal goodness did not prevent his kingdom being plagued by aristocratic 'conspiracies and partakings-with'.[200] Any success achieved by even a good king on behalf of true religion was entirely due to providence, such were the forces of corrupt self-interest with which he would have to contend. Gilby explained that Micah himself was 'of the princely tribe of Judah' and thus was well aware of factional politics.[201] Elite conspiracy would ultimately be confounded:

> You are here likened to Cain, which did lie in wait for his brother's blood. You are likened to Nimrod hunting your brethren to catch them in nets. If you were not such, we should not hear of such sudden fall and ruin of noble houses. But whatsoever you do that must be well done, saith our prophet, so stoutly will you defend your own doings, to make evil good and good evil, as Isaiah saith, and to cloak your wicked works if you do fear any danger.[202]

But meanwhile, ambitiousness resulted in conspiracy and dissimulation, and was succeeded by ruthlessness and cruelty.[203]

Power gained by deceit and ambition showed itself in oppression of the weak. Gilby inverted the standard description of magistrates as 'gods on earth', that is, 'wise men fearing God, yea standing in God's stead to the people, having the truth within them',[204] to show that they had become little tyrants whom none dared criticise; 'blind and deaf' to God's will, not ministers of his judgement; who flayed the people instead of being good shepherds; who were so surrounded by flatterers that if by chance good men were found in their households, they were as 'sheep among wolves', 'derided by my lord's own minions' and at length silenced by them.[205] But oppression was political folly, for the people would not tolerate it for much longer:

> Will you be loved of your subjects? Will you have no uproars nor commotion of your commoners? Then let them see some cause of love in you, for forced

violence and love which cometh by compulsion cannot be long-lasting. The vain imaginations of the late upskips of England to make the people peasants and slaves is not the right pathway to quietness. For even now the commons are so bare and poor that they cry out of the ale bench and openly against the justices of the bench. And what shall follow trow you? In your subtle imaginations and fine wits, O ye upskips, the devourers of the people and destroyers of all public weal, which by wards, by simony, by leasemongering and like merchandise make waste this whole realm, before your time most wealthy. O noble counsellors, see to the safety of yourselves and your subjects in time.[206]

While oppression could not be ended by rebellion, these social plagues clearly went hand in hand. Gilpin too saw the inverse of true nobility in the ruling classes, likening them to biblical oppressors like Nimrod, Ahab and Jezebel:[207]

For falling into ungodliness and framing themselves to the shape and fashion of this world, nobility is turned into vile slavery and bondage of sin, power and dominion are turned into tyranny, authority is become a sword of mischief in a madman's hand, all majesty and honour is turned into misery, shame and confusion; and ever the higher that men be, while they serve sin, more notable is their vice, and more pestiferous to infect, as a cancer, by evil examples; because all men's eyes are bent to behold their doings.[208]

Emulation of the nobility, which if they were virtuous would be a source of social strength, became a threat to order, since the 'inferior members' must always follow the head.[209] The disobedience of the rebels was indeed sinful, but they merely followed the example of their superiors, who had disregarded the statutes and proclamations on enclosure, and refused to provide a preaching ministry. This both flouted the law and revealed a devastating lack of patriotism.[210] This was not a populist account. Protestants clearly had some sympathy for the plight of the commons, but they insisted that the extent of the oppression mirrored the extent of their sinfulness. Domination by 'hypocrites' was a providential and suitable punishment, as Job had prophesied.[211] 'Murmuring' against them would multiply their numbers, rather than removing such a 'scourge'.

Nevertheless, there was some hope of relief, as there would come a time when the 'tyrants' themselves would be judged. Crowley reminded them that though pharaoh and Nebuchadnezzar were sent to punish the sinful Israelites, in the end their oppression of God's people was revenged.[212] No one, however powerful, was exempt from judgement, as God saw all. 'The king in his privy chamber hath this Lord a witness of his doings. The lords of the privy council cannot shift forth of the council chamber this unreprovable witness.'[213] The same God who gave them their authority 'shall examine your works and shall search your very thoughts, because that you being the ministers of his kingdom, have not used right judgement, nor kept the law of righteousness, neither have you walked after the will of God'.[214] The classic Tudor and

A religion of the Word

mediaeval criticism of evil counsellors had an intensified impact in this period of conciliar government – the reference was precise even if no names were mentioned.

Abundant evidence of ambition and oppression badly damaged the protestant image of the leaders of the godly commonwealth. They clearly were placing their own interests before those of the nation. Government was clearly not a stable and sober affair, a council of the wisest heads, but was still at the mercy of unstable and shifting configurations and factions, of deals and conspiracies. No one explicitly referred to Henry VIII's will, to Somerset's self-aggrandisement or to Northumberland's cynical manipulation of Somerset's enemies; but the criticism was as open as protestants could dare to make it. Just as important as the political context was the ideological context: the themes of inversion, conspiracy and repression were all well-developed aspects of the critique of popery, which now had found new guises in an England that was supposedly reformed. Given that many people were, as Gilpin noted, following the example of their social superiors, the continuation of materialism and idolatry, also characteristics of popery, into post-reformation England was not surprising.

Covetousness and carnal gospellers

'Take heed and beware of covetousness', thundered Latimer in his last sermon at Court in 1550. He was not proclaiming a new phenomenon, but voicing an awareness that opportunities for greed to flourish were plentiful. The figure of the 'carnal gospeller' whose enthusiasm for the reformation was merely a front for profit was a source of anxiety from quite early in the reformation.[215] When the dissolution of the monasteries and chantries had been followed not by a radical re-financing of the church, charity and education, but by the wholesale alienation and sale of crown lands, the disillusionment and outrage of the reformers began to build, reaching a peak in Edward's reign when it seemed that the division of the spoils was at its most shameless.[216] 'Piers Plowman's' *Exhortation to parliament* epitomised protestant anxiety that the dissolutions only benefited the rich, who did not intend the land's fair distribution among the 'body of Christ' – notably the poor who suffered from increased unemployment as a result of the dismantling of the old piety.[217] His call to parliament to modify the results of the dissolutions by statutes was, however, unusual; most protestants appealed to individual consciences to restore sacrilegious gains and restrain the impulse to profit at the cost of social justice.[218] Greed damaged the reputation of the reformation; it undermined the Christian commonwealth by denying charity, reviving popish vices, and generating social disorder; in short, it was a plague that threatened to bring further punishment unless restitution was made.

The hypocrisy of carnal gospellers was 'a slander to our religion in these days as it was even in the primitive Church....'.[219] Gilby worried that the charge of papist cynics, that the nobles only supported the reformation for the good of their own purses, would stick.[220] 'Piers Plowman' thought that the impoverishing of England by the activities of selfish entrepreneurs would delight the enemies of the Gospel: 'then would our great enemy the bishop of Rome and all his adherents insult and triumph over us, imputing our destruction as a punishment for the suppression of abbeys and chantries'.[221]

Material benefits accruing from the reformation compromised it. The image of godliness only intensified the sense of betrayal:

> Yet dare you say for these ramping lions have they not banished the popish religion? Is not God amongst us? Have they not set forth the Bible? Are not they gospellers? Yes, to their open shame doubtless, for heretofore there was some pretence of religion, some colourable cloak of virtue and honesty that is shaken off, I do grant, and not so much left as fig leaves to cover their shame. How can God be amongst this people? Amongst whom the devil reigneth and rageth by covetous ambition, whoredom, extortion, contempt of true religion and all civil governance. They have set forth the gospel that all men may see how far they do swerve in life from God his holy Word...[222]

Gilby was convinced that the Gospel had been mocked: 'But you, contrariwise, not repenting, but forgetting how you have offended God with your old idolatry, do abuse his light, now sent amongst you, to the satisfying of your lusts and to the condemnation of your own souls, [and] cause God and his holy Word and the preachers thereof to serve your covetousness.'[223] Hutchinson showed how greed made the reformation not an advance on popery but a confirmation of its corruption:

> We detest the pope, yet we follow him in covetousness. We defy him not for religion's sake, but as one covetous man hateth another; according to the common proverb *figulus figulum odit*. He depraved God's holy Word through shameful covetousness; so it is to be feared lest the same vice do poison us, bring us out of favour with God and disorder the commonwealth, to the oppression and undoing of many thousands.[224]

Greed struck at the heart of the Christian commonwealth because it denied charity, that part of the message of the Gospel which bound society together.[225] The sense that charity was 'growing cold' was an important sign of the last days.[226] Carnal gospellers put private interests, especially individual financial gain, before the welfare of the body of Christ, and forgot that it was the poor who would inherit the kingdom of heaven:

> But ye have despised the poor. Are not the rich they which oppress you and they which draw you before judges? Do not they speak evil of that good name

after which ye be named? I pray you, who in these days are such oppressors, such graziers, such shepherds, such enhancers of rents, such rakers of incomes as are those which profess the gospel. What is this but to speak evil of that good name of Christ after whom we be named Christian?[227]

'Piers Plowman' agreed that charity was farthest from the minds of 'gospellers', who were

> so void of all charity that it shall be taken but for a small matter and for a common practice among us, every man to encroach so much ground into his hands that he shall thereby expel four or five hundred persons from their livings? How doth this trade of living agree with the gospel, seeing that the chief point of our religion, yea, as Christ himself saith, all our religion consisteth in loving of God above all things and our neighbour as our self?[228]

Their denial of charity made hypocrites of such carnal gospellers, but their obsession with financial gain made them idolaters. The disorder this generated allowed protestants to continue to use the language of antipopery in the context of a supposedly newly reformed commonwealth.[229] Though the external forms of popery had been abolished, there was a direct link between popish idolatry and its reformation counterpart:

> As for idolatry (though our governors here in England through the mighty hand of God have for the comfort of his elect banished the outward show thereof) yet one sort making this most godly and glorious fact to serve their lucre and gain to the slander of such a notable enterprise have seemed to change the kind of idolatry, making the muck which they found heaped about those idols, to be their God. So that they may worthily be called idolaters, so long as they have it, keep it, and set so much store thereby.[230]

The idolatry of covetousness originated in the same carnality as popery and was directed at its idolatrous objects and profits. It was likewise a 'dead faith' which destroyed the commonwealth by self-interest – the converse of the charitable 'lively faith' of the true gospeller.[231]

The only difference between the idolatry found in popery and that in covetousness was that the former was found openly in worship. Gilby denounced the secret idolatry of those 'whose God is their belly ... so that in effect idolatry is not banished, but reigneth more cloakedly amongst us ...'.[232] Hypocrisy had not been expelled with popery. Gilpin quoted Musculus on how Satan had replaced popery with 'open impiety': 'for as many of these Ahabs as signify they favour God's Word by reading or hearing it, or with prayer honouring him (as Christ saith, "with their lips, their hearts being far from him" – Matt. 15.8), they are as detestable hypocrites as ever was covered in cowl or cloister'.[233] But the new 'gospellers' took care to conceal their wealth: 'Covetousness hath cut away the large wings of charity, and plucketh all to herself, she is never satisfied, she hath chested all the old gold in

England and much of the new; she hath made that there was never more idolatry in England than at this day. But the idols are hid, they come not abroad'.[234]

The most influential exponent of the idea of covetousness as idolatry was Thomas Lever. In his sermon at Paul's Cross in 1550, he reminded his audience of a text they were familiar with in the context of antipopery – that the Devil was at his most dangerous disguised as an angel of light. What was this, but an allegory for the surface reformation of the despoilers of the church?

> For papistry is not banished out of England by pure religion, but overrun, suppressed and kept under within this realm by covetous ambition. Papistry abused many things, covetousness hath destroyed more; papistry is superstition, covetousness is idolatry. Papistry afore time did obscure the king's honour and abused the wealth of this realm, covetousness at this time doth more abuse and decay them both, making the king bare, the people poor and the realm miserable.[235]

The reformation had brought things from evil to worse, because of the proliferation of idolaters: 'Have ye not read in the prophet Ezekiel how that he which keepeth his idols, meaning covetousness, in his heart, and cometh to hear God's Word, doth thereby provoke God's vengeance to his utter destruction?'[236] It was no use pleading the reformation, because covetousness prevented it taking effect: 'as ye have served superstitious papists, so shall you yourselves be served, being covetous idolaters: yea and have as much advantage at the meeting as is between covetousness and idolatry'.[237]

Lever's sermon culminated in a diatribe against the havoc wreaked by carnal gospellers in the Christian commonwealth, seen in terms of disordered nature:[238]

> All other that have the name and profession of Christ without living and conversation according thereto be fained brethren, in feasts with Christian men to take part of their good cheer, unclean spots among holiest company; clouds without any moisture of God's grace, tossed about with contrary winds of strange doctrine; trees passing summertime without any fruits of good works, twice dead without feeling the corruption of sin, or looking to be grafted in the stock of grace, yea, rooted up from amongst the vines of the Lord; wild waves of the sea frothing forth unshamefast brags; and wandering stars without constancy in judgement and opinion unto whom the dungeon of darkness is ordained for everlasting damnation.[239]

Such disorder resulted from the downward spiral of greed. The plunder of the church resembled the division of Christ's garments, and its impoverishment meant that the people lacked preachers to instruct them, so that they 'without grief of conscience or fear of punishment abuse everything unto the ruin and destruction which God hath ordained to the upholding and increase of a Christian commonwealth'.[240] Ideological purity had been sacrificed to short-term considerations in giving employment and pensions to chantry priests and monks – 'the abuse and misorder of these things is worldly, is wicked, is devilish, is abominable'.[241]

Lever was not alone in considering greed to be the greatest threat to the godly order of the commonwealth. Greed may have benefited the ruling classes, but it infected the whole of society. Cranmer saw it as a madness or poison that affected rich and poor alike: 'We see by daily experience that men be so mad when they once give themselves to covetousness, that they less esteem the loss of their honesty, commonwealth, liberty, religion, yea of God himself and everlasting life than the loss of their riches.'[242] The author of *The praise and commendation of such as sought commonwealths* quoted classical authorities (Epicurus, Aristotle, Ovid) and mediaeval writers (Bede, Vincent) to show the folly of greed, which caused great poverty and distress, destroyed the commonwealth, and eventually brought both worldly downfall and eternal damnation.[243] The intense degree of social conflict led Gilpin to describe both rich and poor as *anthropophagi*, or cannibals, devouring each other with covetousness and envy, the very opposite of civilised behaviour.[244] Crowley saw the squalor of London as symbolic of a disordered commonwealth:

> And this is a city
> In name, but in deed
> It is a pack of people
> That seek after meed
> For officers and all
> Do seek their own gain
> But for the wealth of the commons
> Not one taketh pain.
> An hell without order
> I may it well call
> Where every man is for himself
> And no man for all.[245]

The disorder caused by covetousness was both a plague in itself and an indication that further punishment was imminent. 'This our ingratitude towards God and unmercifulness to the poor will surely accelerate and haste forward the vengeance of God to fall upon us'.[246] In pretending to uphold the reformation, England deceived itself as Israel had done, and God would likewise make an example of the wayward nation.[247] Thus Lever argued that pluralism was a shortlived benefit compared to the lasting loss of God's favour.[248] Many writers threatened woe, in Isaiah's words, to those whose main activity was enlarging their property.[249] 'A pitiful case and great blindness that hearing God's Word, man should fear more temporal punishment than everlasting. Yet hath England had of late some terrible examples of God's wrath in sudden and strange deaths of such as join field to field and house to house.'[250] Outward piety could bear no spiritual fruit – 'This is a plague of all plagues most horrible.'[251] However, the covetous themselves were sent to punish traditionalists, those who rejected the Gospel, calling it heresy and new doctrine.[252] Only if both covetous and conservative were converted would God withdraw the plague of exploitation.[253] If religious traditionalists did not repent, the hypocrites would be given full scope to oppress them.[254]

The repentence of the covetous rich should take the form of renunciation of their ill-gotten profits. This according to Gilby would be in their political interest. Not only would the excuse for further popular unrest be removed (a further plague), but they would restore the bond of charity which their greed had destroyed through mutual suspicion.[255] By such an act of restitution, Lever hoped that the ruling classes would continue to fulfil a providential purpose, as they had done in the dissolutions:

> So dear brethren, hearing and knowing that God hath used your greedy covetousness to destroy abbeys, colleges and chantries, and to plague all this realm, be grieved and sorry in your hearts, seeing that ye have been *vasa irae*, instruments of wrath to execute vengeance, and purge yourselves of this vile covetousness, then shall ye from henceforth be *vasa honoris*, vessels of honour . . .[256]

Outrage at the betrayal of the reformation, which revealed the superficiality of the ruling elite's support for the Gospel, dominated protestant preaching and writing.[257] The rest of the body politic was more openly antagonistic to the reformation – protestants' defensiveness on this front reveals how their 'minority mentality' reflected their actual position.

Resisting the Gospel

Rebellion

The rebellions of 1549 intensified protestant support for the government, but it was a qualified support. On the one hand, protestants needed to distance the gospel from sedition, and indeed some of their tracts were straightforward government propaganda.[258] The western rising, seen almost entirely as a religious revolt, could even be used as a propaganda bonus, linking popery and sedition, but it also confirmed fears that popery had a firm hold on the people which it would be difficult to eradicate.[259] On the other, some of them felt sympathetic to the social and economic grievances of the rebels. The Norfolk rising met with even more of a mixed response, because these rebels seemed to support the reformation.[260] The general discontent increased pressure for more preachers to combat popery and disobedience.[261] Whatever their

A religion of the Word

sympathies, all saw the rebellions of 1549 as the death-knell of any optimism about the rapid acceptance of the Gospel.[262]

The endorsement of religious policy in such circumstances was to be expected. When the 1549 *Prayer Book* was issued, 'R.V.' admonished his readers to 'marvel not at the King's Majesty's proceedings, so long as he hath the Scripture for [i.e. supporting] him'.[263] Richard Finch described the *Paraphrases* and *Injunctions* of 1547 and the 1549 *Prayer Book* as the policies of providence carried out by Edward VI.[264] Cheke indignantly inquired of the rebels: 'But why should ye not like that which God's Word establisheth? The primitive Church hath authorised, the greatest learned men of this realm hath drawn [up], the whole consent of the parliament hath confirmed, the King's Majesty hath set forth.'[265] The official *Message sent by the king's majesty to certain of his people assembled in Devonshire* addressed the rebels as a grieving father would express distress at the opposition of his children.[266] Cranmer's attack on the western rebels was a diatribe which was largely taken up with expressing his shock at their disrespect,[267] and the selective attitude towards the royal supremacy implied in their support for Henrician and not Edwardian religious policies.[268]

Even without the element of official propaganda, the collapse of order showed how superficial the understanding and acceptance of the Gospel was in England. Becon described the rebels as 'brainsick' – mentally unhinged by extreme need so that they failed to understand that dearth and inflation were sent as punishment for their sins.[269] Such a view may have included some degree of sympathy for the desperation caused by poverty, but it was more concerned to inculcate a belief in providence.[270] Their ignorance of scripture meant that the poor failed in their duty of obedience, and the rich in charity,[271] so that social collapse was inevitable. Cheke showed how the actions of the 'unnatural rebels' had widespread repercussions,[272] describing vividly the descent from rebellion to anarchy, economic collapse and disease – which in itself was a metaphor for the sickness of rebellion in the commonwealth.[273] Cranmer saw 'this scourge of sedition' as God's plague on the magistrates for failing to punish sin.[274] 'We have dissimulated the matter, we have been cold in God's cause, and have rather winked at than punished the contempt of both God and his laws.'[275]

Other protestants were less authoritarian in their response. Hooper used the idea of the covenant to show that it was not the imposition of religious reform that gave rise to the rebellions, but the anger of God for the neglect of his law, evident in false religion and injustice.[276] Whatever the cause of rebellion, repentance rather than repression was the only way out, since 'as the people can have no remedy against evil rulers by rebellion so can the rulers have no redress of rebellious people by oppression'.[277] Rebellion plagued the people and repression only produced further unrest.[278] Indeed, the wrath

Signs of the times: hope and fear

to come could take the form of a more serious popular uprising if oppression continued.[279] The suffering of the innocent poor resulting from both the rebellions and the repression that followed them were matters of some concern. As G.R. Elton pointed out, protestants took pains to distinguish between the innocent poor and those malcontents who were eager to rebel.[280] However, Elton played down the ferocity with which protestants belaboured the oppressive masters of the 'deserving poor'. Latimer linked their suffering to that of all Christians in this world,[281] and the conflict as the fulfilment of Christ's prophecy that he came to bring not peace but a sword.[282] Crowley was altogether more aggressive in his defence of the virtuous poor, who trusted in God and not in their own power. The threatening tone in his citation of the story of Judith and Holofernes was unmistakable:

> [D]oubt you not but Judith shall cut off all your heads one after another, and God shall strike your retinue with such a fear that none shall be so bold as once to turn his face. Yea, if there were no men left alive to put them in fear, they should be feared with shadows. And though there were no guns to shoot at them, yet the stones of the street should not cease to fly among them, by the mighty power of God, who will rather make of every grass in the field a man, than such as trust in him should be overrun and kept in oppression. Be warned therefore, and seek not to keep the commons of England in slavery. For that is the next way to destroy yourselves.[283]

While tyrants were sent to punish the sins of the people, the godly would not be tried above their strength.[284] Crowley did not intend a call to revolution, but a prophetic warning of vengeance to come.

Passive resistance – traditionalism, superstition and witchcraft

Resistance to the Gospel could be shown in ways that were less dramatic than open rebellion and yet were in some ways more threatening. The more private and passive resistance shown in attachment to the 'old ways' both underpinned the rebellions and increased the preachers' sense of isolation and hostility. This was as necessary to the self-image of protestants of the persecuted true church as it was a reflection of the beginnings of an alienation caused by the imposition on a largely illiterate people of a religion of the Word preached by a university-educated clergy.[285] Conservative resistance was manifested by the persistence of folk customs and traditional piety. In the protestant mind the two were linked, since popery was conflated with superstition and ignorance. To illustrate this, Latimer related an anecdote about the time he was prevented from preaching one May Day, when the church was locked because the people were 'gone abroad to gather for Robin Hood'. Despite the 'good beginning' of the Edwardian reforms, the ignorance of the people was still fostered by the interests of 'unpreaching prelates'.[286]

A religion of the Word

The superstition and frivolity of the people were fostered by conservative prelates: 'But I tell you, it is far wide that the people have such judgement, the bishops they could laugh at it. What was it to them? They would have them to continue in their ignorance still, and themselves in unpreaching prelacy.'[287]

While they acknowledged the clerical conspiracy, protestants did not underestimate the popular heart of resistance to reformed piety.[288] Hence John Mardely thought that the Gospel was under greater threat from 'the stiff-necked' than it had been since the creation: their malignant activities intended to 'drown the truth alas full piteously'.[289] A more specific occasion impelled Richard Finch to write his *Epiphany of the church*. Attacking the opposition to Ridley's visitation of London, he set out to define the church, since conservative elements in the diocese used 'the church' as their rallying cry:

> For certain overthwart persons (pretending to cleave very earnestly unto the faith of the Church when in very deed they do nothing else but stick to their own wills in following evil custom) coveted divers ways to obscure the praise of your diligent labour. Being moved thereto partly because you examined them by the Scriptures, and partly for that you gave in your visitation injunctions to take away the principal monuments of superstitions, even the altars of the popish Mass.[290]

The visitation was described as a shock to those who thought they could go on worshipping as they had before, or had never been examined in the scriptures, or thought visitations were purely a matter of cash payments. Such 'ingratitude' was dangerous as it might result in the withdrawal of the Word.[291] It was a short step from resentment to rebellion:

> O what murmurings and complainings have they made since their Mass decayed? What lies have these idle brains invented, what slanders have they imagined and what false rumours have they sprinkled abroad in the world against them that have sincerely preached the gospel? How conspire they against good Christian ministers which according to their vocations attend their flocks? What tumults, uproars and rebellions have they raised against their superiors to the great hindrance of God's holy Word?[292]

Finch was describing the antagonism to the work of an active reforming bishop. Others were anxious about a more widespread situation: the imposition of reformed worship without the preaching resources to explain true doctrine to their parishioners. Bernard Gilpin described the incomprehension and hostility this situation provoked:

> [T]hey think Baptism is not effectual because it wanteth man's traditions; they are not taught how the apostles baptised. A great number think it a great offence to take the sacrament of Christ's body in their hands, that have no conscience to receive it with blasphemous mouths, with malicious hearts full

of uncleanness. These come to it by threes of custom, without any spiritual hunger, and know not the end wherefore it was instituted. They come to the church to feed their eyes and not their souls, they are not taught that no visible thing is to be worshipped...[293]

Being able to understand only externals, they fail to regard the spiritual treasures of the church, and refuse to enter, saying they might as well go into a barn, and they preferred to feast on saint's days, 'despising or soon weary of God's Word'. It was not surprising that such ignorance and resentment could easily be mobilised into open rebellion.[294] Lever was less sympathetic. He described the people as so 'envenomed' that is, poisoned or anaesthetised by popery, that they did not realise how wretched they were without the Word of God, so that when it was revealed to them, they 'presumed of their own wilfulness so far as they could or might to withstand the ordinance of God, refused the grace of God, and procured to themselves the vengeance of God'.[295]

Stubborn adherence to custom was not the only manifestation of resistance to the Gospel. Contempt for religion, perhaps encouraged by the iconoclasm of the recent changes, worried Latimer, who lamented the passing of what he called discipline, i.e. respect and reverence:

> I never saw, surely, so little discipline as is nowadays. Men will be masters; they will be masters and no disciples... Men the more they know, the worse they be, it is truly said *'scientia inflat'*, 'knowledge maketh us proud and causeth us to forget all and set away discipline'. Surely in popery they had a reverence, but now we have none at all. I never saw the like.[296]

If Latimer was disturbed by the numbers of people in England who did not 'believe in the immortality of the soul',[297] others saw a disquieting increase in alternative forms of religion. The traditional ways had been dismantled, but the people had not been converted. Thus Bernard Gilpin saw an increasing incidence of belief in magic:

> How great enemies they be to Christ, by keeping away his gospel, it shall appear, if ye consider what superstition and blindness remaineth still among the people, only through lack of faithful preachers; I pass over much infidelity, idolatry, sorcery, charming, witchcrafts, conjuring, trusting in figures, with such other trumpery, which lurk in corners, and began of late to come abroad, only for lack of preaching.[298]

Gilby perceived the increased popularity of witchcraft and astrology as almost as important a source of God's anger as was covetousness. The link with popery was shown both in his connecting of witchcraft to traditional pious practices, and his use of the language of antipopery – he described witchcraft, like idolatry, as 'spiritual fornication'. Witchcraft, like popery, appealed to

A religion of the Word

educated and uneducated alike. He described the Faustus-like fall of learned Cambridge astronomers, first into astrology, then, when that failed to bring the required results, into necromancy and conjuring, using the same meticulous repetition of formulae, and key 'holy' words, as characterised popish devotions. Others chanced success in love or crime on the favourable conjunctions of the planets; they should learn from Saul, who lost his life after consulting the Witch of Endor. At the bottom of the scale, 'wise men and women' used charms to find lost objects or help women in childbirth. These were the delusions of the simple people, which were as dangerous as the Mass; the magistrates and preachers should root them out with as much determination, for: 'Lo, with how sore words and threatenings the lord God detesteth and forbiddeth all the kinds of these devilish inventions whereby men do run a-whoring from God to abuse his creatures in spiritual fornication.'[299] The same human impulse that motivated the worship of 'creatures' in traditional piety, now in the absence of that piety, was propelling men to open devil-worship. Witchcraft was evidence of the Devil's activity in its most obvious and conspicuous form. While modern historians will see in these examples early and specific instances of the alienation caused by the imposition of protestantism,[300] protestants regarded them as signs pointing both to the inadequacy of the missionary effort of the church, and to the wrath of God.

CONCLUSION: ENGLAND IN THE BALANCE

It is possible to discern in the short period of Edward VI's reign a shift in protestant attitudes from the more hopeful to the more fearful. Both of these sentiments were qualified by the understanding of providence and judgement described earlier in the chapter. In the early part of the reign, the promise of reform and the fact that England had the Word implied God's favour.[301] At least the way to repentance had been opened, but such optimism was qualified both by the fact that the Word was God's first visitation and by the need to sustain the reformation impetus if it was to make any difference.[302] From around 1549, existing concern about the motives of those who claimed to support the reformation and about the speed with which it could be accomplished was intensified by political instability, signalling impending judgement. Even this was not unremitting gloom, as the possibility of repentance and restitution was always open, and the faith of the godly at least would protect them from anxiety about their fate in the event of further catastrophes.

The hopefulness of the early part of the reign was exemplified by Philip Gerrard's *Godly invective on behalf of the Gospel*. Gerrard placed great confidence in the combination of youthful sovereign and godly Council and their eventual triumph.[303] Similarly the protestant gentleman in *A dialogue between a gentleman and a priest concerning the Supper of the Lord* hoped that the first parliament of Edward's reign would reflect the godliness of the young king and his Council: 'Ye shall not doubt of good news, yea and godly news as ever was heard of in any parliament.'[304] He dismissed the Henrician reforms as 'wisdom after the flesh' which God would 'confound by weakness' – something which may have included concerted pressure from the godly as well as the youth of the king.[305] Gilpin, like Latimer before him, thought that the deliverance of the English from popery obliged the nation to give thanks as the Israelites did when they were delivered from Egypt and Babylon:

> We must be thankful, lest for our unthankfulness God suffer us to fall into a worse bondage than ever we were in. But most of all it is profitable that we may from our hearts renounce with Babylon all the vices of Bablyon. For what did it profit the deliverance out of Egypt to those that did still carry Egypt in their minds through the desert? What did it avail the deliverance out of Babylon to those that did bring Babylon home to Jerusalem?[306]

Gilpin's sermon was preached in 1552, showing how it was possible to offer hope of national salvation even at a stage when the consensus indicated that England was being plagued for her ingratitude.

The greatest cause for anxiety among protestants was the complacency that prevented the reformation from extending beyond a reform of worship to the establishment of a godly society.[307] God's Word may have been 'daily and purely preached', but to all intents it was being ignored. It was not enough to forsake the pope, abolish superstition and bring back 'universally the order of the primitive Church', for: 'Alas good brethren, as truly as all is not gold that glistereth, so is it not virtue and honesty but very vice and hypocrisy whereof England at this day doth most glory.[308] Indeed the English church was only half-reformed – a situation which left it in a worse state than it had been under popery. 'Will you yet be a Church all alone, O English bishops and priests? Will you neither follow Christ nor his Apostles, neither the Bishop of Rome and his bishops? Are you wiser than the one sort or will you be worse than the other?'[309] demanded Gilby. Lever considered that anyone who persuaded the king and Council that the Church of England was 'honourably, godly or charitably reformed' were but flatterers, since the reality was more dangerous:

> Therefore doth all turn at six and seven, from evil to worse; therefore doth God's word take no place to do good, but is unthankfully refused, which causeth more harm. Is God's word received in England because it is plainly preached and taught, or refused and forsaken because it is not obeyed and followed? Be we in better case than we have been afore time because papistry amongst us is kept under, or else worse than ever we were because covetousness reigneth at liberty?[310]

A religion of the Word

Just as God had rejected the sacrifices of the Israelites, (Isaiah 1:10–11), so he would reject the reforms of the English:

> 'What pleasure have I, yea what care I for all your English Bibles, homilies and all your other books? Set forth no more godly service to honour me with, I hate them with all my heart, they are grievous unto me, I am weary of them, yea it is a great pain for me to suffer them.' 'Why, O Lord, these be good, these be godly and these be necessary things.' 'Truth it is the fault is not in the things that be set forth, but in you that have set them forth, *manus enim vestrae plenae sunt sanguine*, for your hands are full of blood.'[311]

The 'blood' Lever mentioned was the vicious circle of covetousness and negligence leading to rebellion which necessitated merciless repression.[312]

Protestants' frustration both with government policy and with public apathy was indicated by their frequent calls for increase in zeal. Phillip Nichols rejected the argument for caution, declaring that intense religious conviction was the only safe way to get to Canaan:

> But all things must be done with discretion, sobriety and wisdom say they. But I pray you, what greater wisdom and discretion can there be than to do earnestly the commandment of God, and with an earnest zeal to set forth his truth? What is your mind to do? Are ye not minded to set forth God's word with a pure conscience? Are you not minded to do according to the same? Is it not your purpose to root out idolatry? Do you not intend to set up a true worship of God?[313]

Nichols cast doubt on the motivation of those who apparently supported reform. Gilby doubted that they followed the example of the biblical Josiah, despite having 'deposed' the Mass:

> Nay shall I call it deposed which is scantily transposed without any fervent zeal or sign of repentance. We have not felt Moses to make us drink the bitter ashes thereof with tears. We have not had Jehu to avenge God of his enemies the priests of Baal (1 Kings 10). We have not wept and wailed and torn our garments for very anguish of our hearts. We have not cast away the ornaments of our old idols and the vessels that served them as did the good young king Josiah.[314]

Gilby disturbed the sunny assumption that the identification of Edward VI with Josiah was a good sign. Had not Huldah the prophetess warned Josiah that even the intensity of his personal repentance was not enough to placate God for the sins of his people and avert their punishment of defeat and exile?[315] If even Josiah needed the support of his people, how much more vital was the people's repentance in a country led by hypocrites and governed by corrupt officials?[316] While they would have blanched at the thought of a reformation led from below, protestants did not rule out the part the godly (whether lay or clerical) could play in demanding the reformation of manners. Joye's call for the re-enactment of the Mosaic law is a good example of this:

> Forasmuch then as this is truth let neither the secular magistrates wink at this offence, let no man defend the crime, nor the professors of God's word cease to speak or to write, exciting and exhorting all estates to their bounden duties and offices enjoined them of God, putting the word into their mouths and sword into their hands lest for our negligence and winking at so grievous offences, God as he hath done in times past punish both the realms and the head rulers with all the whole subjects thereof.[317]

Lack of zeal and sincerity was evident in the priorities of those who claimed that the public peace was more important than the completeness of the reform, and that the capacity of the people to tolerate change should set the pace. This was particularly true of those with ideologically suspect backgrounds, such as Henrician conservatives who called for unity.[318] Latimer emphasised that unity was a secondary aim to that of doctrinal purity. He was anxious lest 'we would seek peace so much, that we should lose the truth of God's Word'.[319] He suspected the sincerity of many high-ranking 'gospellers':

> There be many reeds nowadays in the world, many men will go with the world, but religion ought not to be subject unto policy, but rather policy unto religion. I fear me there shall be a great many of us reeds, when there shall come a persecution, that we must suffer for God's Word's sake: I fear me that there will be a great number that will change, which will not be constant as John was . . .[320]

Just as the Jews had marvelled at Jesus's teaching, and then turned against him, consenting to his death 'by persuasion of the bishops', so the English would betray the gospel in time of persecution.[321] It was almost easier to deal with open enemies to the gospel than with the lukewarm or indifferent majority.[322]

General calls for repentance and an increase in zeal did not exclude specific remedies. It would be wrong to expect detailed manifestos in sermons and religious tracts, if only because the primary consideration of protestants was the spiritual regeneration of the nation.[323] For instance, as early as 1548, Foxe closed his tract on adultery with the observation that only a faithful ministry, confident in its spiritual powers of exhortation could bring about the restoration of primitive purity in the church.[324] By 1551 he had come to the conclusion that the contentious issue of discipline had to be faced, and he advocated the restoration of a reformed excommunication to combat the disorder and neglect that riddled the contemporary church, sullying the reputation of the English reformation and increasing the imminence of God's vengeance.[325]

A religion of the Word

Foxe was almost unique in envisaging an important role for the church authorities; others took the more conventional approach of looking to the government, both to parliament and to the informal but public example of the nobles. Thus 'Piers Plowman' warned parliament that 'except many inconveniences in this realm be redressed it is rather to be feared lest the gospel be slandered through us',[326] and set out a programme of legislation (principally increasing tillage and import controls) to bring the English economy in line with a justice and prosperity fitting to a nation which purported to uphold the Gospel.[327] Though it would be hard to persuade the covetous to enact these ideas, the catastrophic consequences of their refusal might convince them. Crowley likewise considered that poverty and exploitation (by rentiers, usurers and clergy) were in urgent need of reform by statute. God gave parliament the opportunity to act; if it failed to do so,

> be ye sure that the Lord shall confound your wisdom. Invent decree, establish and authorise what you can, all shall come to nought. The ways that you shall invent to establish unity and concord, shall be the occasions of discord. The things whereby you shall think to win praise through all the world, shall turn to your utter shame and the ways that you shall invent to establish a kingdom shall be the utter subversion of the same.[328]

Given the practical difficulty of enforcing statutes to regulate social behaviour, Crowley's threat of subversion rang uncomfortably true![329]

Both of these tracts were published as 'advice' to the government that if taken would pre-empt God's anger. When the nature of that anger had been made manifest, especially after 1549, more attention was given to the need for public acts of contrition and affirmation of support for the reformed faith. Crowley thought that it was imperative that the aristocracy showed its solidarity with the poor commons in the wake of the rebellions, and gave an unambiguous lead in worship and charity:

> Be not ashamed therefore to proclaim a solemn fast throughout the whole realm, that all at once with one voice we may cry unto God for mercy. Leave off your communions in a corner, and come unto the open temples, that men may see that ye regard the Lord's institution. Break your bread to the poor that all men may see that ye regard fasting.[330]

Hooper urged that everyone should join in a public act of renunciation of the traditional piety: 'restitution' should involve all levels of society.[331] Asking for national acts of repentance was an acceptable approach, as the response of calling for a fast to avert the terrors of the sweating sickness epidemic showed.[332] Such calls for acts of mass repentance showed how there was always a tension in protestant thinking between the imperative for the government to act to complete the reformation and the inability of 'worldly' policy to fulfil the task. Mass sinfulness could only be cured by mass repentance, which human authorities could attempt to enforce in externals, but of which they could only set an example by spiritual sincerity.[333]

England was in a no man's land between imminent reformation and imminent destruction. Whatever course of action was taken would affect the immediate fate of England. While national allegiance to the Gospel was in doubt, so were God's future actions. As Lever pointed out, things could go either way:

> God be merciful to us; for the time is even now coming when as God must needs either of his mercy here in England work such a wonderful miracle unto our comfort as far passeth man's expectation; or else of his righteousness take such a vengeance of this land to the example of all other lands, as shall be to our utter destruction.[334]

However critical they were of the establishment, it was not in protestants' interests to be completely pessimistic. Hence the frequent expressions of hope that God would avert his plagues or that the English would be chastised but not destroyed by them.[335] In an extraordinary outburst of precatory arm-twisting, Ponet asked that if England were to be punished it would be 'according to thy mercy and not after thy fury'. Though they undoubtedly sinned, the fact that the Word was openly preached made the English 'the enemies of the Devil, the Pope and the Turks'. He therefore offered a challenge to God:

> Wherefore awake O Lord God and sanctify thy name, whom they blaspheme, strengthen thy kingdom, which they disturb in us, and let thy will be done, which they will quench in us, and suffer not thyself to be trodden underfoot for our sins' sake, of them that do not correct our sins in us, but would quench in us thy holy Word, name and work, to the intent that thou shouldest be no God and have no people to preach, believe and acknowledge thee.[336]

There was, it seemed, still hope, even in the midst of fear.

NOTES

1 See Introduction, n. 34.
2 *Ibid.*, n. 35.
3 Loach and Tittler, *Mid-Tudor Polity*, 8.
4 See Introduction, n. 36.
5 Notably in *Image of both churches* and *Acts of the English votaries*. His 'influence' did not really take hold until Foxe developed his ideas in *Acts and monuments*; see Fairfield, *John Bale*, 150–6.
6 Cranmer, *Answer*, PS1 310.
7 Gilby, *Answer to Gardiner*, sig. Y2; cf. Lynne, *Beginning and ending of all popery*, 63.
8 Gilby, *Answer*, sig. Y3.
9 *Ibid.*, sig. Y1.
10 *Ibid.*, sig. Y7.
11 *Ibid.*, sig. Y7vo.

12. Bale, *Rank papist*, sig. B4vo.
13. Anon., *A dialogue between a gentleman and a priest*, sig. B6vo.
14. Hooper, *A declaration of Christ*, PS1 29, referring to Luther's doctrine of the Sacrament, which as a loyal Zwinglian he considered to be erroneous.
15. Gilby, *On Micah*, sigs G5–G5vo.
16. Bale, *Image of both Churches*, PS 374.
17. *Ibid.*, 500.
18. Lynne, *Beginning and end of all popery*, 5–6.
19. Gilby, *On Micah*, sigs A7vo–A8.
20. *Ibid.*, sig. A3vo.
21. Notably developed by John Jewel in the disputations with catholics in the 1560s; see J. Booty, *John Jewel as Apologist of the Church of England* (1963), ch. 6. However, some Edwardian writers made extensive use of patristic citations and arguments as evidence of their affinity with the early, pre-papal, church – most notably Cranmer, and also some lesser writers: e.g. see Richard Tracy, *A brief and short declaration* (1548), who cites Augustine, Tertullian, Ambrose, Cyprian – or made compilations of citations from them (e.g. Veron, *Godly sayings*). They may well have used mediaeval florilegia and misattributed sources as well as humanist editions. For the history of an influential compilation, see R. Peters, 'Who compiled the *Unio Dissidentium*?', *SCH* (1965).
22. See A. Ferguson, *Clio Unbound*, 3–4, 163–5.
23. This argument seeks to restore a 'golden age', reminiscent of a humanist approach to history; see D. Kelley, *The Foundations of Modern Historical Scholarship* (1970), 47–9.
24. See above, 'Providence', pp. 178–80.
25. See Chapter 1, 'Inversion', pp. 28–34 and 'Delusion', pp. 41–7.
26. Hooper, *Answer to Gardiner*, PS1 112.
27. Gilby, *Answer*, sig. A4vo.
28. Gilby, *Answer*, sig. H4vo, cites Zwingli, Oecalampadius and Vadian who affirmed mediaeval evidence of the 'spiritual' doctrine of the Sacrament, contrary to Gardiner's assertion that it had not been heard of for 1,500 years. Gilby's apocalyptic dating was an early instance of Bale's influence; see K. Firth, *The Apocalyptic Tradition in Reformation Britain* (Oxford, 1979).
29. Hooper, *Answer*, PS1 112.
30. *Ibid.*, 225–30.
31. John Hooper, *Jonah (fifth sermon)*, PS1 526. Landmarks in the development of the Mass cited by Hooper were: 1215 – papal adoption of the doctrine of transubstantiation; 1226 – institution of the reserved sacrament; 1262 – institution of the feast of Corpus Christi.
32. John Mardeley, *A declaration of the power of God's Word, concerning the holy Supper of the Lord* (1548), sig. D8.
33. Bale, *Rank papist*, sig. C3vo.
34. Hooper, *Jonah (fifth sermon)*, PS1 527.
35. *Ibid.*, 526. 'Wyclif's wicket did open the way to perceive your wilful blindness', according to Gilby, *Answer*, sig. X8, citing Bale, *Mystery of iniquity*, lxii.vo. On the reprinting of Wycliffite texts and revival of Lollard 'heroes', see M. Aston, 'Lollardy and the reformation: survival or revival?' (repr. from *History* 1964), in M. Aston, *Lollards and Reformers: Images and Literacy in Late Medieval Religion* (1984), ch. 7, especially 234–7 on the instrumental part played by Bale. See also *ibid.*, 'John Wycliffe's reformation reputation' (repr. from *P&P* 1965), especially 244–6, 250–4, 257, and Ryrie, 'Problems of legitimacy', in Gordon (ed.) *Protestant History and Identity*, vol. 1: 79–80.
36. For Edwardian reprints of Wycliffe's Wicket, see Aston, *Lollards and Reformers*, 233; for the General Prologue to the Lollard Bible, see *ibid.*, 230–1. For Crowley's editions

of this and of *Piers Plowman*, see King, *English Reformation Literature*, 97–100, 322–40. For the 'Piers Plowman' tradition in mid-Tudor literature, see White, *Social Criticism*, See also A. Hudson, *The Premature Reformation: Wycliffite Texts and Lollard History* (Oxford, 1988), for a more recent survey.

37 *Acts of the English votaries*, dedicated to Edward VI; all references to 1548 edn. See Fairfield, *John Bale*, ch. 4; Parish, *Clerical Marriage*, 105–11.
38 *Ibid*.
39 Bale, *Acts of the English votaries*, 14vo–15.
40 *Ibid*., 16–17.
41 *Ibid*., 18–24. Particular emphasis is placed on Celtic misogyny, sodomy of the priest-kings; but also notes that vows were not compulsory.
42 *Ibid*., 27vo–28.
43 E.g. Saint Illtyd, *ibid*., 20vo; Saint Cuthbert, *ibid*., 41.
44 They 'persevered still in the simple order of the primitive Church, not contented to change it': *ibid*., 33.
45 Bale links the freedom of the early British church from papal jurisdiction with its martyrs as signs of a true church – see *Latter examination of Anne Askew*, PS 188; as a tradition of female British saints, he cited Helena, Ursula and Hilda, *First examination of Anne Askew*, PS 156.
46 See Fairfield, *John Bale*, 95–6, 101, 106; Fairfield points out that Bale does not strictly apply the apocalyptic 'seven ages' chronology to 'England's unique experience'.
47 Gilby, *Answer*, sig. I5.
48 'R.V.', *The old faith of Great Britain, and the new learning of England* (1549), sig. a2vo: AD 185; see also Arthur Kelton, *A commendation of Welshmen* (1546), for a comparison of Lucius and Henry VIII as gospeller kings. See G. Williams, 'Some protestant views of early British church history' (repr. from *History* 1953) in *Welsh Reformation Essays* (Cardiff, 1967), 207–19.
49 'R.V.', *The old faith*, sig. a3. 'New learning' is a somewhat ambiguous term as it refers both to humanist scholarship and to evangelical reformist religion. See M. Dowling, *Humanism in the Age of Henry VIII* (1986), 1–2, 37.
50 'R.V.', *ibid*., sigs a3–a3vo.
51 *Ibid*., sig. a3vo; see also Chapter 1, 'Repression', pp. 47–51.
52 William Salesbury, *A certain case extract out of the law of Hywel Da, king of Wales AD 914* (1550). See Williams, 'The achievement of William Salesbury' (repr. from *Transactions of the Denbighshire Historical Society* 1965), in *Essays*, 191–205.
53 Gilby, *On Micah*, sigs A2–A2vo.
54 *Ibid*., e.g. sigs A4–A6.
55 See especially Latimer, *Third lenten Court sermon*, PS1.
56 But Gilby drew back from making an ecclesiological point out of the prophecy of Zion (Micah 4:1–4), preferring to discourse on the conversion of the Jews: *On Micah*, sigs F6vo–G3.
57 Phillip Nichols, *Copy of a letter sent to master Crispin*, sig. E5vo.
58 Matthew 24:4–6; 2 Thessalonians 2:3–12; 1 Timothy 4:1–3. these prophecies referred to the last days.
59 E.g. Gilby, *Answer*, cxvi; Robert Crowley, *Confutation of the mis-shapen answer*, sigs B8vo, F3vo; Cranmer, *Defence*, PS1 238.
60 Isaiah 1:11–15; Malachi 1:10–11; e.g. Salesbury, *Battery of the pope's buttress*, sig. D1; Gilby, *Answer*, sig. Bb3vo; and in the contrary case of reformed English worship, see below, n. 311.
61 Malachi 2:1–3, Hosea 4:4–6.

A religion of the Word

62 Crowley, *Confutation of Shaxton's articles*, sig. G6vo.
63 Lynne, *Beginning and ending of all popery*, 5–6; Bale, *Image of both churches*, PS 255–8; see also Firth, *Apocalyptic Tradition*, chs 1 and 2.
64 Bale, *Image of both churches*, PS 253.
65 See also Introduction; Chapter 3, 'Preaching and the preacher', pp. 88–94.
66 *Homilies*, sig. O1vo; see below, 'Divine judgement', pp. 187–97.
67 Bale, *Image of both churches*, PS 469.
68 Bale, *English votaries*, sig.*3; for 'the heavenly doctrine of governance', see Chapter 4, 'Introduction' pp. 140–6; cf. Hooper, *Jonah (first sermon)*, PS1 447.
69 Gilby, *On Micah*, sig. K3; cf. Latimer's version of Deut. 17, cited in Chapter 4, 'Introduction', pp. 143–5.
70 See below, 'Judgement', pp. 187–97.
71 Matthew 13:57–8.
72 Thomas Becon, Preface, *The flower of godly prayers*, PS3 10–11.
73 Hooper, *Jonah (third sermon)*, PS1 464.
74 1 Kings 18:17–18, Jeremiah 44:17; Hooper, *ibid.*, PS1 463–4.
75 Gilby, *Answer*, sigs T3–T3vo.
76 Bale, *Image of both churches*, PS 390. See also Chapter 1, 'Inversion', pp. 28–34.
77 Bale, *Image of both churches*, PS 261.
78 *Ibid.*, 251.
79 Lynne, *Beginning and ending of all popery*, 63.
80 It is important to distinguish this belief in the imminence of judgement from the 'hellfire' enthusiasm of later evangelical preaching.
81 *Of declining from God*, in *Homilies*, sig. N4vo.
82 *Ibid.*
83 *Ibid.*, sig. O2.
84 E.g. Hooper to Bullinger, Letter 30, 26 April, in *Original letters*, PS 61; Foxe, *De censura*, sig. A6vo, Becon, *Flower of godly prayers*, PS3 10.
85 Latimer, *Third lenten Court sermon*, PS 148.
86 *Ibid.*, 147.
87 Gilby, *On Micah*, sig. C3vo.
88 See Chapter 4, 'Introduction', pp. 140–6.
89 2 Kings 23. See Chapter 4, 'Godly judgement', pp. 146–58.
90 Hooper, *Declaration of Christ*, PS1 76–7; the allusion is ambiguous: it seems to refer to the godly, but it could include the whole nation. Hooper cites 1 Peter 2:9, 'a royal priesthood, a chosen nation', in support of his contention that the godly should be visibly holy.
91 Nichols, *Godly new story*, sig. B2vo; see Exodus 32; Numbers 11, 21, 25; 1 Corinthians 10. Cf. Bernard Gilpin, *Sermon preached before the Court, at Greenwich, the first Sunday after Epiphany, 1552* (1581), 20.
92 Gilby, *On Micah*, sigs E1–E2.
93 See Stoute, 'Origins,' ch. 2 – the sense of the unity of the covenant in both testaments, first developed by Augustine.
94 Joye, *A contrary*, sig. D3.
95 *Ibid.*, sig. E1vo.
96 Hooper, *Jonah (fifth sermon)*, PS1 512; cf. *Jonah (first sermon)*, PS1 448. See Brigden, *London*, 460, for the effectiveness on some London aldermen of Hooper's preaching.
97 See also Latimer, *A most faithful sermon*, PS 239–42; Lever, *Sermon preached the third Sunday of Lent*, sig. A3.
98 Hooper, *Jonah (first sermon)*, PS1 449–50; cf. Lever, *ibid.*, sigs A2–A3vo, which give almost exactly the same words.

99 Jeremiah 48:1, a prophecy of the destruction of Moab.
100 Latimer, *Sermon on the plough*, PS1 63.
101 Cf. Samuel, *A warning for the city of London*, verses 6 and 7: London compared to Sodom and Gomorrah.
102 Latimer, *Sermon on the plough*, PS1 65. See Beier and Findlay, *London 1550–1700*, and Brigden, *London and the Reformation*, ch. 11.
103 Cf. the distinctions made between the various models of plague and punishment by the Marian exiles, in Joy Shakespeare, 'Plague and punishment', in Lake and Dowling (eds) *Protestantism and the National Church*, 103–123.
104 Latimer, *Fourth lenten Court sermon*, PS1 168, Matthew 24:37. Cf John Bradford, 'A farewell to Lancashire and Cheshire' (1553), in *Sermons*, PS1 453.
105 Latimer, *Fourth lenten Court sermon*, PS1 169.
106 Hooper, *Declaration of the ten commandments*, PS1 281.
107 Joye, *A contrary*, sig. E2; cf. Anon., '... alterations of kingdoms for despising of God' – a damaged broadsheet ballad, detailing the fall of successive Old Testament kingdoms for committing the sins of idolatry, adultery, tyranny and oppression of the poor.
108 Becon, Preface, *Flower of godly prayers*, PS3 4.
109 Hutchinson, *Image of God*, PS 9.
110 Veron, *Godly sayings*, sig. A6; Hooper, *Jonah*, PS1 484.
111 Hooper, *Homily for the pestilence*, PS2 166.
112 Ibid., 159–60. See MacCulloch, *Tudor Church Militant*, 153, for this 'intense but short-lived religious revival'.
113 Becon, *Fortress of the faithful*, PS2 617–8.
114 Cheke, *Hurt of sedition*, sigs D6–E2vo.
115 Crowley, *Way to wealth*, sigs A2–A7.
116 Finch, *Epiphany*, sig. C1.
117 Ibid., sigs C1–C4.
118 Ibid., sig. D3vo.
119 Lever, *Fruitful sermon*, sig. A4vo – he made it clear that he was speaking metaphorically. See Took, 'Government and the printing trade', ch. 1, esp. 30–65.
120 Latimer, *Stamford sermon*, PS2 285; Joye, *A contrary*, sig. A7vo, saw Nebuchadnezzar and Titus as scourges of sexual sins.
121 Anon., 'Piers Plowman', *Exhortation*, sig. B3vo.
122 Gilby, *On Micah*, sig. C7; cf. Walter Haddon, *Exhortation to repentance* (1551).
123 Gilby, *Ibid.*, sig. N7. Mary of Guise visited the English Court in November 1551; Northumberland surrendered Boulogne to the French and arranged a marriage treaty between Edward VI and Elizabeth of Valois, while sending discreet support to the French protestants: Jordan, *Threshold*, 116–34, 153–4 .
124 Lever, *Sermon at Paul's Cross*, sigs H3–H3vo.
125 Latimer, *Sermon preached before the king*, PS1 246.
126 Thomas Becon, *The physic of the soul* (possibly a translation) (1549).
127 Hooper, *Jonah* (sixth sermon), PS1 545.
128 Cf. above, n. 74.
129 Cheke, *Hurt of sedition*, sigs G8vo–H1, see Chapter 1, 'Inversion', pp. 28–34.
130 Becon, *Fortress of the faithful*, PS2 608; cf. Crowley, *Confutation of Shaxton's articles*, sigs I1–I1vo.
131 Roger Hutchinson, 'Sermons on oppression, affliction and patience' (1552, unpublished), PS 306–7; Hooper, *Jonah (fourth sermon)*, PS1 490; Gilby, *On Micah*, sig. K1vo.
132 Latin eulogies about the lives and deaths of the Suffolk brothers were written by their tutors Walter Haddon and Thomas Wilson (1551).

133 Crowley, *Pleasure and pain*, sig. A2vo.
134 See Cohn, *Pursuit of the Millennium*, for a classic study of chiliastic cults; for 'normal' apocalyptic interest, see Firth, *Apocalyptic Tradition*, and R. Bauckham, *Tudor Apocalypse* (Abingdon, 1978).
135 Cf. RSTC 18877, Joye's translation of Osiander's *Conjectures of the end of the world* (Antwerp, 1548), which uses a calculation based on 'great years' of Christ's life. I owe this reference to Bryn Morris.
136 Gilby, *On Micah*, sig. G5vo.
137 Latimer, *Epistle for the first Sunday in Advent (Lincolnshire sermons)*, PS2 20: death and judgement both unexpected.
138 Bale, *Image of both churches*, PS 265; for the layers of Bale's chronology, see Chapter 1, n. 148.
139 Bale listed kings and prelates who turned to the gospel in *Image*, 508–9; he noted the apocalyptic significance of the dissolutions, *ibid.*, 517.
140 *Ibid.*, 325–40.
141 *Ibid.*, 358–66.
142 *Ibid.*, 368.
143 *Ibid.*, 370; see 'Introduction', pp. 1–5.
144 John Bale, *A mystery of iniquity* ('Geneva', i.e. Antwerp, 1545), sig. C6vo.
145 Gilby, *Answer*, sig. C6vo.
146 Crowley, *Confutation of Shaxton's articles*, sig. B1vo. See Chapter 1, 'Inversion', pp. 28–34.
147 Lancaster, *Right and true understanding*, sig. A4; see below, 'Time as revelation', pp. 180–3.
148 Gilby, *On Micah*, sig. A2vo; cf. Nichols, *Copy of a letter*, sig. F7.
149 See the harvest of revenge in Gilby, *On Micah*, sigs H1–H1vo.
150 Bale, *Image of both churches*, PS 625.
151 *Ibid.*, 466; cf. n. 104, above.
152 See Chapter 1, 'Inversion', pp. 28–34.
153 See Chapter 4, 'Introduction'; ' The social bonds', pp. 162–7.
154 Hooper, *Jonah* (third sermon), PS1 468.
155 Crowley, *Voice of the Last Trumpet*, titlepage; see below, Conclusion, pp. 231–3.
156 See Chapter 4, 'The social Bonds', pp. 162–7.
157 Gilby, *On Micah*, sig. O3.
158 *Ibid.*, sigs N6–N6vo.
159 Finch, *Epiphany*, sig. D3vo.
160 See Crowley, *On Joel*, sigs C4–E2, for an application of the apocalyptic prophecies of Joel to the gloom of 1546 – it is interesting how many of his concerns continued throughout Edward's reign.
161 Latimer, *On the Gospel for the second Sunday in Advent (Lincolnshire sermons)*, PS2 51; Gilby, despite his antagonism to miracles, referred to the portents of the sword seen hanging in the air at Boston, and the 'sudden death and murrain of men': *On Micah*, sig. C6.
162 Latimer, *Ibid.*, PS2 51.
163 *Ibid.*, 52.
164 Gilby, *On Micah*, sig. I5vo.
165 Latimer, *First lenten Court sermon*, PS1 102; cf. Becon's hope that the economic crisis would be solved by the king or by the last judgement: *Jewel of joy*, PS2 435.
166 Latimer, *Third sermon on the Lord's Prayer*, PS1 362–3. Latimer doubted that human parliaments could change things.
167 Gilby, *On Micah*, sig. A2vo, cited above, n. 53.

168 See Chapter 4, 'Godly judgement', especially retrospective criticisms of Henry VIII, and those impinging on the royal prerogative; see also Dowling, 'The Gospel and the Court', in Lake and Dowling (eds) *Protestantism and the National Church* Elizabeth too brooked no criticism – see P. Collinson, *Archbishop Grindal, 1519–83: The Struggle for a Reformed Church* (1979), 233–53. For Edward VI, see Introduction, 'A religious revolution?', pp. 1–5.
169 Especially as expressed by Gardiner and princess Mary – see Jordan, *Edward VI*, vol. 1: 206–18; vol. 2: 256–65.
170 Latimer, *Second lenten Court sermon*, PS1 118.
171 Ibid., 113–8.
172 Youth in itself was not a guarantee of godliness, for Manasses (2 Kings 21) and Jehoiakim (2 Kings 23:34 and 24:1–5) were both young kings and notoriously idolatrous. What mattered was that Edward/Josiah followed 'true religion'; see Hooper, 'The epistle', *Jonah*, PS1 437. See also B. Bradshaw, 'David or Josiah?', in Gordon (ed.) *Protestant History and Identity*, vol. 2.
173 Bale, *Frantic papist*, sig. B2vo.
174 Ibid., sig. C7vo.
175 Ibid., sig. B4.
176 Latimer, *First lenten Court sermon*, PS1 92.
177 Latimer, *Third lenten Court sermon*, PS1 133.
178 Latimer, *A most faithful sermon*, PS1 268. See Chapter 4, n. 90.
179 Latimer, *Fifth lenten Court sermon*, PS1 177.
180 'R.V.', *Old faith of Great Britain*, sig. b4.
181 Gilby, *On Micah*, sig. L2.
182 See Chapter 4, 'Godly judgement', pp. 146–58.
183 Collinson, *Grindal*, 61–5.
184 Especially Knox and Horne, SP 10:15, 66; for the alienation of Cranmer, see Strype, *Memorials of Archbishop Cranmer*, vol. 2, Part 1: 383–90, 414–23 – though Cranmer remained a regular attender at Council, and the years 1552–53 saw the culmination of his religious reforms, with the crucial exception of the reform of canon law. Hooper was apparently the least critical, but he was increasingly occupied with diocesan affairs; see F.D. Price, 'Gloucester diocese under Bishop Hooper', *TRHS* (1938): 51–151.
185 See Brigden, *London and the Reformation*, 473–4; note the censorship of Mardeley, and the imprisonment of Curthop in the Fleet for a Court sermon critical of aristocratic plunder of the church.
186 See e.g. Lever, *Sermon preached the third Sunday of Lent*, which was highly critical of Somerset's handling of the 1549 rebellion, exploitation of reformation, building 'gorgeous houses', destruction of educational and charitable provision; but also Ridley's opposition to Somerset's plan to merge Trinity Hall and Clare College into a college for the study of the civil law: SP 10:7, 16; for Latimer on Thomas Seymour, see below, nn. 195–199; on official corruption, see *Third lenten Court sermon*, PS1 128–49. See also above, Introduction, 'Somerset and Northumberland', pp. 10–12; 'Unstable politics?', p. 12.
187 See Conclusion, pp. 231–3.
188 See Chapter 4, 'Introduction', pp. 140–6.
189 Crowley, *Voice of the last trumpet*, sig. A3.
190 Latimer, *On the Gospel for St Andrew's Day* (Lincolnshire sermons), PS2 34. On the necessity of labour in vocations, see *Sixth lenten court sermon*, PS1 214–15; on miraculous or subversive vocations, *On the epistle for 23rd Sunday after Trinity* (Lincolnshire sermons), PS1 517.

191 Robert Crowley, 'Of men that have divers offices', *One-and-thirty epigrams*.
192 See Chapter 4, 'Godly judgement' pp. 146–58; see also Becon, *Fortress of the faithful*, PS2 598–601.
193 Gilpin, *Sermon preached before the Court*, 43.
194 *Ibid.*, 43–4.
195 Latimer, *Second lenten Court sermon*, PS1 113–15; see above, Introduction, 'Unstable politics?', p. 12.
196 Latimer, *Fifth lenten Court sermon*, PS1 183.
197 Latimer, *Fourth lenten Court sermon*, PS1 160.
198 Latimer, *Seventh lenten Court sermon*, PS1 228–9.
199 *Ibid.*
200 Gilby, *On Micah*, sig. A6.
201 *Ibid.*, sig. A4.
202 *Ibid.*, sig. N4vo.
203 Cain and Nimrod; see also Chapter 1, 'Repression', pp. 47–51.
204 Gilby, *On Micah*, sig. F1vo.
205 *Ibid.*, sig. F2vo; cf. Gilpin, *Sermon Preached before the Court*, 46–7. For further references to the Privy Chamber, see Chapter 4, n. 99.
206 Gilby, *On Micah*, sig. D7, also on abuses of courts of wards and augmentations. see Hurstfield, 'Corruption and reform under Edward VI and Mary: the example of wardship', *EHR* (1953): 22–36.
207 Gilpin, *Court sermon*, 51–2.
208 *Ibid.*, 42; see also Chapter 1, 'Inversion', pp. 28–34.
209 Gilby, *On Micah*, B5vo; see Chapter 4, 'Introduction,' pp. 140–6.
210 Crowley, *Way to wealth*, sigs B4–B4vo.
211 Job 34; Gilpin, *Sermon preached before the Court*, 62–3.
212 Crowley, *A New Year's gift*: Cain and Nimrod; Nebuchadnezzar and pharaoh, *Way to wealth*, sig. B6.
213 Gilby, *On Micah*, sigs B1–B1vo.
214 *Ibid.*, sig. B7.
215 Notably Henry Brinkelow, *The complaint of Roderick Mors* (Strassburg, 1542).
216 See Elton, *Reform and Reformation*, 317; W. Hoskins, *The Age of Plunder*, ch. 6. An account of Curthop's sermon, characterising profiteers as 'sponges' of church assets, is in Richard Scudamore, *Letters to Sir Philip Hoby*, Letters no. 19.
217 Anon., 'Piers Plowman', *Exhortation*, sigs A4–A6. This writer thought there was an employment crisis caused by surplus population no longer employed by the monasteries or wars.
218 *Ibid.*, sigs. A8–B3vo: the writer proposed bills to restrain enclosure, encourage the cultivation of marginal lands, and increase self-sufficiency by raising import duties and lowering export duties. see Chapter 3, 'The need for further reformation', pp. 106–14. The economic understanding of these writers was limited, but the exact nature of the mid-Tudor price rise is still debated; see D. Palliser, *The Age of Elizabeth* (1983), ch. 5.
219 'R.V.', *Old learning of Great Britain*, sig. b4vo; cites Eusebius, *History of the Church*, Book 7, ch. 13.
220 Gilby, *On Micah*, sig. F5vo.
221 'Piers Plowman', *Exhortation*, sig. A6vo.
222 Gilby, *On Micah*, sigs. F5–F5vo. Gilby's criticisms are no less damning for being directed generally. For continuity of membership of the Council, see Hoak, *The King's Council*, ch. 2, tables 1–7.
223 *Ibid.*, sig. B7vo.

224 Roger Hutchinson, *Sermons on oppression, affliction, and patience* (1552) PS 324; cf. Robert Crowley, *Philargyrie of Great Britain* (1551).
225 See Chapter 4, 'The social bonds', pp. 162–7.
226 See above, 'Divine judgement', pp. 187–97.
227 Anon., *The praise and commendation of such as sought commonwealths* (?1549), sig. A4vo.
228 'Piers Plowman', *Exhortation*, sigs. B3vo–B4; cf. John Ramsey, *A corosive to be laid hard to the hearts of all faithful professors of Christ's gospel* (?1548) – an anthology of biblical texts to help the reader test the purity of his conversion.
229 See Chapter 2.
230 Gilby, *On Micah*, sig. A6vo; see also Chapter 3, 'The need for further reformation', pp. 106–14.
231 Lever, *Sermon preached at Paul's Cross*, sigs B4–B4vo.
232 Gilby, *On Micah*, sig. A7.
233 Gilpin, *Sermon preached before the Court*, 54.
234 Ibid., 65–6.
235 Lever, *Sermon preached at Paul's Cross*, sigs A3vo–A4; cf. Hutchinson, *Sermons on oppression*, PS 338. See also John Mardeley, *A necessary instrument for covetous rich men* (1548), sig. C1 – see Ephesians 5:5.
236 Lever, *Sermon preached at Paul's Cross*, sig. B2.
237 Ibid., sig. F8.
238 See also Chapter 4, 'Introduction', pp. 140–6.
239 Lever, *Sermon preached at Paul's Cross*, sigs B5–B5vo. This is a protestantised version of the letter of Jude, vv. 12–13.
240 Lever, ibid., sig. A6vo.
241 Lever, *A fruitful sermon*, sig. B8.
242 Thomas Cranmer, 'A sermon on rebellion' (1549, unpublished), PS2 193.
243 Gilpin, *Sermon preached before the Court*, 65.
244 Anon., *Praise of such as sought commonwealths*, sigs A3–A3vo.
245 Crowley, *One-and-thirty epigrams*, sig. A8 – these short poems satirised ambition, greed and idleness, especially in the context of London; e.g. 'A is for Alleys', on urban squalor. See above, nn. 101 and 102.
246 Becon, Preface, *Fortress of the faithful*, PS2 587; cf. Latimer, 'To the reader' (by Thomas Some), *Second lenten Court sermon*, PS1 106.
247 Cranmer, *Sermon on rebellion*, PS2 197.
248 Lever, *Sermon preached at Paul's Cross*, sig. D5vo.
249 Isaiah 5:8–10.
250 Gilpin, *Sermon preached before the Court*, 53.
251 Crowley, *An information and petition*, sig. A7.
252 See below, 'Resisting the gospel', pp. 209–14.
253 Lever, *Sermon preached at Paul's Cross*, sig. F1.
254 Veron, *Godly sayings*, sigs H2–H3.
255 Gilby, *On Micah*, sig. D8.
256 Lever, *Sermon preached at Paul's Cross*, sig. E7.
257 E.G. Gilpin, *Sermon preached before the Court*, 61–5 – he was at pains to point out that the commons were not blameless (see next section).
258 E.g. Cheke, *Hurt of sedition*; Anon., *A copy of a letter, containing certain news and the articles or requests of the Devonshire and Cornish rebels* (1549), sigs A3vo–A4 – this tract, also has useful evidence of the distribution of propaganda. See also Chapter 4, 'Obedience and its limitations', pp. 158–62.

A religion of the Word

259 For the western rising, see J. Youings, 'The south-western rebellion of 1549', *Southern History* (1979). *A copy of a letter*, sig. A4vo, saw the rising as evidence of a wider conspiracy of disorder. For evidence of this, see B.L. Beer, *Rebellion and Riot: Popular Disorder During the Reign of Edward VI* (Kent, OH, 1982), ch. 6; MacCulloch, *Tudor Church Militant*, 121–3.
260 For the Norfolk rising, see D. MacCulloch, 'Kett's rebellion in context', *P&P* (1979): 36–59; J. Cornwall, 'Kett's rebellion in context: a reply', and D. MacCulloch, 'A rejoinder', *P&P* (1981): 160–73. For Somerset's role, see Shagan and ensuing debate in *EHR*, 1999, 2000.
261 See Chapter 3, 'A ministry of the Word', pp. 88–106; Chapter 4, 'Obedience and its limitations', pp. 158–62.
262 Also the 'publishing bulge' of 1548 magnifies the sense of hope, especially in prefaces and concluding paragraphs perhaps tacked on prior to publication – see above, Sources and methodology. But the sense of threat is also there – see e.g. Mardeley, Verse Introduction, sigs A–A2vo; and 'A complaint against the stiff-necked', sigs E3-vo, *Power of God's Word*.
263 'R.V.' *Old faith of Great Britain*, sig. b1; cf. Jean Veron, *The five abominable blasphemies that are in the Mass* (1548), sigs. a2vo–a3.
264 Finch, *Epiphany of the church*, sig. A3vo.
265 Cheke, *Hurt of sedition*, sig. A6.
266 *A message sent by the king's majesty to certain of his people assembled in Devonshire* (1549), sig. A3.
267 See A. Fletcher, *Tudor Rebellions*, 2nd edn (1973), 57–63.
268 See above, 'Royal minority', pp. 198–200.
269 Becon, *Fortress of the faithful*, PS2 594.
270 Ibid., PS2 595–8; Crowley, *Way to wealth*, sigs A4–A5; Gilpin, *Sermon preached before the Court*, 34.
271 Becon, *Fortress of the faithful*, PS2 595–6; Latimer, *A most faithful sermon*, PS1 249–50.
272 See Chapter 4, 'Introduction', pp. 140–6.
273 Cheke, *Hurt of sedition*, sigs D2vo–E8.
274 Cranmer, *Sermon on rebellion*, PS2 191.
275 Ibid.
276 Hooper, 'The epistle', *Jonah*, PS1 441.
277 Lever, *A fruitful sermon*, sig. C3.
278 Ibid., sigs C3–C4.
279 Gilby, *On Micah*, sig. D7; see above, 'Pretending the gospel', pp. 200–9.
280 E.g. Crowley's description of the seditious poor in *The way to wealth*, sigs A3–A3vo; but also note his more sympathetic view of the 'poor idiots', sig. B3vo. 'Piers Plowman', *Exhortation*, sigs A2vo–A3, also takes an anti-'communist' line.
281 Cf. Hutchinson, *On oppression*, PS 302 – 'God's martyrs' were those who suffered uncomplainingly the exploitation of rack-renters, forestallers and regraters.
282 Latimer, *Fourth sermon on the Lord's Prayer*, PS1 377.
283 Crowley, *The way to wealth*, sig. B7vo.
284 See above, 'Divine judgement', pp. 187–97.
285 E.g. C. Haigh, 'Anticlericalism in the English reformation', *History* (1983): 391–407, esp. 405–7.
286 Latimer, *Sixth sermon on the Lord's Prayer*, PS1 208.
287 Ibid.
288 See Chapter 1, 'Conspiracy', pp. 34–7.

289 John Mardeley, 'A complaint against the stiff-necked', *A declaration of the power of God's Word, concerning the holy Supper of the Lord*, sig. E3.
290 Finch, *Epiphany of the church*, sig. A2.
291 Ibid., sigs. A2–A2vo.
292 Ibid., sig. D3vo.
293 Gilpin, *Sermon preached before the Court*, 34–35; see Bossy, *Christianity in the West*, ch. 4.
294 Gilpin, ibid., sigs 35–6.
295 Lever, *A fruitful sermon*, sig. D2vo.
296 Latimer, *Seventh lenten Court sermon*, PS1 230.
297 Latimer, *Fifth lenten Court sermon*, PS1 187; Cf. Hutchinson, *Image of God*, 138.
298 Gilpin, *Sermon Preached before the Court*, 34.
299 Gilby, *On Micah*, sig. K8; Gilby emphasises his own observation of these beliefs and practices, ibid., sigs K4–K8. Cf. Hutchinson, *Image of God*, PS 77–83 for a diatribe against astrology and belief in 'destiny'; Latimer, *Second sermon on the Lord's Prayer*, PS1 345; *On the epistle for the twenty-fourth Sunday after Advent* (Lincolnshire sermons) PS1 534, for resort to witches in times of trouble. One reason why protestants were worried was that the draconian Witchcraft Act of 1542 was abolished in 1547; see K. Thomas, *Religion and the Decline of Magic*, rev. edn (1973), 412–3.
300 Thomas, ibid., chs 8 and 9; C. Haigh, 'Anticlericalism in the English reformation', *History* (1983), 406–7.
301 See also above, 'Royal minority'; Chapter 3, 'Introduction', pp. 87–8; Chapter 4, 'Godly judgement', pp. 146–58. Note that in any case, there is more printed material from the beginning of the reign; see Sources and methodology.
302 See above, 'Divine judgement', pp. 187–97.
303 Gerrard, *Godly invective*, sigs a6vo, E6.
304 Anon., *Dialogue between a gentleman and a priest*, sig. A4.
305 Ibid., sig. A7.
306 Gilpin, *Sermon preached before the Court*, 20; cf. Latimer, *First lenten Court sermon*, PS1 92.
307 And even this was only partial; see Chapter 3, 'The need for further reformation', pp. 106–14.
308 Lever, *A fruitful sermon*, sigs A3vo–A4.
309 Gilby, *On Micah*, sig. D1.
310 Lever, *Sermon preached at Paul's Cross*, sig. C7.
311 Lever, *Sermon preached before the Court*, sigs. B8vo–C1.
312 See above, 'Pretending the gospel', pp. 200–9.
313 Nichols, *A godly new story*, sig. C6vo. For the relative speed with which the Edwardian reforms were carried out, see R. Hutton, *Rise and fall of Merry England: The Ritual year, 1400–1700* (Oxford, 1996), ch. 3.
314 Gilby, *On Micah*, sig. K8–K8vo.
315 Ibid., sig. K8vo.
316 Hooper, *Jonah* (sixth sermon) PS1 542–5.
317 Joye, *A contrary*, sig. A3; see also sigs B1vo, B4vo–B5.
318 Latimer, *On the Gospel for All Saints* (Lincolnshire sermons) PS1 487.
319 Ibid.
320 Latimer, *On the Gospel for the third Sunday in Advent*, PS2 82.
321 Latimer, *On the third Sunday after Epiphany*, PS2 167–8.
322 Confessional arguments are not very well disguised in the historiography of the English reformations. 'Revisionism' tended to be hostile to the aims and achievements

of the Edwardian reformation – MacCulloch, *Tudor Church Militant*, redresses the balance.
323 See Chapters 3 and 4.
324 John Foxe, *De non plectendis morte adulteris*, sig. C7.
325 Foxe, *De censura* (1551), Introduction and ch. 2; see Davies and Facey, 'A reformation dilemma', *JEH* (1988): 37–50.
326 'Piers Plowman' *Exhortation*, sig. A1vo.
327 See above, n. 218.
328 Crowley, *An information and petition*, sigs B6–B6vo. See Chapter 1, 'Inversion', pp. 28–34.
329 See G.R. Elton, *Reform and Renewal: Thomas Cromwell and the Commonweal* (Cambridge, 1973), 162–6.
330 Crowley, *The way to wealth*, sig. B7.
331 Cf. Latimer, *A most faithful sermon*, PS1 262–3; Hooper, *Jonah*, PS1 554–5.
332 SP 10:13, 30.
333 Hooper, *Jonah*, PS1 539–45.
334 Lever, *Sermon preached before the Court*, sig. A2.
335 Becon, *Flower of godly prayers*, PS3 43–4. The insistence on repentance reflected their fear that justification by faith alone was being interpreted as a licence if not actually to sin, then for religious inertia.
336 John Ponet, *A notable sermon concerning the right use of the Lord's Supper*, sig. G8.

Conclusion

WHILE the disparate voices of individual protestant writers should not be denied, what this study has shown is that the characteristics they had in common outweighed those that separated them. In terms of a reformed protestant outlook centred on the primacy of scripture, Edwardian protestants were remarkably united – thus Hooper had more in common with Cranmer and Ridley than has been traditionally assumed. Divisions between them have more to do with political circumstance and incompatibility of character than with absolute theological differences. Personal circumstances were influential – it was much easier to be outspoken as a freelance pamphleteer like Crowley than as a bishop preaching at Court. What is remarkable is the extent to which the two categories were prepared to speak out along similar lines.[1]

Similarly, though English protestants did defer to Martyr, Bucer, Bullinger and Lasco, and though these men were deeply concerned with the progress of the English reformation, and made active interventions in policy to that end, this does not add up to a 'continental phase' for the English reformation, so much as a consciousness that all reformers were participating in a movement which was going to transform Christendom.[2] This would be strengthened in the experience of exile during Mary's reign, and would re-emerge, this time rather more divisively, during the early years of Elizabeth.[3] It is important to bear in mind, however, that the Edwardian reformation grew out of its own particular political circumstances, and that these are reflected in the choice of subjects and the emphasis of contemporary protestant propaganda. The continental theologians were treated as useful guests; meanwhile the formative pressures on the presentation of the protestant case were the reaction to the Six Articles, the need to attack the Mass and make way for the Communion Service, and to provide a plausible case against the formidable and prolific Gardiner, a most effective champion of conservatism; the anxiety created by the rebellions of 1549 and the consequent political instability; and the general constraints of an unreformed church structure and a government with dubious motives for supporting reform. The pressures created by these problems created more of a consensus than would emerge from a study which focuses on theological differences.

What, then, is this consensus? Protestantism in Edward's reign felt itself an embattled creed – which might at first seem paradoxical, for it was at the

Conclusion

same time upheld by the establishment. But protestants faced a profound difficulty in coming to terms with being the representatives of what had become the 'official' religion. They were concerned that 'true religion' had not taken root among the people, who were at best indifferent or ignorant and at worst hostile; likewise that those with wealth and power were misusing it for their own ends. This led to a need to dissociate themselves from the sacrilegious or ungodly activities of the regime, while still maintaining positions in which they could influence policy – as bishops and noble chaplains, for instance. Thus they risked outspoken criticism and exhortation that came very close to constituting a political threat, characteristics made possible for the first time by the political accident of a royal minority. However, the extent to which they could speak out was constrained by their differing perceptions of their various personal positions, their anxiety to maintain order, and by the institutional and practical barriers to a radical reform of the church. Protestants were still in a minority, and continued to have a minority outlook and mental attitude. Unsure of the security of their position, they could only trust in God that he would not have to judge England too severely for its sins.

The fundamental protestant problem of avoiding the charge of inviting schism was pre-empted by their use of inversion, something which was fundamental to their outlook. Protestants validated their case by presenting themselves as opponents of Antichrist. The manifestations of Antichrist included papists and religious radicals – both constituted false religion. However, to start with an analysis of the things protestants hated is not to suggest that protestantism was an entirely negative and reactive phenomenon. Of course, the positive starting-point is doctrine: the revolution of justification by faith alone. However, starting with what they hated and distanced themselves from is a very good way of entering into their worldview, for not only does it reflect the chronological shifts in subject matter in the sources, it becomes clear that their method of dissecting popery is reflected in their views of the unreformed commonwealth. Thus it is not so much that the first two chapters of this book are negative and the second three positive, but that they provide the structure for the whole.

For the problems that nascent protestantism then faced were an unreformed church structure, a doubtfully godly magistracy and an ungodly people. Protestants needed to present a view of true order within this chaos, and yet not be open to charges of sedition. While the prevailing ungodliness appalled them, they maintained the hope that if only the people would repent they could enjoy the benefits of a triumphant nation, blessed by God. This hope was based on their faith in the overwhelming power of the Word gone free in pulpit and press, a high and almost reckless expectation of the profound and speedy change in society that would constitute the true and complete

Conclusion

reformation. Nor was this entirely in the realms of wish fulfilment, for the dramatic changes demanded by the Edwardian religious reforms were carried out remarkably rapidly. The changes envisaged by protestants were thus very different from humanist notions of gradual improvement by a process of education, though they did not of course exclude this. At the same time, they all assumed that human sinfulness prevented the transforming message of the preached Word from getting through. The tensions set up by the change in their circumstances from persecuted, or at least discreet, professors of the Gospel to established church were paralleled by the inherent tension of the role of the prophet, bound to speak out yet rarely regarded.

Thus when Mary did succeed and reversed the Edwardian reforms this tension was to a certain extent resolved.[4] Protestants had to face persecution and exile, and those that accepted that trial rediscovered the strength and confidence of the godly minority.[5] The doubts that had troubled them in Edward's reign had been confirmed; they had been betrayed by the nobility and abandoned by the sins of the people.[6] As Mary's reign wore on, the potential of the doctrine of limited obedience for becoming a doctrine of disobedience became all too clear, and Edwardian prophets became theorists of resistance.[7] The trials of Mary's reign were consciously accepted as the proving of the English church; here was not the doubt and anxiety of Edward's reign, but real, tangible opposition to true religion. In this powerful sense, the triumphant vision of the English church provided by Foxe in the *Acts and monuments* was only made possible by the Marian burnings. Edward's reign was a far more doubtful prospect, and only seen as a new dawn for the church in dewy-eyed retrospect. But apart from the confidence given by the Marian burnings, and the problems and divisions that had opened up in the exile, in many ways the early Elizabethan church faced similar problems to those encountered in Edward's reign.[8] Only late in Elizabeth's reign could the reformation really begin to take hold, and only then, with a new generation, would new solutions – and new antagonisms – arise.

NOTES

1 See MacCulloch, *Tudor Church Militant*.
2 See Introduction, nn. 41, 48.
3 See Collinson, *Archbishop Grindal*, 89.
4 J. Shakespeare, 'Plague and punishment', in Lake and Dowling (eds) *Protestantism and the National Church* (1987), 103, 108–9.
5 E.g. John Hooper, *Letters*, PS2 617–8.
6 E.g. John Ponet, *A short treatise of politic power* (Strassburg, 1556), sigs I3–I3vo, K3–K3vo. Crowley thought that Edward VI had been misled and ultimately destroyed by the 'masking and mumming ... outrageous riding in hawking and hunting' of Northumberland's Court; see Betteridge, *Tudor Histories*, 166–7.

Conclusion

7 See Skinner, *Foundations*, vol. 2: ch. 7; for a different view see M. Walzer, *The Revolution of the Saints* (1966), 92–109.
8 MacCulloch, *Tudor Church Militant*, ch 4; P. Collinson, *The Elizabethan Puritan Movement* (1967), ch. 2.

Appendix: brief biographies of authors

This is a summary guide to most of the authors mentioned in the text, excluding major continental divines. Fuller details may be found in the *DNB* and Fines's *Register*, and in full scale biographies of the more significant figures, as indicated in the bibliography. It should also be noted that 'Anon.' produced seventeen items on my list, and a further five are identified only by initials. Titles of works have been kept to a minimum – please consult bibliography and *RSTC*. The domination of the list by clerics and university-educated men is striking, and raises interesting questions about the 'popular' nature of their work.

ALLEN, EDMUND: *cleric; ?1519–59*

b. Norfolk; fellow of Corpus Christi College, Cambridge (1536); took prolonged 'study leave' in 1540 and gained his BD (Bachelor of Divinity) abroad; also m. with a large family. On return in 1549 was made chaplain to princess Elizabeth; undertook translations of works by continental reformers. Exiled under Mary (1553–59). Because royal chaplain, ambassador and then bishop elect of Rochester after return, but d. in London before he could establish himself in these roles.

BALE, JOHN: *cleric; 1495–1563*

b. Cove[?hithe], Suffolk; 1507 – entered the Carmelite convent in Norwich. 1514 – studying at Cambridge, BD in 1529; 1530–36 – prior of Carmelite convents at Ipswich, Doncaster and Maldon. Converted by Lord Wentworth: renounced vows and m. Dorothy. Rector of Thorndon, Suffolk; wrote plays and received patronage from Cromwell. 1540 – exile; historical and controversial writings. 1547 – returned to rectory of Bishopstoke, Hants; non-resident vicar of Swaffham, Norfolk. 1553 – bishop of Ossory, in Ireland, but made a turbulent voyage into exile again, mostly in Basel. 1558 – returned to England; prebendary at Canterbury.

BECKE, EDMUND: *scholar*

1551 – ordained deacon by Ridley; worked mostly as a translator, notably supervising a revision of John Rogers's 1537 Bible, dedicated to Edward VI, with a chronology from Adam to Christ, and of two works by Erasmus.

BECON, THOMAS: *cleric; 1512–67*

b. Norfolk. 1530 – BA St John's, Cambridge, eventually DD. Converted by listening to sermons and lectures of Latimer and George Stafford. 1538 – ordained, rector of Brenzett, in Kent. Prolific writer on devotional themes (pseud. 'Theodore Basille'). Recanted evangelical views at Paul's Cross 1543; 'internal exile' in the

Appendix

Midlands. 1547 – rector of St Stephen Wallbrook, London; chaplain to Somerset; one of Cranmer's 'six preachers'. 1553 – imprisoned in Tower; 1554–59 – exile in Strassburg. Restored to St Stephen's 1559, plus three other benefices.

BRADFORD, JOHN: *gentleman, cleric;* ?1510–55

b. Manchester, educated at Manchester Grammar School. Entered service of Sir John Harrington of Exton, Rutland, treasurer of the king's camps at Boulogne; 1544 – deputy paymaster at siege of Montreuil. 1547 – Inner Temple; influenced by Thomas Sampson's and Hugh Latimer's preaching, he sold his valuables, gave to the poor and restored money to the crown. 1548 – St Catharine's, Cambridge; 1549 – MA by special grace, also fellow of Pembroke Hall, Cambridge; 1550 – ordained deacon by Ridley, and made his chaplain; 1551 – prebendary of Kentish Town, royal chaplain/itinerant preacher especially in north-west of England. 1553 – arrested, imprisoned in Tower; 1554 – moved to King's Bench prison where he disputed with the free-willers. 1555 – burned as a heretic.

BRINKELOW, HENRY: *mercer; d. 1546*

b. Kintbury, Berks, son of Robert Brinkelow. Became a Franciscan friar, but left the order and m. Margery; son called John. Became a mercer, and citizen of London. Claimed to have been banished from England because of the influence of the bishops. Wrote satirical tracts about social and church reform in 1540s. Left £5 in his will to 'the godly learned men who labour in the vineyard of the Lord and fight against Antichrist'.

CHAMPNEYS, JOHN

b. near Bristol. Lived at Stratford by Bow in London. Unorthodox views recanted before Cranmer in 1548, but survived Mary's reign and replied to Veron's treatise on predestination in 1563.

CHEKE, JOHN: *classical scholar;* 1514–57

b. Cambridge; BA and fellow of St John's College; 1533 – MA. Taught William Cecil, William Bill, Roger Ascham. Royal patronage (via Dr William Butts). 1540 – regius chair in Greek; 1542 – controversy over Greek pronunciation with Gardiner (q.v.) – a thinly veiled debate over 'unwritten verities'? Public orator of Cambridge University, tutor to Prince Edward. 1547 – m. Mary Hill. Given Spalding priory, College of St John, Stoke by Clare. 1547, 1552–3 – MP for Bletchingley; 1548 – provost of King's College – royal mandate dispensed with need for orders. 1549 – visitation of Cambridge, commissioner to revise ecclesiastical law. 1549–50 – witnessed against Gardiner and Bonner. 1550 – gentleman of the Privy Chamber. 1552 – knighted, granted manor of Stoke by Clare (which had belonged to the college), and manors in Suffolk, Norfolk and Lincolnshire which had belonged to the earl of Surrey and duke of Norfolk. Disputed on Eucharist at Cecil's house; severe illness. 1553 – clerk of Council, privy councillor. 1553–54 – arrested and imprisoned; 1554–56 – exile in Italy and Strassburg. 1556

– recaptured in Netherlands and brought home, where he recanted and soon after d.

COLE, THOMAS: *heterodox schoolmaster, cleric;* ?1530–71

1546 – BA King's College; 1550 – MA. 1552 – schoolmaster at Maidstone. Renounced free-willers in a sermon before Cranmer. 1553 – arrested; exempted from pardon at Mary's coronation. Exiled in Frankfurt and Geneva. Returned to preferment in Essex benefices, despite contentious nature of nonconformist views.

COVERDALE, MILES: *cleric, biblical translator;* 1488–1568

b. Yorks. 1514 – ordained at Norwich; joined Austin friars at Cambridge; influenced by Robert Barnes, connections with Cromwell. ?1526 – left his order to remain a secular priest and preacher. 1531 – Bachelor of Canon Law. 1528–35 – exiled on continent, in association with Tyndale; completed his Bible translation in 1535. 1539–40 – oversaw production of Great Bible. Brief stay in England ended with fall of Cromwell. While in Germany m. Elizabeth Macheson; DD Tübingen. 1543 – pastor at Bergzabern, also in Denmark. 1548 – returned, almoner to Katherine Parr, preached her funeral sermon. 1549–50 – actively campaigned against religious radicals, also preached against the western rebels. 1551 – bishop of Exeter. 1552–53 – served on ecclesiastical law commission and attended Lords. Exiled in Denmark and Bergzabern. 1559 – preached at Paul's Cross. 1563 – DD Cambridge and living of St Magnus the Martyr, London. 1566 – resigned over vestments' controversy.

CRANMER, THOMAS: *cleric;* 1489–1556

b. Aslockton, Notts, of minor gentry family. Unhappy schooling, probably in Lincs. 1511/12 – BA Cambridge; 1515 – MA, fellow of Jesus College; 1518/19 – m. Joan ?Black; returned to lecturing in divinity after her death. Ordained by 1520. The need for biblical arguments for the royal divorce brought him to Court (1529), through Gardiner and Edward Foxe. 1530 – archdeacon of Taunton; diplomatic travels in Europe, especially to the emperor. 1532 – m. Margarete, niece of Andreas Osiander's wife; recalled to England to become archbishop of Canterbury and oversaw the royal divorce. Godfather to princess Elizabeth and later prince Edward. King's favour and own considerable political skill allowed him to survive the falls of Anne Boleyn and Cromwell. Weathered the conservative advances of the 1540s, and managed to develop evangelical reform. 1540s – wrote Preface to Great Bible; wrote English Litany; *Homilies*. Eucharistic theology changed to a more sacramentarian view by end of 1547. Sermon apparently preached at Edward VI's coronation anticipated the reforms of a new Josiah. Active privy councillor. 1548 – visitation of Canterbury diocese; translation of Justus Jonas's *Short Catechism* backfired as it appeared to uphold the Real Presence. 1549 – presided over Joan Bocher's heresy trial and the commission (1550–51) depriving Bonner and Gardiner. Fostered contacts with foreign divines, showing especial hospitality to Bucer and Martyr. English Prayer Books of 1549 and 1552 were to have lasting effect on English language, culture and spirituality. Reform of canon law blocked by conflict with Northumberland. A reluctant

Appendix

collaborator in the device for the succession, nominating Jane Grey as queen. November 1553 – arrested; under major pressure to recant, which he did, but withdrew his recantation before being burned, in Oxford, 1556.

CROWLEY, ROBERT: *printer, cleric; ?1518–88*

b. Gloucs. 1534 – Oxford, 1542 – fellow of Magdalen. Late 1540s to London, stationer in Ely Rents, Holborn. 1551 – ridley ordained him deacon. 1553 – exile at Frankfurt. Preached at Paul's Cross on return. 1559 – archdeacon of Hereford; 1560 – prebendary, and other London benefices. 1564 – opposed vestments. 1566 – vicar of St Giles Cripplegate, London – deprived and imprisoned over vestments. 1567 – resigned archdeaconry. 1576–79 – vicar of St Lawrence Jewry, London. 1578 – freeman of Stationers' Company.

FINCH, RICHARD

Wrote a tract on the true and false churches, dedicated to Ridley and commending his 1550 visitation, which was not published until 1590.

FOXE JOHN: *tutor, cleric; 1520–78*

b. Boston, Lincs. 1534–38 – Brasenose College, Oxford; 1538–45 – fellow of Magdalen College, Oxford; vicar of Stewkley; tutor to the Lucy family at Charlecote. m. 1547. Tutor to the children of Henry Howard, Earl of Surrey, in the care of Mary Fitzroy, duchess of Richmond. Met Bale and other leading reformers. Opposed the burning of anabaptists and the death penalty for adultery, but also proposed revived church discipline. 1550 – ordained deacon. 1554 – escaped into exile in Strassburg, Frankfurt and Basel. Early editions of *Acts and monuments*; 1563 – first English edition produced by John Day; revised, expanded version 1570. Canon of Salisbury but objected to vestments.

GARDINER, STEPHEN: *cleric; ?1483–1555*

b. Bury St Edmunds. Educated at Trinity Hall, Cambridge; 1520 – Doctor of Civil Law; 1521 – Doctor of Canon Law. 1524 – lecturer; tutor to Duke of Norfolk's son. 1525 – master of Trinity Hall and archdeacon of Taunton (where he was succeeded by Thomas Cranmer, q.v.). Private secretary to Wolsey. 1527 – diplomatic missions to France and the papacy, to get support for the royal divorce. 1528 – archdeacon of Norfolk, secretary of state. 1530 – visited Cambridge to get support for the royal divorce. 1531 – archdeacon of Leicester; LLD Oxford; bishop of Winchester. 1533 – examined Frith for heresy. 1533 – resigned as secretary, at odds with Cranmer and Cromwell. 1534 – wrote *De vera obedientia*, upholding the royal supremacy. 1535–38 – ambassador at French Court. 1540 – chancellor of Cambridge after fall of Cromwell. Probably not as crucial to the making of the Six Articles as protestant writers have assumed. 1542 – forbade use of new pronunciation of Greek at Cambridge – clashed with Cheke and Smith (q.v.) on this. 1546 – apparent conservative triumph; reversed by 1547, with the exclusion of Gardiner from the regency Council. 1548 – Paul's Cross sermon in which he attacked reform. Imprisoned in Tower; wrote polemical treatises against Cranmer's doctrine of the sacrament. 1549 – deprived of mastership of Trinity Hall; 1551 – deprived of Winchester; 1553 – restored; made Mary's lord chancellor.

GERRARD, PHILLIP: *yeoman of the Chamber to Edward VI*

1545 – dedicated his translation of Erasmus's *Epicureus* to Edward VI. Evangelical sympathies clear in this, but more overtly protestant in his 1547 *Godly invective*.

GIBSON, THOMAS: *physician, printer; d. 1562*

From Morpeth, Northumberland. 1511 – Bachelor of Medicine, Cambridge. ?1535 working as a printer in London, where he was recommended to Cromwell and Latimer as giving good value and for trustworthiness. Produced evangelical and medical works, including a *New Testament Concordance* (1535), a treatise on the plague (1536) and a herbal (1539). 1555 – exile in Strassburg; by 1557 in Geneva, with his wife and daughter. 1559 – given licence from Cambridge to practise as a physician.

GILBY, ANTHONY: *cleric; 1510–85*

b. Lincs. 1532 – BA Christ's College Cambridge; 1535 – MA. Studied classics and Hebrew. m. and beneficed in Leics. 1555 – exiled in Frankfurt, then Geneva. Collaborated on *Geneva Bible* and *Form of Common Order*. Connected with Knox. Patronage of earl of Huntingdon. 1560 – returns to Ashby de la Zouch. Antivestiarian and Calvinist writings. 1571 – involved in the admonition controversy and nearly prosecuted for nonconformity. Revered as 'Father Gilby' by younger generation of puritans.

GILPIN, BERNARD: *cleric; ?1520–83*

b. Kentmere, Westmorland. Relation of Cuthbert Tunstall. 1530s – educated at Oxford. 1549 – debated with Martyr about the Eucharist and began to doubt his conservative views. 1552 – preached at Court; 1553 – given general licence to preach, and was very active in the north of England. Went to Paris 1553–56 (1554–56 – non-resident vicar of Norton, Northumberland); on return Tunstall made him archdeacon of Durham and rector of Easington 1556–60. 1556 – rector of Houghton (the most valuable benefice in Durham). Preached in favour of some protestant doctrine while accepting catholic hierarchy – a course which only the protection of Tunstall made possible; in 1558 he was in danger of arrest. 1559 – refused see of Carlisle and (1560) provostship of Queen's College, Oxford. Renowned for annual preaching tours of Tynedale and Redesdale, some of the most lawless areas of the Borders. 1576 – founded Kepier Grammar School, encouraging a strongly scriptural tradition of learning. Generous in hospitality and charity. Towards the end of his life, a conflict over Bishop Barnes's desire to supplant him at Houghton by a relative was resolved by another hard-hitting sermon.

Appendix

GUEST, EDMUND: *cleric; 1514–77*

b. Northallerton. Educated at Eton. 1544 – MA King's College; 1551 – BTh.; vice-provost. Tracts on privy Masses, Real Presence and free-will (only the first is extant). 1549 – involved in Cambridge disputations on the Eucharist; licensed to preach. Stayed in England during Mary's reign. 1559 – archdeacon of Canterbury. 1560 – bishop of Rochester. 1571 – bishop of Salisbury; DD. Almoner of Queen Elizabeth and chancellor of the Order of the Garter. Reviser of Liturgy.

HADDON, WALTER: *civil lawyer; 1516–72*

b. Bucks, educated at Eton by Richard Cox; 1533 – King's College, Cambridge. By 1549 he was LLD and vice-chancellor of Cambridge University. 1551 – regius professor of civil law; worked on the reform of canon law. Gave Bucer's funeral oration and was an executor of his will. 1552 – master of Trinity Hall, Cambridge, then of Magdalen College, Oxford. Tutor to the young Brandons; wrote Latin obituaries for them when they died of the sweating sickness. Associated with John Aylmer in the education of Lady Jane Grey. Greeted Queen Mary with complimentary verses, but took leave of absence from Magdalen. 1555 – advocate in Court of Arches; 1557 – Gray's Inn and MP. Translated a petition to the pope in favour of Pole, but also wrote Latin verses to Elizabeth on her afflictions. Distinguished government servant in Elizabeth's reign: master of requests, ecclesiastical commissioner and diplomat.

HARTE, HENRY: *layman; d. 1557*

From Pluckley, Kent. Together with a group of Kentish evangelicals in 1538, was interceded for by Cranmer. Layman; teacher of anti-predestinarian evangelical beliefs, separatist and hostile to educated clergy and gambling. Debated with Turner, Cranmer and Ridley in Edward's reign, and Bradford (in the King's Bench prison) in Mary's. Leader of a congregation of increasingly separatist free-willers. Reported dead at the time of sending a warrant for his arrest as a heretic in 1557.

HOGGARD, MILES: *shoemaker/hosier*

Lived in Pudding Lane, London. Active lay catholic controversialist, mostly in verse, during Edward's and Mary's reign. Answered by Crowley, Laurence Humphrey and William Kethe. Associated with Bonner. Dedicated four works (two of them unpublished) to princess/queen Mary.

HOOPER, JOHN: *cleric; 1495–1555*

b. Somerset. 1519 – BA Merton College Oxford. Cistercian monk at Cleeve. Returned to Oxford after the dissolution, where he clashed with Richard Smith. Left to become steward to Sir Thomas Arundel. Went into exile in France and

Strassburg in 1539, returning briefly in 1546. 1547 – m. Flemish noblewoman, Anne de Tserclas, in Basel; to Zurich, where he was closely associated with Bullinger, and studied Hebrew, Greek and natural sciences. 1549 – returned home; chaplain to Somerset. Embarked on a demanding preaching campaign in London, Essex and Kent. Particularly concerned with combatting radical heresy, as well as urging further reformation on the church, but had surprisingly liberal views on divorce. 1550–51 – vestments' controversy with Cranmer and Ridley; of the foreign divines only John à Lasco supported him. Only after imprisonment in the Fleet for three weeks did he submit. Ordained as bishop of Gloucester. Member of commission to revise canon law. Promoted an active programme of reform, clerical education and charity in his diocese. 1552 – became bishop of Worcester in addition. 1553 – stayed in England though sent his wife and two children to exile. 1555 – burned in Gloucester.

HUTCHINSON, ROGER: *cleric; d. 1555*

1543 – fellow of St John's College, Cambridge. 1547 – with Lever in disputation on the Mass. Visited Joan Bocher to persuade her to recant. 1550 – provost of Eton. Married with three children.

JOYE, GEORGE: *cleric, biblical translator; ?1490–1553*

b. Renhold, Bedfordshire. Educated at Christ's College, Cambridge. 1515 – ordained. 1517 – MA, fellow of Peterhouse. 1527 – denounced for heresy. Evaded capture and went to Antwerp and Bergen op Zoom. Worked as a biblical translator in association with Tyndale, with whom he later quarrelled. Though in exile for the rest of Henry VIII's reign and most of Edward's, maintained contact with Cromwell, Latimer and Cranmer. 1535 – his edition of Tyndale's New Testament published. Controversial literature included works against More and Gardiner, on eschatology, persecution and the fate of souls after death, on clerical marriage and adultery. Married with one son. Returned home to Bedfordshire before death.

KELTON, ARTHUR: *poet*

b. Shrewsbury, son of Thomas Kelton. Studied at Oxford. m. Joan Morgan, son called William. Wrote verse chronicles of British and Welsh history, tracing the descent of the English kings from Brutus.

KETHE, WILLIAM: *poet, biblical translator, cleric; d. 1608*

b. Scotland. Lived in Exeter in Edward's reign. Produced protestant broadside ballads. Married. 1554 – exile in Frankfurt and Basel; 1555–61 – in Geneva, where he was a member of Knox's congregation. Produced tract addressed to English nobility; commendatory verses in Goodman's tract on obedience suggested his support for Lady Jane Grey; his metrical psalms included the 'Old Hundredth'. Rector of Upper Okeford, Dorset; 1562 – chaplain to Ambrose Dudley at Le Havre; 1569 – military chaplain in north of England; 1571 – preached at sessions in Blandford forum on sabbath-keeping.

Appendix

LANCASTER, THOMAS: *cleric; d. 1583*

1536 – BTh Oxford. Rector of Offkerque, in Calais, where he was associated with evangelicals, including Adam Damplip; left 1540. Possibly in London and Pluckley, Kent, in early 1540s; may have been imprisoned for importing heretical books. Dean of Kilkenny; 1550 – bishop of Kildare. 1552 – dean of Derry. Deprived for his marriage in Mary's reign, but did not go into exile. 1559 – royal chaplain; treasurer of Salisbury cathedral in succession to Thomas Harding. 1565 – attended on Sir Henry Sidney in his progress through Ireland. 1568 – archbishop of Armagh. d. 1583 at Drogheda.

LATIMER, HUGH: *cleric; ?1480–1555*

b. Thurcaston, Leicestershire. 1510 – fellow of Clare Hall, Cambridge; 1514 – MA; 1524 – BTh. University cross-bearer; 1522 – licensed to preach anywhere. 1524 – converted by Bilney, when preaching against Lutheranism. 1525 – conflict with bishop West and Wolsey, but patronage of Dr William Butts got him to Court; 1529 – sermon on the card at Court. 1531 – rector of West Kington, Wilts. Controversial preaching in London and Bristol. 1534 – royal chaplain; bishop of Worcester. Campaigned against images, preached against fasting and on reform (convocation sermon of 1536). 1539 – resigned his see; imprisoned for a year, then in 'internal exile' mostly in Midlands, but went to London in 1546, where he was arrested and imprisoned in the Tower until the accession of Edward. 1548 – preached at Paul's Cross and at Court. 1549 – member of heresy commission and involved in trial of Joan Bocher in 1550. Refused to be a bishop again and spent increasing time after the fall of Somerset at the duchess of Suffolk's at Grimsthorpe and at Baxterley, in Warwickshire, still preaching actively. 1553 – warned to escape arrest, but accepted imprisonment. 1555 – burned with Ridley at Oxford.

LESSE, NICHOLAS

From London. translator of patristic and reformist works, mostly on predestination but also on divorce. Friend of Bale.

LEVER, THOMAS: *cleric; ?1520–77*

b. Little Lever, Lancs. 1543 – fellow of St John's, Cambridge; 1545 – MA; 1548 – senior fellow and college preacher; with Hutchinson disputed against conservatives on Mass. 1550 – preached at Court; ordained; preached at Paul's Cross. 1551 – master of St John's. 1552 – BTh. 1553 – preached at Court; supported accession of Jane, but allowed to lead party of students to exile. 1554 – exile in Strassburg, Geneva, Wesel and Aarau. 1559 – rector of Coventry. 1563 – master of Shirburne Hospital, Durham. 1564–67 – canon of Durham.

LYNNE, WALTER: *printer*

Flemish; 1533 – printer in Antwerp, 1540 – London. Patronised by Cranmer and other leading protestant clerics. Printed translations of works by continental reformers, including his own translations.

Appendix

MARBECK, JOHN: *musician; d. 1585*

From New Windsor, Berks. Chorister at St George's Chapel, Windsor; 1541 – organist. 1543 – proceeded against for heresy under the Six Articles – condemned but given a royal pardon. 1550 – publication of his *Concordance* and musical settings of the Book of Common Prayer.

MARDELEY, JOHN: *clerk of the Mint*

Author of tracts patronised by Somerset, but in August 1549 had to give recognisance not to print further unlicensed tracts.

MOONE, PETER: *tailor, poet and player; d. 1601*

From Suffolk. Living in Ipswich by 1545–46 (according to the lay subsidy he had land worth £12. m. Anne before 1546 when birth of first of many children recorded. 1548 – took a parish apprentice (Elizabeth Nollys aged 10). Author of antipopish poem; connected with protestant press in Ipswich, and with a group of evangelicals, including John Ramsey (q.v.) and the schoolmaster, priest and physician Richard Argentyne. 1554 – Moone, Ramsey and others were arrested for being part of 'a conspiracy of lewd persons', but were bound over to keep the peace. 1556 – Moone and his wife were examined for heresy by Hopton, bishop of Norwich.; agreed to papal supremacy, but only saved by the sudden departure of the bishop. So distressed by his recantation that he contemplated suicide. Later gave information to Foxe about Marian protestant and catholic factions in Ipswich. 1561 – Elizabeth I visited Ipswich and was entertained by a group of town players led by Moone – possibly performing Bale's *King John*. Continues to perform, in association with Ramsey, in the 1560s. 1562 and 1580–7 – regular duties as town drummer for the militia. 1567 – son William was apprenticed to him. 1552–60 – financial difficulties resulted in his temporary discharge from payment of burgess fine; various disputes with neighbours over living space throughout 1560s. 1568 – assessed at £1 in land, but still owned house in St Lawrence parish. Made clothing for the charitable Tooley Foundation. 1581 – given loan to rebuild his house from the corporation. 1585 – read service at church of St Peter, Ipswich; and helped to discover authors of puritan seditious libels. 1591 – further financial troubles.

NICHOLS, PHILLIP

From Ilfracombe. Answered a sermon by canon Richard Crispyn of Exeter attacking Lutheranism, dedicated to Sir Peter Carew; produced tracts welcoming the reform of the church under Somerset and an unpublished answer to the western rebels. Possibly the author of *A True mirror* (1556) which contained retrospective descriptions of sermons by Latimer, disputations at Oxford, etc. 1557 – exile in Aarau.

PICKERING, PETER

Servant to Sir Anthony Neville, of the Council of the North. 1551 – wrote a handbook for ministers, addressed to friends in Nottinghamshire.

Appendix

PONET, JOHN: *cleric and scholar; ?1516–56*

b. Kent. 1527 – king's scholar with Smith and Cheke at Cambridge. 1532 – BA and fellow of Queen's College, Cambridge; 1535 – MA; reader in Greek; also studied mathematics and astronomy. 1536 – ordained at Lincoln. 1543 – rector of St Michael's, Crooked Lane, London; 1545 – rector of Lavant, Sussex; 1546 – canon of Canterbury; 1547 – DTh and chaplain to Cranmer. 1550 – preached at Paul's Cross and at Court. Translated Ochino's *Tragedy* and defended marriage of priests. 1550 – bishop of Rochester; 1551 – bishop of Winchester. 1551 – member of ecclesiastical law revision commission, and of heresy commission. Divorced for a bigamous marriage and remarried to Mary Hayman. 1552 – produced his *A short Catechism*. 1553 – deprived. Took an active part in Wyatt's rebellion; exiled to Strassburg in 1554, where his two sons were born. 1556 – *Short treatise of politic power*, a major text of the theory of resistance.

PROCTOR, JOHN: *schoolmaster; ?1521–84*

b. Somerset. 1537 – scholar, Corpus Christi, Oxford. 1540 – BA, fellow of All Souls; 1544 – MA. 1553–9 – master of Tonbridge School, Kent. 1549 – conservative views shown in his attack on John Assheton ('Arian') and in his *History of Wyatt's rebellion* (1554). However, by 1578 he had conformed sufficiently to be appointed rector of St Andrew's, Holborn, London.

PUNT, WILLIAM

From Colchester; a relative of Ridley. 1548 – wrote a dialogue against the Mass. Carried letters for the imprisoned Bradford, Ridley and Saunders in Mary's reign; Bradford left him two shirts and the disposition of his books. Involved in illicit book trade.

RAMSEY, JOHN: *joiner, poet and player*

From Ipswich. Witnessed the burning of Peke there in 1539. By mid-1540s was bailiff to Sir Edmund Withipoll of Christchurch Manor, Ipswich. Author of fiercely anticlerical tracts printed in Ipswich; associated with Moone (q.v.) and Argentyne. 1554 – arrested with Moone, but released on bail. 1556 – listed in *Complaint against such as favoured the gospel in Ipswich* by P. Williams. Later, an informant of Foxe about protestantism in the town. 1560s – regular payments from the corporation to 'Father Ramsey' for plays, probably in association with Moone.

RUDDOKE, THOMAS: *cleric; d. 1551*

Cambridge graduate; vicar of Swaffham Bulbeck, Cambs.

SALESBURY, WILLIAM: *lawyer and scholar; d. 1600*

b. Llansannan, Denbigh. m. Catrin Llwyd. Educated at Oxford and Thavies Inn. 1550 – published tracts against altars and supporting clerical marriage. 1551 –

translated gospels and epistles into Welsh. 1553 – in hiding in Wales. 1567– translated and oversaw production of Welsh Bible. Produced a Welsh–English dictionary and book of Welsh proverbs, as well as an unpublished herbal and a work on rhetoric.

SAMUEL, WILLIAM: *poet*

In the service of Somerset. 1550 – author of verse tracts. 1557 – exiled in Geneva. Wrote metrical abridgements of Old Testament books. 1558 – described himself as 'a minister in Christ's church'.

SHEPHERD, LUKE: *physician*

b. Colchester. Living in Coleman St London. Author of antipapist satires, mostly in verse and anonymously. Possibly imprisoned for a short time in late 1540s and under Mary, for production of protestant literature.

SMITH, RICHARD: *cleric; 1500–63*

b. Worcs. Studied at Merton College, Oxford; 1527 – BA; 1530 – MA. 1532 – registrar of Oxford University. 1536 – regius professor of Divinity; DD. 1537 – helped to compile the *Institution of a Christian man*. Master of Whittington College, London; rector of Cuxham; principal of St Alban's Hall and divinity reader at Magdalen College, Oxford. 1546 – produced defences of the Mass and of unwritten verities. 1547 – recanted at Paul's Cross and in Oxford. 1549 – deprived of regius professorship; succeeded by Martyr. Disputations at Oxford with Martyr. Imprisoned; escaped via Scotland to Paris and Louvain. Restored under Mary; also royal chaplain, canon of Christchurch. Disputed with Ridley and Latimer and preached at their execution. 1559 – again deprived; induced to recant by Parker. Exile in Douai; dean of St Peter's church and first chancellor of its new university. Professor of theology. Produced Latin treatises against the reformers.

TILNEY, EMERY

Son of Sir Philip Tilney of Shelley, Suffolk. Educated at Corpus Christi, Cambridge; pupil of George Wishart. Possibly author of *Song of the Lord's Supper* (1550). Gave details about martyrs to Foxe.

TRACY, RICHARD: *gentleman; ?1501–69*

b. Toddington, Gloucs. 1515 – BA Oxford; Inner Temple. 1529 – MP for Wootton Bassett, Wilts. 1532 – successfully took the case of the posthumous burning of his father, William Tracy, by the chancellor of Gloucester to Cromwell for redress. William Tracy's will became a template for evangelical wills and was printed with works by Tyndale and Frith. Richard Tracy was a friend of Latimer and patron of Bartholomew Traheron. 1539 – granted the demesnes of Winchcombe abbey. 1548 – chantry commissioner for Gloucs. 1533–48 – published evangelical

Appendix

tracts, including a supplication to Henry VIII about church reform. 1546 – his books were condemned, but though he was in contact with notable reformers, including Crome, he avoided imprisonment, ironically, until 1551–52, when he was in the Tower for 'a seditious and lewd letter'. Removed from the Bench in Mary's reign; 1555 – before the Council for recalcitrance towards his bishop and for refusing to pay a forced loan in 1557. He did not go into exile. Returned to the Bench in Elizabeth's reign; high sheriff of Gloucs. 1565 – protested to Cecil about the queen's retention of the cross and lights in her chapel.

TURNER, WILLIAM: *naturalist, physician, cleric; ?1512–68*

b. Morpeth, Northumberland. 1530 – BA Pembroke Hall, Cambridge. Friend of Ridley. Translated works by von Watt (Vadian) in 1534 and by Urbanus Rhegius in 1537. Ordained deacon; m. Jane Auder. 1540 – oversaw publication of Purvey's Prologue to the Wycliffite Bible. 1542 – imprisoned for unlicensed preaching. On release he went into exile in Italy (where he graduated MD), Switzerland and the Low Countries. Attacked Gardiner and the Six Articles in *The hunting of the Romish fox*; 1546 – his books were burned. 1548 – returned home to become physician and chaplain to Somerset. 1550 – ordained. 1551 – dean of Wells. Wrote against anabaptism. 1553 – exiled again; produced tracts against Mary's policies, but was critical of the incomplete nature of the Edwardian reforms and proposed major reorganisation of the ministry. Reinstated in 1559, but deprived for nonconformity in 1564. Author of the first English herbal and other works of natural history.

VERON, JEAN: *cleric; d. 1563*

b. Sens. 1534 – studied in Orleans. 1536 – to Cambridge. Lived in Worcester. Translated works by Zwingli and Bullinger against the anabaptists. 1551 – ordained. 1552 – rector of St Alphege, London Wall. 1553 – imprisoned with Bradford, and remained in prison until 1559. 1559 – preached at Paul's Cross and at Court. Continued to write against anabaptists and free-willers – explicitly denounced Champneys (q.v.). Rector of St Martin's, Ludgate, and prebendary of St Paul's.

WILSON, THOMAS: *civil lawyer; ?1528–81*

b. Strubby, Lincs. 1546 – BA King's College Cambridge; 1549 – MA. Tutor to young Brandons and Northumberland's children. 1555–60 – exile in Italy, in Padua, Rome (where he was briefly imprisoned) and Ferrara (where he graduated LLD). Became a diplomat on return to England, also wrote and translated. 1578 – secretary of state. 1580 – lay dean of Durham.

Bibliography

A note on the referencing of early modern printed books: Before numerical pagination became standard, books were paginated according to the section or 'signature' (abbreviated to sig.) Each book was made of a number of sections of folded sheets. Most of the works in question here were octavo, so there were eight pages in the section. Each signature was identified alphabetically in either upper or lowercase (I have followed originals), and numbered (1–8, and sometimes 1–4, leaving the rest to be inferred) on the right side (recto) of the page only. The numbering restarts with every signature. The back of the sheet (verso, abbreviated as vo.) would be left unmarked. If the number of signatures exceeded the number of letters in the alphabet, then double letters would be used. Usually roman numerals were used, but in all but a few cases I have standardised this to arabic. I have not abbreviated recto but left it assumed and only used verso: thus sig. A6 means front of sixth page in first signature; sig. A6vo means sig. A, back of sixth page, while A6-vo means front and back of sixth sheet. Roman numerals used on their own have been left, referring to consecutive (if not front and back of page) pagination. A *used with sig. refers to prefaratory or end matter, as in originals.

PRIMARY SOURCES

Manuscript sources

Public Record Office, SP 10 – State Papers (Domestic) for the reign of Edward VI

Early printed works by RSTC no

360	Allen, Edmund, *A Catechism, that is to say, a Christian instruction now newly corrected* (1551).
683	Anon. (?Luke Shepherd), *Antipus* (?1548).
920	Augustine (tr. N. Lesse), *A work of the predestination of the saints* (1550).
1035.5	'B., J.', *A brief and plain declaration of certain sentences in this little book* (1547).
1271	Bale, John, *The acts of the English votaries* (1548).
1274	Anon. (?John Bale), *An answer to a papistical exhortation* (Antwerp, 1547).
1275	Bale, John, *The apology of John Bale against a rank papist* (1550).
1294	Bale, John, *An expostulation or complaint against the blasphemies of a frantic papist of Hampshire* (1551).
1303	Bale, John, *A mystery of iniquity contained within the heretical genealogy of P. Pantobalus* (Antwerp, ?1545).
1709	Becke, Edmund, *A brief confutation* (1550).
1741	Becon, Thomas, *The physic of the soul* (1549).

Bibliography

3258.5	Anon. (?Luke Shepherd), *John Bon and master parson* (1548).
3760	Brinkelow, Henry, *The complaint of Roderick Mors*, 2nd edn (1548).
4048	Bullinger, Heinrich, *The Christian state of matrimony* (1543).
4059	Bullinger, Heinrich (tr. J. Veron), *An wholesome antidotus against the anabaptists* (1548).
4068	Bullinger, Heinrich (tr. J. Veron), *A most necessary and fruitful dialogue between the seditious libertine and the true Christian* (Worcester, 1551).
4069	Bullinger, Heinrich (tr. J. Veron), *A most sure and strong defence of the baptism of children* (Worcester 1551).
4463	Calvin, Jean, *A short instruction against the anabaptists* (1549).
4812	Anon. (?J. Ponet), *A short Catechism or plain instruction* (1553).
4956	Champneys, John, *The harvest is at hand* (1548).
5109	Cheke, John, *The hurt of sedition* (1549).
5195	Anon., *A caveat for the Christians against the archpapist* (1548).
5539	Cole, Thomas, *A godly sermon made at Maidstone* (1553).
5605a	Anon. (?Luke Shepherd), *The comparison between the antipus and the antigraph* (?1548).
5894	Coverdale, Miles, *The order that the church in Denmark doth use* (?1550).
6082	Crowley, Robert, *The confutation of the mis-shapen answer* (1548).
6083	Crowley, Robert, *The confutation of the xiii articles to which Nicholas Shaxton subscribed* (1548).
6085	Crowley, Robert, *An information and petition against the oppressors of the poor commons* (1548).
6088	Crowley, Robert, *One-and-thirty epigrams* (1550).
6089	Crowley, Robert, *The opening of the words of the prophet Joel* (1546; pr. 1567 – though a possible edition in 1547 – see Addenda RSTC vol. 1).
6089.5	Crowley, Robert, *Philargyrie of Great Britain* (1551).
6090	Crowley, Robert, *Pleasure and pain, heaven and hell* (1551).
6094	Crowley, Robert, *The voice of the last trumpet* (1549).
6096	Crowley, Robert, *The way to wealth* (1550).
6802.5	Anon., *A dialogue between a gentleman and a priest* (1547).
7071	Anon. (?Luke Shepherd), *Doctor double ale* (1548).
7506	Edward VI, *A message sent by the king to certain of his subjects assembled in Devonshire* (1549).
9181.5	*Copy of a letter sent to licenced preachers* (1548).
10087.5	*Injunctions given by the most excellent prince Edward VI* (1547).
10430	Anon., *An epistle exhortatory* (?1547).
10532	'Esquillus, Publius' (M. Flacius, tr. W. Baldwin), *Wonderful news of the death of Paul III* (1552).
10877.5	Finch, Richard, *The epiphany of the church* (1550, pr. 1590).
11233	Foxe, John, *De censura, sive excommunicatione ecclesiastica* (1551).
11235	Foxe, John, *De non plectendis adulteris* (1548).

Bibliography

11235.5	Foxe, John, *De lapsis in ecclesiam recipiendis consultatio* (1549).
11590	Gardiner, Stephen, *A detection of the devil's sophistry* (1546).
11593.5	Gardiner, Stephen, *'Their deeds in effect my life would have . . .'* (?1548).
11797	Gerrard, Phillip, *A godly invective in the defence of the gospel* (1547).
11802	Guest, Edmund, *A treatise against the privy Mass* (1548).
11842a	Gibson, Thomas, *A brief chronicle of the bishop of Rome's blessing* (?1548).
11884	Gilby, Anthony, *An answer to the devilish detection of Stephen Gardiner* (1547).
11886	Gilby, Anthony, *A commentary upon the prophet Micah* (1551).
11897	Gilpin, Bernard, *Sermon preached before the Court at Greenwich* (1552; printed 1581).
12020	Goodman, Christopher, *How superior powers ought to be obeyed of their subjects.*
12564	H[arte], H[enry], *A consultory for all Christians* (Worcester, 1549).
12594a	Haddon, Walter, *De vita et obitu H. et C. Brandoni epistola* (1551).
12887	Harte, Henry, *A godly new short treatise* (1548).
13051.7	Anon. (?Luke Shepherd), *A poor help* (?1548).
13560	Hoggard, Miles, *A new treatise which showeth the excellency of man's nature* (1550).
13639–62	*Homilies appointed to be read by the king's majesty* (1547; edition cited here is 1549).
14822	Joye, George, *A contrary to a certain man's consultation* (1549).
14828.5	Joye, George, *The refutation of the bishop of Winchester's false articles* (1546).
1483	Anon., *The true judgement of a faithful Christian* (1548).
14919	Kelton, Arthur, *A commendation of Welshmen* (1546).
14941	Kethe, William, *Of misrule's contending* (1553).
14942	Kethe, William, *A ballad, declaring the fall of the Whore of Babylon, entitled 'Tie thy mare, Tom Boy'* (?1548).
14999.5	Anon., *. . . alterations of kingdoms for despising of God* (1550).
15109.3	L., R. ('R.L.'), *Copy of a letter containing news of the western rebels* (1549).
15188	Lancaster, Thomas, *The right and true understanding of the Supper of the Lord* (1550).
15462	Anon., *The recantation of Jack Lent* (1548).
15543	Lever, Thomas, *A fruitful sermon preached at St Paul's in the Shrouds, 2nd February* (1550).
15546	Lever, Thomas, *A sermon preached at Paul's Cross, the 14th December* (1550).
15547	Lever, Thomas, *A sermon preached the third Sunday in Lent before the king's majesty* (1550).
17115	Lynne, Walter, *The beginning and ending of all popery* (1548).
17137	Anon., *A brief recantation of mistress Missa* (?1548).
17317	Mardeley, John, *A declaration of the power of God's Word* (1548).
17318	Mardeley, John, *A short recital of certain holy doctors* (?1548).
17319	Mardeley, John, *A necessary instrument for all covetous rich men* (1548).
17630	Anon. (?Luke Shepherd), *The upcheering of the popish Mass* (?1548).
18056	Moone, Peter, *A short treatise of things abused* (Ipswich, 1548).

Bibliography

18575	Nichols, Phillip, *The copy of a letter sent unto one master Crispin, canon of Exeter* (1548).
18576	Nichols, Phillip, *Here beginneth a godly new story of xii men that Moses . . . sent to spy out the land of Canaan* (1548).
18770	Ochino, Bernadino (tr. J. Ponet), *A tragedy or dialogue of the unjust primacy of the bishop of Rome* (1549).
19463	Anon. (?Luke Shepherd), *Pathos, or an inward passion of the pope for the loss of his daughter the Mass* (1548).
19897.3	Pickering, Peter, *A mirror or glass for all spiritual ministers* (1551).
19903	'Piers Plowman', *A godly dialogue concerning the Supper of the Lord* (1550).
19905	'Piers Plowman', *Exhortation unto the lords, Knights and burgesses of the parliament house* (?1550).
20176	Ponet, John, *A defence of the marriage of priests* (1549).
20177	Ponet, John, *A notable sermon, concerning the right use of the Lord's Supper* (1550).
20178	Ponet, John, *A short treatise of politic power* (Strassburg, 1556).
20182	Anon., *The praise and commendation of such as sought commonwealths* (1549).
20406	Proctor, John, *The fall of the late Arian* (1549).
20499	Punt, William, *The inditement against mother Mass* (1548).
20661	Ramsey, John, *A corrosive to be laid hard to the hearts of all faithful professors of Christ's Gospel* (1548).
20662	Ramsey, John, *A plaster for a galled horse* (1548).
20827	*A report of Dr Redman's answers* (1551).
21305	Anon., *The fall of the Romish church* (1548).
21435.5	Ruddoke, Thomas, *A remembrance for the maintenance of the living of ministers* (1551).
21612	Salesbury, William, *Case extract from the law of Hywel Da* (1550).
21613	Salesbury, William, *The battery of the pope's buttress commonly called the high altar* (1550).
21690.2	Samuel, William, *The abridgement of God's statutes* (1551).
21690.6	Samuel, William, *The practice, practised by the pope and his prelates* (1550).
21690.8	Samuel, William, *A warning for the city of London* (1550).
22818	Smith, Richard, *Divers truths* (1547).
22819	Smith, Richard, *Confutation of Cranmer* (1550).
22822	Smith, Richard, *Recantation* (1547).
22823	Smith, Richard, *Of unwritten verities* (1548).
22824	Smith, Richard, *Declaration at Oxford* (1547).
24078	T[ilney], E[mery], *Here beginneth a song of the Lord's Supper* (1550).
24162	Tracy, Richard, *A short declaration made . . . what is a sacrament* (1548).
24165.5	Tracy, Richard, *A supplication to Henry VIII* (1545).
24355	Turner, William, *The rescuing of the Romish fox* (Bonn, 1545).
24361.5	Turner, William, *A new dialogue, entitled the examination of the Mass* (1548).
24368	Turner, William, *A preservative against the poison of Pelagius* (1551).

Bibliography

24566	V., R. ('R.V.'), *The old faith of Great Britain and the new learning of England* (1549).
24676	Veron, Jean, *Certain little treatises for the learning of the simple* (1548).
24679	Veron, Jean, *The five blasphemies that are in the Mass* (1548).
24682	Veron, Jean, *The godly sayings of the fathers on the sacrament* (1550).
25816	Wilson, Thomas, *De vita et obitu duorum fratrum Suffolkensium* (1551).

Reprints

Acts of the Privy Council of England, ed. J.R. Dasent (1890–1907), 32 vols (vol. 3, for 1550–52, cited in the present work).

Bale, John, *Select works*, PS, ed. H. Christmas (Cambridge, 1849).

Becon, Thomas, *Works*, PS 3 vols, ed. J. Ayre (Cambridge, 1843, 1844).

Bradford, John, *Writings*, PS 2 vols, ed. A. Townsend (Cambridge, 1848, 1853).

Cranmer, Thomas, *Works*, PS 2 vols, ed. J.E. Cox (Cambridge, 1844, 1846).

Foxe, John, *Acts and monuments*, ed. G. Townsend and R.S. Cattley (1837–39), 8 vols.

Holt, R. et al., *Birmingham wills and inventories, 1551–1600* (University of Birmingham, Department of Extramural Studies, 1985).

Hooper, John, *Writings*, PS 2 vols, ed. S. Carr and C. Nevinson (Cambridge, 1843, 1852).

Hutchinson, Roger, *Works*, PS, ed. J. Bruce (Cambridge, 1842).

Latimer, Hugh, *Sermons and remains*, PS 2 vols, ed. G.E. Corrie (Cambridge, 1844, 1848).

The two liturgies of 1549 and 1552, with other documents set forth by authority in the reign of Edward VI, PS, ed. J. Ketley (Cambridge, 1844).

Original letters relative to the English reformation, PS 2 vols, ed. H. Robinson (Cambridge, 1846, 1847).

Ridley, Nicholas, *Works*, PS, ed. H. Christmas (Cambridge, 1841).

Scudamore, Richard, *Letters to Sir Philip Hoby*, ed. S. Brigden, Camden Miscellany vol. XXX (1990).

SECONDARY SOURCES

Aston, M., *Lollards and Reformers: Images and Literacy in Late Medieval Religion* (1984).

Aston, M., *England's Iconoclasts*, vol. 1: *Laws Against Images* (Oxford, 1988).

Aston, M., *The King's Bedpost: Reformation and Iconography in a Tudor Group Portrait* (Cambridge, 1993).

Avis, P., 'Moses and the magistrate', *JEH* (1975) 26.

Bailey, D.S., *Thomas Becon* (1952).

Baskerville, E., 'John Ponet in exile – a Ponet letter to Bale', *JEH* (1986) 37(3): 442–7.

Bauckham, R., *Tudor Apocalypse* (Abingdon, 1978).

Beer, B.L., *Northumberland; The Political Career of John Dudley, Earl of Warwick and Duke of Northumberland* (Kent, OH, 1973).

Beer, B.L., *Rebellion and Riot: Popular Disorder During the Reign of Edward VI* (Kent, OH, 1982).

Beer, B.L. and Nash, R.J., 'Hugh Latimer and the lusty knave of Kent: the commonwealth movement of 1549', *BIHR* (1979) 52(126): 175–8.

Bibliography

Beier, A. and Finlay, R., *London 1500–1700 – the Making of the Metropolis* (1986).
Bennett, H.S., *English Books and Readers, 1475–1557* (Cambridge, 1969).
Bernard, G. (ed.) *The Tudor Nobility* (Manchester, 1992).
Betteridge, T., *Tudor Histories of the English Reformations 1530–83* (Aldershot, 1999).
Bindoff, S.T., *Tudor England* (1950).
Bond, R.B., '"Dark deeds darkly answered": Thomas Becon's *Homily against whoredom and adultery*, its contexts and its affiliations with three Shakespearean plays', *SCJ* (1985) 14(2): 191–205.
Booty, J., *John Jewel as Apologist of the Church of England* (1963).
Booty, J. (ed.) *The Godly Kingdom of Tudor England: Great Books of the English Reformation* (Wilton, CT, 1981).
Bossy, J., 'The Mass as a social institution', *P&P* (1983) 100: 29–61.
Bossy, J., *Christianity in the West, 1400–1700* (Oxford, 1985).
Bradshaw, B. and Duffy, E. (eds) *Humanism, Reform and the Reformation: The Career of Bishop John Fisher* (Cambridge, 1989).
Brigden, S., 'Religion and social obligation', *P&P* (1984) 103: 67–112.
Brigden, S., *London and the Reformation* (Oxford and New York, 1989).
Brooks, P.N., *Thomas Cranmer's Doctrine of the Eucharist* (1965).
Burrage, C., *The Early English Dissenters in the Light of Recent Research (1550–1641)* (Cambridge, 1912), 2 vols.
Bush, M., *The Government Policy of Protector Somerset* (1975).
Carlson, E., *Marriage and the English Reformation* (Oxford and Cambridge, MA, 1994).
Carlson, E. (ed.) *Religion and the English People 1500–1640: New Voices, New Perspectives* (Kirksville, MO, 1998).
Carter, P., 'Clerical polemic in defence of ministers' maintenance during the English reformation', *JEH* (1998) 49(2): 236–56.
Chester, A., *Hugh Latimer. Apostle to the English* (Philadelphia, PA, 1954).
Chester, A., 'The new learning: a semantic note', *Studies in the Renaissance* (1955) 2: 139–47.
Christianson, P., *Reformers and Babylon* (Toronto, 1978).
Clark, P., Smith, A. and Tyacke, N. (eds) *The English Commonwealth: Essays Presented to Joel Hurstfield* (Leicester, 1979).
Clark, S., 'Inversion, misrule and the meaning of witchcraft', *P&P* (1980) 87: 98–127.
Clasen, C.P., *Anabaptism: A Social History, 1525–1618* (Ithaca, NY, 1972).
Clebsch, W.A., *England's Earliest Protestants, 1520–35* (New Haven, CT, 1964).
Clifton, R., 'The popular fear of catholics during the English revolution,' *P&P* (1971) 52: 23–55.
Cohn, N., *The pursuit of the millenium* (rev.ed 1978).
Coleman, C. and Starkey, D. (eds) *Revolution Reassessed: Revisions in the History of Tudor Government and Administration* (Oxford, 1986).
Collinson, P., *The Elizabethan Puritan Movement* (1967).
Collinson, P., *Archbishop Grindal, 1519–83: The Struggle for a Reformed Church* (1979).

Collinson, P., *The Birthpangs of Protestant England: Religious and Cultural Change in the Sixteenth and Seventeenth Centuries* (1988).

Collinson, P. and Craig, J. (eds) *The Reformation in English Towns* (1998).

Coolidge, J.S., *The Pauline Renaissance: Puritanism and the Bible* (Oxford, 1970).

Cressy, D., *Literacy and the Social Order: Reading and Writing in Tudor and Stuart England* (Cambridge, 1980).

Cross, C., '"Great reasoners in scripture": the activities of women Lollards, 1380–1530', in D. Baker (ed.) *Medieval women* (Oxford, 1978).

Davies C., 'A protestant gentleman and the English reformation: the career and attitudes of Richard Tracy', in *The Sudeleys – Lords of Toddington: Proceedings of the Manorial Society of Great Britain* (1987).

Davies, C.S.L., 'Slavery and protector Somerset: the Vagrancy Act of 1547', *EcHR* (second series) (1966) 19: 533–49.

Davies, W.H., *Worship and Theology in England from Cranmer to Hooker, 1534–1603* (Princeton NJ, 1970).

Davies, C. and Facey, J., 'A reformation dilemma: John Foxe and the problem of discipline', *JEH* (1988) 39(1): 37–65.

Davis, J.C., *Fear, Myth and History: The Ranters and the Historians* (Cambridge, 1986).

Davis, J.F., 'Joan of Kent, Lollardy and the English reformation', *JEH* (1982) 33(2): 225–33.

Davis, J.F., *Heresy and the Reformation in the South-East of England* (1983).

Dawson, J., 'The foundation of Christ Church, Oxford, and Trinity College, Cambridge, in 1546', *BIHR* (1984) 57(136): 208–15.

Dickens, A.G., 'Peter Moone, the Ipswich gospeller and poet', *Notes and Queries* (1954) December: 513–14.

Dickens, A.G., *The English reformation* (revised 1976; 2nd edn 1989).

Dinsmore Briggs, W., 'On a document concerning Christopher Marlowe', *Studies in Philology* (1923) 20(2): 153–9.

Duffy, E., *The Stripping of the Altars: Traditional Religion in England 1400–1580* (New Haven, CT, 1992).

Dowling, M., *Humanism in the Age of Henry VIII* (1986).

Dugmore, C., *The Mass and the English Reformers* (1958).

Elton, G.R., *England Under the Tudors* (1955).

Elton, G.R., *Reform and Renewal: Thomas Cromwell and the Commonweal* (Cambridge, 1973).

Elton, G.R., *Reform and Reformation: England 1509–58* (1977).

Eisenstein, E., *The Printing Press as an Agent of Change: Communications and Transformations in Early Modern Europe* (Cambridge, 1979), 2 vols.

Fairfield, L., *John Bale. Mythmaker for the English Reformation* (West Lafayette, IN, 1976).

Fairfield, L., 'John Bale and the development of protestant hagiography in England', *JEH* (1973) 24(2): 145–60.

Febvre, L. and Martin, H.-J., *The Coming of the Book: The Impact of Printing, 1450–1800*, tr. D. Gerard, ed. G. Nowell-Smith and D. Wootton (1976; repr. 1984).

Ferrell, L.A. and McCullough, P. (eds) *The English Sermon Revised: Religion, Literature and History, 1600–1750* (Manchester, 2000).

Bibliography

Ferguson, A., *Clio Unbound: Perceptions of the Social and Cultural Past in Renaissance England* (Durham, NC, 1979).

Fideler, P. and Mayer, T. (eds) *Political Thought and the Tudor Commonwealth* (1992).

Fines, J., *A Biographical Register of Early English Protestants and Others Opposed to the Roman Catholic Church* (Part 1, A–C, Appleford, 1980; Part 2, D–Z, Bognor Regis 1984: both temporary formats).

Firth, K., *The Apocalyptic Tradition in Reformation Britain* (Oxford, 1979).

Fletcher, A., *Tudor Rebellions*, 2nd edn (1973).

Ginzburg, C., *The Cheese and the Worms: The Cosmos of a Sixteenth Century Miller*, tr. J. and A. Tedeschi (1980).

Gordon, B. (ed.) *Protestant History and Identity in Sixteenth Century Europe* (Aldershot, 1996), 2 vols.

Greenblatt, S., *Renaissance Self-Fashioning from More to Shakespeare* (Chicago, IL, 1980).

Guth, D. and McKenna, J.W. (eds) *Tudor Rule and Revolution: Essays Presented to G.R. Elton by His American Friends* (Cambridge, 1982).

Guy, J., *Tudor England* (Oxford, 1988).

Guy, J. and Fox, A., *Reassessing the Henrician Age: Humanism, Politics and Reform, 1500–30* (Oxford, 1986).

Hadwin, J., 'Deflating philanthropy', *EcHR* (second series) (1978) 31: 105–38.

Hageman, E., 'John Foxe's Henry VIII as "Justicia"', *SCJ* (1979) 10(1): 35–44.

Haigh, C., 'The recent historiography of the English reformation', *HJ* (1982) 25(4): 995–1007.

Haigh, C., 'Anticlericalism in the English reformation', *History* (1983) 68: 391–407.

Haigh, C. (ed.) *The English Reformation Revised* (Cambridge, 1987).

Haigh, C., *English Reformations: Religion, Politics and Society Under the Tudors* (Oxford, 1993).

Hale, D.G., *The Body Politic* (The Hague, 1971).

Hannay, M.P., *Silent But For the Word: Tudor Women as Patrons, Translators and Writers of Religious Works* (Kent, OH, 1985).

Heal, F., *Of Prelates and Princes: A Study in the Economic and Social Position of the Tudor Episcopate* (Cambridge, 1980).

Heal, F. and O'Day, R. (eds) *Church and Society in England: Henry VIII to James I* (1977).

Hoak, D., *The King's Council in the Reign of Edward VI* (Cambridge, 1976).

Hopf, C., *Martin Bucer and the English Reformation* (Oxford, 1946).

Höpfl, H., *The Christian Polity of John Calvin* (Cambridge, 1982).

Horst, I.B., *The Radical Brethren: Anabaptism and the English Reformation to 1558* (Niewkoop, 1972).

Hoskins, W.G., *The Age of Plunder* (1976).

Houlbrooke, R., *Church Courts and the People During the English Reformation, 1520–1570* (Oxford, 1979).

Houlbrooke, R., 'Henry VIII's wills – a comment', *HJ* (1994) 37: 901–14.

Hudson, A., *The Premature Reformation: Wycliffite Texts and Lollard History* (Oxford, 1988).

Hudson, W.S., *The Cambridge Connection and the Elizabethan Settlement of 1559* (Durham, NC, 1980).

Hughes, C., 'Two sixteenth century northern protestants: John Bradford and William Turner', *Bulletin of the John Rylands Library* (1983–84) 66(1): 104–38.

Hurstfield, J., 'Corruption and reform under Edward VI and Mary: the example of wardship', *EHR* (1953) 68(266): 22–36.

Hutton, R., *The Rise and Fall of Merry England: The Ritual Year, 1400–1700* (Oxford, 1994; 1996).

Ives, E., Knecht, R. and Scarisbrick, J. (eds) *Wealth and Power in Tudor England: Essays Presented to S.T. Bindoff* (1978).

Ives, E., *Faction in Tudor England*, Historical Association Pamphlet (1979).

Ives, E., 'Henry VIII's will: a forensic conundrum', *HJ* (1992) 35(4): 779–804.

Ives, E., 'The protectorate provisions of 1546–7', *HJ* (1994) 37(4): 901–14.

Janelle, P., *Obedience in Church and State* (Cambridge, 1930).

Jones, W.R.D., *The Tudor Commonwealth 1529–1559* (1970).

Jones, W.R.D., *The Mid-Tudor Crisis 1539–1563* (1973).

Jones, W.R.D., *William Turner: Tudor Naturalist, Physician and Divine* (1988).

Jordan, W.K., *Philanthropy in England 1480–1660* (1959).

Jordan, W.K., *Edward VI*, vol. 1: *The Young King* (1968).

Jordan, W.K., *Edward VI*, vol. 2: *The Threshold of Power* (1970).

Kelley, D., *The Foundations of Modern Historical Scholarship* (New York, 1970).

Kendall, R.T., *Calvin and English Calvinism to 1649* (Oxford, 1979).

King, J.N., 'Freedom of the press, protestant propaganda and protector Somerset', *HLQ* (1976) 40(1): 1–10.

King, J.N., *English Reformation Literature: The Tudor Origins of the Protestant Tradition* (Princeton, NJ, 1982).

King, J.N., *Tudor Royal Iconography: Literature and Art in an Age of Religious Crisis* (Princeton, NJ, 1989).

Knappen, M.M., *Tudor Puritanism: A Chapter in the History of Idealism* (Chicago 1970 repr.).

Knowles, D., *The Religious Orders in England* (Cambridge, 1961), vol. 3.

Knox, D.B., *The Doctrine of Faith in the Reign of Henry VIII* (1961).

Krahn, C., *Dutch Anabaptism: Origin, Spread, Life and Thought, 1450–1600* (The Hague, 1968).

Kreider, A., *The English Chantries: The Road to Dissolution* (Cambridge, MA, 1979).

Kyle, R., 'John Knox and the purification of religion: the intellectual aspects of his crusade against idolatry', *Archiv* (1986) 77: 265–80.

Lake, P., 'The significance of the Elizabethan identification of the pope as Antichrist', *JEH* (1980) 31(2): 161–78.

Lake, P., *Anglican and Puritan? Presbyterianism and English Conformist Thought from Whitgift to Hooker* (1988).

Lake, P. and Dowling, M. (eds) *Protestantism and the National Church in Sixteenth Century England* (1987).

Loach, J., 'The Marian establishment and the printing press,' *EHR* (1986).

Loach, J., *Edward VI*, ed. P. Williams and G. Bernard (New Haven, CT, 1999).

Bibliography

Loach, J. and Tittler, R., *The mid-Tudor polity, c.1540–60* (1980).

Loades, D.M., 'Anabaptism and English sectarianism in the mid-sixteenth century', *SCH* (1979), Subsidia 2: *Reform and the Reformation*, 59–70.

Loades, D.M., *John Dudley Duke of Northumberland, 1504–1553* (Oxford, 1996).

MacCulloch, D., 'Kett's rebellion in context', *P&P* (1979) 84: 36–59 and debate (1981) 93: 160–73.

MacCulloch, D., *Thomas Cranmer: a Life* (New Haven, CT, 1996).

MacCulloch, D., *Tudor Church Militant: Edward VI and the Protestant Reformation* (1999).

MacDonald, M., *Mystical Bedlam: Madness, Anxiety and Healing in Seventeenth Century England* (Cambridge, 1981).

Macek, E., 'Richard Smith: Tudor cleric in defence of traditional belief and practice,' *CHR* (1986) 72(3): 383–402.

McGiffert, M., 'William Tyndale's conception of covenant', *JEH* (1981) 32: 167–84.

Maconica, J.K., *English humanists and reformation politics under Henry VIII and Edward VI* (Oxford, 1968).

Marcombe, D., 'Bernard Gilpin: anatomy of an Elizabethan Legend', *Northern History* (1980) 16: 20–39.

Martin, J.W., 'English protestant separatism at its beginnings: Henry Hart and the free-will men', *SCJ* (1976) 7(2): 55–74.

Martin, J.W., 'The publishing career of Robert Crowley', *Publishing History* (1983) 14: 85–98.

Martin, J.W., 'The first that made separation from the reformed Church of England', *Archiv* (1986) 77: 281–312.

Mason, E., 'The role of the English parishioner, 1100–1500', *JEH* (1976) 27(1): 17–29.

Moller, J., 'The beginnings of puritan covenant theology', *JEH* (1963) 14(9): 46–67.

Muller, J.A., *Stephen Gardiner and the Tudor Reaction* (1926).

O'Day, R., *The Debate on the English Reformation* (1986).

O'Day, R. and Heal, F., *Princes and Paupers in the English Church* (Leicester, 1981).

Opie, J., 'The anglicizing of John Hooper', *Archiv* (1968) 59: 150–75.

Ozment, S., *The Reformation in the Cities: The Appeal of Protestantism to Sixteenth Century Germany and Switzerland* (New Haven, CT, 1975).

Ozment, S., *The Age of Reform* (New Haven, CT, 1980).

Ozment, S., *Protestants: The Birth of a Revolution* (1993).

Palliser, D., *The Age of Elizabeth* (1983).

Parish, H., *Clerical Marriage and the English Reformation: Precedent, Policy and Practice* (Aldershot, 2000).

Parry, G., 'Inventing "the good duke" of Somerset', *JEH* (1989) 59: 150–75.

Pearse, M.T., 'Free will, dissent and Henry Hart', *CH* (1989) 58: 452–9.

Peters, R., 'Who compiled the *Unio dissidentium*?', *SCH* (1965) 2: 237–56.

Pettegree, A., *Foreign Protestant Communities in Sixteenth Century London* (Oxford, 1986).

Pettegree, A. (ed.) *The Reformation World* (2000).

Phillips, J., *The Reformation of Images: Destruction of Art in England, 1535–1600* (Berkeley and Los Angeles, 1973).

Pineas, R., *Thomas More and Tudor Polemic* (Bloomington, IN, 1968).

Pocock, N., 'The condition of morals and religious belief in the reign of Edward VI', *EHR* (1895) 10(39): 417–44.

Pollard, A.F., *The History of England from the Accession of Edward VI to the Death of Elizabeth* (1910).

Porter, H.C., *Reformation and Reaction in Tudor Cambridge* (Cambridge, 1958).

Potter, G., *Zwingli* (Cambridge, 1976).

Price, F.D., 'Gloucester diocese under Bishop Hooper', *Transactions of the Bristol and Gloucester Archaeological Society* (1938) 60: 51–151.

Primus, J., *The Vestments Controversy* (Kampen, 1960).

Primus, J., 'The role of the covenant doctrine in the puritanism of John Hooper', *NAK* (1967–68).

Redworth, G., 'A study in the formulation of policy: the genesis and evolution of the Act of Six Articles', *JEH* (1986) 37(1): 42–67.

Redworth, G., *In defence of the Church Catholic: The Life of Stephen Gardiner* (Oxford, 1990).

Ridley, J., *Nicholas Ridley. A Biography* (1957).

Ridley, J., *John Knox* (Oxford, 1968).

Rupp, E.G., *Studies in the Making of the English Protestant Tradition* (Cambridge, 1965).

Scarisbrick, J., *The Reformation and the English People* (Oxford, 1984).

Scribner, R., *For the Sake of Simple Folk: Popular Propaganda for the German Reformation* (Cambridge, 1981).

Shagan, E., 'Protector Somerset and the 1549 rebellions: new sources and new perspectives', *EHR* (1999) 114: 34–63; debate (2000) 115(460): 103–33.

Simon, J., *Education and Society in Tudor England*, 2nd edn (Cambridge, 1979).

Skinner, Q.R.D., *The Foundations of Modern Political Thought* (Cambridge, 1978), 2 vols.

Slack, P., *Poverty and Policy in Tudor and Stuart England* (1988).

Slack, P., *From Reformation to Improvement: Public Welfare in Early Modern England* (1998).

Smyth, C., *Cranmer and the Reformation Under Edward VI* (Cambridge, 1926; repr. Greenwood, CT, 1970).

Spalding, J.C., *The Reformation of the Ecclesiastical Laws of England, 1552* (Kirksville, MO, 1992).

Spufford, M., *Contrasting Communities: English Villages in the Sixteenth and Seventeenth Centuries* (Cambridge, 1974).

Spufford, M., *Small Books and Pleasant Histories* (1981).

Starkey, D.M., *The Reign of Henry VIII – Personalities and Politics* (1985).

Strong, R., 'Edward VI and the pope: a Tudor antipapal allegory and its setting', *Journal of the Warburg and Courtauld Institutes* (1960) 23: 311–13.

Strype, J., *Ecclesiastical Memorials* (Oxford, 1822).

Strype, J., *Memorials of Archbishop Cranmer* (Oxford, 1848).

Tawney, R.H., *Religion and the Rise of Capitalism* (1926; repr. 1943).

Thomas, K., *Religion and the Decline of Magic: Studies in Popular Beliefs in Sixteenth and Seventeenth Century England* 2nd edn (1973).

Todd, M., 'Humanists, puritans and the spiritualised household', *CH* (1980) 49: 18–34.

Bibliography

Tudor, P., 'Religious instruction for children and adolescents in the early English reformation', *JEH* (1984) 35(3): 391–413.

Tyacke, N. (ed.) *England's Long Reformation 1500–1800* (1998).

Verkamp, B., *The Indifferent Mean: Adiaphorism in the English Reformation to 1554* (Athens, OH, 1977).

Walzer, M., *The Revolution of the Saints* (1966).

Watt, T., *Cheap Print and Popular Piety 1550–1640* (Cambridge, 1991).

Webb, J., 'Peter Moone of Ipswich (d. 1601): a Tudor tailor, poet and gospeller, and his circle', *Proceedings of the Suffolk Institute of Archaeology* (1993) 38: 35–55.

White, H., *Social Criticism in the Popular Religious Literature of the Sixteenth Century* (New York, 1944).

Whiting, R., 'Abominable idols: images and image breaking under Henry VIII', *JEH* (1982) 33(1): 30–47.

Whiting, R., *Local Responses to the English Reformation* (Basingstoke, 1998).

Wiener, C.Z., 'The beleaguered isle: a study of Elizabethan and early Jacobean anticatholicism', *P&P* (1971) 51: 27–62.

Williams, F.B., *Index of Dedications and Commendatory Verses in English Books Before 1641* (1962).

Williams, F.B., 'The lost books of Tudor England', *The Library* (1978) 33(1): 1–14.

Williams, G., *Welsh Reformation Essays* (Cardiff, 1967).

Williams, G.H., *The Radical Reformation* (1962).

Youings, J., 'The south-western rebellion of 1549', *Southern History* (1979) 1: 99–122.

Unpublished theses

Bowler G., 'English protestant resistance theory, *c.* 1535–1600' PhD thesis, University of London (1981).

Clements, C., 'The English radicals and their theology', PhD thesis, Cambridge University (1980).

Hildebrandt, E., 'A study of the English protestant exiles in north Switzerland and Strassburg, 1539–47, and their role in the English reformation', PhD, University of Durham (1982).

Johnston, A., 'The eclectic reformation: vernacular pamphlet literature in the Dutch-speaking Low Countries 1520–65', PhD, Southampton University (1987).

Ryrie, A., 'English evangelical reformers in the last years of Henry VIII', DPhil, Oxford University (2000).

Stoute, D., 'The origins and early development of the reformed idea of the covenant', PhD, Cambridge University (1979).

Thompson, S., 'The pastoral work of the English and Welsh bishops, 1500–58', DPhil, Oxford University (1984).

Took, P.M., 'Government and the printing trade, 1540–60', PhD, University of London (1979).

Tudor, P., 'Changing private belief and practice in English devotional literature, *c.*1475–1550', DPhil, Oxford University (1984).

Index

Note: 'n' after a page number indicates a note number on that page.

Abraham 99
absolution 101
Acts of the Apostles 160
Adam 36
adultery 103, 133 n 144, 153, 167
Allen, Edmund 121, 123, 160–1
almsgiving 163
altars 19, 25, 53 n 7, 172 n 115
anabaptism 67, 68, 73, 78, 79, 97, 98, 160
Antichrist 21, 28, 31, 35, 40, 42, 51–2, 92, 152, 181, 185, 194, 232
anticlericalism 32, 35, 52, 94
antinomianism 71, 89
apocalypse 42, 177
apostles 201
Arian heresy 69, 70, 72, 74, 161
Ascham, Roger 8
Askew, Anne 34, 48, 69, 150
Assheton, John 69
Augustine, Saint
  of Canterbury 183
  of Hippo 27, 35

Baal, priests of 42
Babylon 28, 39, 92, 195
Bale, John 22, 27, 29, 32–4, 37, 40, 48, 87, 94–5, 141, 144, 150, 152, 179, 185–6, 195–6, 198
ballads xiii, 20
baptism 27
  infant, justification of 75
Barnes, Robert 36
Becke, Edmund 74, 78
Becon, Thomas xvii, 42, 78, 119, 155, 157, 160–1, 190, 210
Beer, B. 11
Belmain, Jean 8

Bernher, Augustine 101
Bible xv
  in English 36, 52, 87, 126
  reading 72–3, 179
Bilney, Thomas 196
bishops 37, 96, 179
  and secular office 105
B., J. 73, 77–8
blasphemy 38
Bocher, Joan 67, 69, 70, 72, 74
Bocking conventicle, the 67, 72
Brandon
  Henry and Charles 193
  Katherine (Duchess of Suffolk) 149
Bride of Christ (Jerusalem, the true church) 28
Brinkelow, Henry 6
broadsheets xiii
Brigden, S. xiii
Bucer, Martin 5, 20, 231
Bullinger, Heinrich 67, 74–5, 77, 120, 231

Cain 47, 196, 202
calendar, religious 2
Calvin, Jean 75
Cambridge xii, 107
Canaan 189
canon law, reform of 3
Canterbury xii
Carew, Sir Peter 149, 151
catechism 116, 118–19, 125
celibacy, clerical 18, 33, 40, 49, 181
censorship xii
  relaxation of xii, 19
ceremonies 26, 32
chamber, privy 37
Champneys, John 69, 70–2
chantries, dissolution of 2, 7
chaplains, noble 113, 149
charity 7, 161
Cheke, John 8, 9, 159, 191–2, 210

Index

Christ, Jesus 43, 70, 87, 205
Christology 70, 75
chronology 181, 194
church, Celtic (British) 182–3
church, of England 215
church, Fall of the Romish 42, 49
church
  invisible 115
  visible 114
churches, true and false 26–9, 33, 47, 51, 179
clergy wives 97
Cole, Thomas 81 nn 14, 15
Collinson, P. 200
'commonwealth men' 6
  ideology 168
communion service 117, 123, 231
confession 100–1
confraternities 2
congregation 123
consensus 231
Cooche, Robert 68, 77–8
Corinthians, first letter to the 71, 105, 161
corruption, official 155
council, privy 11, 198–9, 203
court 148, 201
covenant 164, 169 n 29, 188–9, 192, 197
Coventry 7
covetousness 204–9
Cox, Richard 8
Cranmer, Thomas xv, xvi, xxiii, 1, 3, 4, 22, 27, 29, 31, 35, 37, 42–3, 45, 50, 68–9, 87, 92, 102, 115–16, 124, 125, 146, 178, 208, 210
crisis, mid-Tudor 5
Cromwell, Thomas xi, 7
Crowley xii, xiii, 6, 19, 20, 24, 48, 89, 95–6, 98, 105, 108–11, 113, 142, 145, 157, 164, 182, 185, 191, 195, 201, 203, 208, 211, 218
culture, oral xiv, 89, 56 n 28
custom 213

Daniel 157, 160–1, 186
David 147, 198
Davies, C.S.L. 10
Day, John xii
dedications xii
Deuteronomy 122, 143

dialogue between a gentleman and a priest, A 179, 215
Dickens, A.G. 1
discipline 116–17
disobedience, lawful 159
disorder 207
disputations 19, 92
dissent 126
divorce 133 n 144
Dorset, Henry Grey, Marquess of 149–50
Duffy, E. 1
duty 161

economy 6–7, 226 n 218
ecumenism xxiii, 56 n 37
Edgeworth, Roger 3
education 7–8, 106–7
Edward VI 8–10, 143, 146, 148, 157, 188, 195, 198, 210, 215–16, 141
Egypt 189
Elijah 22, 71, 93, 109, 186
Elizabeth
  princess 12, 144
  queen 198, 233
Elton, G.R. 1, 6, 10, 41, 211
enclosure 7
  commission 13
England 181, 188
episcopacy 103
Erasmianism xxii, 87
eschatology 193
Essex 69
excommunication 103, 117, 217
Exhortation to parliament 145, 204, 206, 218
exiles 52, 53 n 4
  Marian 192–3
Ezekiel 95

faction 5, 12, 200
faith 30–1, 72
famine 191
fasting 218
fees, clerical 109
Finch, Richard 196, 210, 212
Fines, J. 5
Fisher, John 106
Fitzroy, Mary, Duchess of Richmond 149
flesh 24–6

260

Index

forgiveness 101
Forty-Two Articles, the 97, 116
Foxe, John xv, 95, 101, 103, 117, 153–4, 167, 217
   Acts and monuments 9
France 11, 191
free-willers 72, 78
friars 97

Gardiner, Stephen xii, xvi, 9, 12, 19–20, 22, 27–9, 45, 48–50, 54 nn 11 and 14, 104, 179, 231
Garter, order of the 9
Germany 188
Gerrard, Phillip 36, 39, 147, 155, 214
Gilby, Anthony 24–5, 27, 33, 42, 49, 91, 95–6, 112, 119, 122, 148, 161, 178, 180, 183–4, 186, 188–9, 191, 195, 197–8, 202, 206, 209, 213–14, 216
Gilpin, Bernard 201, 203, 206, 212, 215
Gildas 182, 185
glosses 38
godly 23, 26
Goodman, Christopher 161
Gospel, 93, 148, 205
   gospellers, carnal 205–9
Gregory VII, Pope 40, 49
Grey, Jane 13
Guest, Edmund 24, 108, 119

Haigh, C. 1
Haddon, James 149
Hales, John 7
Harte, Henry 69, 71–2
Henry VIII 36–7, 52, 87, 144, 148, 198
   will of 12, 204
heresy xi, 73
   Commissions 68
Hezekiah 150, 202
history 180–3
Hoak, Dale 11
Hoggard, Miles xvi, 3, 19
Holbein, Hans 9
Homilies, The xii, 89, 90, 126
   Of obedience 140
   Of declining from God 185, 187
Hooper, John xvi, 4, 19, 20, 26, 29, 30–1, 35, 39, 42, 67, 74, 76, 78, 89–92, 95, 99, 102–4, 108, 115–16, 118–20, 149, 154–6, 161–2, 164, 184, 186, 189, 198, 218
hospitals 7
humanism xxii, 233, 150
Hutchinson, Roger 68–9, 76, 92, 112, 120, 190, 192
hypocrisy 206

iconoclasm 2
idolatry 27, 32, 37, 39, 44, 46, 112, 151, 200, 206, 216
ignorance 213
illiteracy 89
imagery, biblical 23
impropriations, monastic 109
incorruptibility (of the magistrate) 147
Injunctions, royal (1547) 95, 112, 126
Interim (German religious settlement of 1548) 159, 188
Ipswich xiii
Isaiah xv, 29, 36, 184, 188–9, 199, 216
Israel 147, 154, 161, 184, 208

Jehosophat 155
Jeremiah 91, 109, 192
Jerusalem 28
Job 203
Joel 196
John, first epistle of 33
Jonah 89, 90, 93, 95, 155, 189, 192
Jones, W.R.D. 5
Jordan, W.K. 6–7, 10
Joseph 160
Josiah 151, 188, 199, 200, 216
Joye, George 20, 30, 101, 103–4, 117, 153, 167, 189
Judas 155
Judith 211
judgement, the last 197
Judges (Old Testament) 143, 156
justification by faith alone 18
justice 161, 164
   social 157, 197
   divine 154

Kent 69
Kethe, William 47
keys, power of the 102
King, J.N. xi–xii

Index

laity 114
Lancaster, Thomas 98, 125–6, 142, 195
Lasco, John à 5
last days 184
Lateran Council, Fourth 187
Latimer, Hugh 6, 8–9, 37, 76, 80, 89, 90, 92–4, 96–7, 99, 100, 102, 104–9, 113, 118, 120, 126, 143, 147, 152–3, 155, 157–8, 163, 166, 184, 188, 194, 197, 200, 204, 211, 213, 217
law of God 167
Lesse, Nicholas 38, 78
Lever, Thomas 6, 8, 96, 98, 106–7, 111, 113, 141–2, 153, 191–2, 207, 209, 219
Levitical priesthood 92
liturgy
    Latin 29
    vernacular 122
Loach, J. xii, xxiii, 9, 10, 11
Lollardy, Lollards xi, 3, 69, 74, 220 nn. 35, 36
London xiii, 3, 5, 7, 68, 189
Lord's Prayer 163, 165
Lord's Supper 3
Luke, gospel of 201
Luther, Martin xi, 197
    argument against vows 33
    doctrine of sacrament 179
    Lutherans xvii, xxii, 28
Lynne, Walter 180, 185

MacCulloch, D. xxiii, 1, 4, 9–11, 13
magic 45
magistrates 77, 202
maintenance, clerical 108
Mardeley, John 38, 181, 212
marriage 40
    clerical 2, 96, 59 n 131
    royal 144, 199
Martin, J.W. 67, 72
Martyr, Peter 5, 231
Mary
    princess 9, 13, 144
    queen 67, 200, 233
Mass, sacrament of the xxiii, 3, 18, 27, 31, 36, 43, 46, 78, 122–3, 161, 166, 179, 184, 216, 231
    private Masses 19

Matthew, gospel of 73
May Day 211
Melanchthon, Philip xxiii
mercy of God 219
Micah 96, 183, 185, 193–4
Mierdman, Stephen xii
ministry, lay 71, 98
minority, royal 146, 198–200
miracles 183, 200, 202
monarchy 141, 145
monasteries, dissolution of 18, 110, 205
Moone, Peter 47
More, Sir Thomas 179
Moses 91, 143, 147, 150
    law of 217
Münster 77

Nebo 189–90
Nebuchadnezzar 156, 203
Netherlands xi–xiii, 68, 77
Nichols, Phillip xiv, 49, 98, 111, 147, 151, 156, 184, 216
Nineveh 90, 95, 156, 190
Noah 190
nobility 148
non-residence 113

obedience 77, 158
obscurantism 44
Ochino, Bernadino xiii
oppression 206
optimism 177
order 32, 160
    divine 140
Oswen, John xiii
Oxford xiii

papacy 41–2, 159, 180
Paraphrases (of Erasmus) xii, xxii, 2, 126, 210
Paris, George van 67
parliament 215, 218
Parr, Katherine xxii, 12, 149
patriarchy 34
patristics 220 n 21
patronage 171 nn 80, 82
Paul, Saint 39, 50, 180
Pelagianism 74, 78
    Pelagius 182
persecution 47–8, 50, 179

Index

pessimism 177, 186, 219
pestilence 97
Pettegree, A. 5
Peter, first letter of 150
pharaoh 160, 203
Phineas 99
Pickering, Peter xvi
Piers Plowman 182
plague and punishment 187, 208
pluralism 112
Pole, Reginald 143
Ponet, John xiii, 10, 20, 44, 49, 116, 219
pope xv, 40, 215, 219
   power of 18
poverty 157
praise . . . of such as sought commonwealths, The 208
prayer, private 118
Prayer Book
   of 1549 xii, 2, 100, 118, 210
   of 1552 2, 118
preachers 94
preaching 71, 88–9
predestination 136 n 247
Presence, Real 25, 27, 29, 31, 38, 184
priesthood of all believers 35
priests 26, 94
Proctor, John 69, 70, 75
prophecy 183–7
providence 178–80
purgatory 18
purpose of events 178

radical protestantism 3
Ramsey, John 25, 33, 41
rebellions, 1549 3, 7, 158–9, 209–11
   Norfolk 13
   Rising, Western 13
reformation 145, 205
repentance 101, 166, 186, 191–2, 198, 217
resistance, passive 159
restitution 155, 204
retribution 166
Revelation, book of 27–8, 185–6
revelation, providential 180
Rhineland xxiii
Ridley Nicholas 3, 4, 68, 105
ritual 35
Ruddoke, Thomas 106, 110

sabbath 120–1
sacrilege 111
Sacrament, the xvii, 19, 24, 27, 29, 31, 50, 88, 121–2, 124
Salesbury, William 19, 36, 183
salvation 154, 180
Samuel, William xiii, 37
Satan 21, 43, 78, 93, 181, 197
scandal, sexual 33, 133 n 144
scholasticism 22, 29
schools 7–8
Scotland 11, 144
scripture 21–3, 88
secularisation 108
sedition 76, 191, 232
separatism 76, 79
Seymour
   Jane 9
   Thomas 12, 201–2
Sharington, Sir William 155
silences, polemical 18
Simon, J. 7
Six Articles, act of xii, 231
Skinner, Q. xxi n 43, xxii
Smith, Richard 19, 22
Smith, Sir Thomas 6
Smyth, C.H. 67
Solomon 148, 199
Somerset, duke of 10–12, 146, 148, 200–1, 204
   Stanhope, Anne, duchess of Somerset 149
Song of the Lord's Supper 117, 150
'soul murder' 49
spirit 23–4
Spufford, M. xiii–xiv
'Stranger churches' 1, 5
statute 204
stewardship, Christian 165
Strassburg xiii, 18
superstition 212
supremacy, royal 2, 7, 18, 34, 146, 158
sweating sickness 190, 193
sword
   spiritual 102–3, 152–3, 154
   temporal 150, 152–3

Testament
   New *see* Gospel
   Old 50

Index

theft 165
Thessalonians, second letter to the 73
Timothy, letter to 103
tithes 109–10
Titus, letter to 91
tradition, church 21–2
translations xvii
transubstantiation 25, 31, 38, 45, 181
treason 40
Tudor, P. xvii
Turner, William 46, 68, 75, 77–8, 150
Tyndale, William 36–7

universities 8
unrest, social 202–3

verities, unwritten *see* tradition, church
Veron, Jean xvi, 19, 31, 36, 68, 76–8, 80, 115, 125, 151
vestments controversy 4, 104, 152
via media 1
visitation of God, dual 187
vocation 99, 142, 201
vows 33
V., R. xv, 151

Wales 183
war 157
Watt, T. xii
wealth
 church 32, 46
 royal 144
West country xiv
Westminster 2
Whitehall 9
witchcraft 213–14, 229 n 299
Wittenberg 18
whoredom 95
Whore of Babylon 28, 32–4, 41, 194
Wolsey, Thomas 7
woodcuts xi
 of Latimer preaching 9
 Lutheran 28
works 30
Worcester xiii, 2
worship 118
Wyclif, John 182, 185, 194

Zion 197
Zurich 18
Zwingli xxiii